Sacred Journeys

Sacred Journeys

The Anthropology of Pilgrimage

Edited by ALAN MORINIS

Foreword by Victor Turner

Contributions to the Study of Anthropology, Number 7

Greenwood Press
Westport, Connecticut • London

Library of Congress Cataloging-in-Publication Data

Sacred journeys : the anthropology of pilgrimage / edited by Alan
   Morinis ; foreword by Victor Turner.
         p.   cm.—(Contributions to the study of anthropology, ISSN
   0890-9377 ; no. 7)
      Chiefly papers delivered at a conference held in May 1981 at the
   University of Pittsburgh.
      Includes bibliographical references and index.
      ISBN 0-313-27879-2 (alk. paper)
      1. Pilgrims and pilgrimages—Cross-cultural studies—Congresses.
   I. Morinis, E. Alan.   II. Series.
   BL619.P5S23   1991
   306.6'91446—dc20   91-36833

British Library Cataloguing in Publication Data is available.

Library of Congress Catalog Card Number: 91-36833
ISBN: 0-313-27879-2
ISSN: 0890-9377

First published in 1992

Greenwood Press, 88 Post Road West, Westport, CT 06881
An imprint of Greenwood Publishing Group, Inc.

Printed in the United States of America

The paper used in this book complies with the
Permanent Paper Standard issued by the National
Information Standards Organization (Z39.48-1984).

10 9 8 7 6 5 4 3 2 1

Contents

Foreword

VICTOR TURNER

In 1970, when I was invited by the American Council of Learned Societies to deliver six lectures on pilgrimage in the series entitled "The American Lectures in the History of Religion," I found that the study of pilgrimage had a very low priority in the anthropological agenda. Yet hundreds of millions of people go on pilgrimage every year, while abundant documentation proves that the practice is ancient indeed. Dr. Preston, in this volume, has mentioned several reasons for this neglect, almost amounting to rejection of pilgrimage as a legitimate object of study for anthropologists and also for historians, sociologists, historians of religion, and social psychologists. He cites the reluctance of social scientists to study transitory phenomena, the "particularistic holism" of anthropologists, the "studious avoidance" by behavioral scientists of phenomena that smack of "mysticism," and, perhaps most "insidious" of all, disciplinary compartmentalization that balks at the interdisciplinary teamwork necessarily involved in the study of such multileveled mass phenomena as pilgrimage and, indeed, other modes of large-scale motivated travel. It seems that some of these resistances have been overcome. I am sure that Dr. Morinis's splendid initiative in convening the Pittsburgh Conference on pilgrimage in 1981, of which this multidisciplinary book is one of the fruits, has been a major factor. One might also mention the cognate rise of the anthropology of tourism, whose guiding spirits, Nelson Graburn, Erik Cohen, and Dean MacCannell, have been sensitively responsive to recent developments in the anthropology of pilgrimage. As Edith Turner and

I wrote in *Image and Pilgrimage*, "A tourist is half a pilgrim, if a pilgrim is half tourist."

Sacred Journeys contains a wide variety of approaches to the pilgrimage process. Examples are drawn from most of the major world religions. Detailed case studies of the genesis and operation of specific, localized pilgrimages are interdigitated with social-historical surveys of the influence of international pilgrimages on the economic and political structures of wide sociogeographical regions. Some pilgrimages are viewed from the perspective of the pilgrim participants, their categories and cosmology. Others are viewed in the radically different terms of western social science. Some of the authors are themselves believers in, other skeptics of, the religious worldview validating the pilgrimages they discuss. This variability and ambiguity are all to the good, indeed, a healthy sign. Not only is it a marker of the nativity of a new subfield of interdisciplinary study, but it also reflects the laminated character of pilgrimage itself.

We hear that other volumes on pilgrimage are gestating. Among them is a German collection of essays significantly entitled *Wallfahrt kennt keine Grenzen*, which means "Pilgrimage Knows No Bounds." This title perhaps holds a clue to the new scientific interest in pilgrimage and tourism, for these have become metaphors for a world on the move, where rapid transportation and the mass media are moving millions literally or mentally out of the stasis of localization. The perennial tension between social structure and communitas is now being greatly amplified and simplified. Pilgrims, seeking an ancient meaning in a far place, have often found new sources of meaning along the roads they travel. The "sacred journeys" related with such scrupulosity and affection in this volume make up a crisscross pattern, not a tangle of disparities. As several of the authors suggest, this pattern may as readily be one of sociocultural growth as of invariant tradition. The anthropology of pilgrimage may be in its infancy, but on the evidence of this book it is a lusty, fast-growing infant.

Preface

The idea for this book originated with the conference "Pilgrimage: The Human Quest" which was held at the University of Pittsburgh in May 1981. This symposium drew international participants representing the disciplines of anthropology, history, geography, sociology, literature, religious studies, and tourism to discuss the many dimensions of sacred journeys. This interdisciplinary dialogue was fruitful, largely because pilgrimages themselves are, indeed, literary, spatial, geographical, cultural, social, demographic, ritual, and ideological institutions. Although the present volume is aimed primarily at anthropologists, it has drawn inspiration and insight from workers in other fields, and the lessons of this effort will, we hope, be of use to our colleagues investigating pilgrimages from the perspectives of their own disciplines. It is especially desirable that future research on pilgrimage be conducted within a multidisciplinary frame.

The case studies in this book represent a broad selection of pilgrimage traditions. It is hoped that each chapter contributes to the analysis and understanding of pilgrimage in general and to the increasing involvement of anthropologists in the study of sacred journeys, especially in areas where no work has been done to date.

It should also be made explicit that the study of pilgrimage is much more than the microscopic examination of a sample of humanity on the move. Pilgrimage is a paradigmatic and paradoxical human quest, both outward and inward, a movement toward ideals known but not achieved at home. As such, pilgrimage is an image for the search for fulfillment of all people, inhabiting an imperfect world. The metaphor is well used, but there is still an important perspective to be gained from seeing both pilgrims and anthropologists as people of culture. An anthropological study of pilgrimage is a conversation about life, suffering, and the pursuit of ideals and salvation.

Many people have helped along the journey of this book. There are the authors themselves, whose diligence and steadfastness made possible my job of marshaling all of us to our collective goal. Most of the authors attended the Pittsburgh conference, and to all participants in that extraordinary event thanks are due for inspiring the commitment to undertake and complete this project. I must especially single out James Preston, who supported the idea of a conference from the beginning and has been unfailingly helpful since, and Fred Clothey, who hosted the Pittsburgh meetings so graciously and made possible the exchange of ideas of which this book is the fruit. Appreciation is also due to Simon Fraser University and the University of Pittsburgh for their financial assistance to our meetings. Thanks as well are due to my editor, Mildred Vasan, for patience and faith.

I dedicate this book to my parents, in respect and with gratitude for their guidance along a way that they told me about in my childhood but that I am coming to recognize, only as I walk it, is as they said it would be.

Introduction:
The Territory of
the Anthropology of Pilgrimage

ALAN MORINIS

Pilgrimage is born of desire and belief. The desire is for solution to problems of all kinds that arise within the human situation. The belief is that somewhere beyond the known world there exists a power that can make right the difficulties that appear so insoluble and intractable here and now. All one must do is journey.

In every era and society people have set out and crossed the boundaries of their familiar territory in search of the earthly home of their god. Their motives and the form of their journeying have varied, as each culture has fashioned its own version of the pilgrimage, and every pilgrim has interpreted this cultural model to suit his personal life and spirit. Through its transformation from a great austerity fraught with real danger and well-justified fear to modern, efficient, comfortable journeying, the quest for the sacred remains a fascination to humankind. Contemporary pilgrimages draw together the largest regular human assemblages on earth. The Kumbha Mela, held every twelve years at the sacred river confluence at Allahabad, India, attracts over ten million people to bathe at the auspicious moment. Mecca now attracts over a million Muslims annually from every corner of the Islamic world. Holy Week in Rome, Passover in Jerusalem, Perahara at Kandy, the global tide of pilgrims is still unabating, propelled by desire, guided by belief.

Pilgrimage suggests unlimited possibilities for anthropological analysis, drawing on the ideas, symbols, behavior, social forces, and experiences woven into the practice. Sacred journeys are an important aspect of the world's complex religions,

1

and the ethnographic record shows actual and prototypical pilgrimages in many nonindustrial societies. Australian aborigines are reported to have maintained and visited sacred places: "In the Walbiri desert country, the snake is pictorially represented at several sacred sites, such as Ngama (mother) cave thirty miles west of the Yuendumu settlement and the Wanayara waterholes, its mythical home thirty miles to the north" (Cawte 1974: 79-80).

The Zuni Indians of the southwestern United States would visit shrines on their sacred Corn Mountain. They would perform rituals at one shrine if they were supplicating for a daughter, at another for a son (Stevenson 1904).

Serious anthropological interest in pilgrimage has only been recent, though it has been slowly increasing. Anthropologists have tended to neglect pilgrimages because they were, by definition, exceptional practices, irregular journeys outside habitual social realms. Pilgrimage eludes the attention of the traditional researcher who takes a fixed socio-cultural unit, such as a village, as the subject of study. Pilgrimage also tends not to fit into conventional anthropological categories. It is rather a composite process pieced together from elements of mythology, ritual, belief, psychology, social roles, architecture, geography, literature, drama and art, and spiritual concerns. Pilgrimage partakes of the mystical, and nothing is less amenable to investigation by social science.

This volume is a step toward rectifying this neglect. The chapters that follow take as their territory the concept and practice of undertaking sacred journeys. In most cases these journeys have specific, revered sites as their goal, but some pilgrimages are wanderings with no certain goal (e.g., Basho 1966). What is essential is the setting out on a quest for the "sacred."

The term sacred has been problematic since Emile Durkheim tried to use it so globally. I use it to refer specifically to the valued ideals that are the image of perfection that a human being sets out to encounter or become on a pilgrimage. The deity of the shrine is frequently an embodiment of cultural ideals, but it is the pursuit of the ideal (whether deified or not) that defines the sacred journey. The ideals that are the pilgrim's goal are usually—but not always—fixed in space within the perceptible world. Cultures have provided many pathways to seek ideals, and some non-geographical goings-forth also fall within the territory of the anthropology of pilgrimage. The reason is that the terrestrial journey tends to be infused with the significance that derives from the expressive archetypes of the spiritual quest, while, conversely, the metaphorical language needed to speak of the ineffable spiritual path draws on the imagery of the pedestrian earthly pilgrim. Meaning, metaphor, practice, and experience are separable for the purposes of discourse but tend to meld into one another in the development of a cultural category of sacred journeys.

Indigenous categories tend to merge geographical and non-geographical aspects of sacred journeying. The 108 sacred "seats" of the Goddess in India includes many famous pilgrimage shrines such as Kamrupa in Assam and Kalighata in Calcutta but lists as well "light in the solar orb" and "the Gayatri mantra in grammar" (Sircar 1973). These are all "places where the Goddess can be sought." Hindu mystics and the Sufis have developed a concept of the inner pilgrimage by which one visits sacred places within the microcosm of the mind and body (cf. Morinis 1984; Stanley, Chapter 3; Thayer, Chapter 9). The earthly Christian Jerusalem partakes of the heavenly City of God, like Vrndavana, the north Indian city to which pilgrims flock because of its association with the youthful Krishna. Krishna lives today in a celestial, transcendental Vrndavana located in the god-realm. The theologian Radhavallabha-dasa asks, "What of the Vrndavana of the mind?" and answers that it is manifested in the mind of the devotee who perfects the practice of devotion (Sen cited in Dimock 1966: 1690).

The fact of the merger of geographical and non-geographical aspects of pilgrimage is essential to establishing the boundaries of the territory being explored here. The pilgrimage category open to anthropological investigation contains a wide variety of practices, but also images and meanings, that are more extensive and touch on more areas of cultural and personal life than is immediately evident when one calls to mind the image of the pilgrim, with cloak and staff and dusty feet.

How, then, are we to define pilgrimage for anthropological purpose? It seems the term can be put to use wherever journeying and some embodiment of an ideal intersect. Frank Lloyd Wright says of museums that "the collections become shrines for the artist pilgrims in need of worship or in search of light" (1967: 77). Other usages that have recently caught my eye and reveal something of the semantic range of the contemporary English "pilgrimage" include soldiers returning from a battlefield, Ku Klux Klansmen on parade, and children on the treat rounds of Halloween. Compare the Hindu *tirtha* (sacred ford, or place of pilgrimage), which can be applied to the shrine at the end of a sacred journey, but as well to a devoted wife, a spiritual preceptor, one's parents, and virtues such as truth and honesty.

It is an important task for anthropology to plot the boundaries and analyze the meanings that different cultures assign to the sacred journey.

It is also important to note and trace the connections, both ideological and practical, that relate a pilgrimage to the socio-cultural, political, and economic context in which it is embedded. Jonathan Sumption has described how the medieval European pilgrimage tradition achieved cultural mesh with the overarching traditions of which it was an aspect. In his term, pilgrimage casts an "image" of the culture. This is not surprising, considering that the cornerstone of the sacred journey is the quest for the culturally validated ideal (often depicted as a deity). James Pruess's description (Chapter 11) of the creation of a Thai Buddhist pilgrimage center illustrates how historical forces operating within the cultural context generate a sacred place of culturally and historically appropriate characteristics. The pilgrimage complex tends to have different meanings, depending upon the general meaning a culture gives to the key themes of "going forth," "journeying," "communion," and so on.

Despite this variation among pilgrimage traditions, there is also cross-cultural homology. It is at this level that a workable general definition must be sought. While there is little dispute labeling as a pilgrim a devout Muslim who has journeyed to Mecca for the *hajj* or a Catholic attending Holy Week in Rome or a dutiful Hindu performing ancestral rites at Gaya, the clear definition of pilgrimage starts to fray in the cases of the provincial Russians who bring their newborn babies for the blessing of contact with Lenin's Tomb in Red Square and the pilgrimage-like aspects of tourism, such as visits to Disneyland (Moore 1980), seaside paradises (Cohen 1982b) and other touristic "Meccas."

Erik Cohen addresses some of these issues in his discussion of the distinction between pilgrimage and tourism in Chapter 2 of this volume. What is certain, as Richard Niebuhr (1981) has pointed out, is that the boundaries of the pilgrimage category are defined solely by the limits of the human imagination. Anthropologists tend to pay more attention to actual ritual goings-forth on sacred journeys in geographical space, but the other sorts of venturing toward ideals undertaken by humans are equally pilgrimages. It is, indeed, questionable to distinguish between terrestrial and "metaphorical" pilgrimages. This distinction portrays the earthly journey as somehow more real, when, in fact, most cultures subsume physical journeys and other quests into one more inclusive category: the spiritual life is a pilgrimage, the ascetic learns to visit the sacred shrines in his own body, devotion is a journey to God. The notion of pilgrimage is polysemous (cf. Holloway 1981). While most of the chapters in this book address the terrestrial journey, it is a challenge to contemporary anthropology to be able to address the pilgrimage as an important motif of the human imagination, that takes on a variety of forms in thought and practice.

With these considerations in mind, I tender a definition: the pilgrimage is a journey undertaken by a person in quest of a place or a state that he or she believes to embody a valued ideal. At its most conventional, the end of the pilgrimage is an actual shrine located at some fixed geographical point. The place has acquired a reputation that draws pilgrims (Preston, Chapter 1 calls this the center's quality of "spiritual magnetism"). One who journeys to a place of importance to himself alone may also be a pilgrim. The allegorical pilgrimage seeks out a place not located in the geographical sphere. Some sacred journeys are wanderings that have no fixed goal; the pilgrimage here is the search for an unknown or hidden goal.

The destinations at the end of all of these pilgrimages share being an intensified version of some ideal that the pilgrim values but cannot achieve at home. The Mary of Lourdes or Fatima is the same as one can worship in the local church, but at the sacred shrine she is found in a more potent form because she is reputed actually to have appeared at these places as an apparition. The pilgrimage that has developed following an apparition of Mary at Saut d'eau, Haiti, is described and discussed as a case in point by Stephen Glazier (Chapter 7). Allah is worshiped in prayer and in the local mosque, but one is most truly an accomplished Muslim when one has visited the earthly places of His own Prophet, and the mind of devotion one pursues at a sacred place outstrips what is possible amid the involvements and turmoil of domestic life. Matsuo Basho captures the image of the ideal in the pilgrim's goal when he writes of the Atsuta shrine as having a polished surface of divine glass without a flaw, "Chaste with flowers of snow" (1966: 75).

Recognized pilgrimage places embody intensified versions of the collective ideals of the culture. Most typically, these have been religious ideals, and so pilgrimage places have often been considered sites where the divine issues forth into the human realm. The shrine is a rupture in the ordinary domain, through which heaven peeks. Considering the pilgrimage center as a place where cultural ideals (rather than gods alone) are enshrined permits secular journeys to fall within our territory. Reverential visits to Lenin's Tomb, Mao's Mausoleum, or the Washington Monument can be considered pilgrimages if we view these founders of nations as contemporary symbols for national ideals. Similarly, visits to Cape Kennedy to witness space flights or Las Vegas to sport with money are journeys undertaken to places that have come to be repositories of collective ideals. As well, the pilgrimage of life and the spiritual quest can be seen to be journeys directed toward a way of being that embodies the ideals the traveler now holds but cannot manifest.

The ideal at the center can be a sectarian or even an heretical ideal, as in the example of the shrine of an excommunicated group of Catholics in Wisconsin (Wood, Chapter 6). In this case, one of the principal ideals enshrined at the pilgrimage center is the traditionalist, conservative stance of Catholics who oppose what they see as the liberal, revisionist, humanistic tendencies of the modern Roman church. The ideals at the core of the Thai shrine discussed by Pruess (Chapter 11) are both the Buddha as a perfected being and, more immediately, a saintly monk who incarnates the valued ideals of the culture. The pilgrimage center can house ideals of national identity (as in the Haitian case in Chapter 7), the identity of ethnic groups (as in the case of the Maori discussed by Sinclair, Chapter 12), regional cultures (the Thai-Lao group considered by Pruess), or transnational religious groups, which are the focus of chapters by Thayer (Chapter 9) and Bowman (Chapter 8).

This view of the pilgrim's destination allows us to consider the pilgrimage to a collectively designated goal and also to places that somehow represent a store of one's personal ideals. This fashioning of the sacredness of the shrine allows us to see how some secular activities (such as certain forms of tourism) share in many of the older, deeper cultural paradigms and processes of pilgrimage.

It is because pilgrimage centers are repositories for a culture's ideals that they have been so commonly and extensively supported. Political patronage has been common, as is evidenced in the discussion of Thai pilgrimage by Pruess (Chapter 11). Celebrated pilgrimage places often enshrine relics of the most revered saints or most authenticated apparitions of the divine. These centers have been glorified with the highest expressions of religious art and architecture that cultures have evolved. The result is that the shrine incarnates the ideals it embodies. The message that this place is the holy of holies is strongly reinforced for the pilgrim in the art, architecture, music, drama, and so on that embellish the center. In fact, once the "spiritual magnetism" of the place develops (to employ James Preston's term), it can become so powerful that it overwhelms group or cultural boundaries and so draws pilgrims of many affiliations, who come because of the reputation for power the place projects and manifests through material representations.

We can note here one reason that pilgrimage places so often (although certainly not always) are located at places of geographical splendor. Mountaintops, sea vistas, great rivers, and springs are easily translated into images of greatness and so reinforce the message about collective ideals enshrined in the pilgrimage places.

Relics and traces of the saintly or divine also have a role in representing the ideal that is the goal of pilgrims. The individual who has left these traces—Buddha, St. Paul, Caitanya—epitomizes the human ideal to the cult. It may not be that he is a founder, for many relics are not those of founders, but that in his hierophany he was an ideal incarnate. The trace is a sign that identifies itself as such. It calls attention to the reality that the ideal has been achieved and is therefore realizable still. No attempt is made to represent this ideal realistically; that representation would be futile, for the ideal must remain an abstract that is realized only by the devout in their lives. Basho says of the Ise shrine that it is a "picture of Nirvana" (1966: 80). The picture is the trace and Nirvana is the ideal to be witnessed by the heightened sensitivity of the poet and the devout.

The cult of traces affects pilgrimage in another way. Pilgrims, regardless of the religious tradition, tend to carry souvenirs away with them. Pilgrim trinkets tend to be cheap, tawdry representations of the shrine or some aspect of it. It is not that the shrine artists are incapable of better artistic productions—the art and architecture of the shrines themselves are often the highest achievements of the culture—but that they are creating traces of the shrine. In the home or with the returned pilgrim, the cheap souvenir symbolizes the ideals of the shrine but in no way attempts to rival or reproduce the perfection it contains. That attempt would be to negate the uniqueness of what is situated far off and make tangible what is ideal.

The message of ideals is an inner voice, or implicit paradigm, of the shrine. Not all pilgrims come to hear this voice, although some do. In most cases, the core notions of the shrine are translated into religious, ritual, or spiritual imagery that gains popularity. The pilgrimage place becomes known as a place of power. In Pruess's case study from Thailand (Chapter 11), the belief in the sacred power of a holy relic is made clearly explicit, since the overt purpose of the pilgrimage is to capture some of that very power.

What is this sacred power? It could be plausibly argued to arise from the collective investment in the ideals that are enshrined at the pilgrimage center. Emile Durkheim would have it otherwise, the god of the shrine representing society itself, rather than its more epiphenomenal values and ideals: "The god of the clan, the totemic principle, cannot therefore be anything other than the clan itself hypostasized" (Durkheim 1915: 206). Durkheim's theory overly stresses the social determinacy of religion and neglects the cultural factors. In fact, the sacred place draws potent force from its celebrated position in terms of both the social and the cultural realms.

The distinction must be made between those who are drawn to the pilgrimage place by hopes of grasping that force, to make themselves over into the ideals it embodies, and those who merely seek to tap the force for instrumental or other effective ends. Those who would hear the inner voice of the pilgrimage place are journeying to encounter the abstract ideals it embodies; those who would use the power of the concentrated greatness are journeying in search of aid along their life's way.

These reflections point to the boundaries of the territory of the anthropology of pilgrimage. In some cases, especially of tourism, the boundary between pilgrimage and other cultural journeying cannot be clearly demarcated. There are clear differences between the most typical forms of these practices, but many cases are not typical. The insights gained by studying pilgrimage will have some utility for understanding phenomena such as tourism, although less in some cases than others.

Distinguishing pilgrims from other travelers on significant journeys is made easier by the fact that in most cultures pilgrims tend to be self-labeling as such. Length of journey or the nature of the destination are lesser factors compared with the individuals's view of the activity he sees himself to be undertaking. A resident of Rome who regularly visits the Vatican for Mass is not a pilgrim; nor is the tourist who visits Jerusalem, even from a long distance, if the intent of the journey does not involve a quest for an ideal.

We are justified in including non-geographic sacred journeys in the territory of the anthropology of pilgrimage, largely because most cultures make this inclusion. But we must be careful not to become too mentalistic. Belief systems and concepts are important, but not to the neglect of the more mundane side of pilgrimage, which also deserves anthropological attention. The economic consequences, social arrangements, and political implications of pilgrimage fall fully within the scope of study. The territory of the anthropology of pilgrimage can extend to every dimension of human questing after ideals. Most typically, though not exclusively, it involves traversing earthly miles to terrestrial sacred places.

THE ANTHROPOLOGY OF PILGRIMAGE

The history of the anthropological study of pilgrimage is not deep, nor has it been comprehensive. Despite early ventures into the field (e.g., Robertson-Smith's *Religion of the Semites* [1907]; Hertz 1983 [orig. 1913] on St. Besse), Bharati (1963; 1970) and Turner (1973; 1974a; 1974d; Turner and Turner 1978) first gave the subject serious attention within the anthropological mainstream. One recent collection that focuses on Christian pilgrimage (Sallnow and Eade 1990) has pursued a theoretical approach to the subject.[1] Most anthropological research on pilgrimage has, however, been of one of three kinds: ethnographic, fragmentary, or typological.

Considering the number of sacred places that regularly draw pilgrims, the number of ethnographic studies is small, though increasing. A recent and welcome contribution adding to the ethnographic record is the volume *Pilgrims and Sacred Sites in China* (1992; edited by Naquin and Yu). Most ethnographic research has tended to focus on the sacred place rather than on pilgrimage itself. L. P. Vidyarthi (1961; 1979) and his students (e.g., Jha 1971) have contributed studies on pilgrimage places. Noteworthy studies that have considered the sacred journey itself are Irawati Karve's article concerning a Maharashtrian pilgrimage (1962), Ann Gold's study of Rajasthani pilgrims (1988), and J. A. Works's book on the Hausa making *hajj* (1976).

By fragmentary studies, I mean research that has considered elements of pilgrimage as aspects of other ethnographic categories, such as religious specialists or ritual. Jonathan Parry's study of death-related beliefs and practices at Banaras (1982) and my own paper concerning a pilgrimage ritual (1982) fall under this heading.

More general in intent have been the typologies that have been put forward by Agehananda Bharati (1963), Victor Turner and Edith Turner (1978), and Preston (1980). These typologies are not of pilgrimage but of sacred places. None is generally applicable. Bharati's and Preston's lists concern India alone; the Turners's typology admits of many exceptions (see Morinis 1984). A preliminary typology of sacred journeys is put forward in the next section of this chapter.

Most of the chapters in this volume are ethnographic. They address pilgrimage directly and so tend not to be fragmentary. None presents a unified theory of pilgrimage.

The only significant theory of pilgrimage that has been put forward to date is that of Victor Turner. He is owed credit for bringing pilgrimage to the forefront of anthropological consideration. Despite the valid criticisms that have been made, his work has been seminal and contains much that is insightful.

The principal proposition put forward by Turner is that the pilgrimage is like a rite of passage, bringing forward a modified version of the theory of ritual he developed (1969), following Arnold van Gennep. The central notion of Turner's theory is that pilgrimage as a performance stands as the anti-structural counterpart to the structured organization of society, with its rigid roles and statuses. Pilgrimage, in its essence, is an opportunity for the expression of the "communitas" experience: the "direct, immediate, and total confrontation of human identities" (1969: 131), breaching the bonds of structure. Pilgrimage is anti-structural, although not to the extreme of what he calls "existential communitas." Pilgrimage is a form of "normative communitas," that is, the destructuring communitas experience "organized into a perduring social system" (1969: 132). He states, "Though pilgrimages strain in the direction of universal communitas, they are still ultimately bound by the structure of the religious systems within which they are generated and persist" (1974: 205-6).

Turner's theorizing has been put to the test in Morocco (Eickelman 1976), Thailand (Pruess 1974), Nepal (Messerschmidt and Sharma 1981), north India (Van der Veer 1984), Peru (Sallnow 1981), Sri Lanka (Pfaffenberger 1979), and Bengal (Morinis 1984). None of these studies has confirmed Turner's hypotheses. In place of the recurrence of a leveling "communitas" situation, a wide variety of behaviors and experiences has been described. In many cases, pilgrimage was found to be a highly individualistic practice in which a person sought to establish direct contact with his deity, in contrast to the group event emphasized by Turner.

Pilgrimage has some formal similarities to a rite of passage, just as in some cases it resembles a rite of intensification (as pointed out by Coon 1958), but this similarity does not justify the analytical reduction of pilgrimage by assimilating it to another ritual of simpler structure. The complexity and diversity of the assemblages of meaning and action that are pilgrimages prove such reduction futile. Pilgrimage may be initiatory, like a rite of passage, or reinforcing, like a rite of intensification, and a quality of "communitas" may be identifiable in some cases, but, equally, pilgrimage can, and frequently does, take the form of a personal therapeutic act or an explicitly instrumental plea for divine intervention to sort out some earthly woe. Pilgrimage is too varied in content to be analyzed as if there were a single, recurrent, common, manifest factor.[2]

Though "communitas" has not been found to be a universal aspect of pilgrimages, Turner has pointed to a crucial facet of pilgrimage that contemporary anthropological theory is not well equipped to handle—the realm of individual experience. "Communitas" may not be *the* pilgrimage experience, but Turner has pointed to the fact that experience itself is of central concern to pilgrims. The goal of most Hindu pilgrims is the *darsana* (sight) of the deity's image. This idea is echoed in the words of Bishop Leo of Rome, who commented on the experience of the pilgrimage to the Holy Land, "Why need the mind toil, when *sight* is the master" (cited in Hunt 1982: 248). The recent dominance of symbolic analysis in the anthropological study of religion has obscured the importance of direct, sensory, non-intellectual experience in socio-cultural life. The majority of participants in ritual and pilgrimage do not pay nearly as much attention to symbols and meaning as do anthropologists. Their concerns lean to practical effect and direct experiences. One case that demonstrates some of the importance of experience is the study of the heretical sect "For My God and My Country Incorporated" of Wisconsin (Wood, Chapter 6). The group depends on the attraction of converts for its growth, and the impetus to conversion is always the direct, "religious" experiences had by the interested when on pilgrimage to the shrine.

An important task before anthropologists is to investigate in greater depth the experiential correlates of ritual participation (see Gell 1980 for a study that effectively argues for a central place for experience in anthropological analyses). In the following chapter Preston considers more broadly some of the methodological directions that the study of pilgrimage must pursue.

The conclusion, then, is that pilgrimage is a socio-cultural institution that bears analysis from whatever theoretical perspective an anthropologist chooses to bring to it. Michael Sallnow and John Eade (1990) have stated the most contemporary of social scientific perspectives on pilgrimage and look at the institution as "above all an arena for competing religious and secular discourses." Understanding of pilgrims and their pilgrimage, however, demands that social perspectives be supplemented by an appreciation for the direct experiences had by pilgrims. Structure and experience are inseparable components of the institution and process of sacred journeying. Victor Turner has encouraged exploration along both these lines, and so despite the questionable aspects of his theory, he has pointed to the two-pronged approach the study of pilgrimage requires. The stress on the complementarity of structure and experience is one of the main contributions the study of pilgrimage stands to make to contemporary anthropological theory in general.

A TYPOLOGY OF SACRED JOURNEYS

There is wide variation in what can validly be called a pilgrimage. It is not that there are many types of pilgrimage, because there are not, but there do exist significant differences among the types.

A true typology of pilgrimages focuses on the pilgrims' journey and motivations, not on the destination shrines. Although the pilgrimage journey has been given many forms in different cultures and eras, these can be sorted into a number of basic types, according to differences in individual motivations and aspirations. In every case, we see the movement away from the accustomed place toward a place or state that is held to embody ideals of importance to the pilgrim, but this basic formula has been applied to the accomplishment of a range of purposes. The principal types of sacred journey are (1) devotional; (2) instrumental; (3) normative; (4) obligatory; (5) wandering; and (6) initiatory.

Devotional

Psalm 84, "A Pilgrim's Song," says:

Happy those who live in your house
and can praise you all day long;
and happy the pilgrims inspired by you
with courage to make the Ascents.

Devotional pilgrimages have as their goal encounter with, and honoring of, the shrine divinity, personage, or symbol. Most Buddhist pilgrimage, especially to the holiest sites where the Buddha himself was present (Bodh Gaya, Lumbini, Kusinara and Sarnath), is fashioned as an honoring of the sacred traces of the Enlightened One. Hindu pilgrimage, especially that of the Vaisnava sect (worshipers of Krishna), tends also to stress the devotional aspect (*bhakti*) of the sacred journey. The pilgrimage to Pandharpur (Stanley, Chapter 3) is of this type. In both Hindu and Buddhist devotional pilgrimage, the goal is often the accumulation of merit that can be applied in this or future lives. Devotional pilgrimage has motivated much of the traffic of Christians seeking out the places that witnessed Christ's life and passion. Jerome encourages visitors to the Holy Land by saying "To worship at the place where the feet of the Lord have stood is the task of faith" (cited in Hunt 1982: 87). The pilgrim Paula who accompanied Jerome prostrated in devotion before the Cross. And it was of devotion that Paulinus of Nola said, "No other feeling draws men to Jerusalem, save to see and touch places in which Christ was bodily present."

Instrumental

Instrumental pilgrimages are undertaken to accomplish finite, worldly goals. A common example found in all religious traditions is the journey to the shrine in hopes of obtaining a cure for illness. In ancient Greece pilgrims would seek out the shrines of the mythic healing divinity Asklepios when illness persisted. Under the guidance of the shrine priests, the pilgrims would spend the night lying in the sanctuary awaiting a dream that would reveal the cause of their illness and/or provide a remedy. Hindu pilgrims also practice dream incubation as a healing rite of pilgrimage (Morinis 1982), as well as other rituals intended to restore health. The Christian pilgrimage center at Lourdes is only the most famous of pilgrimage places to which pilgrims journey in hopes of a cure. In this present volume the chapters on Velankanni in South India (Chapter 4), Saut d'eau in Haiti (Chapter 7), and Lac Ste.-Anne in Canada (Chapter 5) concern healing Catholic shrines. Fatima in Portugal, Guadalupe in Mexico, Esquipulas in Guatemala, Ste.-Anne de Beaupre and St. Joseph's Oratory in Quebec City and Montreal, Canada (Laperriere 1981), and the Black Virgin of Czestochowa, Poland, are all renowned for cures. We find the tombs of Muslim saints being sought out for the same purpose (cf. Betteridge, Chapter 10 and Crapanzano 1973). Many of the chapters in this book (especially Chapters 4, 5, and 10) are concerned with healing pilgrimages.

Aside from pursuit of cures, instrumental pilgrimages are undertaken for almost any conceivable reason. Since the shrine deity is an especially potent version of the cult deity, anything for which one might call on God is done better through a pilgrimage. The alleviation of barrenness is a common instrumental goal of pilgrims (cf. Betteridge Chapter 10). My research on pilgrimage in Bengal found pilgrims undertaking sacred journeys for reasons as diverse as restoring lost hair to the head, altering an astrological chart, finding a good marriage partner for a daughter, desiring success in examinations, helping an ailing business, and so on (Morinis 1984).

Normative

This type of pilgrimage occurs as a part of a ritual cycle, relating to either the life cycle or annual calendrical celebrations. In the Hindu tradition it is appropriate to undertake pilgrimage at any major life passage. Feeding a child his first solid food, cutting a child's hair, or investing a boy with a sacred thread are all important rites that are given higher value when performed at a recognized pilgrimage center. Newly married couples frequently seek out a shrine to request the blessings of the deity on their union. Death in a pilgrimage center is said to free the deceased from further rebirth. The elderly congregate at sacred places like Banaras, and the ashes of the dead are frequently brought for immersion in the sacred rivers of India (Gold 1988). Hindu belief in the excellence of death at a pilgrimage place has given rise to the practice of ritual suicide at places like Puri and Allahabad (Prayaga; cf. Chattopadhyaya 1937). The eastern sacred city of Gaya has come to specialize as a pilgrimage place where one can perform ancestral rites for the recently departed (Vidyarthi 1961).

The Old Testament assigns pilgrimage to calendrical rituals. The three festivals that today are still known as the Pilgrim Feasts—Weeks, Tabernacles and Passover—were occasions when all of the men of the Hebrew tribes would converge on the temple at Jerusalem. Annual community pilgrimages are to be found in the Muslim (Eickelman 1976), Buddhist (Pruess 1974), and Latin American Catholic (Crumrine 1991) traditions.

We can note here that there is a tendency to undertake pilgrimage at a critical point in a cycle. Certain times of the month or year, a particular period in the agricultural calendar, or a juncture in an individual life cycle are turning points when people commonly embark on sacred journeys. As a cycle enters a new phase, there is a breaking open of routine that frees people to step out of habitual structures temporarily. The uncertainty bred of change also makes it desirable to seek out the powerful god of the shrine as a new phase begins. The turning point is both honored and hopefully defused by reference to the higher, enduring, stable level of order represented at the shrine. Individual life, community fortunes, the seasons, and culture all change, but the pilgrimage place located outside of the boundaries of the settled community endures. In fact, pilgrimage shrines are, of course, subject to all the forces that breed socio-cultural change, but they do tend to be less affected by the tides of change, and they do tend to be more enduring than most socio-cultural institutions. Jerusalem is an excellent example of the enduring appeal of the pilgrimage place throughout eras of social and cultural change.

Obligatory

The most famous of the obligatory pilgrimages is the *hajj*, the fifth pillar of Islam that enjoins all Muslims to visit Mecca once in their lives. The *hajj* is a set of prescribed rites that are performed at fixed times at assigned locations in and near Mecca, Saudi Arabia. Thayer's chapter (Chapter 9) concerns the impact of this practice on one corner of the Muslim world, but it is fair to extrapolate that similar influences have been felt from Morocco to Indonesia. It was Muhammad's genius to recognize that an annual gathering of representatives from every segment of the dispersed Islamic religious world would have a significant impact on the solidarity of the international Muslim community. Being obligatory, the *hajj* has drawn Muslims together in every year since its inception. Since the Second World War the number of pilgrims has grown steadily, currently reaching over one million per year.

Obligatory pilgrimages in Christianity were commonly imposed by ecclesiastical or secular authorities as a punishment or penance. Frotmond, an early Christian pilgrim, was convicted of killing his uncle, an ecclesiastic. He was bound with chains, clothed with a hair shirt, covered with ashes, and sent to walk to Jerusalem. He spent four years in the holy city practicing austerities. He then went to Egypt, where he lived among rigid, self-torturing hermits. He hoped by this penance to earn the pardon of Rome, but despite his efforts, pardon was twice refused (Besant and Palmer 1899: 136-37). Santiago de Compostela, the famous shrine in northern Spain, was a pilgrimage place to which convicted criminals were commonly sent on penitential journeys in the Middle Ages. Some pilgrims were condemned to wander from shrine to shrine until their chains were worn away by the friction of dragging along the roadways.

Wandering

This type of pilgrimage has no predetermined goal. The pilgrim sets out in the hope that his feet will be guided to a place that will satisfy his inner craving. The journey of Basho, the Zen poet-pilgrim of the Seventeenth century in *The Narrow Road to the Deep North*, is a wandering quest for the ideal of timeless eternity, which he hopes to find in the beauty of nature in the unopened northern reaches of Japan (1966). An echo of Basho's journeying is to be found in the tradition of the beggar pilgrims of Edo Japan, who wandered from shrine to shrine throughout their lives.

Early Christian theologians interpreted the pilgrimage (*paroikos, peregrinus*) as the search for solitary exile. The pilgrim abandoned the cities of the world to become a hermit or wanderer in the wilderness, an image of Abraham, who received God's commandment to leave his homeland. The pilgrimage was a dying to the world to inherit heaven. The tradition of shrine-worship emerged much later and led to such corruption of the spiritual intent of pilgrimage as the selling of thousands of years of indulgence at shrines. The excesses of Catholic pilgrimage were one of the failings of the Church that fueled Luther's rebellion and the Reformation.

A contemporary example of Christian wandering pilgrimage is the journeys undertaken by Spiritual Baptists in Trinidad, named "closed pilgrimages" by Glazier in his chapter in this volume (Chapter 7). In this case, the social goals of massing and leading a group far overshadow the geographical goal of the pilgrimage, which is usually an ordinary church located beyond the pilgrimage leader's sphere of influence.

In general, wandering pilgrimages reflect the fact that the ideals that are pilgrims' goal need not be located in time and space. Still, a journey is undertaken because in some way movement from here to Other is called for to realize the quest of the pilgrim, be it social, instrumental, salvic, or whatever. We know that here is incomplete and unsatisfactory, and so we set out, hoping to find the Other through the act of going forth itself.

Initiatory

This category includes all pilgrimages that have as their purpose the transformation of the status or the state of participants. Important here is the "journey" that a seeker undertakes to work a transformation of self. The pilgrimage of the Huichol

Indians of Mexico, for example, is a terrestrial journey on which the individual seeks a hallucinogenic cactus. The visions that follow eating the cactus are considered an initiation, both in the social sense and in terms of the awakening of a higher level of consciousness (Meyerhoff 1974).

The *hajj* to Mecca can also be considered initiatory insofar as the returned pilgrim is then classified as occupying a new social rank, with the title *hajji*. In the Hindu tradition, pilgrimage is incorporated into many life-cycle initiations (*samskaras*). It is common to give children their first solid food or their first haircut at a sacred place, for boys of the twice-born castes to be invested with the sacred thread at a shrine, and ultimately for the rites of transformation and repose of dead ancestors to be performed at a pilgrimage place, all initiatory functions.

Because the essence of pilgrimage is concerned with the pursuit of ideals and salvation within the human condition, many pilgrimages are oriented toward initiation, in the sense of both change of social status and transformation of personal state.

This typology has no pretense of being totally exhaustive. It is meant as a step toward refocusing attention onto the sacred journeys of pilgrims themselves and away from the shrines and deities that are important to, but not the essence of, pilgrimage. I also want to show that different types of pilgrimage occur within the same religious tradition, while similar practices can be noted cross-culturally. Having sorted out the ethnographic record in this way, I turn to sketching a theoretical frame for the analysis of all types and varieties of sacred journeys.

TOWARD A COMPARATIVE STUDY OF PILGRIMAGE

Pilgrimages range in structure from the highly formal to the highly informal. There is a continuum from, at one pole, very formalized, even obligatory behavior to the opposite pole, at which informality and non-institutionalized behavior are dominant. Pilgrimages can be located along the length of this continuum.

At the pole of high formality we find that the stress in pilgrimage is on social ritual. At the other extreme the emphasis is on authentic, direct, individual experience. Formal pilgrimages stress the repetition of formula and ritual, while informal pilgrimages are oriented toward personal expression. The collective symbolic content of formal pilgrimages tends to be much higher than that of the informal. The format of formalized pilgrimages tends to be fixed and rigid, while informal pilgrimages tend to be more flexible. The behavioral code enjoined on participants tends to be much more restrictive in the former case:

Formal	*Informal*
rigid format	flexible format
stresses formula and ritual	stresses direct experience
highly symbolic	low symbolic content
moral	personal
highly restricted behavioral code (e.g., re: emotions and body)	open behavioral code

One example of a pilgrimage tending to the formal pole is the *hajj* to Mecca, which is performed annually according to a highly specified formula, in fulfillment of a religious obligation. A second case is the Alandi *palkhi* (pilgrimage group), described by Stanley (Chapter 3). At the informal pole we find the wandering ascetic pilgrimages of Basho. Early Christian pilgrimage also tended toward the individual and away from the collective performance now more typical of Christian sacred journeys.

Even at the informal pole, though, pilgrimage does not take place outside of culture. Basho recorded his journeys in the conventional forms of haiku poetry. The hermit monks situated their practices within the doctrines of the church. By its nature pilgrimage reflects the social and cultural environment that generates and sustains it and gives motive for pilgrims' journeys.

This linkage of pilgrimage to its environment gives rise to the specific content of the pilgrimage and is the source of the major differences among pilgrimages. Switching our focus from differentiation to commonality, we see that there are essentially two invariable components to be found in every pilgrimage: the journey and the goal.

The Journey

The essence of the journey is movement. The analysis of pilgrimage movement is, to an extent, typological, but it is more as well because movement encompasses significant aspects of meaning and experience that are central to sacred journeys.

The common journey is of a linear type, taking the pilgrim from home to shrine and home again. Massing pilgrimages are also linear, insofar as people go from home to a massing point and then proceed en masse to the shrine, afterward dispersing to home. A case of this type of pilgrimage is given by Stanley (Chapter 3) in his discussion of the Pandharpur pilgrimage. Massing pilgrimages often take the form of processions, which transform movement from a functional, physiological act into a cultural performance. Processions permit many sorts of organization, each of which depicts socio-cultural themes. It is common, for example, to organize the participants in a pilgrimage procession as a manifest replication of the social rankings of groups in society (e.g., Obeyesekere 1966). In the Velankanni pilgrimage in South India Younger (Chapter 4) describes "the movement of the near-ecstatic vow-keepers into the presence of the image."

Then too, the movement of the procession contains other forms of movement that might be significant. Do the pilgrims dance (cf. Poole 1991), walk on their knees, or measure the length of their bodies in prostrations?

The journey can also be circular or spiral. Rounds of pilgrimage, which take the pilgrim on a journey encircling a feature or territory such as a mountain (e.g., Tiruvanamalai, South India) or an island (as in Shikoku, Japan; cf. Statler 1983) or to a set of sites in one city or region (e.g., the Via Dolorosa in Jerusalem; see also Stanley Chapter 3) are circular. Circular movement can also be an aspect of pilgrimage ritual, such as the circumambulation of a shrine, as is common in Tibetan Buddhism and Hinduism.

In spiral journeys one does not proceed directly to the shrine, but goes round and round until the center is reached. This form of movement can be a symbolic ascent (e.g., Falk 1977) or can be an actual pathway to ascend a height. Since many pilgrimage places are located on mountaintops, the ascent by spiral movement is common.

These and other forms of movement on pilgrimage are ripe for symbolic analysis. The sacred journey is always subject to cultural molding and so is a stage for the depiction of whatever meaning the culture attributes to various sorts of territorial action.

The symbolic meaning of movement is also informed by its opposite, stasis, and a good part of the meaning of sacred journeys is to be uncovered in the analysis of this central structural opposition. In many cases the deity is static; in some cases the deity moves. Whether the god travels or remains fixed or the pilgrim journeys to or with the deity are important questions of symbolism at the foundation of meaning for the pilgrimage performance. Pilgrimage is woven out of the structural opposition of stasis/movement, in whatever diversity this theme might be depicted. The relationship of stasis and movement figures centrally in the legend of origin of the Pandharpur pilgrimage, which sees the moving Krishna become fixed standing on a brick (Stanley, Chapter 3).

There is a time element of movement that creates frequency and repetition of journeys through space. Pilgrimages are often timed to occur within monthly, annual, seasonal, or other cycles. Individuals can undertake to make pilgrimages at specified intervals. Symbolism is involved here. So, too, is the relationship of pilgrimage movements to other cycles and movements, such as those of the day, sun, moon, seasons, and so on. The Yucatec Mayan term for pilgrimage also refers to the journey of the stars through the heavens (Konrad 1991: 123). Pilgrimage can link human movement through space and the progression of life through time to other dynamic spheres of the universe.

History has time and again recorded the practical and social implications of the large-scale movements of people through territory. The formation of pilgrim parties, their leadership, the development of pilgrim ritual specialists, the providing of goods and services, and other such practical matters are important aspects of study. Important, as well, is the relationship of pilgrimage routes and traffic to trade routes and the paths of refugees, conquerors, Crusaders, and other travelers. The ties between sacred and secular journeys have been considerable and contributed to the social importance of pilgrimage.

A last and more inchoate aspect of journeying is the question of the experience itself. Anthropologists have given little attention to the psychophysical aspects of pilgrimage performance, yet there are obvious implications to practices that demand that mountains be climbed, fasts endured, austerities performed, and so on. Turner has called attention to the fact of experience with his concept of "communitas," but we are yet to investigate the broad range of psychosomatic sensations that accompany sacred journeys and are often the most significant aspects of pilgrimage in the view of participants themselves (Aziz 1987 treats this issue more fully). The analysis of symbols offers only a limited understanding of the concern of pilgrims pictured by Gregory of Nyassa as they approach a casket of relics: "those who behold them embrace them as though the actual body, applying all their senses, eyes, mouth and ears; then they pour forth tears for his piety and suffering, and bring forward their supplications to the martyr as though he were present and complete" (cited in Hunt 1982: 133).

Pilgrims need not, and seldom do, understand a great deal of the symbolism and meaning packed into the churches, shrines, and temples they seek out. Social structure, cultural configurations, and symbolism are only the building blocks out of which the creators of culture fashion the pathways that participants follow. For pilgrims, their experiences while following the stipulated path loom significant. I call attention to the interaction of individuals (with their given structure of physical and psychological responses) and cultural frameworks that incorporate a meaningful code but, at the same time, serve to induce specific, direct experiences in those who follow the steps of the conventional procedure. More research is needed to document the range of pilgrims' experiences and the mechanisms by which these are induced. Experience must be analyzed in relation to social and cultural patterns, in the attempt to make sense of why certain experiences are common to some pilgrimages and not others. There are methodological difficulties in trying to understand the highly individualized world of sight, sound, and smell, but we cannot neglect what the pilgrim may view as of utmost importance, what might motivate his journey, and what, in the end, may leave the most lasting impression.

The sacred journey deserves primary attention because it is the essence of pilgrimage. Implicit in most types of sacred journey, however, is the goal at journey's end. The journey is always a quest, and the quarry is usually an extraordinary place.

The Goal

Pilgrimage to a sacred place is the most common form, though not every temple, shrine, or tomb attracts pilgrims. A pilgrimage place is elevated above ordinary religious establishments, usually because it lays claim to an exaggerated relationship to the divine; the divine might be represented in the ordinary place of worship, but the divine has been or still is actually present in the pilgrimage center. The most visited Catholic pilgrimage shrines today are associated with apparitions—direct sightings—of Mary: La Salette, Lourdes, Fatima, Guadalupe. Many Hindu sacred places are sites where saints (representing humans who have ascended to the divine) or *avataras* (the deity descendant to the human realm) have dwelt. The four sites in India associated directly with the life of the Buddha are the most sacred of Buddhist pilgrimage places. Pruess (Chapter 11) discusses a common icon of the Buddhist pilgrimage center: the footprints of the Buddha and his predecessors. Hindus also enshrine footprints in their sacred centers (e.g., the Gayapada at Gaya and the footprint of Caitanya at Puri). Mecca and Medina are cities that witnessed the Prophet in his life. The tomb shrines of folk Islam, as well as shrines in all of the other major religious traditions, frequently house the relics of revered saints, again a feature of the actuality of the divine presence in that place.

The pilgrimage center must achieve a reputation for having a unique character and offering something available at no other place with which it competes for patronage. But there are constraints on how differentiated a shrine can be. It must remain within the known boundaries of its culture. Sacred centers accomplish this balancing of familiarity and differentiation by developing and projecting an image that is a magnification of some accepted ideals of the culture. They represent a higher or purer or more ideal version of what the potential pilgrim already values and seeks by dint of membership in a culture. Cultural intensification of this sort is the central force in the creation, maintenance, and success of pilgrimage shrines. A center that ceases to embody an intensified version of cultural values goes into decline. New values and new representations of values spawn new centers. Professor Preston picks up this theme in the following chapter.

This description of the general character of the pilgrimage center implies two sorts of fields in which it participates. There is the social field, in which the pilgrimage center is a locus for human gathering. Second, there is the informational field, in which the pilgrimage center is an encoded image broadcast through the social field in legend, story, song, poem, film, and so on. Each of the ethnographic chapters in this volume deals with a center sought out by a pilgrim population of certain, specified social characteristics. The stream of information that flows within the social field and catalyzes members of the cultural group into pilgrims encodes the core images—the intensified ideals, the sacredness—of the center. The legends, miracle tales, reports of cures, stories of saintly lives, and the like make up an interesting corpus of ideas, writing, art, and speech, which also recur as a focus of attention in many of the chapters of this volume. More research is to be done on the informational fields of pilgrimage shrines. One subject that has hardly been studied at all is the relationship between pilgrimage beliefs and behavior (i.e., the tales of the sacred place and the rituals performed there).

Pilgrimage fields define the area within which the center is known and from which pilgrims are drawn. Where shrines share similar or overlapping fields, they may compete directly for pilgrim trade or, more commonly, either accept a ranking (in which case similar ideals are intensified but are acknowledged to be more concentrated in the higher-ranked shrine) or embody differing ideals. This pattern is given form, for example, in India, where shrines sacred to the cult of Siva can exist near equally popular shrines appealing to the followers of Krishna. Lesser shrines to both deities fall within the fields of the major centers. The fields of the most important shrines can encompass entire nations or go beyond that scope to the field of all believers, as is the case for Mecca and Rome.

It is conventional to refer to sacred places of pilgrimage as centers, and from a social and especially a cultural point of view, the image of the center is valid. But centrality is only one spatial concept that is tapped in locating the sacred place in relation to its fields. Geographically, the sacred place is actually seldom central. Most commonly, the journey takes the pilgrim to the top (mountain peak), edge (seashore, forest), or beyond (desert, uninhabited region). The pilgrimage is a cultural construct that is woven out of, and so displays, basic cosmological principles, especially regarding the space dimension. Since cosmologies are culturally relative, it is important to consider where in space—center, top, beyond—the sacred place is situated and what meaning might be attached to this positioning of the most sacred locus.

These comments relate only to aspects of sacred places that are relevant to sacred journeys, since the study of shrines, temples, and churches is already highly developed compared with our knowledge of pilgrims and their journeys. To date, most studies of pilgrimage centers have been made by disciplinary specialists who have considered only the aspect of the shrine that was relevant to their academic field: architects on architecture, historians on history, geographers on spatial arrangements, and so on. The direction of future research on pilgrimage shrines should be collaborative. Understanding the multidimensionality of these places in their full complexity demands a collective effort that combines the methods and insights of several disciplinary perspectives.

Pilgrims

Pilgrims tend to be people for whom the sacred journey is a limited break from the routines and familiar context of an ordinary, settled social life. This contrast prompted Victor Turner to draw an opposition between life within everyday society as "structure" and pilgrimage as the context (still socially patterned) of moving outside structure to reach goals through the enactment of breached structure: "anti-structure." What prompts individuals to move out of their daily orbit to undertake a sacred journey? What is the nature of their undertaking? What are its results? These three questions guide us through an investigation of pilgrims' motives, actions, and the impact of their journeying.

Almost any conceivable purpose can motivate a pilgrimage. Explicitly religious pilgrimages tend to be initiated out of strongly felt personal needs that are culturally channeled into pilgrimages. Throughout history, though, "sacred" journeys have been undertaken for reasons relating more to social, political, and economic circumstances than to ostensible religious intentions. The pilgrim's goal can be the acquisition of greater wealth, political power or prestige. Of the tendency for those involved in church politics in the Middle Ages to make pilgrimages to the Holy Land, Hunt (1982: 203) says, "The capacity of the holy places to attract to themselves, in the guise of piety, the central figures of ecclesiastical controversy proved considerable." Writers on Meccan pilgrimage have frequently referred to the social motives for pilgrimage. Joseph Hickey, Gregory Stats and Douglas McGaw (1979: 223), for example, found that the *hajj* of the Nigerian Fulani tends to be undertaken by men of wealth, as measured in numbers of wives, children, and sons. Their pilgrimage is intended to convert wealth into social prestige. Cohen (1968: 171), al-Naqar (1972), and Charles Frantz (1978) have made similar findings on the social factors that impinge on the religiosity of the *hajj*.

The motives pilgrims give for their pilgrimage reveal the conscious model of the pilgrimage within which the individual plans and executes actions. We find here statements about the power of the divine, notions of the efficacy of thought and action, and, more generally, statements of belief in the nature of the pilgrimage quest. The anthropology of pilgrimage has given too little attention to the personal side of pilgrimage, of which motives are one aspect. Methodological innovations will be needed to probe the personal history, thought, experience, and belief that give rise to pilgrim behavior.

Pilgrims on their quest are seeking a relationship with an ideal, often culturally-defined but sometimes fully personal. The relationship with the ideal can be of many types, although two overarching patterns are (1) to become the ideal (to have direct insight, to experience, to know) in the way in which one affirms one's aspiration to become Christ through the Blessed Sacrament and (2) to tap the power that the ideal possesses, often for practical or even mundane ends. Pilgrims tend to talk about the "power" of sacred places. Some individuals seek identification with a locus of extrinsic power, while others desire to make use of the power available from that source.

Motivation is the first of a series of thoughts and actions that a pilgrim goes through on a sacred journey. It is followed typically by setting out, going, arrival, communion, and return. The content of each of these stages will show distinct cultural patterning. As well, there is usually a degree of cultural regulation of the full process, so that the parts are integrated in a practical and meaningful way. From the point of view of pilgrims, the composite of these stages *is* the pilgrimage.

The journey can be studied as a social process. Identification of a core process of stages of action makes possible cross-cultural comparison. The contents, as well as the patterning of the stages of the journey, can be set beside each other for comparative purposes.

The stages of the pilgrimage are a framework for personal action. Each culture will specify the content of each stage differently, and, in fact, different pilgrimages within a single culture can have distinct rules and norms of behavior. Pilgrimages of the more formal type are more closely stipulated, while there is more latitude for variation in informal pilgrimages. In all cases the individual works the socio-cultural institution to accomplish intended ends. An individual negotiates the specified actions, meanings, and experiences of each stage of the pilgrimage according to ability and need and achieves experience and reward in reflection of this negotiation process.

Pilgrims (unlike anthropologists) do not spend much of their time on pilgrimage unpacking the meaning of symbols. Symbols tend to be built into the environment or to be encoded in behavioral prescriptions that the pilgrim follows. The pilgrim follows prescriptions and is delivered the information and experiences appropriate to his or her motives and actions. The information given is often little; sacred journeys tend not to be intellectual quests. It is experience that counts. Many pilgrimages specify what a pilgrim must see, hear, touch, and taste. Austerities like fasting, self-mutilation, fire-walking, hook-swinging, and the like, which are common features of pilgrimage, also concern direct experience. It is valid to conceptualize pilgrimages as cultural channels along which individuals pass, carrying out actions (often specified) in pursuit of predictable experiences.

Most pilgrimages are goal-oriented, if not overtly instrumental, and direct experience can be the goal itself (as in the case of the Hindu *darsana*, where the "sighting" of the deity can be the total goal of a sacred journey) or the means to the goal. Experiences can affect psychological and physical aspects of pilgrims' lives, working impact on health, well-being, and spiritual life. Pilgrims' personal acts and experiences can, as well, be connected to social goals. In the Maori pilgrimages discussed by Sinclair (Chapter 12), personal experiences (especially visions) are part of a pilgrimage which has as its explicit goal the reworking of a collective ethnic identity.

Pilgrimage, in turn, can have an impact on the social structures and processes of home. Trade, transfers of wealth, and changing employment opportunities can result. Less tangible but equally significant can be changes in general norms, values, and behaviors that come about because of contact with the diverse influences at a pilgrimage center. Change is not the only possibility; existing normative and behavioral patterns can be reinforced by visits to the cultural capitals of society. All of these effects are mediated through the lives and actions of individual pilgrims. Glazier (Chapter 7) describes another way in which pilgrimages are applied to social ends: Trinidadian Spiritual Baptists use pilgrimages to raise money and develop a following as leaders within the church community.

CONCLUSIONS: THE PLANES OF PILGRIMAGE

Thus far in this discussion I have flipped back and forth among a variety of anthropological vantage points on pilgrimage. Sometimes I have adopted a psychological perspective, sometimes a structuralist or functionalist view. I have adopted concrete categories as targets for analysis ("pilgrims," "journeys," "places") to lay down a basis for cross-cultural comparison. It has been possible to use contrasting theoretical positions to analyze within each of these categories. I turn now to an attempt to make this diversity systematic and examine the "planes" of pilgrimage.

Ego Plane

Pilgrimage in its inception and continuing popularity is a personal act, giving rise to the traveler's personal impressions and experiences. At this ego plane, pilgrimage is situated in the context of the pilgrim. The principal means to gain access to this plane is to investigate the personal tales and attend to the written, autobiographical memoirs of pilgrims themselves. Glenn Bowman's treatment of pilgrims' narratives reveals that they contain a systematic, ideological formulation of the Otherness of the sacred place, and James Thayer draws on such accounts to make sense of the impact of the *hajj* in West Africa. Colin Turnbull's accounts of his own Himalayan pilgrimages (Postscript) stand for all pilgrims whose footsteps echo through this volume.

The level of ego-plane must be emphasized to appreciate why people set out on their sacred journey and what they learn, see, and experience on the way. Comparison at this level will reveal the cultural continuities and individual variants within and between pilgrimage traditions.

At this plane are situated the important psychological mechanisms that operate in the processes of different pilgrimages. The pilgrimage experience can give rise to pain, concentration, suggestion, change, and reinforcement in the human mind, to temporary or lasting effect. In turn, the efficacy of pilgrimage in healing, settling a troubled mind, or helping an individual resolve a difficulty in life may be a function of operations at this level.

Cultural Plane

At the more generalized level of culture, individual belief, action, and experience in pilgrimage take on a more consistent general patterning. A complex relationship links a pilgrimage place with its cultural field. This relationship is complex because it contains the two opposing tendencies of closely identifying the center with the culture of its population, while somehow distinguishing it from the more accessible forms of the ideal that is enshrined at the pilgrimage center. This paradoxical status is achieved by configuring the accepted ideals of the culture in an extraordinary way. Important in this process of image-making is the web of tales, legend, history, and miracle stories that spins out from the sacred center. Bowman (Chapter 8) describes how the image of Jerusalem propagated in Europe was more a reflection of the European culture of the time than it was an accurate representation of the Holy City itself. In Shiraz, Iran (Chapter 10) the legendary life histories of various Imams are invoked to account for why pilgrims take certain problems to one and not another shrine.[3]

At this level, too, the question of meaning arises. The symbolism of the pilgrimage and the symbols that are integrated into the sacred journey and center are all features of culture. More generally, here we find what can be called the code of pilgrimage, which underlies the concept and practice of pilgrimage within a culture. Through song, art, narrative, drama, and so on, this code conveys messages about the relative importance of pilgrimage as a personal practice, the schemes of levels of sacred sites within the culture, and the semantic linkages of pilgrimage with other cultural categories. Earlier on I mentioned the semantic range of the Hindu term *tirtha*, which links the pilgrimage shrines of the Indian subcontinent to renunciates, wives, scriptures, parents, virtues, and organs of the body. All these share the pilgrimage code, which in this case specifies that a *tirtha* is any intermediate location across which one can move to gain access to another, more ideal cosmological realm, whether the movement is somatic and territorial or is another sort of change semantically assimilated to movement, for example, approaching the state of consciousness of one's *guru*.

Similarly the Latin root of the English *pilgrimage—per ager*, through the fields—is an aspect of the Christian pilgrimage code that gives rise to terrestrial pilgrimages but equally informs St. Augustine, who said that the City of God is a pilgrim on earth, and Samuel Purchas, who gives expression to the common image of life as a pilgrimage:

And thus is Man's whole life a Pilgrimage,
either from God as Cain's or from himself as Abel's (1905-1907: 138).

The pilgrimage code makes terrestrial pilgrimage sensible, creates the image of the pilgrimage that is a motif of other sorts of culturally-sanctioned journeying, and differentiates one pilgrimage tradition from another cross-culturally. Culturally-derived meaning is invested in the common aspects of the sacred journey, such as departure, arrival, communion, and return, which become part of the pilgrimage code and so are important to understanding the indigenous concept of the sacred journey in its many forms.

Another issue at the level of culture is the dynamic aspect of cultural change in sacred journeys. Sacred power is not always the same, and patterns of journeying change through time. Pruess's chapter deals directly with this issue by describing how a new sacred place emerges from old by a transference of culturally approved artifacts that carry with them some of the sacred essence of the original, revered site. The trade and movement of relics in the Christian world reflect the same process of translating sacred power through space and time. In my own chapter (Chapter 5) I consider aspects of social and cultural continuity that link contemporary Canadian native Indian pilgrimages to pre-missionary ceremonial gatherings. Pilgrimage institutions and processes do tend to have extraordinary persistence, through periods of internal and external change. Besides my chapter, the contributions by Paul Younger, James Thayer, Peter Wood and Karen Sinclair all deal with the processes of change that alter but also preserve the practice of pilgrimage through time.

Social Plane

A pilgrimage complex incorporates a number of social groups into sets of relationships that are essential to the operation of the institution. At the broadest, the pilgrimage has its social field, defined by the catchment area from which it draws pilgrims. Social ties link pilgrims into pilgrim parties in ways specific to the culture or even the pilgrimage. Sometimes pilgrims set off alone, most commonly in the company of friends and family and occasionally in a party of strangers. The social composition of the group strongly influences behavior and experiences on the pilgrimage. Examples of social groups on pilgrimage are the *ko*, a Japanese village confraternity that tithes members and uses the accumulated funds to sponsor pilgrimages, traditionally to the Ise shrine but now to Shikoku as well, and the *cofradias*, ceremonial sodalities among the Mayo in Mexico.

Another important relationship links pilgrims to shrine priests. Almost every sacred center has a group of ritual specialists who mediate the relationship of pilgrim to shrine deity. There are also non-ritual specialists, such as traders, innkeepers, and guides, with whom pilgrims interact.

The sacred center is itself a social institution and so embodies a structure of roles and relationships that anthropologists can fruitfully analyze. The center is sustained—or destroyed—by virtue of the social links among the priests or other ritual specialists, resident ascetics, politically powerful patrons, and other parties who have an interest in the center and its operation.

The pilgrimage complex will reflect changing social patterns. Pilgrimage places can be valuable resources in sociopolitical processes. Groups may attempt to capture the power of the sacred place by associating it with their cause or community, dramatic examples of this process being the Islamicization of Mecca and the campaigns to take Jerusalem during the Crusades.

There are, as well, social impacts arising from the practice of pilgrimage. The *hajj*, for example, has been responsible for the diffusion of new ideas, the legitimization of new regimes, and other effects documented by Thayer (Chapter 10). Early pilgrims from West Africa contributed to the Islamicizing and Arabizing of West Africa more than did traders because of the influence wielded by the pilgrims, who were almost exclusively royalty or respected clerics. Later pilgrims carried reform movements current in Arabia back to their distant outpost of the Muslim world. The point to note is that the same pilgrimage can have different impacts in different eras, depending on social conditions.

Because pilgrimage places tend to enshrine collective ideals, pilgrimage is usually a conservative force that reinforces the existing social order. This result is not inevitably so, however. Wood (Chapter 6) considers the role of pilgrimage in an excommunicated Roman Catholic group, and Sinclair describes a Maori pilgrimage that is explicitly a search to change the group's relation to the dominant social order (Chapter 12).

The pilgrimage place stands apart from society but is nevertheless sensitive to, and reflective of, forces at work in society. Its position outside ordinary social boundaries lends power to the pilgrimage center, yet, ironically, belief in the power of the place makes it a target for social manipulations.

Physical Plane

Of concern here are the physical structure of the pilgrimage place and the spatial factors that have bearing on the relationship of the place to its field. The architecture and physical arrangements of the shrine center are both a practical arena for pilgrims' actions and a representation of the symbols, deities, and ideals that are the central focus of pilgrimage practice. The architecture thus takes inspiration from, and gives form to, the code of the pilgrimage, and represents important aspects in physical space. Of special note in this regard are the cosmological schemes built into the Hindu temple or Buddhist *stupa*.

The social and cultural fields of the pilgrimage have their counterpart in a geographical field. The relationship of a place to its surrounding space is an important factor in determining the path of the sacred journey and the obstacles a pilgrim must overcome. The physical setting, as well, provides symbols, such as river confluences and mountain peaks. Space itself is subject to conceptualization and so there will be culturally-derived meaning given to territorial space, as is true of the notion of "wilderness," which is a major motif of pilgrimage to the heretical American Catholic shrine in Wisconsin (Wood, Chapter 6).

The physical arrangements of the sacred place and its territorial field are integral practical and semantic aspects of the process of sacred journeying that cannot be neglected in an anthropology of pilgrimage and are themselves rich subjects for the study of pilgrimage institutions and the process of sacred journeying.

Meta Plane

Each plane of pilgrimage has its place as a component of the institution and process of sacred journeying, however, the planes of pilgrimage cannot be clearly distinguished, as evidenced in the fact that the physical plane is endowed with meaning arising from the cultural plane. Movement through culturally construed space, with its different categories of territory, is a central feature of pilgrimage.

Each plane takes account of the other planes with which it intersects, and a relationship among the planes must be established. The matrix of this relating is the Meta plane of pilgrimage.

At its most elementary the pilgrimage matrix is constructed of two poles and movement between them. The two poles of the meta-plane are culturally construed. In general, they represent the key polarities that concern the socio-cultural group that patronizes the pilgrimage. These are not the oppositions familiar from structuralist theory, but, more simply, they represent the perfect (which is the unknown ideal) and the imperfect (which is the all-too-well-known circumstances of human life).

Although each culture casts these poles in its own image, in general they contrast as:

Familiar	Other
known	mysterious
human	divine
social	ideal
imperfect	perfect
mundane	miraculous

The key to the pilgrimage process is the movement between these two poles. Pilgrimage mediates the opposition between them and permits various sorts of resolution. The pilgrim is a cursor that shifts from problem to answer, in the hope of working a mediation and resolution between the imperfection he knows and the ideal he seeks.

Movement (physical or otherwise) is inherent in the transcendence of constraints. Most commonly, movement by the pilgrim links two static poles: the fixed place of home and the fixed place of the ideal. This pattern takes advantage of the power of movement to join the poles by crossing the gulf that separates them. This pattern is not universal in pilgrimage because not all homes are static (as in the case of nomadic peoples), nor are all deities fixed in space (e.g., the gods of the Trinidadian Spiritual Baptists are highly mobile; Glazier, Chapter 7). In every case, movement is employed in pilgrimage to represent the route of transformation toward perfection, but there is no inherent rule that this mediation take the form of stasis-movement-stasis.

The pole of Otherness is out of time and space. In the most mundane sense, it is always located away from the known territory of home, and a visit is usually a breach of ordinary time cycles. But it is also a feature of the codes of pilgrimages to depict the perfect Otherness of the sacred center by locating it outside the constraints of space. There are many cases of pilgrimage places being assimilated to non-earthly realms: heavenly Jerusalem, celestial Vrndavana. But more striking and significant is the emphasis on the collapse or cancellation of time and history that is so central to pilgrimage.

Basho's wanderings had no certain goal, except the quest for the timeless eternal. The passage of time Here leads to the suffering and problems that drive the pilgrim to set out for There, where death and the trials of reaching that end no longer threaten. The relics, tombs, mausoleums, and other remains that are common features of sacred centers work to cancel time by representing continuing presence. The very concept of apparition or *avatara* represents an undying presence here and now. The legends that are an essential component of any pilgrimage system always tell that the saint or deity is eternally accessible there to the faithful. At Shikoku, Kukai is believed to be ever alive and continuing his pilgrimage. The Bordeaux Pilgrim (quoted by Bowman, Chapter 8) tells of Christ visiting the pilgrim in the holy places where he lived in the past. The description of the trees believed to have been planted by Jacob echoes the Buddhist tradition of the continuing vitality of the tree under which the Buddha achieved Enlightenment. Reputed shoots of the ancient tree are revered by present-day pilgrims in India, Thailand, Sri Lanka, and elsewhere. Pilgrimage deities in Bengal are described as being *jagrata*, "awake". The justification for today's rites of the *hajj* is that they are the same as done by Muhammad. Historical continuity is another way of denying the effect of time, which ordinarily breeds change.

Many of these examples are concerned with the connection of present to past, but by so doing or by more explicitly asserting that the past is now, too, all time is collapsed into an eternal moment in which perfection overcomes the incompleteness of mundane lived time. This is salvation.

Sometimes the quest for salvation that is pilgrimage is made explicit, as in the case of journeys to Banaras to avoid rebirth or the purchase of indulgences at medieval Catholic shrines to shorten the time a soul would have to spend in purgatory. Cases from this volume include the spiritual messages about salvation received by Maori pilgrims in New Zealand (Chapter 12) and the doctrine of the Wisconsin shrine, which asserts that the shrine is an Island of people guaranteed eternal salvation when the great divine Chastisement sweeps all sinners to damnation (Chapter 6). More commonly, the search for salvation is implicit in people's attempts to deal with life's imperfections by taking themselves on pilgrimage to attain the aspects of their lives they sorely miss: health, children, peace of mind, comfort, wealth, gain.

Salvation can be either the total transformation attained through transcendence or the more piece-meal and earthly acquisition of solutions to the powerlessness, discomfort, and weakness of an afflicted life. Pilgrimage is inclined to vows and promises because the solutions to the seemingly insurmountable difficulties that motivate a sacred journey must come from a higher order of power.

The individual does not stand alone, and so in many cases salvation is contingent on social forces. The Crusaders were promised salvation for their deaths in the taking of holy places. The colonized Maori and Plains Indians seek resolutions on their pilgrimages, but the social and cultural pressures of the recent centuries of domination have made the working out of personal fate dependent on collective ethnic salvation.

The return to the everyday is a component of almost every pilgrimage. While the sacred place is the source of power and salvation, it is at home once again that the effects of power are incorporated into life and what salvation is gained is confirmed. The return journey and the reincorporation of the pilgrim into social life are the test of the pilgrimage. Has there been change? Will it last? In Chapter 12 Sinclair puts it clearly: "Salvation and grace depend only partially upon transcendence. Ultimately moral redemption lies in the creation, by whatever symbolic sacred means, of a positive place within the mundane social order." The mountain is climbed, the peak tested, but the knowledge of what has occurred awaits the descent.

Anthropologists, including all the contributors to this book, have seen the search for salvation written into creased faces, clenched in joined hands, carried in ordinary voices rising up in the prayers of the thousands of pilgrims we have encountered and with whom we have shared the road. Their song is the theme melody that has played in hearts and minds since the dawn of consciousness. Life is hard, uncertain, fearful. I suffer. I am incomplete. But I have heard tales, in my childhood I heard legends, and I recall scraps of stories about another place, hundreds of difficult miles away, where all answers abide and problems dissolve as the chains of time and space are lifted from this soul. I set out—on foot, in my heart—to find that jeweled place, to tap that boundless power that will solve the dilemma of my life.

Turnbull ends this book with his bare feet in icy Himalayan water. From this point at the outset of this volume to that final voice at the end, an echo of the personal nature of the quest weaves through these pages. Between these two points we will join many a pilgrim, walk some miles on their journey, sit close as tea is shared. Many of the chapters to follow are analytical, as is much the purpose of this volume, but even as the intellect "accounts" for what occurs, the solitary pilgrim setting feet along the path to meet his god is sounding a theme melody of the human soul. Pilgrim's quest is the human quest.

NOTES

1. My earlier work (Morinis 1984) contains a more extensive analysis of anthropological theories of pilgrimage.

2. The same criticism can be brought to bear against any attempt to apply Durkheim's concept of "collective effervescence" or "effervescent assemblies" to account for pilgrimages (1961: 62). Durkheim's concern was to find social functions in religious performances, and collective emotional displays were easily argued to be effective in reinforcing social integration. When one focuses on the full range of types of pilgrimage, however, it becomes clear that there is great variety in patterns of sacred journeying and that it is the exceptional pilgrimage that involves the collective effervescence Durkheim describes, just as it is the exception rather than the rule to discover what might be called "communitas" among pilgrims.

3. See also Slater 1991 for a model study of the oral and written literature of pilgrimage.

I
THEORETICAL ISSUES

Spiritual Magnetism: An Organizing Principle for the Study of Pilgrimage

JAMES J. PRESTON

Pilgrimage has been a neglected subject, despite the important place it occupies in world religions. Professor Preston suggests some cogent reasons for this situation, especially the fact that sacred journeys often involve a mystical aspect which is difficult—although not impossible—to penetrate analytically. The problem is methodology. He calls for an interdisciplinary approach to the study of pilgrimage because the multi-faceted nature of sacred places and of pilgrims' quests demands a comprehensive approach that no single discipline can provide. The author also develops several concepts that should prove useful for conceptualizing the less easily accessed dimensions of sacred journeys. In particular, the notion of "spiritual magnetism" to account for the drawing power of the sacred center, and "tracing" as a methodology for analyzing ever-changing pilgrimage patterns through time and space should find a place as useful theoretical tools for the researcher of the future who will tackle the sort of interdisciplinary study pilgrimage demands.

It is curious that until recently pilgrimage has been neglected as a topic of inquiry by social scientists and historians of religion. What is the reason for this lack of interest over the years? Pilgrimage is not an esoteric phenomenon. It is manifested in one form or another in virtually all the world's religions. Nor is there an absence of documentation, since for centuries many shrines have kept elaborate and meticulous attendance records, biographical histories, and pilgrim travel guides.

What has impeded the study of this important religious custom? The problem is at least partially methodological. Something is intrinsically difficult about studying transitory phenomena like pilgrimage. In anthropology, for instance, there has been a strong inclination to focus on spatially bracketed phenomena at village levels or within particular religious complexes. Unlike village studies that involve clearly defined communities, pilgrimages are unbounded phenomena involving strands of behaviors that transcend geographically confined groups. Another factor that has impeded the study of pilgrimage has been the dominance of Boasian Particularism in anthropology, a school of thought that has insisted on "holism" and neglected the elaborate networks characteristic of complex social systems.

These reasons alone do not fully explain the neglect of pilgrimage as a focus of research. A further aspect of the problem is suggested by Victor and Edith Turner, who characterize pilgrimage as "extroverted mysticism, just as mysticism is introverted pilgrimage" (1978: 33). This apparent kinship with mystical experience has rendered pilgrimage unfashionable as the social sciences have swept the more subjective side of human experience off center stage. Although there is a long and distinguished anthropological tradition associated with the study of mysticism (especially shamanism), exemplified by the classic works of Radin, Wallace, Lowie, and LaBarre, the dominance of behaviorism and particularism has pushed mysticism from the foreground of research. A survey of the psychological literature on "religious experience" reveals an almost thorough retreat from serious investigations of the topic after a period of initial enthusiasm in the early part of the twentieth century (see Preston 1984). Following the widespread use of psychedelic drugs and the popular "discovery" of eastern religions in the 1960s, religious experience has once again attained legitimacy as an appropriate topic for scholarly research. The recent readmission of subjective aspects of human nature as a focus of anthropological inquiry has contributed greatly to the present burgeoning interest in the study of pilgrimage (Preston 1991).

The neglect of pilgrimage in the scientific study of religion is related to an even more insidious problem than the narrow scientism of either behaviorism of Boasian particularism. Pilgrimage defies the kind of compartmentalized analysis associated with the present style of Western thought that organizes everything into discrete disciplines of inquiry. The social sciences are ill-equipped to cope with sprawling, processual phenomena. On the other hand, the physical sciences have been forced to overcome disciplinary compartmentalization by creating multidisciplinary methodologies to resolve the fragmentation of Western knowledge. Medicine, biochemistry, archaeology, and other materially oriented fields of inquiry have synthesized methodologies for investigating complex phenomena. Multidisciplinary research strategies require abundant funding. Unfortunately, generous resources for research projects in comparative religion are rare.

We are challenged both to work within our disciplinary biases and to transcend them. Pilgrimage can be approached from a number of different theoretical orientations, such as structuralism or cultural materialism. Today, however, these once fashionable theories are inadequate for the study of pilgrimage. No single discipline or theoretical perspective can do it justice. We are challenged, then, to contemplate the potential power of a multidisciplinary methodology.

SPIRITUAL MAGNETISM AND THE PROBLEM OF LEVELS

Many scholars have noted the tendency for pilgrimages to be arranged in hierarchies, circulating devotees among different levels of sacred centers (Bharati 1970; Bhardwaj 1973; Turner and Turner 1978). The pilgrim flow is usually, though not always, patterned along increasingly more complex levels of sociocultural integration, from local peripheral folk centers toward national or international shrines. While no one doubts the existence of these levels, scholars disagree about how to define them. One common denominator is *spiritual magnetism,* which can be defined simply as the power of a pilgrimage shrine to attract devotees.[1] It is not an intrinsic "holy" quality of mysterious origins that radiates objectively from a place of pilgrimage; rather, spiritual magnetism derives from human concepts and values, via historical, geographical, social, and other forces that coalesce in a sacred center. It develops at a particular place of pilgrimage because of the interplay of traceable forces that seem mysterious to participants but have measurable referents in empirical reality. This attribution does not diminish or in any way disregard attributes of mystery, miracle, or sacrality assigned to the phenomenon by devotees.

Folk explanations of the spiritual magnetism attributed to a sacred center are valid from the participant's point of view. Nor can we neglect extrinsic variables that make a pilgrimage shrine attractive. Places of pilgrimage are endowed with spiritual magnetism by association with (1) miraculous cures, (2) apparitions of supernatural beings, (3) sacred geography, and (4) difficulty of access. The following are brief descriptions of each variable.

Miraculous Cures

Sacred streams, hot mineral springs, and other natural sources of water are frequently associated with healing. Miraculous cures attract large numbers of pilgrims to sacred centers. Some involve the reported intervention of a deity or saint; others occur by the mere presence of an ill person in the sacred precincts of a pilgrimage site. The range of cures attributed to divine intervention is extensive, including miraculous healings of syphilis, leprosy, tuberculosis and stress-related disorders like asthma, arthritis, delirious fevers, and various mental conditions. Miraculous cures may also involve forms of "social healing," such as the healing of family solidarity or the attainment of jobs. Many of the great Christian pilgrimage centers that developed in the nineteenth century derived from miraculous cures. These centers include the shrines at Knock (Ireland), Fatima (Portugal), Lourdes (France), and La Salette (France). Hundreds of thousands of pilgrims flock to these shrines every year. Miraculous healings enhance spiritual magnetism even after the introduction of modern medicine. In India, for instance, the eradication of smallpox has not diminished pilgrimage to shrines devoted to the smallpox goddess Sitala. Instead, this goddess has started specializing in the cure of pilgrims who suffer from general fevers and other afflictions. The significant question is how pilgrimage shrines become centers of wholeness for fragmented people and provide atmospheres of physical and psychological healing.

Apparitions of Supernatural Beings

Deities are believed to speak directly to those persons who, as mediums for divine encounters, deliver messages to humanity or reveal holy laws. Inevitably such revelations call for a shrine to be built where the apparition has occurred, sometimes at the insistence of the deity. Here the original vision is reenacted (Turner and Turner 1978: 210). Pilgrimage sites associated with apparitions are imbued with strong mystical powers. Once the miraculous descent of the supernatural into the world has happened, it is believed it can occur again.

Prophets, saints, and deities may have visited these pilgrimage sites, either as mythological or historical personages. Caitanya, the great Bengali Vaisnava saint, made frequent pilgrimages to the shrine of Lord Jagannath in Orissa, one reason for its elevation to the status of an all-India shrine. The major Islamic pilgrimage center at Mecca is located where Muhammad destroyed pagan icons and established the monotheistic focus of Islam. In Christianity numerous pilgrimage shrines have been founded after apparitions of the Virgin Mary have occurred. Typically she delivers messages to "common folk" (sometimes children) about how to confront problems of corruption, decadence, and evil in the world.

In those cases where the appearance of a supernatural being has taken place or a holy person is believed to have performed some crucial act to found a new religion, special shrines are erected. Spiritual magnetism is enhanced in these places of pilgrimage by the performance of rites of renewal. Pilgrims typically reenact the original experiences reported to have occurred at holy sites, rites that link them back to the core values of their tradition. There is something energizing about locations where encounters with deities once happened, even though these events may have taken place thousands of years ago.

Sacred Geography

In those traditions where the earth is associated with powerful religious sentiments, spiritual magnetism is strongly linked to sacred geography.[2] The land of Israel is imbued with sacrality for Jews, Christians, and Muslims alike. Similarly, sacred geography is expressed in the Hindu concept of Bharat—the place where the Mahabharata, Ramayana, and Puranas were lived out during mythological times. The holy wells, islands, and mountaintops of Ireland represent a Christianized sacred geography superimposed over older, pagan Celtic traditions.

Pilgrimage sites are often found in the most dramatic locations on the globe and inspire lofty emotions and high spiritual values. Hiroshi Tanaka describes eighty-eight sacred places on mountain peaks and in valleys scattered throughout the four major islands of Japan (1978: 2). Himalayan sites (like Mount Kailasa, Tibet) and other mountain peaks in the world (Doi Suthep, Thailand; Sri Pada, Sri Lanka; and Croagh Patrick, Ireland) attract thousands of pilgrims each year. Sacred topography is ubiquitous in India, where certain mountains, ponds, lakes, rivers, trees, and abodes ascribed to deities (*dhamas*) are selected for particular reverential treatment (Bharati 1963: 161, 165; Bhardwaj 1973: 95; Clothey 1972: 88-92; Singh and Singh 1987). The Ganges River, from its source in the Himalayas to its mouth on the Bay of Bengal, is laced with pilgrimage sites that demarcate the contours of Indian civilization. Visits to local villages in India spontaneously evoke tales of sacred places in the surrounds where deities and heroic figures from the epic scriptures once roamed.

Sacred geography is not always defined in terms of dramatic features of land-scape. There is nothing particularly beautiful or extraordinary about the geographical locations of Mecca, Rome, or Jerusalem, yet they are located at the crossroads of previous civilizations that have been transformed and synthesized time and again into new worldviews by saints or prophets. A principle of *spiritual synthesis* is operative here. These shrines are focal points for movements of large numbers of people toward centers of civilization. Pilgrimage sites strongly associated with sacred geography may diminish in importance as civilizations decline. Many of the great places of pilgrimage of antiquity have faded away after periodic episodes of stellar florescence.

Difficulty of Access

Some pilgrimage sites attain a high degree of spiritual magnetism because they are difficult to reach due to either intrinsic or extrinsic factors. A shrine located in a precarious place attains some of its spiritual magnetism from *intrinsic* dangers associated with the pilgrimage journey itself. Other shrines impose rigorous *extrinsic* rites of penance for pilgrims to perform as they approach the inner sanctum. In either case, the pilgrimage requires sacrifice, an important ingredient for enhancing spiritual magnetism.

India's Amarnath cave shrine is a place of pilgrimage located in a difficult place of access. This Shaivite shrine has an extraordinary *lingam* of Lord Siva, composed of an ice stalagmite. The shrine is located ninety miles northeast of Srinagar (Kashmir) at 12,729 feet above sea level. It attracts thousands of pilgrims each year who travel to the high Himalayas, where they pay tribute to Lord Siva. Over the years pilgrims have willingly journeyed there, despite the risks of danger along a final thirty-mile trek over a precipitous bridle path. Bad weather in 1928 killed 500 people on pilgrimage to the sacred cave. In 1970 a blizzard took the lives of 18 others.

Instead of discouraging devotees, these events have actually elevated the spiritual magnetism of the pilgrimage.

Factors of risk inherent in journeys to remote locations were also evident in Christian pilgrimages to the Holy Land during the Middle Ages. Danger experienced during pilgrimage is a source of spiritual magnetism even today. Young and old alike ascend Ireland's Croagh Patrick once each year on a dangerous three-and-a-half mile climb to the summit at 2,510 feet. In 1972 fifteen accident victims were carried down by stretchers, and in 1106 the Bishop of Ardpatrick was struck by lightning and killed. Seven years later on the eve of St. Patrick's festival, thirty people were hit by a thunderbolt while fasting and praying at the summit. All of them died (Turner and Turner 1978: 208). The irony of these tragic events is that they attract rather than repel pilgrims, due to the widespread folk belief that dying while on pilgrimage is auspicious.

Sometimes the difficulty of a pilgrimage may be imposed through traditional obstacles created deliberately for pilgrims to endure. These places are not necessarily remote. Extrinsic hardships often take the form of penances. Individuals are expected to demonstrate acts of contrition for sins or to purify themselves through elaborate devotions, including self-flagellation, crawling on one's knees during a specific phase of the journey, or licking the ground while approaching the sanctuary. Exhausted pilgrims may faint, have convulsions, or enter into delirium trances. During the Feast of the Madonna of the Arch near Naples, Italy, pilgrims work themselves into a state of frenzy, exhaustion, and trauma from self-inflicted wounds. Each year over a thousand need special treatment at first-aid stations (Tentori 1982: 100). The penitential aspect of pilgrimage is not unique to Christianity. It is widely articulated in pilgrimage traditions throughout the world.

Modern tourism erodes the penitential dimension of pilgrimages. During field-work in India priests and older pilgrims expressed concern about attenuated rites at many contemporary shrines. In their view the decline of spiritual magnetism at some pilgrimage sites can be attributed to the "softness" of an increasing number of "tourist pilgrims." Accustomed to urban comforts, these tourists are typically reluctant to undergo the hardships of long journeys on foot or the routine penances once expected of all pilgrims. One cannot help but speculate that busloads of "tourist pilgrims" and attenuated penitential customs have negative effects on the spiritual magnetism of pilgrimage shrines. The opposite result may also occur as tourism and pilgrimage are forged together, amplified, and orchestrated to reinforce nationalistic/ethnic identities. The recent apparitions in Yugoslavia reflect a fascinating combination of tourism and pilgrimage. Highly touted by the media, this pilgrimage has become a major attraction for hundreds of thousands of tourists, many of whom are also attending as pilgrims. While spiritual magnetism is clearly related to the numbers of people who attend a shrine, it also involves more profound measures of religious experience, such as the pilgrim's sense of being in the presence of the supernatural.

In recent years many shrines have abandoned the imposition of penitential hardships on pilgrims. Others have not, such as the Irish pilgrimage to St. Patrick's

Purgatory in Lough Derg, County Donegal, where an ancient penitential pilgrimage continues to thrive despite minor attenuations. The St. Patrick's Purgatory pilgrimage is nearly 1,500 years old and has undergone many changes. At several points in history it was closed by Protestants. It reached its peak during the famine years but today continues to attract large numbers of pilgrims despite hardships imposed by penitential customs. St. Patrick's Purgatory is located on a small island in a lake. It is easy to reach, and during the summer months as many as 20,000 people spend three days of penance there. Pilgrims must remove their shoes, engage in extensive fasting (only bread and water), stand all-night vigils, and repeat endless prayers and rounds to the various small shrines on the island. It is believed by pilgrims that the more they suffer deprivation on the island, the easier will be the torment their beloved ones will endure in purgatory (Turner and Turner 1978: 121). The willingness of pilgrims to undergo these hardships suggests that even today penance enhances spiritual magnetism at some shrines.

Not every pilgrimage site is endowed equally with the four variables that contribute to the development of spiritual magnetism. Some sacred centers attract large numbers of pilgrims even though they are associated with only a couple factors. For instance, Ireland's popular pilgrimage to the shrine of Our Lady of Knock has nothing to do with sacred geography. Nor is it difficult to reach, being located in the gentle hills of County Mayo with easy access by car, train, bus, or plane. The Knock shrine is not situated on the main crossroads of urbanizing culture like some places of pilgrimage. It is located instead in an unmistakably rural setting, like other Irish pilgrimages to places of sacred geography, such as holy wells, rivers, or mountain-tops. The Knock shrine became a pilgrimage site in 1879 at the end of the second Irish famine after the appearance of the Virgin Mary to over a dozen people. Ten days following this dramatic event, visitors to the site reported miraculous healings. The first instance was the case of a twelve-year-old girl cured of deafness and sharp pain in her left ear. The child's mother removed a piece of cement from the gable of the small church where the apparition had occurred, made the sign of the Cross, and placed the cement in the afflicted ear. The pain reportedly ceased at once with no remaining traces of deafness (Walsh 1967: 15). After this incident Knock became a place of intense spiritual magnetism for the Irish people and rivaled the already well-established shrine at Lourdes in France.

The intensity of spiritual magnetism may increase as a shrine becomes better known for miracles or when it develops a focus of intensifying cultural activity. Unfortunately, there are not enough ethnohistorical studies of pilgrimage sites to know exactly how this intensification occurs. It would appear, however, that during certain historical periods some sacred centers become increasingly associated with supernatural efficacy. Sometimes the notoriety of a pilgrimage shrine develops at an almost exponential rate, as if it were involved in a positive feedback system that peaks and then diminishes as dramatically as it flourished.[3] Most intriguing is why spiritual magnetism is more intense in one sacred place compared with another, a fact that establishes the relative stratification of shrines in pilgrimage networks. These questions must await further research to be answered with any degree of certainty.

The four variables associated with spiritual magnetism are not exhaustive. Other factors should be investigated, such as the role of national identity in forming spiritual magnetism, as in many Catholic Marian shrines like Czestochowa (Poland), Guadalupe (Mexico), and Copacabana (Bolivia) (Preston 1982: 333). Also, the presence of relics at a shrine may enhance its spiritual magnetism. This effect was particularly true in the past, especially in Europe where the cult of relics flourished during the High Middle Ages.

RESEARCH STRATEGIES

The value of spiritual magnetism as an analytical tool must await empirical testing through systematic fieldwork. Different research methodologies yield a variety of results. What is the best approach for the study of pilgrimage? Some research strategies place emphasis on attendance at shrines; others stress participation of the individual pilgrim. Each approach reveals another facet of this complex phenomenon.

The Statistical Method

At first glance pilgrimage would seem to be an ideal subject for statistical analysis. Many shrines and communities keep records of pilgrim activities. These data are usually inaccurate, however, and need to be supplemented by systematic strategies designed by professional researchers. In his classic study of Hindu pilgrimage, Surinder Bhardwaj (1973) has employed statistical methods to avoid the subjective factors associated with other types of classification. He relies heavily on counting the actual numbers of pilgrims who attend a pilgrimage, including the distances they travel to a shrine and the diversity of pilgrims (in terms of caste, class, gender, or other variables). Bhardwaj delineates five levels of classification for Indian pilgrimage shrines. He is correct to observe that the "...sanctity (of a shrine) cannot be easily quantified" (1978: 15).

When relying on statistical methods, one tends to emphasize the distance traveled to pilgrimage shrines as a measure of spiritual magnetism. This measure may be quite misleading. In Orissa (India), for instance, virtually everyone would agree that Sarala Temple (located in a small village thirty miles east of Cuttack city) is a major place of sanctity because of its association with Sarala Das, Shudra author of the Oriya *Mahabharata*. Yet few devotees are attracted to this shrine from beyond the district where it is located. The small number of pilgrims who attend the shrine is due to poor access. It is located outside the main transportation corridors running north and south. Nor is Sarala Temple situated in a place of particular beauty or unusual challenge. It is out of the way and consequently attended infrequently. Other shrines in Orissa, believed by devotees to have less spiritual magnetism than Sarala

Temple, are visited more frequently by pilgrims because of their convenient locations. Despite its shortcomings, the statistical method has the important advantage of objectifying otherwise unclear phenomena. It also yields a potential for correlations between different variables of pilgrimage.

The Indigenous Literary Method

This research strategy employs both linguistic terms and classification schemes found in the sacred literature to extract insights about different levels of sacred centers. Agehananda Bharati (1970: 97) is correct when he insists that indigenous classification schemes should be considered before new ones are constructed from the outsider's point of view. Nevertheless, indigenous schemes are limited, since many of them are dated and do not apply to contemporary pilgrimage cycles. These schemes may have little value because they are frequently vague and poorly defined. In the Indian case, for instance, there are rich epic and Puranic sources that classify pilgrimage shrines, but they are so vague as to be relatively useless with respect to current shrines.[4]

The Contextual Method

The placement of a pilgrimage tradition within a civilization's religious and political history constitutes the contextual method. In this research strategy the level of spiritual magnetism of a shrine is determined by its place of centrality with respect to the Great Tradition. While some shrines are peripheral to the civilizational core, others are at the epicenter, supporting divine right kingship and the elaborate hierarchy of bureaucracy that reinforces the system. A. Eschmann (1978: 84) uses a contextual methodology to study the multiple levels of sacred centers in Orissan Hinduism. She classifies Orissan shrines along an axis extending from tribal cult temples through higher levels of sociocultural integration, culminating in the great Hindu temple complexes at the core of Indian civilization. In this approach the icon becomes a focus and an instrument of increasing acculturation. This approach is a diachronic rather than a synchronic view of pilgrimage and sacred centers. Several problems are evident. In the first place, the contextual methodology is difficult to apply without good historical records. There is also the danger of placing too much emphasis on large, politically important pilgrimage centers (because of available data) while neglecting other shrines by classifying them as peripheral. Furthermore, a question could be raised as to whether the historical/political context of a shrine tells us anything about its spiritual magnetism. Some of the great Christian centers of healing, such as Lourdes and Fatima, are not particularly important centers of European civilization. These shrines serve a purely religious function for devotees, one that transcends historical and political contexts.

The Psychological/Linguistic Method

This research strategy has considerable potential for the study of pilgrimage. The psychological/linguistic approach would include a series of intensive interviews with pilgrims to determine levels of spiritual magnetism of shrines in a particular region. In anthropology this method of research is similar to ethnoscience—the development of cognitive models using linguistic categories and concepts carried around in people's heads. The psychological/linguistic approach is employed by anthropologists during fieldwork to elicit the cognitive contours of cultural systems. Are there differences in the mental maps of sacred centers among people from various social classes and different regions? Anthropologists have found cognitive categories to be useful for the study of small groups in complex societies, such as bars, elevators, hospitals, and other social institutions. The method has also yielded intriguing results among tribal peoples, particularly for the classification of color terminology and folk taxonomies of animals and plants.[5]

Each of the methodologies noted here has its advantages and disadvantages. None is sufficient alone for delineating the parameters of a pilgrimage network. Spiritual magnetism is determined by a multiplicity of factors in different religious traditions. Many questions need to be addressed. How does a pilgrimage shrine influence the surrounding secular field? How does it contribute to the economy of the locality? Does it spawn a tradition of miracles? How much of the spiritual magnetism of a shrine is generated by commercial, economic, and political factors?

One of the most critical tasks in the study of a pilgrimage tradition is to establish the hierarchy of shrines and the appropriate relationship among them.[6] This preliminary exercise is crucial for a comprehensive understanding of the role of pilgrimage in a religious system. Sacred journeys are like filaments that constitute the superstructure within a civilization. Thus, while pilgrimage is a private and personal event at one level, at another it transcends the individual and links him into the interconnecting fibers represented in the process of sacred journeying.

THE SACRED TRACE

The key to pilgrimage is found in the flow of people along linkages between different levels of sacred centers. A unique methodology is required for the study of religious movement. I call this methodology *tracing*—a term borrowed from nuclear physics, where the invisible world of atomic structure becomes tangible through traces left in other media. The invisible dimension of pilgrimage is the overall process, a pattern visible only when all pieces of the puzzle have been assembled. Since pilgrimage is always in flux, it requires a methodology that captures its periodicity and the flow of behavior ascending in networks of increasing ritual and cultural complexity toward a point of religiocultural integration.

Patterns of pilgrim movement are best assessed in the broader cultural context of the pilgrim field. This general background information brackets the pilgrimage process and places the phenomenon in clear relief, as in the relationship of figure to ground. Since all pilgrimages are stratified spatially and temporally, tracing, of necessity, should be achieved through the movement of a team of experts following the pilgrim flow at various levels. Tracing the flow is essential because pilgrimage is a circulation of people, ideas, symbols, experiences, and cash. Pilgrimage extends humans beyond parochial horizons, as they move both vertically and horizontally into increasingly wider religiocultural spheres. On the vertical axis pilgrimage is a dual process; pilgrims move upward to higher and higher levels in the religious network, then return to their villages (or urban neighborhoods) with new perspectives that have important influences on local traditions.[7] This feedback mechanism widens horizons for individual pilgrims and occurs at various levels. Pilgrimage cycles connect people on the horizontal axis to large geographical entities. Pilgrims enter extensive marketplaces associated with pilgrimage routes, participate in vibrant religious traditions that extend beyond parochial horizons, come in contact with persons of different classes (who would otherwise remain segmented from each other), experience ethnic groups other than their own, and gain a clearer sense of their own uniqueness.

Tracing probes still further to the very deepest levels of religious experience. Elsewhere I have defined the sacred trace found at the core of the world's religions as follows:

> The phenomenon of an invisible reality made visible in the world is what I call the *sacred trace*. Trace is defined in the dictionary "as a visible mark or sign of the former presence or passage of some person, thing or event." It also means, in its archaic usage, "a path or trail through a wilderness."…. The sacred trace is located at the core of every pilgrimage. It takes many different forms. In some cases it is the relics or tomb of a saint; it may be the place where Muhammad delivered his sermon, calling together the Brotherhood of Islam or where Jesus of Nazareth rose from the dead. The trace is the source of spiritual magnetism of a shrine, its powerhouse, so to speak. By participating in the epiphany manifested at a particular place of pilgrimage, the pilgrim ingests and carries home the trace of his tradition, then anchors or implants it in his home community. This is part of the reason why sacred objects (sacramentals) of all sorts are purchased and brought home from pilgrimage shrines (Preston 1990: 22).

TOWARD A MULTIDISCIPLINARY METHODOLOGY

Ideally, the tracing of a pilgrimage cycle would involve a team of experts who conduct research on various aspects of spiritual magnetism. Several disciplinary approaches and dimensions of pilgrimage are sketched briefly here. No single scholar could cover all of them alone. Thus, a multidisciplinary approach is critical.

Geographical Dimension

A crucial first step in the study of pilgrimage must be to map the pilgrim field. Several types of surveys are valuable: (1) maps of the distribution of pilgrimage sites; (2) visits to major pilgrimage shrines to determine their locations, indigenous categories of classification, configurations of diffusion, and so on; and (3) maps of pilgrimage circulation patterns. Modes of transportation in the pilgrimage process need to be determined. How are vehicles of transportation linked into the civilization as a whole (Bharati 1970: 126)? The geographical dimension requires technical skills in the analysis of spatial networks and demographic movements.

Historical Dimension

Pilgrim records and other historical documents need to be examined to trace the evolution of a pilgrimage from its point of origin through various phases of sociopolitical and religious change. This information is particularly valuable for "syncretic pilgrimages," which blend two or more religious traditions. It is also useful for the study of "founder pilgrimages," where pilgrims trace the sites of the founder's original vision. This "reenactment of the generating vision" (Turner and Turner 1978: 210) becomes a symbolic vehicle for the paradigmatic pilgrimage. The tracing of historical changes should yield insights about how pilgrimage shrines become transformed in different historical periods.

Sociocultural Dimension

Several issues are critical in tracing the sociocultural dimension of pilgrimage. To what extent, for instance, does a universal pilgrimage, like the *hajj* to Mecca, entail the dissolving of ethnic boundaries or the imposition of a dominant acculturating motif? A number of studies (Gross 1960: 145; Bharati 1970: 87; and Turner and Turner 1978: 129) have noted a feudal paradigm associated with pilgrimage, the patron being the deity at the pilgrimage site, the client being the pilgrim. In Gross's study of the Bom Jesus de Lapa shrine (Brazil), the vehicle for the patron-client relationship is the *promessa*, or vow of payment. "Worship and the paying of *promessas* correspond to the fealty and labor which a client owes his superior" (1960: 145). This relationship of dependency in the sacralized dyadic contract is a significant element of pilgrimage. Why does the feudal paradigm exist in some pilgrimages and not others? Perhaps the most important issue associated with the sociocultural dimension has to do with how the pilgrimage process fuses together otherwise disparate social groups under a single umbrella. Mexico's Guadalupe shrine is a typical syncretic pilgrimage conceived in a grand "mestizo synthesis" that forges the roots of Mexican national identity (Campbell 1982).

Economic Dimension

Virtually every pilgrimage is associated with a field of economic exchange, as in fairs, carnivals, and permanent or temporary marketplaces. Materials are redistributed as pilgrims enter sacred centers, then disperse. A relationship of debt between deity and pilgrim, the institution of begging, and the temporary incorporation of peripheral tribal peoples in the process of exchange are examples of secondary (in some instances primary) motives for pilgrimage behavior. The economic dimension is connected to the widespread custom of sightseeing, which has always had some influence on pilgrimage. Tourist activities are common interludes on pilgrimage journeys. It would be useful to trace the general scope of commercial stimuli provided along pilgrimage routes and within sociopolitical spheres.

Psychological Dimension

Numerous psychological factors contribute significantly to the pilgrimage process. The following represent a few questions that might be addressed in a psychological study of pilgrimage. What motivates people to undertake sacred journeys? How does the pilgrimage change people psychologically? What role do perceived salvation, suffering, and penance play in the pilgrimage process? Psychological studies should consider the important dimension of healing as a by-product of pilgrimage. How are illnesses, both physical and mental, influenced by visits to sacred centers?

Religious Dimension

The reenactment of the founder's original religious experience is often a potent method for periodically revitalizing a particular religion. Invariably, contact with the sacred center is an act of "rupture" in which the pilgrim crosses a series of thresholds and returns to the source where humanity and divinity are believed to intersect. This "coming into the presence of the sacred" is often experienced as miraculous. We need to know more about sacred thresholds. Critical questions arise concerning the nature of sacrality. As the Turners have observed, all pilgrimage sites are "believed to be places where miracles once happened, still happen, and may happen again" (1978: 6). Even where miracles occurred only in the past, contact with the sacred center in such a place may continue to have religious value.

Other questions about levels of pilgrimage need to be addressed. In the Indian case, for instance, Bhardwaj (1973: 158-60) has observed an important difference in the purposes of visits to higher-level as compared with lower-level places of pilgrimage. Higher-level shrines are visited for *darsana* (viewing the deity) and the attainment of merit, while lower-level shrines (often devoted to goddesses) are attended mainly to fulfill vows (*sukkna*) associated with the meeting of specific needs. How broadly can we generalize these findings to pilgrimages in other parts of the world? The Turners note an opposite configuration for Christian pilgrimages, where Marian shrines are primary rather than secondary places of pilgrim activity (1978: 201-2). Even in the Indian case, it is doubtful Bhardwaj can generalize his findings beyond the north Indian context where he gathered most of his data. My own research in the state of Orissa suggests opposite findings from those of Bhardwaj. Many of the most influential pilgrimage sites in Orissa are associated with the goddess worship tradition. Pilgrims attend these shrines for the fulfillment of vows, not just for a *darsana* or view of the deity.[8] We need to use caution about generalizing from typologies based on clusters of traits that may shift from one region to another.

The "root paradigms" embedded in religious traditions and articulated differently in various cultures are often associated with important pilgrimage sites such as Banaras (Eck 1982) and the holy Ganges River in India (Bharati 1970: 107). At Biraja Temple, an important goddess shrine in Orissa, the sacred well in the temple compound is said to be connected underground to the Ganges River, located several hundred miles to the north. Thus, the local shrine becomes an extension of the great paradigmatic pilgrimage center at Kashi (Banaras). Similar underground connections to the Ganges are reported from a wide range of shrines in South India. The holy city of Jerusalem, a major focus of pilgrimage for Judaism, Christianity, and Islam, contains the root paradigms at the core of the religions of the West. A multidisciplinary study of Jerusalem as a pilgrimage center would reveal profound insights into these religions.

The religious dimension of pilgrimage is enhanced by creative imagination. Pilgrimage is concerned with elevation and display, magnification and miniature, awe and terror. Entering the sacred center both enhances the mystery and dissolves it. Even in America, where secular pilgrimages flourish, this same element of revelation is generated as we watch men journey into outer space, explore the awe, beauty, and terror of nuclear fission, and project into nature a romantic vision of Eden. These ventures all involve the crossing of successive thresholds, the rupture of old worldviews, a transcendence of brackets, and reentry shock. The religious imagination operates by both universal and culturally specific principles shaping a wide variety of pilgrimage experiences.

TOWARD A NEW COMPARATIVE STUDY OF RELIGION

Multidisciplinary studies have been infrequent and much less broadly funded in the social sciences as compared with the physical sciences. Pilgrimage is a natural topic for pioneering research among scholars from a variety of disciplines. This point is evident from the highly successful multidisciplinary conference on pilgrimage held at the University of Pittsburgh in 1981. Since that landmark event the topic has become increasingly popular as a focus of research.

The study of pilgrimage is a particularly challenging field of investigation for anthropologists, as we move away from the study of clearly bracketed social groups, like tribes, peasant communities, or communes, toward the analysis of culture as process. Giant strides have been made in the anthropology of religion since Malinowski's classic work on Trobriand magic. Structuralists have investigated common symbolic themes underlying distinct religious systems. In recent years, we have discovered the important role of metaphor, symbolism, and imagery in the relationship of religion to culture. Our attention is drawn increasingly to an appreciation of religion as process. We are now ready to return to a more sophisticated comparison of religions, instead of studying them as discrete entities. More important is the recent interest in the great world religions, not just treating them as "folk religions" or conducting village-level investigations but considering also the powerful symbols they generate as connecting links to the civilizations in which they are embedded.[9] We are on the threshold of a new synthesis in the comparative study of religion. This new approach must be built on a foundation anchored in several disciplines. The emphasis placed here on tracing, spiritual magnetism, and levels of shrines, suggests common points of departure for the integration of disciplinary differences. If we concede that something of religious and cultural significance occurs in pilgrimage and that the root paradigms of the world religions can be revealed in the study of peregrination, then pilgrimage can be a rallying point for the complementary interchange of different disciplines.

What practical steps are needed to launch this new synthesis? Classification schemes and surveys of pilgrim fields are not enough. We must also study individual pilgrimage shrines in depth. It is imperative to emphasize *process* and examine carefully *religious movement* as an expression of transcendence. Why are certain types of movement considered mechanisms for communicating with the supernatural? Since civilizations are linked into the pilgrimage process, it is essential to investigate the subtle distribution of power and political control implied in the movement of disparate peoples into ceremonial centers, along with their dispersal back to local peripheries. Most critical is the pattern of patronage associated with different pilgrimage traditions. Who pulls the purse strings? How much is pilgrimage a residual mechanism by which powerful elites utilize mystical concepts of devotion to land, kin, crown, and deity to impose their suzerainty over subject peoples? These questions cannot be answered from the perspective of a single discipline. They require the insights and methodologies from a multidisciplinary effort.

The field of comparative religion was initiated in the late nineteenth century by scholars like Muller, Lang, Durkheim, Tylor, Weber, and Freud, each of whom contributed to the founding of the major disciplines in the social sciences and humanities as we know them today. They drew on a wide variety of methods and paradigms, asked broad, sweeping questions about human nature, and nurtured elaborate correspondences with colleagues from different disciplines. Their bold, intuitive speculations framed issues that have echoed for over a century in the disciplines concerned with the comparative study of religion. Grand themes were their favorite vehicles for exercising armchair speculations about human nature. A necessary correction for such intuitive abandon was instituted during the early part of the twentieth century in virtually every discipline they founded. Along with this significant correction, the large comparative questions vanished as each discipline retreated into its own territory and established the rigid boundaries encrusted in present-day academia. The new comparative religion urges us to break out of this entrapment, to reestablish the broad, comparative base of its origins, while retaining the caution and rigor of the more systematic methodologies developed during this century.

Pilgrimage challenges the present canons of academia. It forces us to contemplate the value of more imaginative applications of our various methodologies. It calls for the complementary fusion of our disciplines to forge a deeper, more penetrating analysis of religion. Countless millions of pilgrims have traversed the globe throughout the centuries. The irony of our time is that we know less about them than we do about the remote planets of our solar system. It is now time to remedy that situation.

NOTES

1. I am greatly indebted to Alan Morinis for his assistance in clarifying the definition of spiritual magnetism.

2. "Sacred geography" is a useful concept developed by Vidyarthi for the study of Hindu pilgrimage sites (1961 and 1979).

3. For a discussion of the transformation of an obscure Hindu shrine into a major focus of religion in Cuttack city, Orissa, India, see my study of Chandi Temple (Preston 1980a).

4. The Puranic term *tirtha* (place of pilgrimage) and *pitha* (seat or Tantric center) are of little value for the analysis of pilgrimage in Hinduism. The numerous listings of these places of pilgrimage in the Puranas are not very helpful since most no longer exist.

5. For a discussion of problems associated with the ethnosemantic approach see Harris (1968: 579-92). Folk taxonomies include classifications of color categories (Conklin 1955), kinship terminology (Goodenough 1965), and diseases (Frake 1961).

6. For a comprehensive discussion of levels of analysis and classification of Hindu sacred centers see my article (Preston 1980b).

7. The literature is replete with examples of the prestige gained by individuals who have returned home from the *hajj* to Mecca. A particularly valuable documentation of this is found in Antoun (1989).

8. Alan Morinis has observed similar reversals in pilgrimages of West Bengal (see Morinis 1984).

9. For a thematic approach to the new comparative religion see the concluding chapter of my book *Mother Worship: Theme and Variations* (1982).

2

Pilgrimage and Tourism: Convergence and Divergence

ERIK COHEN

Drawing distinctions between the pilgrim and their close relative the tourist points out important characteristics of both types of traveler. These differences are not merely "academic" (in the derogatory sense) or semantic because they throw up the crucial issues of the definition of pilgrimage. In reflecting on the relationship of pilgrimage to practices such as tourism, we ascertain the boundaries of the pilgrimage category.

The following chapter by Erik Cohen, a leading theoretician of the sociology of tourism, takes major steps toward answering these questions. Applying a structuralist approach, he develops the contrast between the pilgrim, whose journey is to a center of his world, and a tourist, who travels away from a center to a periphery. Notwithstanding that there are inevitable exceptions to these generalizations and that a degree of uncertainty must remain since no one will assert that there is a clearly demarcatable boundary between pilgrimage and tourism, Professor Cohen's thoughtful essay should be carefully considered for a better understanding of ritual travel, in whatever form it might take.

Besides being the basis for differentiating pilgrimage from tourism, the quest for the Center and the search for the Other have been recurrent motifs throughout the imaginative history of humankind. This chapter highlights these themes and so provides an opportunity to contemplate the place of sacred journeying in all civilization, from Ur and Chichen Itza to Las Vegas and the French Riviera.[1]

THE PROBLEM

Historians of tourism have argued that religious pilgrimages are one of the principal forerunners or historical sources of modern tourism (Sigaux 1966). This argument, however, leaves open the analytical differences between tourism and the pilgrimage as social phenomena. The subject has received little, if any, careful systematic treatment in the literature,[2] though various theoretical arguments concerning their relationship have been forwarded. Here I depart from these arguments, state my own position, and explicate it on three analytical levels: the deep-structural, the phenomenal, and the institutional; thereby the points of convergence, as well as the directions of divergence, between tourism and pilgrimage will be clarified. I illustrate my analysis with data from my study on youth tourism to Thailand—the kind of tourism that is often given as an example of contemporary touristic "pilgrimages."

THEORETICAL POSITIONS ON THE RELATIONSHIP OF PILGRIMAGE AND TOURISM

Two principal theoretical positions can be distinguished in the literature—the one tending to identify pilgrimage and tourism (convergence), the other tending to see them as fundamentally dissimilar (divergence).

Convergence

Some authors (e.g., Nash 1981), striving to establish an "etic," cross-culturally applicable concept of tourism, tend to subsume under it all non-instrumental (Cohen 1974: 532, 540-44) kinds of travel, including the pilgrimage (Cohen 1981). More relevant for our purposes, however, are those authors who discover some intrinsic, theoretically crucial similarities between the two phenomena—in particular N. H. H. Graburn (1977), who analyzed tourism as a sacred journey, and Dean MacCannell (1973, 1976), who sees in tourism a modern substitute for religion. For both these authors tourism is essentially the pilgrimage of modern times.

Divergence

Those authors who conceive of tourism as a modern, mass-leisure phenomenon find it devoid of any deeper spiritual or cultural significance; for them, the tourist is an aberration of the earlier, serious traveler (Boorstin 1964: 77-117), and the modern pleasure trip an aberration of the Grand Tour (Turner and Ash 1975: 137). Though they might have originated from the same source, tourism and pilgrimage have profoundly diverged in the modern world. These authors conceive of tourism as a shallow traveling for pleasure, devoid of deeper meaning and, as such, antithetical to the profound spiritual quest of the past epitomized in the ancient traveler or pilgrim.

Chronologically, divergence was the earlier position; first formulated by Boorstin, it informs the popular writings of "culture critics" both in the United States (e.g., Fussell 1979) and in Europe (e.g., Turner and Ash 1975; Armanski 1978; Prahl and Steinecke 1979). Convergence emerged largely as a criticism of the elitist position of the cultural critics themselves (MacCannell 1973: 598-601); by evaluating rather than understanding tourism, the culture critics are said to have failed to realize the more profound cultural meaning of tourism, which allegedly makes it a functional equivalent to the pilgrimage of traditional society. According to MacCannell, "tourism absorbs some of the social functions of religion in the modern world", while "sightseeing is a ritual performed to the differentiations of society" (MacCannell 1976: 13). The latter are symbolized by the touristic "attractions"; the tourist's attitude to these attractions is characterized by "respectful admiration" (40) and his visit to them is expressly called a "pilgrimage" (43). Tourist attractions, then, are the shrines of modernity. Graburn similarly notes that the traditional division of time into profane and sacred periods found in tourism a novel expression: the modern profane time is everyday life, the "daily humdrum often termed a 'dog's life', since dogs are not thought to 'vacation'" (1977: 22), whereas sacred times are the "holidays (holy, sacred days now celebrated by travelling away from home)" (22); such times "make life worth living as though ordinary life is not life or at least not the kind of life worth living" (22).

While in some respects the work of these authors suffers from the shortcomings of every theorizing based on loose analogies, it is both stunning in its flashes of insight and highly appealing as a refutation of the often smug and facile, commonplace condemnation of the superficiality and banality of modern tourism. For this reason it merits a serious examination.

The contrast between the opposing positions on the relationship between pilgrimage and tourism derives primarily from a basic difference in the level of analysis. Protagonists of divergence relate to the "phenomenal" level; while aware of a deeper meaning of travel or pilgrimage in the past, they emphasize the aberrations of those ancient cultural forms in contemporary touristic practice. The modern mass tourist, according to authors like Boorstin or Fussell, is differently motivated and behaves differently, while his superficiality and frivolity are themselves symptomatic of the alienation of the age, which thrives on "pseudo-events" (Boorstin 1964). Their antagonists, who advocate convergence, relate to a deeper, structural level. While not necessarily denying that many tourists are frivolous and superficial, they discern, beneath the surface of modern tourism, general human concerns or universal cultural themes, such as the quest for "authenticity" (MacCannell 1973, 1976: 91-107) or for "life" (Graburn 1977: 22; cf. Schober 1975: 17). Alienated as they are from the modern world, tourists are said to look elsewhere for real life or authenticity "in other historical periods and other cultures" (MacCannell 1976: 3).[3] According to the advocates of convergence, though the tourist may be unaware of it, his is a modern form of the quest for the re-creating and revitalizing "Center," which is also "the pilgrim's goal" (Turner 1973). We are thus left with the bland conclusion that, on a superficial, "phenomenal" level, tourists may often be "superficial"; but on a "deep-structural" level, they appear to be "deep," their "real" motives being identical with those informing the pilgrimage in traditional society.

This conclusion is unsatisfactory. Leaving both positions intact, it does not tell us anything on the relationship between the deep-structural themes and the motivational, behavioral, or institutional manifestations of contemporary tourism. It does not reconcile the multifariousness of concrete touristic phenomena with the singleness of their underlying structural theme, nor does it account for some important differences between tourism and pilgrimage at various levels of analysis. Hence, a more discerning approach should address each of the different levels of analysis separately as well as expressly raise the problem of their interrelationship. Specifically it should ask three basic questions:

1. Are the deep-structural themes informing the pilgrimage and tourism indeed identical?

2. How far are these deep-structural themes reflected, on a phenomenal level, in the actual motivations and behaviors of various types of tourists and pilgrims? How do tourists differ from pilgrims phenomenally?

3. How are the deep-structural themes and the characteristic motivations and forms of behavior of tourists and pilgrims reflected in the respective patterns of institutionalization of tourism and the pilgrimage? Are these patterns basically similar, or do they differ significantly?

PILGRIMAGE AND TOURISM: A STRUCTURAL ANALYSIS

Basing my analysis on the work of Mircea Eliade (1969: 27-56; 1971), Paul Wheatley (1967), and others, I proceed on the assumption that the model of the world prevalent in traditional society can be conceived, perhaps at the risk of some oversimplification, as consisting of a sacred Center, an ordered, hallowed cosmos, and a surrounding dangerous but alluring chaos. Expanding my previous analysis (Cohen 1979a: 180-3), I now argue that within this socially constructed space, two prototypical, non-instrumental movements can be distinguished: pilgrimage, a movement toward the Center, and travel, a movement in the opposite direction, toward the Other,[4] located beyond the boundaries of the cosmos, in the surrounding chaos. Both these deep-structural themes are multivocal (Turner 1974: 48; Turner and Turner 1978: 246); though conceptually distinct, they are not completely discrete, as each possesses some qualities of the other. The Center is the source of the hallowed (socio-moral) order of the cosmos. It is the point at which the charismatic divine power penetrated the chaos and created the phenomenal world; but this power itself is, in R. Otto's (1959: 39-44) term, a "Wholly Other"—the indescribable, since categorically incomprehensible, unity behind the differentiations of the phenomenal world.

The Center is the most sacred place on earth, the meeting point of the heavenly and the earthly planes (Eliade 1971: 12); it attracts the pilgrim either as the source of religious merit, divine blessings, and "the inward transformation of spirit and personality" (Turner 1973: 214) or as the source of miraculous healing and rejuvenation. The pilgrim, whose ordinary abode is in profane space, ascends, both geographically and spiritually, from the periphery toward the "Center out there." The modal experience of the ideal type of the pilgrim at the Center is "existential" (Cohen 1979b: 189-91)—an experience of re-creation, revitalization, grace, and exaltation.

While the Center is well-defined and frequently discussed in the literature, the Other is a much more ambiguous and relatively rarely considered deep-structural theme. Ambiguity belongs to its very nature (Kenny 1981: 486); it stands for the strange and the attractive, the threatening and the alluring, in short, the fascinating, primordial, unformed, and unknown, lurking in the recesses of chaos surrounding the ordered, "civilized" cosmos. In its malignant aspect it is monstrous (Friedman 1981), the embodiment of evil as cognitive and moral confusion; it is appalling and repelling, but even as such it fascinates an intrepid traveler, like Richard Burton, who was, by his own testimony, driven by the Devil, and "dwelt fascinated upon all things accounted devilish" (Brodie 1971: 13). In its benign aspect, the Other is alluring, promising the seeker the innocent happiness of losing himself in the primordial pre-creational (or prenatal) unity of all things,[5] often identified with an effortless, creaturely satisfaction of all desires, unhindered by the restriction of the socio-moral order.

The Center and the Other, though in a sense opposites, also possess some common traits. Both are liminal (Turner 1974a: 81-82); at both the center of the world and at its margins, form and order dissolve. The Center, however, is "pregnant with order": it possesses a creative, cosmicizing potential, of which the Other, dwelling in the chaos on the margins of the cosmicized world, is completely devoid (Eliade 1971: 9; cf. Kenny 1981: 488).

The Pilgrim's journey to the Center, though perilous, is in traditional cultures and societies ultimately legitimate; the Traveler's, in these societies, is ordinarily not. If the Traveler merely desires to escape order and to lose himself in the primordial chaos—even if only to achieve a better perspective on the ordered world (Duerr 1985)—he will be considered a deviant; contact with the chaotic Other is generally anomic on the social level and defiling on the religious level. But if the Traveler departs into the chaos out of despair of his own society and in search of a new, alternative Center in the recesses of the Other, he becomes socially positively dangerous and religiously a heretic, since his endeavor represents a threat to the accepted Center and, thereby, to the established social order. Such a Traveler is an antinomian figure; while his adventures may excite the fantasy of many of those who stay behind, he is a lonely hero, imitated by only a daring few.

With the coming of modernity, the Traveler's role gradually becomes socially more acceptable. Here lie the roots of the contemporary traveler-tourist as a legitimate modern cultural role (Boorstin 1964). Within the constraints of this chapter, its genesis may be outlined only in most general and somewhat schematic terms.

Paralleling the progressive "disenchantment of the world" (Weber 1920: 94), the mythico-religious worldview has given way to a modern, "rational" one, with neither a Center nor an Other of any great primeval, mystical significance. Both are retained, however, in a "secularized," enfeebled, form, and with them, the modern versions of both the pilgrimage and travel. Alongside the traditional centers of religious pilgrimage, new centers of political and cultural pilgrimage have now emerged, symbolizing the basic values of the polity (e.g., the Lenin Mausoleum, the Lincoln Memorial, Mount Herzl) or the roots of western society's culture (e.g., the great monuments of classic antiquity or of the Renaissance, visited on the Grand Tour). As the range of such centers multiplies, most become gradually transformed into disenchanted "attractions," and their visitors, the one-time pilgrims, become "tourists." This view is one version of "the tourist" as conceived by MacCannell (1976: 42-42)—that of the "pilgrim-tourist."

With the gradual geographical denouement of the world, much of the mystical quality of the unknown lying beyond the boundaries of the individual's world has also greatly diminished. Even remote "paradises" became gradually disenchanted (Cohen 1982c). But the strange, wild, and pristine world beyond the boundaries of civilization preserved some of its attractiveness; with the modern legitimation of a generalized interest in, and appreciation of, things strange and novel for their own sake (Cohen 1979b: 182), it became a culturally acceptable motive for travel. As travel is popularized, the Traveler of old becomes a "tourist" (Boorstin 1964: 77-117) in search of novelty and, eventually, only mere change (Cohen 1974: 544-45). In the process, far-off people, cultures, and landscapes are transformed into "attractions," not because they symbolize one's own culture but precisely because they are different, allegedly harboring an "authenticity" that modernity has lost; one can say that they are "museumized" into modernity (MacCannell 1976: 8). This view is the second version of "the tourist" as conceived by MacCannell, that of the "traveler-tourist," moving away from the centers of his culture and society, unlike the "pilgrim-tourist," who moves toward them. Turner and Ash poignantly characterize this version: "Tourism is an invasion outwards from the highly developed and metropolitan centers into the uncivilized peripheries" (1978: 129). This version grew in importance as modern man became increasingly alienated from his world and departed, or escaped, in search of recuperation and relief, into its periphery (129). For those most alienated from modernity, indeed, the search is crowned by the discovery of a new, personal or "elective" Center (Cohen 1979b: 190), not shared by the co-members of their society of origin. Here the periphery is not merely "museumized" into modernity to savor its authenticity; it becomes an alternative to it. The pendulum swings fully, and the Other, encountered in the periphery of the modern world, is transformed into a Center for the escaping modern individual.

Structurally speaking, modern tourism is thus rooted not in one, but in two dialectically opposed deep cultural themes, the Center and the Other; it developed from the originally contrary movements of pilgrimage and travel. Moreover, even as the traditional pilgrimage becomes "mere" tourism, tourism, as a modern version of travel, becomes for some the new pilgrimage. While both versions of tourism are present in modern society and are often empirically hard to distinguish, it is important to keep them analytically apart. The second of these versions, travel-tourism, is the focus of the following analysis of touristic experiences.

PILGRIMAGE AND TOURISM: A PHENOMENAL ANALYSIS

Students of tourism have emphasized the highly heterogeneous character of touristic phenomena (e.g., Cohen 1972, 1979b; Noronha 1977: 6-9; Smith 1977; Nash 1981). This work has shown the senselessness of loose talk about the tourist as a general type, whether in the manner of Boorstin or of MacCannell. Pilgrimage is no less a heterogeneous phenomenon, although a comparable typology of pilgrims has not yet been proposed. The pilgrim in an "existential" quest of the Center, which serves as a reference point in the following analysis, is merely an idealized type, approximated only by a minority of deeply committed individuals. Still, the exuberance and exaltation manifested by ordinary pilgrims at important pilgrimage centers witness that their experience frequently possesses an existential quality, even if this may become diluted by routinization and by recreational or other accompanying activities (Turner and Turner 1978: 36-37). As Nash (1979: 9-10) has noted, even in traditional societies there were many "false pilgrims," whose conduct was remote from the ideal and resembled that of many contemporary tourists. Indeed, in modern mass-pilgrimage, paralleling mass-tourism, the actual behavior of pilgrims often becomes indistinguishable from that of tourists (Dupont 1973).

Culturally speaking, there is an important difference in the institutionalized expectations between the experience of the pilgrimage and that of tourism: the pilgrimage is traditionally expected to provoke religious "rapture" or "exaltation," that is, the existential experience referred to above, even if it frequently fails to do so in practice. Tourism, however, is expected to give mere pleasure and enjoyment, derived from the novelty and change provided by the destination (Cohen 1974: 540-41). The legitimacy of that attitude is of recent origin; earlier tourists had to justify their trip by more exalted motives, such as a quest for health or healing (Lowenthal 1962), itself a reflection of the religious quest for the life-and-health-endowing Center.

The culturally approved mode of the touristic experience, then, is *"recreational"* (Cohen 1979b: 183-85). It assumes a conforming individual who, while adhering to the central values of his society, nevertheless experiences strains and tensions in his everyday life; a vacation or holiday in the periphery serves to recreate him—to restitute him, physically and mentally, for the performance of his ordinary roles. Mere relaxation is frequently the main motive of tourism in some destinations, especially resorts, where the desire of the visitors to relax largely determines the ambience of the place, as, for example, it does on the islands of southern Thailand visited by youth tourists (Cohen 1982b: 208-9).

Not only passive relaxation or vacationing, however, but also active holidays and sightseeing can be of recreational significance, like trekking excursions into remote hill-tribe areas in northern Thailand for those youth who engage in them mainly for the fun of the physical exercise involved.

We turn now to the touristic experiences of alienated individuals. I distinguish four modes of such experience, depending on the extent of the individual's desire and success to overcome his alienation through the medium of travel (Cohen 1979b).

The *diversionary* mode is similar in quality of experience to the recreational but does not perform the restitutive function of the latter. This mode is common among alienated young tourists. For example, in Thailand, there are many young tourists who escaped from modern industrial society but do not engage in a quest for authenticity in the host setting (cf. Cohen 1984 [1986]); they are essentially "decentralized" individuals (Kavolis 1970) whose catchword is "to enjoy" and who live in the here and now without any clear purpose or direction in life.[6]

The *experiential* mode, deeper and more searching than the preceding ones, consists of the conscious quest for the vicarious experience of the authentic life of others (Cohen 1979b: 186-88). It is encountered most often in sightseeing and is common among young tourists in far-off places. This mode is well illustrated by a young Frenchman trekking among the hill tribes in northern Thailand, in search of things that would be "as different as possible" from those in Europe. He sought to find the "original life," the life of the "tribes not yet degraded by civilization"; similarly, a young English-speaking tourist came to visit a remote tribal village to ascertain "that such places still exist." Unlike the recreational tourist, the experiential tourist tends to be "a stickler for authenticity" (Desai 1974: 4); the Frenchman, for example, complained that the tribals in one of the villages used commercial plastic glasses instead of their traditional bamboo cups. But he himself did not want to live as the tribals do. He came to experience, not to experiment. This type comes closest to the second version of MacCannell's notion of the tourist, that of the traveler-tourist, who observes the authenticity of the life of others but does not seek to live it himself. Not all alienated tourists, however, desire to experience authenticity merely vicariously. Rather, they differ in the depth of their quest. Hence, I distinguish two additional modes of touristic experience—the experimental and the existential.

In the *experimental* mode, the tourist tries out various alternative life-styles in an effort to discover the one that he would like to adopt for himself (Cohen 1979b: 189). The frequently repeated claim that people travel "to find themselves" is the inward-looking facet of that mode. The mode is well illustrated by a young German tourist who professes not merely an interest in the life of various peoples but also a hope that he may eventually find a place where he would want to settle down. The desire "to find a place that suits me" has been frequently voiced by young travelers.

For some travelers, however, the quest itself may become the goal; thus, a young Australian, who, after a long period of distressful wandering, finally found peace and warmth living with a Thai woman on a small island in Thailand, nevertheless claimed that for him only a traveling life is satisfactory, and he refused to settle down. "New places, new things" was his motto. In its extreme, the experimental mode may thus turn the quest itself into a way of life.

In the *existential* mode, the tourist commits himself to an alternative that becomes for him a new, "elective" center (Cohen 1979b: 189-92). His existential experience at that center is homologous to that of the idealized pilgrim. This mode is less frequently encountered or is, at least, less expressly verbalized among contemporary young tourists in Thailand, or even in Asia as a whole. Many became disenchanted with the East, which so mightily attracted an earlier generation of Western youth. As one German tourist put it: "Five years ago there were 'travelers' who sought the meaning of life in the East. Now, the time of the Herman Hesse traveler is over." A most compelling testimony of an existential experience comes from an American female traveler who lived for some years in Ladakh in India, which for her was an elective center. On lonely treks in the Ladakh mountains, surrounded only by "the skies and rocks," she reports to have had an experience of "natural meditation"; she thought neither of the past nor the future—"only the now" existed. This natural mystical experience is similar to that reported by Admiral Byrd on sighting the polar light in the Antarctic (Byrd 1935: 194-95). It relates a sensation of timelessness-in-time, an eternal now, a dissolution of the structure of time characteristic of the experience of liminality (Turner 1974a: 238; see also Wagner 1977: 41-42).[7]

While the experience of the existential tourist at the elective center is homologous to that of the idealized pilgrim, his structural position is not. The pilgrim's center is within his own society or culture, whereas that of the existential tourist is not; rather, the latter transforms a point in the periphery of that world into his elective center. Moreover, unlike MacCannell's attractions, that Center is here not "museumized" into modernity (MacCannell 1976: 8). Rather, the existential tourist opts out, spiritually, from modernity; his center lies outside it—in the wide spaces of Ladakh, a primitive tribe, an Indian *asrama*, or an Israeli kibbutz; he returns home, if at all, only for instrumental purposes. He is the obverse of the "sojourner," whose spiritual center remains at home, though, for instrumental or other reasons, he is forced to live abroad (Siu 1952; Bonacich 1973).

In conclusion, the different modes of tourist experiences express varying degrees of intensity and profundity in which the underlying deep-structural themes are actually experienced and realized by the tourist; they thus embody different stages of the transformation of the Other into an elective center.

PILGRIMAGE AND TOURISM: AN INSTITUTIONAL ANALYSIS

The difference between the deep-structural themes from which pilgrimage and tourism are derived leads to different expectations concerning the modes of experience appropriate for each; these in turn have important implications for their respective patterns of institutionalization: tourism is less thoroughly institutionalized than the pilgrimage, though tourism may well be, as in mass tourism, highly routinized. This difference is inherent in its social definition; the conception of tourism as a leisure-time activity precludes its rigorous institutionalization.

In contrast to the pilgrimage, the deeper cultural significance of tourism is socially not widely recognized. It is instructive in this respect that the alleged discovery of deep-structural themes, beneath the frivolous, superficial appearance of tourism, by writers such as MacCannell or Graburn, comes as a surprise to modern readers in a measure in which the discovery of similar themes in the pilgrimage, for example, by Victor Turner, never would—precisely because their existence in the latter is commonsensically taken for granted. The difference in the commonsense view of these two forms of travel is analytically significant: while the traditional pilgrimage has an explicit, culturally recognized meaning, modern tourism has not. Its meaning, like that of the "hidden myth" encoded in advertisements (Leymore 1975), has to be revealed by analysis.

Since it is less rigorously institutionalized, tourism is in all respects more "open" than the pilgrimage. This fact can be seen from a comparison along several principal parameters:

Obligatoriness While the pilgrimage is obligatory in some instances, as for example, the Islamic *hajj*, universally it is at least semi-obligatory, combining voluntariness with obligatoriness (Turner 1973: 204) and reconciling the tension between (binding) status and (voluntary) contract "in the notion that it is meritorious to choose one's duty" (Turner 1973: 200). Tourism, as a leisure activity, however, is by definition non-obligatory, "freedom from obligations" being, according to J. Dumazdier (1968: 250), one of the defining characteristics of leisure; it is the voluntary type of travel *par excellence* (Cohen 1974: 536-37). The individual is, hence, free to decide for himself whether to travel at all or to stay at home (Graburn 1977: 19-20). To engage in tourism may bring prestige, but touring in itself is not a meritorious activity, as is the pilgrimage. "Sacralized" tourist attractions, as Mac-Cannell has argued, may have "a moral claim on the tourist" (1976: 45). But as such they become centers of the modern pilgrimage, and their visitors pilgrim-tourists; the traveler-tourist derives his pleasure—and prestige—precisely from moving away from the touristic "musts," into areas the journey to which is not morally sanctioned by his society.

Itineraries and Seasons Not only the goal but also the itinerary of the pilgrimage are set in custom. The itinerary is not a simple geographical route, but a symbolic ascent from the profane daily existence to the sacred (Turner 1973: 204, 211). Though pilgrimage centers can be visited at any time throughout the year, most have their appointed seasons, during which pilgrimage is most meritorious (cf. Sallnow 1981: 169). Modern tourism has no culturally set destinations or itineraries and no appointed times—even if both may, in actual practice, become routinized to the extreme, like the "summer migration" of the French (Cribier 1969). Such routinization, however, is frequently criticized as an aberration of the spirit of tourism (e.g., Hiller 1976; Fussell 1979) and often satirized (e.g., in films such as *It's Tuesday, So It Must Be Belgium*). Visits of great numbers of tourists are usually believed to spoil a destination, while the presence of tourists at a site is seen as detrimental to the experience of its authenticity. In the pilgrimage, the presence of other pilgrims is often felt to enhance rather than detract from the experience (Turner 1973: 217-18). Pilgrims are not accused of spoiling the goal or destroying its authenticity; rather, they belong to its ambience. Hence, while pilgrims are encouraged to depart on established itineraries and appointed seasons to their common goal, in tourism originality of destinations and itineraries is appreciated. The visiting of little-known attractions endows the tourist with a special prestige (Boorstin 1964: 106). Remote and pristine locations are more attractive than the more routine, touristic destinations. This cultural attitude engenders a centrifugal tendency in tourism (Christaller 1955) and its penetration of ever new, more peripheral areas; this tendency is the very opposite of the expressly centripetal tendency of the pilgrimage—the orientation of a system of pilgrimage itineraries, like the spokes of a wheel, toward a common center (Turner and Turner 1978: 6, 40-102). Indeed, those tourists who are most keen on authenticity will manifest the strongest centrifugal tendency—for example, the original drifters (Cohen 1973) or wanderer (Vogt 1976)—and travel along off-the-beaten-track routes; admittedly, they may thereby pioneer new itineraries and destinations for less enterprising tourists.

Patterns of Demeanor Both pilgrimage and tourism have a "getting out" character (Turner and Turner 1978: 7) in addition to "getting to." "Getting out" means abandoning accustomed social structures and daily routines (Graburn 1977: 20-23). The pilgrims' demeanor, however, like their itineraries, is ritually more strictly organized and disciplined; in pilgrimage "the absolute communitas of unchanneled anarchy does not obtain" (Turner 1973: 195). The demeanor of the tourist, in contrast, may legitimately remain completely unstructured or "anarchical." True enough, much of mass tourism is regimented, and the participants' behavior and attitudes are homogenized and synchronized by prior expectations, preparations, explanations and instructions of guides (Cohen 1982a). Such mass tourist regimentation, however, is not culturally prescribed and indeed draws caustic comments from critics of tourism (Hiller 1976; Fussell 1979) of a kind that mass pilgrimage does not at all provoke. The freedom from obligation encourages the tourist to "do his own thing" in terms of dress, association, activities, meals, and so on; he is sometimes castigated for not making use of his liberty. The idea of liberty from obligation finds expression in language in the term vacation (from "vacant," i.e., empty time, free from prescribed activities) and is in fact most fully realized in vacation resorts. An utter lack of any imposed order or fixed timetable is the outstanding characteristic of such places and one of the principal sources of enjoyment; it often transfixes the visitor and puts him into a mild trance in which he loses his sense of time. This ambience was observed by U. Wagner (1977: 41-42) on a Gambian beach and by myself on the islands of southern Thailand (Cohen 1982b). Its importance for young tourists is well illustrated by the complaint of a German on one of the islands against the presence of a clock in the restaurant of his bungalow, which, he said, reminded him of the strict allocation of time at home. He commented that in Germany time is "quantitative"—every period of time is allocated to a prescribed pursuit—on the beach, however, he sought "qualitative" time and strove to achieve a state of mind in which he would do nothing throughout the day and not feel guilty in the evening. This attitude is a forceful expression of liminality. It differs, however, from that in the pilgrimage. There, the liminal anti-structure is allegedly transformed anew in the process of restructuring; liminality is "embedded" in the institutional structure of the pilgrimage process as a whole (Turner 1973: 204). No such restructuring process exists in tourism; the liminal state is simply terminated by departure, often followed, particularly in the case of youth tourists, by the re-entry shock of homecoming.[8] Moreover, the liminal experience is not culturally interpreted in terms of contact with a center and hence is not, as in the pilgrimage, considered of major significance to the individual's life plan; the beaches on the islands of southern Thailand are only "marginal paradises" (Cohen 1982b).

Relations with Co-travelers Both pilgrims and tourists tend to travel in groups. Indeed, co-travelers, for both, are frequently the principal role-partners in their journeys. There is, however, an important difference in the cultural significance of the group: for pilgrims, the group is part and parcel of the experience of the pilgrimage. The assembled pilgrims "belong" to the destination; they are part of its ambience in a sense in which tourists are not.

In contrast, in tourism the groups have no culturally defined significance. Though tourists may enjoy the company of co-travelers, the latter are not necessary for the specifically touristic experience, and the more keen a tourist is on experiencing authenticity, the more he is disturbed by the presence of other tourists. Youth tourists trekking in Thailand in the jungle frequently complained about the presence of other trekking parties in a tribal village who, in their view, spoiled the ambience. Many drifters or travelers therefore refused to join organized trekking parties, and hoped to be able to reach alone a "non-touristic" tribal village, while others purposely segregated themselves from their party during a stay in the village to enjoy, undisturbed, the native surroundings. Even on the southern islands, some tourists were disturbed by the presence of a few score of vacationers, although the beach was miles long. Whether they perceived the beach as crowded or not was a principal determinant of their satisfaction. As one French woman paradoxically put it, "A place is not good for tourists if it is too touristic." Indeed, the search for solitude is one of the principal motives of young tourists for penetrating ever more remote beaches or islands in southern Thailand.

CONCLUSION

On the basis of the foregoing analysis we may now formulate the answers to the three theoretical questions on the relationship between pilgrimage and tourism.

(1) Two dialectically opposed deep-structural themes are the ultimate sources of non-instrumental travel (Cohen 1974: 532)—the Center, which is the goal of the pilgrim, and the Other, which is the goal of the traveler. Tourism is, in principle, a

modern metamorphosis of both pilgrimage and travel. Secularization, however, has robbed both deep-structural themes of much of their symbolic significance and mystical power and transformed their loci into attractions or mere destinations. Pilgrimage then often becomes indistinguishable from tourism, so that the analytical distinction between pilgrim-tourists, who travel toward the religious, political, or cultural centers of their cultural world, and traveler-tourists, who travel away from them into the periphery of that world, tends to become empirically blurred.

(2) The deep-structural themes reverberate, on the phenomenal level, in varying degrees of profundity in the modes of experience of both pilgrims and tourists. My typology of such modes relates expressly to tourists, but it is, at the extremes, synchronized with that of the pilgrims. At the one extreme are the recreational and diversionary modes, the least profound ones, characteristic not only of many contemporary mass traveler-tourists, but probably also of many mass pilgrim-tourists. At the other extreme is the existential mode, the most profound one, expressing the experience of the center. This is the ideal mode of experience of the pilgrim, but it is also found in those tourists who, alienated from their own society, find an elective center in its periphery; they transform the Other into their center. By embracing it, they opt out spiritually from their society of origin. In the extreme, they "switch worlds" (Berger and Luckmann 1966: 144).

(3) The differences in the deep-structural themes underlying pilgrimage and tourism and in the respective culturally expected and approved modes of experience of each explain their divergent patterns of institutionalization. Tourism is in all respects less institutionalized than the pilgrimage, owing to the non-obligatory character of its principal, socially recognized motive—traveling for pleasure. In comparison with the pilgrimage, tourism is a more voluntary activity; its destinations, itineraries, and seasons are less fixed; the demeanor of tourists is normatively less regulated; and the group of co-travelers has no cultural significance. This difference in the degree of institutionalization reflects the difference between the deep-structural themes on which pilgrimage and travel are predicated. While the quest for the Center is socially not only legitimate but also meritorious, that for the Other is at best semi-legitimate; the traveler is a lonely, antinomian hero, following his own lights. This feature of the traveler is transmitted into the cultural image of the ideal-typical traveler-tourist as a lonely individual penetrating the mysterious periphery of the cosmicized world. The pilgrim, on the contrary, traveling to the society's Center, partakes in a culturally sanctioned enterprise. His role is therefore legitimate and more readily institutionalized. This is not to say that much of modern tourism is not highly routinized, organized and regimented; but the society itself often considers this state an aberration, and not desirable.

This difference in the deep-structural themes also explains the difference in functions. Since the pilgrim's center is that of his own culture, a visit to it not only recreates and revitalizes the individual but also reinforces his commitment to basic cultural values; he is restituted to, and reconciled with, his role and position in society. Pilgrimage is, hence, functional. This outcome is explicitly the case in religious pilgrimages, but it also holds true for the political and cultural ones.

The serious touristic quest for authenticity, however, rests on alienation: insofar as the existential tourist embraces an elective center, he, too, will be re-created and revitalized. He is not, however, restituted to, or reconciled with, his own society but remains alienated from it; he may continue to vegetate in it, but his "real" life will be at his elective center.[9] Hence, while the less profound, recreational tourism is socially functional, serious existential tourism is not—except perhaps in the oblique sense that it deflects away deeply alienated individuals who might otherwise engage in activities aimed at the destruction or revolutionary transformation of the existing order of their society of origin.

NOTES

1. This paper develops further some ideas stated originally in Cohen 1979b. The empirical illustrations were collected within the framework of a study on youth tourism among the hill tribes of northern Thailand and on the islands of southern Thailand in the summers of 1977-1980, under grants from the Harry S. Truman Research Institute at the Hebrew University of Jerusalem (1977-1978, 1980) and Stiftung Volkswagenwerk (1979), whose support is here gratefully acknowledged. For further details on the study see Cohen 1979a, 1983a, 1982a, 1982b, and 1983b. Thanks are due to M. Heyd, D. Mittelberg, and D. Shulman for their helpful comments on an earlier draft of this paper.

2. For some earlier treatments, see Pitt-Rivers 1964; Dupront 1967; and Dupont 1973.

3. This insight is neatly illustrated by a newspaper article significantly entitled "A Traveler's Lament: Always Too Late." The author remarks that "it does not matter *when* you go to a place. As soon as you get there, someone will smugly tell you that you should have been there yesterday, a month ago, last year". (Peper 1980: W7). While the author revolts against such smugness, he unconsciously hits upon a deeply-set theme in the structure of modern consciousness, so ingeniously analyzed by MacCannell.

4. This distinction was developed following a suggestion by Graburn in a personal communication (see also Cohen 1982c: 1-4).

5. The two aspects of the Other are strikingly united in R. M. Rilke's third "Duino Elegy", in which the lover declares his love for the terrible primeval monster, his mother, in which he himself was "dissolved" in the prenatal state (Rilke 1972: 45).

6. For some, however, mere enjoyment becomes a new "liminal center"; see Cohen 1984 [1986].

7. One of the most vivid, though probably at least partially fictionalized, accounts of the discovery and adoption of an elective center is T. Schneebaum's (1969) description of his life among the "Akarama" Indians in Peru. Schneebaum, after describing his ecstatic meeting with the Akaramas, claims, "Now, living within their lives, I have become what I have always been and it has taken a lifetime, all my own life, to reach this point where it is as if I know finally that I am alive and that I am here, right now" (69). He admits, however, that, as much as he might strive, he can never completely shed civilization and go fully native (69-70). His book is replete with similar statements, as well as with testimonies of a sense of timelessness, characterizing his sojourn with the Akaramas.

8. This is akin to the "reverse culture shock" experienced by the returning anthropologist (see Meintel 1973: 52).

9. A parallel phenomenon was noted among anthropologists who frequently "come to life only when a field trip is in prospect for them" (Nash 1963: 163, quoted in Meintel 1973: 53).

II
CASE STUDIES

3

The Great Maharashtrian Pilgrimage: Pandharpur and Alandi

JOHN M. STANLEY

Movement is a key to understanding pilgrimage. Every other artifact commonly associated with pilgrimage such as shrines, saints, rituals, and all save pilgrims and their journeying is not universal to the pilgrimage category. Motion carries the pilgrim away from home, and movement leads him across physical and metaphysical boundaries. These aspects, simply put, are the essence of both earthly and metaphorical notions of sacred journeying.

This central theme emerges clearly in the following study of one of the most famous of Hindu pilgrimages. Dr. Stanley describes the devotions of pilgrims to Pandharpur and concludes that their devotion is embedded primarily in their acts of movement. The pilgrims see their pilgrimage as an experience of being devotees in motion toward the deity. While this study concerns a thoroughly Hindu pilgrimage, embodying many aspects unique to that culture, it has a universal relevance because the theme of movement is so explicit. This explicitness is a feature both of this pilgrimage and of Professor Stanley's analysis, which is ground-breaking for emphasizing bare movement as an essential motif of the sacred journey.

Professor Stanley also ventures into one of the frontier fields of anthropology— the study of personal experience. At Pandharpur we find an ideology of movement (embodied in sacred literature) and ample symbolic expression given to the theme of movement, but in the end the author stresses that the sensations and feelings experienced by the pilgrims play so important a role that these actually constitute their pilgrimage. All else is abstraction.

In Maharashtra, as throughout India and, indeed, the world, pilgrims make their ways to sacred places in a variety of patterns and for a variety of reasons. Pilgrims travel singly or in groups, at special times or at unspecified times. Some go for particular reasons, to perform a life cycle ritual, as atonement for a wrong deed, to recieve or be "recharged" with power, to seek ritual purification, or to request some particular wish or favor; some go only to express their devotion to their god and seek no reward or benefit beyond the sheer joy of going. Some pilgrimages are once-in-a-lifetime events; some are repeated each year, some every twelve years, some whenever a new moon or full moon (*purnima* or other lunar day happens to correspond to a special solar day.[1]

Some pilgrimages follow the pattern of a circuit, the pilgrims moving from one holy place to another in a rough circle—always moving around to the right with their right shoulders pointed toward an invisible center. Other pilgrimages are more linear, following a wandering line moving in one direction, like the course of a river, and, also like the course of a river, converging from various starting points over an entire "catchment area"[2] toward a common goal. This chapter is the story of a pilgrimage primarily of this catchment area pattern; more accurately, it is the story of the converging of two such pilgrimages, one large and one small, both occurring at special times each year and sharing an overlapping mythology and a common set of ritual patterns. It is also an account of a pilgrimage that pilgrims undertake for no reward or special merit but (at least ideally) only to offer their devotion (*bhakti*) to their god and to experience the joy of that act of offering. The larger of the two pilgrimages culminates each year on the bright eleventh day of the lunar month of Asadha at Pandharpur, normally a town of barely 1,000 people, on the banks of the Bhima River in Sholapur District, Maharashtra. The smaller pilgrimage occurs four and one-half months later in the temple town of Alandi on the banks of the Indrayani River in Poona District (see map).

MYTHOLOGICAL CHARTERS OF THE PILGRIMS' MOVEMENT

There are three principal myths (preserved in both oral and written forms) chartering the presence of Vithoba and his devotees at Pandharpur and Alandi. One tells how Krishna came to be at Pandharpur in the form of Vithoba. A second tells how Pundalik, the first *sant*[3] in the cult, came to Pandharpur and how it became a place of pilgrimage. A third establishes the presence of Vithoba at Alandi, the place of the *samadhi*[4] of Jnanesvar, one of the early historical *sants* in the cult and its premier pilgrim.

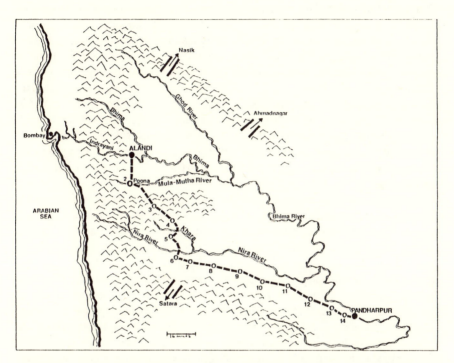

Plate No. 1: Route of the Jnanesvar *palkhi* with traditional halting points. Specific points may vary from year to year because of the way the lunar days fall. Map derived from Deleury (1960) plate 6.

1. Alandi	4. Jejuri	7. Taradgaon	10. Natepute	13. Shegaon
2. Poona	5. Valhe	8. Phaltan	11. Malsiras	14. Wakri
3. Sasvad	6. Lonand	9. Barad	12. Velapur	15. Pandharpur

Krishna Comes to Pandharpur

There are several versions of the myth establishing the presence of Krishna at Pandharpur. According to one of the most popular of these, the mature ruler Krishna—not baby Krishna loved by his mother, not the young prankster and butter thief loved by the women of Vrindavan, not the youthful, beautiful, flute-playing Krishna loved by the *gopis* and Radha, not even the warrior god of the *Bhagavad Gita* respectfully adored by Arjuna, but a mature, responsible ruler Krishna who had settled down as the king of Dwarka and married the goddess Rukmini—who embodied the qualities of all the previous Krishnas, was visited one day by a vision of his youthful love, Radha. She told him in the vision that he would find her in the great forests of Maharashtra. He should leave his home and his kingdom, go on a pilgrimage there, and join her. In another version of the myth, equally popular in the cult and preserved in written form in the *Panduranga Mahatmya*, as well as in oral traditions, Radha (who, in this version, is the *avatara*[5] of the wife of Indra) actually comes to Dwarka and is discovered in tryst with Krishna by Rukmini. Rukmini then leaves Dwarka in anger to go into the wilderness and "undergo severe penance." Krishna abandons Radha to search for Rukmini to persuade her to return, but he does not find her.

In one version of the myth it is Radha whom Krishna is looking for in the forests of Maharashtra; in another version it is Rukmini; in either version Krishna gets only as far as Pandharpur on the banks of the Bhima River, where he comes upon a humble hut in which he notices a young man in the act of expressing great devotion (*bhakti*) to his father. The man, named Pundalik, is sitting massaging his father's feet and doing so with such devotion that he does not seem to notice the presence of Krishna. Krishna begins to glow and radiate his energy so that his presence would be inescapable. Still Pundalik does not look up. Finally Krishna glows brightly enough that Pundalik can no longer ignore his presence, but Pundalik's devotion to his father is so intense that he is not distracted even by so great a presence as Krishna. Still, not wanting to be discourteous to a god who is waiting at the door as a guest, Pundalik, without interrupting his attention to his father's feet, picks up a brick and tosses it over his shoulder for Krishna to stand on.

The throwing of the brick to Krishna, though variously explained, is best construed as a gesture of hospitality, a kindness from a host to a guest: let the guest wait, but while waiting, at least give him something to stand on, off the wet ground. Krishna is so impressed by Pundalik's devotion to his father that he decides to remain in that place, in the presence of such remarkable filial devotion, forever. He abandons his search for Radha, leaves her waiting in the forest, and sends a message for Rukmini to come and join him standing on the brick in front of Pundalik's hut.[6] And there they stand to this day.

The symbolism of the brick is especially interesting. Later Varkari tradition will interpret the brick as a symbol of Pundalik's devotion to Vithoba, and, by extension, the brick becomes the symbol of every Varkari's individual devotion.[7] In the original story, however, the brick seems to point first to the intensity of Pundalik's devotion toward his parents and second to the stability that that devotion provides for Krishna himself. The god who had himself been impatient at home and was wandering to find Radha (or, in the other version, to recover Rukmini) becomes so impressed by Pundalik's act of human devotion that he stops and decides to wait forever in its presence.[8] His mobility fixed, he becomes the ritual goal of his devotees' ritual movement. The brick, in fact, becomes the god's vehicle (*vahana*). Krishna in the form of Vithoba no longer moves at all but remains in this one place,[9] arms akimbo, standing on his brick forever, transformed by human devotion into the premier god of devotion.

How Pundalik Comes to Pandharpur

The story of how Pundalik gets to Pandharpur is an important secondary myth in the cult. Not only does it provide the charter for the ritual visit to Pundalik's *samadhi* during the pilgrimage, but it also provides an interesting counterpoint to the basic founding myth. Like that basic founding myth, it is a story about movement and stasis and their relation to devotion (*bhakti*). According to this story, Pundalik has been a profligate and inconsiderate son, paying no attention to his parents' infirmities and needs but only to his own desires. Even on a holy pilgrimage to Kasi (Banaras), he ignored the needs of his parents. He rode to Kasi in luxury in a carriage, while his old and infirm parents walked. He ate in elegance and splendor, while they begged for crumbs. (Pundalik's irresponsibility is variously and elaborately developed.) Then one day, just before the pilgrimage party was to arrive at Kasi, a vision came to Pundalik, and he reformed. He suddenly wanted to do everything for his parents that he had previously neglected to do, even to find new ways to express his filial devotion. He gave up his pilgrimage to Kasi as he realized that devotion to his parents was more important, and he returned home to devote his full attention to their care. At the particular moment when Krishna appeared in the clearing and looked into the hut, Pundalik was in the process of massaging his father's feet with such devotion that Krishna was amazed and transformed.

The symbolism of Pundalik's abandoning his pilgrimage to Kasi to return home and become the super-devoted son to his parents parallels the symbolism of Krishna's abandoning his wandering search for Radha. Indeed, the devotional act that symbolized the profligate human's reform is the very same act that arrests the wandering of the god. Pundalik's devotion transforms Krishna into the static god, Vithoba,[10] who, in this new static form, becomes the object of centuries of devotion expressed through the ritual movement of his pilgrims to his fixed place.

Jnanesvar and the Coming of Vithoba to Alandi

This new form of the lord Krishna became known throughout Maharashtra and northern Karnataka as the premier god of the highest form of *bhakti*.[11] He attracted many devotees, among them certain saints or holy men (*sants*)—charismatic devotees who expressed their devotion eloquently in songs and hence came to be known as *sant kavi* (poet saints). Some of these *sants* lived in Pandharpur, but others who were not from Pandharpur began to make pilgrimages to Pandharpur from all over Maharashtra to express their devotion to Vithoba and, singing on the way, brought with them the devotional songs they composed as offerings to their god.

Jnanesvar in the late thirteenth century came from Alandi, Eknath in the sixteenth century from Paithan, and Tukaram in the seventeenth century from Dehu, and there were others. Pundalik, the mythological first *sant*, seems originally to be vaguely associated with Karnataka, but his *samadhi* is in Pandharpur, as are those of several other historical *sants* in the cult, including the thirteenth century contemporary of Jnanesvar, Namdev. In the present day the geographic distribution of the *sants* forms a geographic model of the pilgrimage, as the *samadhis* of the *sants* are the starting points of each of the organized groups of pilgrims called *palkhis*, a name they take from the Marathi word for the palanquin in which they carry silver replicas (called *padukas*) of the feet of their respective *sant*.

The story of how Jnanesvar became a devotee of Vithoba and subsequently both a *Varkari*[12] and a *sant* differs somewhat from the character of the charter myths about Pundalik and Krishna. Jnanesvar was an historical figure, perhaps the most important and most influential of his age, and some of the elements of the stories about him have the characteristics of historical fact. He was one of four children of an outcaste Brahmin father. His father was outcasted by the Brahmin authorities for lapsing back into the status of a householder after taking the vows of *samyasa*.[13] Even his subsequent ritual suicide by throwing himself into the waters at the *sangama* of Ganga and Jumna at Prayaga[14] was not enough to erase the outcaste stigma from his children; and certainly that unrelenting attitude of the Brahmin community toward Jnanesvar and his brothers and sister may have influenced his championing of several popular, non-Brahmin causes. Jnanesvar was probably initiated into the ritual of "going to Panduranga"[15] by his brothers in the early thirteenth century. Subsequently he not only became the most famous pilgrim to Pandharpur but dignified the pilgrimage by writing numerous *abhangas*,[16] which set the mood for the "total devotion" with which even today the pilgrim "sings his way to Pandharpur." He also wrote the *Jnanesvari*, a now famous commentary on the *Bhagavad Gita*; and he wrote it in Marathi, thereby establishing himself as the "Dante of Marathi Literature" and providing the impetus and momentum for what came to be called "the Marathi Renaissance." The *Jnanesvari* was finished in 1290 A.D.; Jnanesvar died some years later in Alandi by voluntarily entering *jivant samadhi*.[17] Soon afterward his followers began the practice of venerating his *padukas* and carrying them on their pilgrimage to Pandharpur;[18] at about the same time large numbers of pilgrims began visiting the place of Jnanesvar's own *samadhi* in Alandi.

Other elements of the story about Jnanesvar are less historically verifiable, merging into the legendary and mythical—for example, that he wrote the entire *Jnanesvari* at the age of fifteen or (in another version) at the age of nine, that he refuted the Brahmins in Paithan by teaching a buffalo to recite the Vedas, and that

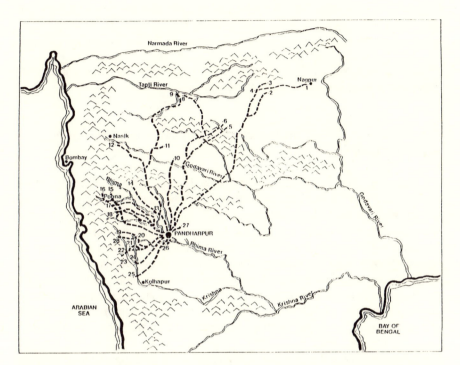

Plate No. 2: The "catchment area" and traditional route of 28 *palkhi*s. Map derived from Deleury (1960) plate 4.

No. Name	Starting point		
1. Sri Bhutesvar	Nagpur (Nagpur dt.)	15. Jnanesvar	Alandi (Poona dt.)
2. Rukmini	Kondanpur(Umaravatti dt.)	16. Tukaram	Dehu (Poona dt.)
3. Sankara Maharaj	Mahuli (Umaravatti dt.)	17. Laksminarayana	Saswad (Poona dt.)
4. Sesanarayana	Umaravatti (Umaravatti dt.)	18. Sopandev	Saswad (Poona dt.)
5. Svarupananda	Dhanegaon (Buldhana dt.)	19. Tukaram Maharaj	Trepute (Satara dt.)
6. Nrsimhasarasvati	Mahekar (Buldhana dt.)	20. Sekujibova	Sirasvadi (Satara dt.)
7. Muktabai	Edalabad (East Khandesh dt.)	21. Jayaramswami	Vadgaon (Satara dt.)
8. Muktabai	Mehun (East Khandesh dt.)	22. Ghadgebova	Kale (Satara dt.)
9. Muktabai	Jalgaon (East Khandesh dt.)	23. Goraksnath	Sirale (Satara dt.)
10. Eknath	Paithan (Aurangabad dt.)	24. Macchindranath	Macchindranath (Satara dt.)
11. Janardanaswami	Daulatabad (Aurangabad dt.)	25. Purnananda Maharaj	Bhognul (Belgaon dt.)
12. Nivrttinath	Trimbak (Nasik dt.)	26. Damaji Maharaj	Mangalvedhe (Solapur dt.)
13. Balbhima Maharaj	Sade (Solapur dt.)	27. Jnanoba Maharaj	Tuljapur (Usmanabad dt.)
14. Limbaraj Maharaj	Dahithan (Ahmednagar dt.)	28. Ramdas	Sajjadgad (Satara dt.)

he actually is, himself, an *avatara* of Vithoba, born on the traditional day of Krishna's birth, the dark eighth (*Kal astami*) of the month of Sravana, and possessing from birth the "true understanding" of the *Bhagavad Gita* which he promulgates anew in the *Jnanesvari*. These legendary and mythical elements of the Jnanesvar story, passed on through generations of devotees' songs, including many by the popular seventeenth century saint poet, Tukaram, establish Alandi as a powerful place of Vithoba, second only to Pandharpur, and charter the extremely important second movement in the pilgrimage: the return to Alandi.

THE SHAPE OF THE PILGRIMAGE: GEOGRAPHY, ORGANIZATION, AND MOVEMENT

Geography The pilgrimage to Pandharpur is principally a pilgrimage of the Marathi *desh* (the central plain of Maharashtra),[19] but it attracts pilgrims from all over the state, including large numbers of Kolis (fisher caste) from the coastal region (Konkan), large numbers of Dhangars (shepherds) from the hills, and smaller numbers of Kanada- and Telegu-speaking peoples from northern Karnataka and Andhra Pradesh. Late in the lunar month of Jyestha all over Maharashtra devotees of Vithoba begin making plans to act out their devotion to their god by making the journey to his principal city on his special day. The day on which they plan to enter the city in one long procession is the *sukla ekadasi* (bright eleventh), the eleventh *tithi* (lunar day) of the bright (waxing) fortnight of the month of Asadha. Many will go part of the way, some even all the way, by bus, but the 75,000 to 100,000 who comprise the core of the pilgrimage will walk. Pilgrims will come from as far north as the Narmada river valley, from as far west as Bombay and Ratnagiri on the Konkan coast, and from as far east as Nagpur and Bhandara. Some will travel individually or in small groups all of the way from their homes to the village of Wakri, just outside of Pandharpur, but most will join along the way one of the thirty or forty organized groups coming from points forming a large semi-circle around the city of Pandharpur (see map, plate 2).

Organization

Palkhis. Some of the *palkhis* are rather small and are not subdivided further into smaller groups. The larger *palkhis* are divided into *dindis*, somewhat homogenous groups organized by caste grouping, village origin, or family. Some *dindis* are even further divided, at least in their pattern of march, into sub-*dindis* and sometimes even into smaller units within the sub-*dindi*. In some *dindis* males and females are separated. In others both male-female separation and caste division are, at least temporarily, overcome.[20] Each *palkhi* has a prescribed route that it will follow. Some are quite rigidly organized, having both stopping points and stopping times rigidly determined as well as the precise order of the *dindis* and sub-*dindis* in the line of the march. For example, in the Alandi *palkhi* (the largest and most rigidly organized), the stopping places for each night are set at precise points along the route (see map, plate 1). The stopping times are set by lunar days. Since the lunar day does not correspond precisely to the solar day and since the starting and stopping hours for the march are determined by the solar day, on some days the *palkhi* will move very slowly over a short distance, while on other days a rather longer distance must be covered before the night's halt. The result is considerable variation of both the speed and the arduousness of the procession throughout the fourteen days of the journey. Some of the smaller *palkhis*, especially from the eastern districts, are much less compulsive in their organization, having only a specified departure time and the arrival goal of *sukla dasami* (the bright tenth lunar day) at the village of Wakri on the outskirts of the holy city of Pandharpur.

The *palkhis* also vary a great deal in other aspects of organization. In the larger *palkhis* some of the *dindis* will have an organizational leader who arranges for a truck with fresh water, food, and cooking fuel to be available at each night's stopping point and at each midday pause. Each member of the *dindi* will have paid a set amount for these support services, arranged, usually rather efficiently, by the organizer of the *dindi*. In some *dindis* the organizer is very much like a modern tour guide,[21] while others have much looser arrangements. Some *dindis* will follow the traditional pattern, requiring each pilgrim to carry his or her own provisions (to be supplemented only by begging) all the way to Pandharpur.

Movement

Movement toward Pandharpur. Prescribed members of each *palkhi* carry silver replicas of the feet of one of the saints of the cult. The silver feet, called *padukas*, are carried in a palanquin (*palkhi*). At times the *palkhi* is placed on a bullock cart and at times carried by hand. The *padukas* symbolize the feet of the *sant* on his original pilgrimage. Hence the pilgrimage as a whole can be seen as having a dimension across time as well as space, as each pilgrimage becomes the joining across time of the pilgrimages of all of the saints in the cult. Since each of the members of the *palkhi* identifies with the *sant* whose *padukas* his *palkhi* is carrying, a common expression on the pilgrimage becomes, "We are all *sants* together."

A riderless horse is led at the head of the larger *palkhis*. In the Alandi *palkhi*, and some others, he is joined by a ridden horse, the riding of which is assigned according to a tradition, usually honoring a certain family.[22] The riderless horse also symbolizes the *sant*'s original pilgrimage as well as his presence in this one. The redundancy of the symbolism does not bother the pilgrims, nor does the implied contradiction that the *sant* could not have made his original pilgrimage both on horseback and by walking barefoot. According to the pilgrims I interviewed, the *sant*'s presence is believed to be both in the *padukas* carried in the *palkhi* and on the riderless horse at the head of the column, and indeed those two places mark the principal points of attraction for all of the spectators who gather on the side of the road as the pilgrims pass by. The spectators will take *darsana*[23] of both the horse and the *palkhi* and thereby add their participation to the pilgrimage. Many will also take *darsana* of the feet of the pilgrims as they pass, believing that they are taking *darsana* of the feet of all of the *sants* at once. Even the dust of the road on which the pilgrims' feet trod comes to be regarded as especially sacred. Spectators will collect the dust after the pilgrims have passed and mix it with *bukka*, the black powder sacred to Vithoba, which they use to mark their foreheads.[24]

The entire movement of the pilgrimage, from the starting points of the individual pilgrims, to the starting points of each *palkhi*, to the joining of the routes along the way, to the final joining of all the *palkhis* at the village of Wakri, resembles very closely the catchment metaphor model of the pilgrimage that Victor Turner has articulated. There are even rituals of joining at the point where the route of two *palkhis* meet,[25] as there are ritual markers at the point where two rivers meet (*sangama*). On the tenth day of the month, when the *palkhis* have gathered from all over the catchment area at the tiny village of Wakri, there is a great deal of mingling between groups and random, spontaneous performance of various rituals of joining, after which the entire procession begins to move, turns round on itself in one large circle, and flows into the holy city. The procession lasts all day, the smallest *palkhis* going first, the largest and most important, the Jnanesvar *palkhi* from Alandi, entering last in the position of greatest honor.

Queue for the *darsana* of Vithoba. Many pilgrims will stand in queue all through the night for the opportunity of spending a few seconds directly in front of Vithoba to take his *darsana* and touch his feet.

Queue for *darsana* of Pundalik's *samadhi*. If the heavy rains have not begun, the queue for *darsana* of Pundalik's *samadhi* is formed on the dry ground near the edge of the river. Often by Asadhi Ekadasi, however, the monsoon has arrived in force and the Bhima is in full spate. Devotees from the fisher caste (Mahadev Kolis) provide boats to Pundalik's *samadhi*.

Once in the city, the pilgrims make their way to the temple of Vithoba and join the queue to take *darsana* of their god. The taking of *darsana* will last all night and throughout the entire course of the eleventh day, which is regarded as the most auspicious time to complete the *darsana*.[26] After taking *darsana* of Vithoba, however, the pilgrims' goal is not quite completed. A few hundred feet closer to the river, indeed, sometimes engulfed by the river, is the *samadhi* of Pundalik, the legendary first *sant* in the cult. Most serious pilgrims will not be satisfied until they add the *darsana* of Pundalik's *samadhi* to their pilgrimage.[27]

If the monsoon has already begun by this time, as it often has, the temple of Pundalik will be half under water, and this last leg of the pilgrims' journey must be completed by boat (see photo). Hundreds of boatmen (Mahadev Kolis) will be employed to take the pilgrims some fifty yards out into the swollen river to the half-submerged temple door, where they can catch a glimpse (*darsana*) of the *samadhi* of the man whose original act of devotion fixed the wandering of their god at this place and made their pilgrimage possible. For many of the pilgrims the *darsana* of Vithoba and of Pundalik's *samadhi* is the culmination of the "Great Maharashtrian Pilgrimage." These pilgrims will come once a year, or perhaps less often, to express their devotion to Vithoba. They feel now that their offering is complete. They will return to their villages either individually or in groups, considerably less organized in the return than in the coming, taking with them *prasada* from Vithoba and holy water (*tirth*) from the Bhima River.[28]

Movement toward Alandi. For some of the pilgrims, however, the pilgrimage to Pandharpur is only part of a larger story. For them there is another ritual movement that must be made, and, without that second movement, the pilgrimage to Pandharpur is felt to be incomplete.[29] On the *Krishna ekadasi* (dark eleventh) of the lunar month of Kartika, just four months and one fortnight after they enter the city of Pandharpur, many of these pilgrims will make a similar pilgrimage to the village of Alandi, the special place of Jnanesvar, the premier *sant* in the cult. Some of these pilgrims will converge individually and in groups on Alandi from their various home villages in much the same pattern as they came to Pandharpur. Some, however, will make the journey to Alandi in a special way. On the bright eleventh day of the month of Kartika they will come first to Pandharpur, where they will participate in a small festival. They will take *darsana* of Vithoba of Pandharpur and of the *samadhi* of Pundalik and then make the fourteen-day journey to Alandi, essentially retracing the steps of Jnanesvar on his return from Pandharpur to Alandi. They will enter the village of Alandi and take *darsana* of the image of Vithoba and *samadhi* and *padukas* of the saint Jnanesvar on the dark eleventh of the month, and, taking with them *prasada* from Jnanesvar's *samadhi* and *tirth* from the Indrayani River, they will return home.

Those who "promise always" to make this double pilgrimage to Vithoba and Pundalik at Pandharpur and to Vithoba and Jnanesvar at Alandi are called Varkaris.[30] They are considered to be especially devout pilgrims, and, unquestionably, their devotion to Vithoba constitutes the heart and soul of the pilgrimage.

Moreover, for a few of these Varkaris there is still more to the pilgrimage. Those who make the extreme promise of the Mahinemaha Varkari will commit themselves to making the pilgrimage to Pandharpur on the *sukla ekadasi* (bright eleventh) of every lunar month and to Alandi on every dark *ekadasi*. Since the journey between Alandi and Pandharpur requires about two weeks, the Varkaris who have made this extreme vow, have, in effect, made their entire lives into a pilgrimage. Without taking any vow of *samyasa*,[31] without ceasing to be householders, they have turned their lives into the lives of *bhakti sadhus*, constantly moving between the two fixed poles of their devotion: Pandharpur and Alandi.[32]

THE FRAME OF THE CHATURMAS

One final thing to note about the shape of this pilgrimage system is that the two pilgrimages form a ritual frame around the *chaturmas*, the four and one-half especially holy months in the Maharashtrian ritual calendar. These months, during which most marriages are suspended and which are loaded with the major religious festivals, correspond to the months of the rainy season. It is a common folklore notion in Maharashtra that the beginning of the *chaturmas* is marked by the pilgrimage to Pandharpur and the end marked by the pilgrimage to Alandi, much in the same way that popular American culture sees the summer vacation period framed by Memorial Day and Labor Day. The three basic elements of the shape of this pilgrimage can be briefly summarized as follows: (1) the movement of pilgrims from all over Maharashtra to Pandharpur and to Alandi (two separate instances of the catchment metaphor); (2) the movement back and forth between Pandharpur and Alandi[33] (pulsating metaphor), expressed especially by the Mahinemaha Varkaris; and (3) the framing of the holiest time of the Marathi year by those two ritual movements.

THE *BHAKTI* CHARACTER OF THE PILGRIMAGE

Maharashtrian culture distinguishes clearly between two kinds of *bhakti*: *sakam bhakti* (wish-granting devotion) and *niskam bhakti* (desireless devotion). In performing *sakam bhakti*, the devotee makes a vow (*navas*) to the god to demonstrate the intensity of his *bhakti*. Sometimes the vows are to perform simple rituals of devotion, such as going on a certain day to take *darsana* or performing a pilgrimage. Occasionally the vows are more extreme, involving, in some of the *sakam bhakti* cults, various forms of self-torture. The assumption is that the god will not refuse any request if the intensity of *bhakti* is sufficiently demonstrated by the vow. Pilgrimages are often undertaken to gods of *sakam bhakti* to gain power, prosperity, children or success in a business or political venture. Gods of *sakam bhakti* are numerous in Maharashtra, and one or two will normally be on the circuit of any pilgrim performing a circuit pilgrimage.[34] Nearly all pilgrims to Pandharpur and

Alandi, however, will make it clear that *sakam bhakti* has no part in their pilgrimage. Even the Varkaris, who have made a promise "always to go to Vithoba," have made it as an unconditional promise, not a conditional vow. They go to Vithoba out of love, not desire; they are seeking only the opportunity to express their devotion to him and the sheer experience of the joy of going, and, though occasionally someone will seek to use the pilgrimage for profit, he is usually rigorously criticized, as was a recent politician who attempted to use his pilgrimage to Pandharpur for political gain.

Not only *sakam bhakti* but also the goals of *dharma* or *moksa* have no place in the Pandharpur and Alandi pilgrimages, for, while theoretically not antithetical to the goal of *niskam bhakti*, such *bhakti* is not a means to a higher goal. It is itself the principal goal and really the only goal for most pilgrims.

"WE SING OUR WAY TO PANDHARPUR"

Although Maharashtrian *bhakti* is not elaborated as thoroughly as Bengali and other north Indian *bhakti*, it has developed along the same theoretical lines. There are several popular moods (*rasas*) corresponding to the standard *bhakti* relationship (mother-child, wife-husband, lover-beloved, friend-friend, servant-master). In the devotional songs, which become the principal expression of *bhakti* for the people on their journey, the experience of the singers reflects these various moods. Thus, for example, the song that Iravati Karve (1962) reports hearing so often on her way to Pandharpur,

> The quality of compassion is to love—
> to love without thought of return—
> as a mother loves her child.

would be sung in the mood expressing a mother's love for a child. Other songs would be sung spanning the full range of the possible *bhakti* moods, sometimes even mixing them. The moods of utter adoration, however, dominate. The *abhangas* are usually composed in the voice of a fictional person, the poet assuming the persona and writing the song to his lord as if he were that person. The devotees singing that song identify with that persona, assume the mood of the appropriate relationship, and experience, as they sing, the feelings associated with that mood. One pilgrim put it this way: "We make our pilgrimage as we sing our songs—for the love of Vithoba. There is no other reason.... We sing all the way to Pandharpur because of our love of Vithoba."

THE EXPERIENCE OF THE PILGRIMAGE: AN ANALYSIS

Normative Communitas

Many of the accounts of the experience of going on the pilgrimage reported to me in interviews could be interpreted through the category of what Victor Turner called "normative communitas"—a heightened sense of camaraderie, of closeness, of specialness, a significant reduction in the normal structures of society that separate group from group, but lacking the full "communitas" character of "existential communitas." Turner has written at length about this phenomenon. Indeed, in his treatment of the Varkari pilgrimage in *Dramas, Fields and Metaphors* Turner sees the Varkari's experience as the exception to the rule of normative communitas and claims that the Varkari's promise is so unconditional that it takes him altogether out of structures, even the modified ones of normative communitas, and into a more rarefied aura of "existential communitas." Turner was, as we have seen, wrong about that. Elaborate structures remain in the organization of the pilgrimage, including an order of march, prescribed stopping times and places, and sometimes elaborate eating arrangements. All of these structures preserve abbreviated but still definite separations. Here, as in most pilgrimages, normative communitas reigns. An excellent example of this can be seen in Karve's (1962) account of her encounter with Maratha women. Herself a Brahmin, she is participating in the pilgrimage as a member of the Alandi *palkhi*. At first frustrated by the structure separations that remained in the normative communitas atmosphere of the pilgrimage, she gradually felt some of them relax. She writes:

> I joined now one group and now another, trying to construct a bridge at least as far as I was concerned. After I had taken my meal with them, I felt that they were more friendly. Many of them walked alongside of me, held my hand, and told me many things about their life. Toward the end, they called me "Tai," meaning "sister." A few of them said, "Mark you, Tai, we shall visit you in Poona." And then one young girl said, "But will you behave with us then as you are behaving now?"

Both Maratha girl and Brahmin woman hoped that she would but knew that she would not—not because of a lack of will but because the structures of their culture were by no means overcome, only partially and temporarily suspended. Still, the temporary suspension of those structures and the cooperative sharing of values such suspension engenders, even temporarily, are seen by the pilgrims as both edifying and inspiring.

Moving and Standing: The Feet of the Pilgrims

Much of the imagery in the pilgrimage focuses on feet. This focus is clear in the charter myths for both pilgrimages. Pundalik is massaging his father's feet when

Krishna discovers him; Krishna's wandering feet become fixed on the brick; Jnanes-var's feet are symbolically carried between Pandharpur and Alandi by his devotees, and so on. This focus is even clearer in the rituals within the structure of the pilgrimage. The feet of the pilgrims are holy. Spectators take *darsana* of the feet of the pilgrims, the feet of the horses, and the replicas of the feet of the *sants*. Moreover, the dust from the pilgrims' feet, as well as the dust the horses' feet stepped on in the *ringan* ritual, is regarded as holy and is either mixed with, or applied to, the forehead in place of Vithoba's holy powder (*bukka*).

A. K. Ramanujan has discussed the opposition of standing and moving (*sthavara* versus *jangama*) in the Virashaivaite religion of northern Karnataka. Gods, idols, and temples "stand"; a human devotee "goes" or "moves" to express his devotion: "*Sthavara* is that which stands, a piece of property, a thing inanimate. *Jangama* is moving, movable, anything given to going and coming. Especially in Virashaiva religion a *jangama* is a religious man who has renounced world and home, moving from village to village, representing god to the devoted, a god incarnate" (1973: 20-21).

Ramanujan comments on a poem by Basavanna:

The rich will make temples for Shiva.
What shall I,
a poor man,
do?

The answer is, the poor man can make himself into a moving temple, a temple that will be even richer than the one that merely stands and cannot move. Much the same contrast between stability and mobility is expressed in the pilgrimage to Vithoba. The god has become fixed. Even Vithoba's vehicle, the normal symbol of a god's mobility, is an immobile brick. Temples could be built, and indeed are, around the image of the stable god. But even greater than the fixed temple is the institution of the moving devotees. Indeed, the moving back and forth of the pilgrims between the two fixed poles of the object of their devotion becomes itself an even superior object of devotion. The feet of the pilgrims and the movement of the pilgrims are a religious reality of which spectators take *darsana*. The pilgrims themselves experience in their going the divinity that the spectators so honor. Even Karve, careful scientist and seasoned observer, remarks of the experience of this feeling of movement.

Everything was in motion in the wind-swept atmosphere—the ends of the saris of women, the branches of the trees, the stalks of millet in a few unploughed fields, the walking crows, and the clouds overhead. I was walking on and on in a space filled with colour, sound, and wind. When I looked down, I saw innumerable feet moving up and down onward to the rhythm of *tal* and *mrdang*.

I felt I was a drop in this vast stream of human beings, that instead of walking, I was being carried forward by the surrounding motion. Even at night when I slept, I was surprised that I lay still at the spot where I had fallen asleep.

The Experience of *Vari* as *Bhakti:* Joy, Total Joy

The action of going on the pilgrimage is technical work (*karma*), but it is offered and experienced as devotion (*bhakti*). The pilgrim is offering his own "going" as both emblem and instance of his devotion ("We are all *sants* together"), and, most important of all, he is aligning his going with the devotional goings of all of the *sants* across history, and he is contributing to the goings of all subsequent pilgrims. This corporate *karma*, which produces a shared, corporate joy, manifests itself in individual pilgrims in various ways at various times during the pilgrimage. It can be seen when they are especially "into" the spirit of a devotional song. It can be seen during the *ringan* performance when the pilgrims, beaming with smiles, pick themselves up off the ground after diving recklessly under the hooves of a horse to catch, before it falls to the ground, some of the dirt the horse has stepped on or when they throw themselves with abandon into the other ritual games of joining, often spinning in circles until dizzy and giddy. It can be seen when a pilgrim becomes lost in the spirit of the movement and is carried along with glowing countenance on the waves of motion "infused," as one informant put it, "into the bliss of the *vari*."

Moreover, the joy, both the individual experience of the joy and the contribution one makes to the corporate joy of the going, is intensified by hardship. The harder the going, the more discipline it takes to give the act of going as a gift, hence the greater the joy. One informant put it this way: "Sometimes the going will be hot and dry. Good! all the more joy! Sometimes it will be impossible to sleep because of the rain. Good! All the more joy! A *vari* is never really thought to be a success without some hardship."[35]

Hardships offer the pilgrim the opportunity to add the discipline of *yoga* to his going, just as the ringing of the cymbals (*taks*) and the work of the going offer him the opportunity to add *karma* and as the performance of the various rituals (taking *darsana*, chanting the *haripath*, performing *ringan*, and so on) offers the opportunity to add *upasana* (observance or performance of ritual). But the *upasana*, the *yoga*, and the *karma*, however intense, are not sufficient—in fact, they are nothing—if they are not offered and experienced as *bhakti*. If they are experienced as *bhakti*, then one is infused into total joy. This, to be sure, must be the final word about the experience of the pilgrimage: it is finally the joy of giving to God. "I wonder if you have understood what we experience in the pilgrimage," one of my informants inquired of me. "I wonder if you have understood what you said you have seen in the pilgrims' faces? These [westerners][36] who go on the pilgrimage—their faces don't show it because they don't experience it. You can talk to them about the pilgrimage, but what will you learn? Their faces look tired. A [true] pilgrim's face is the face of joy. Even when they are ill, even if dying, they experience the *vari* as joy, total joy—[the joy] of giving to God."

NOTES

1. A Hindu lunar day (*tithi*) is 1/30th of a lunar month. The division, however, is made geometrically rather than chronometrically. The apparent course of the moon against the background of the fixed stars is divided into thirty equal, elliptical segments rather than thirty equal time segments. One *tithi* is the amount of time, however long, required for the moon to regress twelve degrees in its path along the ecliptic. Since the moon's apparent motion against the background of the fixed stars is extremely erratic, the length of *tithis* varies as much as four and one-half hours, and their beginnings and endings seldom correspond to the beginning and ending of a solar day (*var*), measured from sunrise to sunrise (see Stanley 1977: 27ff.). An elaborate mythology assigns influences of various gods to both *tithi* and *var*. In many cases the correspondence of a particular *tithi* with a particular *var* can result in a special access of power at the place of a specific deity and hence be the occasion of a pilgrimage. The pilgrimage to Khandoba at Jejuri when the no-moon *tithi* corresponds with Monday (*Somavar*) is an example.

2. Victor Turner (1974a) has elaborated the "catchment area" metaphor as a model for understanding the course of pilgrimages. The catchment area is the geographical area from which pilgrims come to a particular goal at a particular time. The catchment area for any pilgrimage usually varies from time to time. Turner's contention that the goal of a pilgrimage usually lies at the periphery of the catchment area has been challenged by religious geographers such as David Sopher. The catchment area for the Pandharpur pilgrimage in the month of Asadha is shown in plate 2. The catchment area for the Alandi pilgrimage in the month of Kartika is considerably smaller.

3. *Sant* is a Marathi word connoting a particularly holy person. It is roughly the equivalent of the English word *saint*. Usually it denotes a set of popular charismatics of historical importance who composed songs to the god Vithoba and made pilgrimages to his temples.

4. A *samadhi* is the burial place of a Hindu holy person. The term derives from the name for the eighth level of *yoga*, a state of deep trance usually characterized by peace and bliss. Since it was assumed that holy persons sometimes died in such a state, it was further assumed that they could be buried or immersed in a river (cremation not required since a body in the state of *samadhi* was already purified) without polluting the ground or river. The term is also used loosely to designate a memorial to a holy person even if the person is not buried there.

5. *Avatara* is the descent, rebirth, incarnation of a god.

6. In the variant version Rukmini gives up her penance and mysteriously appears by Vithoba's side, sometimes on her own brick.

7. A Varkari is a special pilgrim in the cult of Vithoba (see note 12). In later Varkari traditions the throwing of the brick is regarded as an act of devotion, and the brick itself becomes a symbol of every Varkari's devotion to Vithoba. Thus Lokhande writes: "the brick under the feet of Vithoba has come to mean prayer, dedication, and surrender to Vithoba. To become a brick, in the Varkari terminology, means to devote oneself body and soul to Vithoba. The brick became a symbol of one who wanted to belong totally to god" (1976: 146). In the case of the Mahinemaha Varkari, who is always moving between Pandharpur and Alandi, the brick can be seen as the nexus between the fixed feet of the god and total devotion of the Varkari expressed through his constantly moving feet.

8. According to another variant of the story, told by Maharashtrian parents to charter filial piety for their offspring, Krishna was told by a messenger that a former devotee named Pundalik had forgotten Krishna in his over-zealous performance of serving his parents.

Krishna came in the form of Vithoba to Pandharpur to remind Pundalik of his duty to him. Pundalik throws him the brick to stand on but tells him he must wait to talk until he is finished massaging the feet of his father. So great is his devotion to his father, however, that he never finishes, and to this day Vithoba stands there, waiting for Pundalik's acknowledgment.

9. Though most of the traditions in the Vithoba cult emphasize the stability of Krishna at both Pandharpur and Alandi and the immobility of the brick *vahans*, there are two important, though minor, instances of Vithoba's mobility. One is ritual; the other mythological. There is a ritual procession at Pandharpur in which an image of Vithoba is taken out of the temple and carried around the city. This practice is not as common as at other Hindu temples, but it is performed occasionally, and there is an *utsava murti* (festival image) of Vithoba for that purpose. The second exception is the mythological story that Vithoba leaves the city Pandharpur precisely on the holiest day of the pilgrimage (Asadhi Ekadasi). The story is alluded to by Karve (1962) at the conclusion of her account of her own pilgrimage. According to one version of the story, it is an anti-Varkari story, implying that the Varkaris themselves have made going on the pilgrimage a substitute for true *bhakti* and the pilgrimage itself a substitute for true spirituality. Another interpretation is that it is a pro-Varkari, story making fun of many of the non-Varkari pilgrims who come only to enjoy the festival and to have a "valuable *darsana*." According to this version Vithoba is walking out of the city and the temple (where everyone had queued up to take *darsana*) to be available to his true devotees, who will know that the importance of the pilgrimage is in "the going," in the performing of the *vari*, in the walking itself, and not in the *ekadasi darsana*. All of the Varkaris I interviewed about this story agreed that they had heard similar versions; they stressed that the import of the story is not that Vithoba is not in his temple on Asadhi Ekadasi but that he can be elsewhere as well and, most important, that he will always be wherever his *bhaktas* are singing.

10. Other frequently used names are Vithal and Panduranga.

11. Maharashtrian culture makes a sharp distinction between *niskam bhakti* (surrendering devotion) and *sakam bhakti* (wish-granting devotion). In Maharashtra Vithoba is the premier god of *niskam bhakti* while Khandoba is the premier god of *sakam bhakti*. See J. M. Stanley 1977: 31.

12. The term *Varkari* means one who makes a pilgrimage. The usual term in Marathi for pilgrimage is the Sanskrit word *yatra* or *tirtha-yatra*. Pilgrims to Pandharpur and Alandi eschew this term and refer to their pilgrimage as *vari*. The root of the word is *var*, meaning "special period of time" (cf. Note 1). *Vari* thus denotes the "regular" appearance of a person at a certain place at a certain time. A Varkari denotes one who "does" or "performs" (*karne*) a *vari* to Vithoba. By most definitions, however, just making a pilgrimage is not a sufficient condition to become a Varkari. N. B. Langde, president of the Varkari Mahamandal, makes the following distinctions. There are four levels of Varkaris. First, there are those who go to Pandharpur and Alandi once a year—always to Pandharpur in the month of Asadha and usually to Alandi in the month of Kartika, though some will go to Alandi during another month. They could also go to any one of the other *palkhi* locations (see note 33). There are from 75,000 to 100,000 Varkaris at this level. Second, there are those who go both to Pandharpur and to Alandi two times a year. These number about 7,000. Third, there are those who go both to Pandharpur and to Alandi four times a year, numbering about 1,000. Fourth, there are those who go to Pandharpur and Alandi every month. These are called Mahinemaha Varkaris. They number about 600 people, and they are considered the heart and soul of the *vari*. They are the most highly respected of all the Varkaris. Their numbers are growing, especially among the educated. They travel singly, not usually joining *palkhis* or *dindis*, though at Pandharpur and Alandi they have subgroups into which they occasionally gather (thirty in some; twenty in

others; as few as five or six in some) after reaching the holy city. It is said if one of their subgroup does not arrive by the tenth day of the fortnight at the anticipated goal, the rest are concerned. If the man has not arrived on the eleventh day, they assume he has died. If he has not arrived on the twelfth day, they perform the funeral rites. Mahinemaha Varkaris are considered very special and infuse inspiration into the rest of the Varkaris. Varkaris are loosely organized. There is a school in Alandi in which their traditions are carefully taught to future generations.

13. The vows of *samyasa* include the renunciation of possessions and attachments and the giving up of the life of the householder in terms of both material possessions and life-style.

14. The present-day city of Allahabad is considered the most sacred of all of the *sangamas* in India. It is the joining of the Ganges and the Jumna rivers, and, according to mythology, it is actually a triple *sangama* because the waters of the mythological Saraswati River join at the same point. It is an important pilgrimage place in India, especially for the atonement of misdeeds. Pilgrimage to Prayaga for the purpose of the ritual of suicide is considered a "pilgrimage unto death" and is traditionally the most powerful eliminator of sins.

15. One of the names of Vithoba connoting special intimacy.

16. A particular form of religious poetry favored by the poet saints.

17. *Jivant* means "living." A *jivant samadhi* is a living *samadhi*. The assumption is that the saint voluntarily, in a conscious state, entered a place of entombment and assumed the condition of *samadhi* with the intention of remaining in it forever. From one point of view it is a special form of ritual suicide. From another point of view it is not suicide at all because it is not really death, the assumption being that the saint is still in a state of *samadhi* and therefore alive.

18. Until recently the *padukas* that were carried on the pilgrimage were made of stone and were quite small. Individual devotees tie them around their necks. The practice of carrying life-size silver *padukas* in a palanquin dates from the early nineteenth century. See H. B. P. Neurgoankar 1936; cf., D. D. Kosambi 1962.

19. See plate 2.

20. It is the overcoming of caste and sex barriers that led Victor Turner (1974a), following the ethnography of G. A. Deleury (1960) and S. V. Dandekar (1927), to see the pilgrimage as an example of existential communitas. Thus Turner concludes that there is *"no hierarchy* among the members of the procession," that "the pilgrimage has no director," and that there is "no distinction between priests, officiants, clerks and faithful." Although Turner was, to a large extent, correct about the spontaneous character of the promise made in the pilgrimage, he is clearly wrong about the lack of hierarchy. Indeed, in the Alandi Palkhi even the devotional songs that are sung along the way are strictly regulated. *Kirtankars* (song leaders) are assigned by tradition to lead the singing of the songs (*abhangas*) on the pilgrimage. Each *kirtankar* is fixed for each day's journey and night's stop. They take their assignments very seriously. There is a tradition among them that a *kirtan* program can never be canceled, however ill the *kirtankar* might be. Indeed, there is a saying among the *kirtankars* that the *kirtan* must be performed on time "whether we live or die." (See Neurgoankar 1936: 37.) Any change in the *palkhi* program is allowed only if "absolutely necessary" and must be approved by the *panchayat* committee of Alandi.

21. Karve (1962: 13-14) offers a colorful account of this.

22. Both the riderless horse and the horse that is ridden participate in a very important ritual from three to five times during the procession. The ritual is call *ringan*. There are two kinds of *ringans*. They are usually performed serially. One is an *ubhe ringan*, performed in a straight line; the other is an *adave ringan*, performed in a circle. In both cases the members of the

palkhi form a corridor, either in a straight line or in a circle in the middle of the field. The *palkhi* is set either at one end of the corridor or in the center of the circle. In the *ubhe ringan* the horses race at a gallop up to the *palkhi*, stop suddenly, bow down, and touch their heads to the side of the *palkhi*. In the circular *adave ringan* the horses run four or five times at a gallop around the circle, then proceed into the center of the circle where the *palkhi* is at rest, and perform there the ceremony of bowing to the *palkhi*. In both cases pilgrims will dive to the ground behind the horses and try to catch clumps of dirt before they fall to the ground. They then treat the dirt ritually in the same way that they treat the dust from the pilgrims' feet. They apply it to their foreheads, keep it as *prasada* (see note 28), or mix it with *bukka* and apply it to their forehead. The *ringan* ceremonies are performed at set places, often just after two or more *palkhis* have joined together. Hence, they can be considered rituals of joining. They are happily anticipated by the pilgrims and frequently become the occasion for the spontaneous outbreak of a number of other rituals of joining, include *phagdi* (see note 25).

23. *Darsana* is the act of seeing (and simultaneously being seen by) a god or an auspicious person. *Darsana* is "given" by the god and "taken" by the person. It is often explained as a discharge of power mediated by sight or touch.

24. Karve, performing the pilgrimage as a participant observer in the 1950s: "Tai bent down and took up the dust on the road. The dust under their feet was sacred. I too dipped my finger in dust and put it to my forehead" (Karve 1962: 15).

25. In a typical ritual a representative from each group will meet each other and exchange coconuts (similar to a minor ritual in a wedding ceremony). In another very popular ritual called *phagdi*, members from each group meet, cross arms, right over left, grasp hands, and swing each other round in a circle. Sometimes many members of the groups will join in this ritual in a very playful spirit; sometimes the rituals of joining are preceded by antiphonal calls from one *palkhi* to another as the two approach each other toward the meeting point.

26. There are three different kinds of *darsana* taken by pilgrims at Pandharpur and Alandi. The most powerful *darsana* is actually physical *darsana* where the pilgrims not only see but touch the image of Vithoba or the *samadhi* of the *sant*. Queues for this kind of *darsana* are extremely long. People wait in queues sometimes all night for an opportunity to touch the deity. The second kind of *darsana* is sight *darsana*, which is taken at close proximity in front of the image. The majority of pilgrims to Pandharpur will stand many hours in queue for an opportunity to be directly in the line of sight of the deity for a few seconds. The third kind of *darsana* is *darsana* of the *sikar* (spire) of the temple, which can be taken from almost any point in the city. All pilgrims will take at least the *sikar darsana* before returning to their homes. Many will set aside time to stand in the queue for one of the more powerful forms of *darsana*. I am indebted to Raymond Crow, Ph.D. candidate, University of Pennsylvania, for this observation.

27. There are a number of other sacred places in the city of Pandharpur, including the *samadhi* of Namdev (a poet-saint and contemporary of Jnanesvar), Janabi (Jnanesvar's sister), and Cokamela (a popular low-caste *sant*). Many pilgrims will make a circuit pilgrimage around the city (*nagar pradaksina*) and take *darsana* at each of these holy places.

28. *Prasada* is food that has been offered to the god, "taken" by the god (which means that it has come in contact with his digestive juices and by the principle of contagion contains his substance), and then returned to the devotee. It is presumed to contain some of the power of the god and can be either ingested or taken home and shared with others.

29. Varkaris estimate the number of pilgrims who make this second pilgrimage at 60,000 to 75,000 a year. Non-Varkari estimates are more conservative. In any case, it is clear that the ideal of returning to Alandi on the dark eleventh day of the month of Kartika is well established

in the cult. Most Varkaris consider it a necessary condition of being considered a Varkari. See note 12.

30. See note 12.

31. Since the time of Jnanesvar, the concept of *samyasa* (renunciation) has been transvalued in the Vithoba cult. One of the principal teachings of the *Jnanesvari* is that one can accomplish the full heights of *niskam bhakti* without renunciation, that, in effect, one can be the most holy of persons while still remaining a householder.

32. Pilgrimages to Pandharpur and Alandi attract a number of *sadhus* and holy men who, while not claiming to be Varkaris, claim to have the power to "mentalize" (spiritually enact) the pilgrimage in a *yogic* trance without actually performing it. Some do this in a normal posture. Others perform more rigorous and dramatic demonstrations of their *yogic* powers by burying themselves alive in a pit of loose earth for three or four hours or by putting their bodies into a *yogic* trance while aligned with the two sacred cities of the pilgrimage. The following photo shows such a *sadhu* with head pointed toward Pandharpur and loins pointed toward Alandi moving a mound of mud from one point to the other on his body with slow, stylized movements of his hands and arms. When I asked why he was doing this, the response was: "It is his *vari*. He does this instead of 'going.'" He was regarded as an auspicious phenomenon by many pilgrims who "bought into" his mentalized *vari* by making a contribution. Interestingly, however, he was not so regarded by Varkaris.

Mentalizing the pilgrimage. In yogic trance with slow stylized gestures, head pointing toward Pandharpur, loins toward Alandi, this devotee 'acts out' the movement of the pilgrims by moving a mound of mud back and forth from his head to his loins.

33. The fact that there is a ritual return only of the Alandi *palkhi* and not of any of the others is interesting. Some regard this as a phenomenon of the Jnanesvar cult. Indeed, Jnanesvar is the only one of the *sants* to be regarded as an *avatara* of Vithoba. Others, including many Varkaris, regard the return to Alandi as representative of the return of all the *sants* to their respective places. A small number of Varkaris will actually perform the return either occasionally or regularly to the place of one of the other *sants*, for example, to Tukaram at Dehu or to Eknath at Paithan.

34. The two best-known gods of *sakam bhakti* in Maharashtra are Khandoba and Tuljupur Bhavani. Interestingly, both the Tuljupur temple and the Khandoba temple at Jejuri are normally scheduled stopping points for the Alandi *palkhi*, both to and from Pandharpur. Many pilgrims will ask for boons or favors from these gods and even give vows (*navas*) to them. They will not, however, confuse these practices with their surrendering devotion (*niskam bhakti*) to Vithoba. See note 6.

35. N. B. Langde gives the following account of this phenomenon: "This year when we stopped in Phaltan it rained all night—from 5:00 P.M. to 4:00 A.M. We could not sleep the whole night. *Yoga* was required to go on the full next day without sleep. Those of us who control our bodies through *yoga* welcome this adversity as a test; we feel that the *vari* has not really been successful without some adversity and inconvenience."

36. In the summer of 1983 for the third time in five years a westerner had made the entire pilgrimage on foot from Alandi to Pandharpur. All of the Varkaris I interviewed were very proud and pleased that westerners were not only studying but experiencing the pilgrimage. Several of my Varkari informants, however, especially the one quoted here, were concerned that in the tedium of the journey the westerners were missing its essential joy.

INTERVIEWS CITED

Joshi, K. V., Trustee, Vithal Mandir, Alandi.

Khandke, Smt. S. D. and Narayan, Master K. N., Varkari Shiksham Samstha, Alandi.

Langde, N. B., President, Varkari Mahamandal, Poona.

4

Velankanni Calling:
Hindu Patterns of Pilgrimage at a Christian Shrine

PAUL YOUNGER

This chapter documents an interesting pilgrimage situation. Most of the pilgrims are Hindu and ritual patterns are closely aligned with Hindu traditions, but the shrine is Roman Catholic. As Dr. Younger points out, the existence of this sort of pilgrimage testifies to the vitality and adaptability of human religious life.

This is a fascinating case study of a far from unique phenomenon. Many pilgrimage centers attract members of sects or religions other than that attached to the dominant cultus of the shrine. Hindus and Muslims frequently visit each other's sacred places in north India, Muslims visit the tombs of Jewish saints in North Africa, Protestants pray at Catholic shrines, and so on. These situations are not uncommon, for reasons intrinsic to the general structure of pilgrimage. Being peripheral (notionally, if not always physically) and radiating an other-worldly, mystical attraction, sacred places often have the capacity to attract individuals of many affiliations. Pilgrimage inherently suggests the crossing of boundaries, and so it is not surprising—though very significant nonetheless—to find that sacred places, with their reputations for miracles and direct access to the divine, attract pilgrims from different religious groups. More research is needed to document the impact of intergroup contact that occurs in the context of pilgrimage.

The shrine of Velankanni in south India is managed by the Roman Catholic church, but most of the million persons who go there on pilgrimage during the first week of September each year are scarcely aware of the shrine's Catholic connections. The faith expressed in the worship activity of that week is deeply rooted in the patterns of goddess worship among the lower classes of south India, and yet it has some elements not found in those well-established patterns that give it a different emphasis and a special appeal.

PLACE

Velankanni is the name of a tiny village seven miles south of the city of Nakapattanam on the southeast coast of India looking out toward the island of Sri Lanka. In the village, there are about 600 homes of fishermen, divided almost equally among the three communities of Hindus, Muslims, and Christians. The Hindus still go out fishing, but the Muslims have become somewhat more prosperous as traders and seldom go fishing these days, and most of the Christians are now employed looking after the vast crowds that come to the shrine, so that they, too, have little time for fishing. The three communities live in separate sections of the village, with the Hindus clustered tightly around a Mariyamman temple in the center, the Muslims with streets of newer homes to the north, and the Christians scattered in clusters to the south.

The sacred geography of the village is a bit complex. The southern boundary of the village is formed by a branch of the sacred Kaveri River, which breaks into a delta of numerous streams about fifty miles upstream. In the midst of the Christian homes is a small, muddy tank of fresh water called the Ampa Kulam or Mother's Tank, where the first vision of the sacred Mother and Child is said to have taken place. North of both the Hindu and Muslim sections on the northern outskirts of the village stands the shrine.

The shrine is now a huge, European-style church complex. The largest part of this structure was built only in 1975 and is a plain, two-storied church. On each level there is a sanctuary large enough to hold a thousand or more worshipers, and there is a normal Roman Catholic altar in each sanctuary. During the festival week an orthodox Roman Catholic mass is said throughout the day on both levels of this church. Back-to-back with this "church," which faces west, is the "shrine," which contains the image of the Mother and Child and faces out to sea or toward the east. This shrine was originally a tiny structure 12 feet deep and 24 feet across. Later a 70-foot nave was set in front of it, and still later 24-foot rooms were set on either side and to the rear. With still further additions the whole shrine now forms a Latin cross 182 feet east to west and 112 feet north to south, with a windowed dome rising to 93 feet over the central room and spires on the front corners rising to 82 feet each. A flagstaff in the northeast corner of the compound flies a gigantic, sacred blue flag, and it towers over the whole scene.

The image in the shrine is a more-than-life-size Mother and Boy Child high up against the back wall. Both Mother and Son wear large crowns and are decked in rich brocade. The standing figure of the Mother holds the child in her left arm and a scepter in her right hand.

The stories about the shrine in the official literature are similar to stories connected with shrines of the Virgin Mary across the world (Turner and Turner 1978), but they did not seem to be widely known among the worshipers to whom I talked. The base story is of a shepherd boy who was on his way back to the home of his master with a pot full of milk when he stopped at the tank of water in the village to have a drink of water. While resting under the banyan tree beside the tank, he had a vision of a beautiful mother and child, and the mother asked him for some milk for the child. He hesitated, fearing what his master might say, but eventually gave her some milk. Rushing on home, he sought to explain the missing milk to his master, but the master found the pot full to the brim. Together they rushed back to the water tank and bowed to the ground in worship. Later they built a small shrine on that spot and called the tank Ampa Kulam, or Tank of the Mother.

Unlike the first story, which appears to be set in a time before the arrival of Christian missionaries, the second one is set in the sixteenth century after Christian churches had been established in the city of Nakapattanam. This story is about a widow and her son, who was lame from birth. A small thatched hut was constructed under the banyan tree by the tank in order that the boy could sell buttermilk to passersby suffering from the heat of the day. One day a beautiful lady with a boy child approached and asked for buttermilk. The lame boy provided some. Then she ordered the boy to go to a specific Catholic gentleman in Nakapattanam and ask him to build a chapel on this spot for her. The boy explained that he could not walk, but she ordered him again. Trying to obey, he found that he was healed, and he ran off to the city with joy. The chapel was built, and the Lady came to be called Velankanni-Arokkiyam Mata or the Healing Mother of the village Velankanni.

The third story is a story of Portuguese sailors who were on their way from China to Sri Lanka and became lost in a storm. Praying to the Virgin Mary, they were eventually shipwrecked onto this shore and led to the little thatched chapel by fishermen. The Portuguese sailors then built a brick and mortar chapel near the spot where they had been shipwrecked, and they presented the Virgin with the Chinese porcelain plates that still form the backdrop of her image. Their shipwreck took place on September 8, the date when the festival is now timed to climax each year.

FESTIVAL

While the physical layout of the shrine and the stories described thus far are similar to worship patterns one finds elsewhere in the Catholic tradition, the worship activities of the majority of the worshipers during the festival week (as observed in 1981) generally follow patterns found in the goddess temples of the Hindu tradition. The general structures of a goddess festival are present in that the festival lasts ten days; it features a procession of images pulled on decorated carts or *vahanas* every evening; and it finds its focus of worship in the movement of near ecstatic vow-keepers into the presence of the image (Whitehead 1921; Beck 1980; Younger 1980).

The pattern of worship is that of a pilgrimage that begins in the home village with a vow to go and worship Arokkiyam Mata, Velankanni or Healing Mother, Velankanni. For a few devout Catholics from far-off Calcutta, New Delhi, or Bombay that journey means three days on a train. For a larger number it means joining in a company from their home village in a walking pilgrimage. For the vast majority, however, it means a bus ride over hundreds of miles of twisting roads in a bus jammed with three or four times its capacity. During the first half of the ten-day period buses arrive bumper to bumper throughout the day and night, as the population of the little village swells from 5,000 to what the police estimate to be over a million. The people packed into the buses are generally the poorest of the poor, the landless laborers of Tamil Nadu and the neighboring states of Kerala, Andhra Pradesh, and Karnataka who normally do not leave their local area even to go on pilgrimages to the great Hindu temples. Frightened in spite of the large group of relatives with whom they travel, the people on the bus trips frequently suffer nervous sickness and vomiting, and the bus parking lot is full of bus conductors and drivers trying to clean up their buses while the police urge them to get back on the road to make room for those pouring in.

Once at the pilgrimage site a fever of frenetic activity begins. Government-placed water taps are everywhere, but toilet facilities are almost nonexistent, and commercial food supplies are minimal. Eventually most groups end up moving toward the southern end of the village in search of a shrub around which they can camp, with virtually no shelter from the scorching sun. A few thousand find accommodation in thatched partitions near the shrine, and a few hundred are accommodated in a church-run hostel. Many more ignore the need for food and sleep and begin immediately a feverish round of worship activity.

For many worship begins with a total shaving of the head. Rows of church-run barbershops shave men, women, and particularly children, who want to offer their hair to Velankanni. Probably 20 percent of the worshipers make this their first offering, which is made by a similar percentage of the worshipers at the temples of Hindu goddesses. The next step, in which almost everyone participates, is to bathe at the beach to the north of the shrine where one can usually walk far out in the shallow water. Few of the worshipers seem sure of what they want to do about these unfamiliar experiences of shaving the head and bathing. The sea bath especially is a problem, for in south Indian folklore the sea is a place of danger and many villagers have never seen it before. Anxiety hangs heavy in the air as people move back and forth to barber and sea, watch others, and try to resolve their doubts.

With the shaving and the sea bath behind them, the worshipers start to buy offering materials to supplement those they might have brought from home. Chickens and goat kids can still be bought in an emergency. Coconuts, bananas, incense, packets of rice or gram, sweets, flowers, and candles are all on sale. People eventually join the mile-long lineup to see the image but often rush out only moments later to buy more materials, visit some small shrine on the wayside, or rush to the flagstaff when the flag is moved up and down at fifteen-minute intervals. (Fifty-feet-long extra ropes are attached to the ropes on the flag, and they are passed about among the crowd as people touch them to their forehead and frequently go into ecstatic trance at the foot of the flagstaff.) Back in the lineup the crowd within a few hundred yards of the shrine starts to rush like the water approaching a waterfall. Many by this time are dancing, falling, or tugging at their clothes. A hundred yards from the shrine the crowd unexpectedly finds itself inside a tiny auxiliary shrine, and people hurriedly worship the image of the saint there, much as they would a Ganesa image at the entrance to a Hindu temple. At the entrance to the shrine itself bodies press solidly against one another until the pressure seems unbearable and everyone struggles to raise his or her offerings or child aloft. Young men at the entrance snuff out all candles and push the crowd along. After another set of doorways the Mother comes in view high above the crowd, and folded hands go up in worship as a delicate sound of "ah" fills the air. Young priests sprinkle the crowd with holy water as it progresses through the hallway. Suddenly the young men are pushing the crowd to either side of the central shrine room while flower garlands are taken by other young men to be touched to the feet of the image before being returned. Other offerings are received by still another group of young men and put in huge piles of similar offerings in the side rooms.

Once outside the shrine the worshipers move off for more activity. Shops sell colorful pictures of the Mother and Child and of the shrine. Others sell necklace charms, *yantras* or psycho-somatic diagrams, and charts of the zodiac. The loudspeaker plays lilting music in which the name Velankanni is repeated over and over and invites people to booths where they can hear stories of people miraculously healed or get the magazine of such stories, entitled *Velankanni Calling*. In the new, two-storied church to the rear of the shrine, masses are being said as crowds mill around and people sleep at the back in one of the few shady spots for miles around. At the front, as a relatively small group gathers around, the priest explains over and over that only Catholics should take the wafer. Outside, the priests at the confessionals have almost no customers, but the seller of holy oil is usually very busy.

By evening the anxious activity of individuals and small groups takes on a more organized pattern as all seek the best vantage from which to witness the images and decorated carts as they proceed around the worship complex. Here the activity is less frenetic as the worshipers wait with hundreds of thousands of their fellows and know for the first time the larger solidarity of pilgrimage experience. As the moment for catching a glimpse of the images comes, a new tension fills the air and the crowd surges as one in the expression of joyous excitement.

All through the festival the loudspeakers plead with people who have finished their worship to return home on the thousands of buses leaving empty. Few leave, for as in any festival of the goddesses it is the ninth day that is considered sacred, the time when her power will be at its peak. Finally, on the evening of the ninth day the flow of packed buses starts in the other direction, as a tired, hungry, and hopeful mass of humanity reluctantly heads back into the constraints of village life.

ANALYSIS

The underlying pattern of worship in the Velankanni pilgrimage festival is that found in the worship of the goddess Mariyamman. The preparatory vows, the shaving of the hair, the presentation of offerings, the frenetic worship and sharing in the worship of others, and the ecstatic moments around the central shrine make up a pattern these villagers would have known from childhood in connection with shrines of Mariyamman.

The logic underlying the worship of the goddess Mariyamman seems to rest on a Tamil worldview defined in terms of a series of structured polarities. In poetic convention the polarity is drawn between *akam*, or the expression of an interior romantic urge usually set in the mouth of a heroine, and *puram*, or the heroic action of a king (*Tolkappiyam* 1916). In caste classifications it is between the "right-hand" castes, which work on the land and are concerned with its fertility, and the "left-hand" castes, which take care of the crafts, trade, and other services that keep society functioning (Beck 1972). In ritual symbolism the polarity is between the "hot" red of blood sacrifice and life, and the "cool" white of knowledge and that which is beyond death (Shulman 1979; Clothey 1983). In village worship the polarity is between the goddess inside the village and male gods who guard the outer world (Dumont 1959).

Patterns of worship may be designed from this underlying logic in a great variety of ways. The medieval landlords and kings designed a temple ritual in which the goddess married the cosmic Lord Siva, and they were worshiped together with their sons Vinayakan and Murukan in an elaborate and carefully balanced system (Younger 1982a). In another pattern the devotees of the male deities Murukan and Visnu have carefully developed stories of the relationships of those deities to mother, sister, and wife figures, so that it is in terms of those relationships that the worship patterns are understood (Clothey 1978; Hudson 1978). In some cases famous goddess temples appear to be variations on these royally sponsored patterns, so that we find, for instance, that the worship of Minakshi, the "royal" goddess in Madurai (Fuller 1984), or Akilanteswari, the dominant figure in the "family" of Siva in Tiruvanaikka (Younger 1982a), involves both sides of the polarity even though the goddess is the dominant figure. More often goddess worship involves an altogether different or third pattern that has little to do with either the rulers or the priests but is the product of the passionate attachment the villagers have with the land on which they work (Whitehead 1921; Beck 1972, 1980; Brubaker 1978; Younger 1980). In the logic of the original polarity goddess worship was the pole that clung to "nature" and was set in opposition to the more varied pursuits of craftsmen and traders who were concerned more directly with human accomplishments or "culture." When government and Brahmanical priests later came to set up the structure of society in such a way that it left those attached to the land little by way of either power or status, goddess worship came to be the central symbolic form of those powerless groups, and in that sense it became an enduring expression of "anti-structure" (Turner 1969). When subsequent changes in political authority brought Muslim, British, and then democratic rule, the traditional "structure-anti-structure" pattern was disrupted in certain ways, but the result was that those who had earlier found refuge in the system of goddess worship were left even more uncertain of where they stood in the system (Diehl 1956).

In modern contexts goddess worshipers are no longer always confined to the village setting. A temple such as the popular one in Samayapuram, on the outskirts of the large city of Tirucirapalli, involves the worshipers of Mariyamman bringing to the goddess not only the traditional petitions of the village setting, which involve a cry for rain, fertility, and freedom from smallpox epidemics, but also their newer concerns with health in the family and the witchcraft of their job rivals and other "enemies" (Diehl 1956; Younger 1980). Velankanni worship provides an opportunity for traditional goddess worshipers to extend this growing range of goddess worship in even newer directions. Velankanni's reputation as a "mother" focuses the attention on the personal and family-based nature of the "troubles" the poor face in the contemporary situation; the seacoast setting provides the widest possible sense of the mysterious, primordial realm that the goddess controls; and the triumphant tone of the Mother-Son synthesis that the image manifests gives the basic Tamil polarity a sufficiently new form so that it provides hope and confidence to those who feel distraught and oppressed. Each of these "new" elements in this worship pattern needs to be examined more thoroughly.

Early missionary reports on the problems the goddess Mariyamman was thought to deal with focus primarily on the smallpox epidemics that were dreaded killers, sometimes wiping out whole villages during the hot, dry months from January to June (Elmore 1915; Whitehead 1921). The goddess worshipers in the dry regions of south India during these difficult summer months feared that the absence of rain and the presence of this disease were somehow related to the anger of the goddess Mariyamman. They did not blame her for this situation but felt that somehow they as a community were at fault. They had not been in proper touch with the natural order with which they worked or with the Goddess who personified it. Pronouncing vows, slaying scarce animals, and engaging in wild, ecstatic dances, the community sought to propitiate the goddess and draw the "heat" away from both her and the natural order, so that the worst of all consequences, the dreaded epidemic, might not visit their village.

More and more as the poor of Tamil Nadu moved out of the village setting, the problems of life came to be seen as family problems: the health of the children, the unemployment and frequent depression of the father, the quarrelsomeness and selfishness of the in-laws and other relatives, and the indifference and arrogance of the potential employers and undefined others in society. According to the logic of the older pattern, the cause of the problem continued to be blamed on the inadequacy of one's past worship, except that now the mother of the family (rather than the village community) assumes the responsibility and makes a vow to the goddess with which she hopes, through the "power" (Wadley 1980) of her will and ritual action, to propitiate the goddess and restore the well-being of her family. For many women the return to the village Mariyamman shrines no longer seems the most natural way in which to deal with their family's new problems, and the option of going to the "new" goddess, Velankanni, while keeping much of the same ritual energy, seems the most acceptable way of dealing with the problem.

If the first new dimension of Velankanni worship is that she is thought to deal with family problems more than village problems, the second is that the seacoast setting provides a symbolic statement of the limitlessness of her range of authority. In traditional Tamil symbolism the universe was divided among the five types of terrain: mountains, deserts, forests or pastureland, fertile river valleys, and seacoasts. Although seacoasts are included in this list, the emphasis is on types of land environment, and Tamil myth involved a fear of the mysterious sea, which was thought to have already encroached on two-thirds of what had been the Tamil land. In the most extended mythic treatment of the sea theme, the epic "Manimekalai" portrays the heroine, Manimekalai, as an anti-structural figure in the tradition of the sea goddess of the same name. Born the daughter of the dancing-girl prostitute Matavi, Manimekalai stays on the edge of society and taunts the king, who falls in love with her but is unable to touch her. Eventually she becomes a Buddhist nun, a figure who forever remains "on the edge."

For south Indians the sea surrounded them on three sides and was never far away. For a certain percentage of them the sea provided a livelihood through both fishing and trade, but for the majority it was the unknown boundary that added mystery to a tightly structured system of agriculture and social relationships. With the arrival of the European powers the sea lost some of its mystery and came to have a new impact on daily life, but the awesome reputation of the sea was at least partially transferred onto the Europeans who brought strange new goods and ideas to these seacoasts. When many of the fishermen converted to Christianity, new forms of worship became part of the religious universe and held out the promise of allowing the more adventurous worshipers to gain ritual influence over the once mysterious powers of the sea. As the worship of Velankanni became more and more popular, this wider range of her influence came to be interpreted to mean that she could meet any need and that nothing in the primordial deep was beyond her range. The one who could rescue shipwrecked sailors was, indeed, a powerful figure of unbounded scope. Paradoxically, what is remembered is not the fact that the sailors served a colonial and ruthless European power but the fact that Velankanni is not limited to the tightly structured village environment that these worshipers have found so oppressive. It is precisely because Velankanni is situated on the seacoast and her worship includes foreign symbols that the pilgrimage to her has an open-ended and powerfully anti-structural tone.

The third new dimension of the worship of Velankanni is evident in the ease and confidence with which she is pictured as holding the already crowned child in her arm. As far as I have been able to find out, Mariyamman is never pictured with a child. In the symbolism of Tamil Nadu, Mariyamman is, in many ways, a fertility figure who brings rain and crops, but she is usually pictured alone or, at most, with some shadowy male figures (Beck 1980), and she symbolizes the potential refusal of the land and the Tamil woman to bear the burden of fertility. On the other hand, a goddess such as Parvati is so submerged in the life and action of her sons Vinayakan and Murukan that she is never pictured in a Madonna-like pose where the mother is still responsible for and upholds the child. The stories of Vinayakan and his mother are full of tension and involve a potentially incestuous relationship that frequently angers the boy's father. Murukan is often pictured as a child in the Somaskantan image, but there he is almost always seated between both parents, and the mother's power is not particularly evident. The polar character of the Tamil symbol system had tended to encourage a portrayal of the goddesses as if they were either militant and independent upholders of the realm of fertility or co-opted wives and mothers supportive of the goals of their husbands and sons.

The triumphant and heroic ideal in the Tamil symbol system was thought of as a male role and was ideally embodied in kingship. In the Catholic tradition the symbolic poles were not separated in this same way, and the kingly and youthful Christ was always thought of as upheld by the Mother. While in the Tamil tradition the king was thought of as having sacred dimensions (Hart 1973, 1975) and the male deities Siva and Visnu are regularly worshiped in ritual forms that address them as royal beings (Younger 1982b), goddesses were not normally associated with kingship. The crowns on the heads of both Velankanni and the child in her arms bring to the image this triumphal character (Bayly 1989) without in any way taking away from the central focus on the feminine nature of the image.

In the actual worship practice of the present-day festival the triumphalist note is still somewhat muted. When I asked the worshipers who poured out of the shrine about the child in the arm, they often failed to remember that there was one. For many of the worshipers the presentation of their petitions to Velankanni has much the same note of fear and anxiety that one finds in the propitiation of Mariyamman. When I pointed out the child in the picture on the cover of the booklets, worshipers then talked about the crowns, the golden clothes, and the happy child and often wondered aloud about this different note of royal splendor and joyful, this-worldly triumph. The Roman Catholic organizers of the festival pilgrimage make every effort to encourage this triumphal tone in the worship. They forbid, for instance, the women who go into trance and tell fortunes at Mariyamman festivals to operate openly, and while that practice continues to some degree, the anxiety at the close of a Mariyamman festival as worshipers rush from one fortune-teller to another is not reproduced here. The organizers also make a major push late in the festival to introduce a note of "action-in-the-world" and try to steer worshipers to health clinics, social action workshops, and the local Velankanni worship centers in their area. A relatively small percentage of the worshipers actually respond to these efforts of the organizers, but in general the triumphalist tone is evident in the peaceful aura that marks the close of the festival, in marked contrast to the anxious tones that remain evident at the close of a Mariyamman festival.

CONCLUSION

The pilgrimage-festival of Velankanni is a vivid example of the widely attested fact that people of different traditions sometimes worship together in a pilgrimage situation (Voinot 1948; Obeyesekere 1966; Morinis 1984). This fact in itself lends support to a number of the newer lines of interpretation in religious studies. It supports, for instance, Wilfred Cantwell Smith's contention that religion is better thought of as an activity of persons than as so many blocks of reified tradition labeled Hinduism, Christianity and the like (1963). Because the vast majority of the worshipers of Velankanni are from socially disenfranchised and marginal segments of society, the mixture of traditions can also be seen as support for Mary Douglas's point that patterns of loyalty to "group" and "grid" or ritual form are lower among those from disenfranchised sections of society than they would be for those who have a stake in upholding the political and ritual leadership in their society (1973). As Victor Turner has shown in other pilgrimage sites, the pilgrim experience itself clearly opens the Velankanni worshipers up to a series of "liminal" experiences in which they take delight in seeing the structures of village life temporarily fade away while they find themselves sharing with others of different background in a free community or "communitas" (1969, 1974a). The evidence of the pilgrimage to Velankanni is certainly a dramatic example of two traditions being blended together in the pilgrimage situation, and in that sense it clearly supports each of these three lines of interpretation. By focusing our attention, however, not so much on this general feature of the mixture of traditions but on particular features of the worship pattern that results, we have tried to penetrate further inside the worship experience and point out some of the processes involved in the formation of this new worship experience.

In the analysis above an effort was made to present the basic pattern or structure involved in the Tamil tradition of religious meaning and then to analyze the religious activity around the shrine of Velankanni as a transformation of that pattern. Against the polar pattern of Tamil thought, the role of goddess worship was shown to be an expression of loyalty to the pole of nature, of the fertile and maternal power manifest in the productivity of the land and the conception of the child. The worship of Velankanni, while meaningful only within this general pattern, transforms the pattern in important ways: by identifying the worshiper's problem more clearly in terms of individual or family misfortune; by extending the domain of the goddess by establishing her control of the primordial sea that lies beyond the forces of nature and society encountered in everyday life; and by providing a clearer answer to life's problems in the triumphant unification of symbols in the crowned mother and child image. In identifying these transformative processes operating within the basic pattern of goddess worship, we are able to watch a society generating religious meaning. Without our knowing the structure of the well-known pattern of goddess worship, the many activities at the Velankanni shrine would be like a baffling gibberish of meaningless sound. With the structure understood, the process of generating a new expression of religious meaning becomes an articulate and meaningful statement in spite of the million voices (Habermas 1979).

In serving as a context in which people of Hindu and Christian background can worship and as an example of how a well-known pattern of religious meaning can be transformed into an intelligible new statement, the worship of Velankanni becomes an important testimony to the vitality and adaptability of the religious life of humankind. The religious statement being made by these crowds cannot be dismissed as a clinging to tradition, for whether one thinks of recent years when the crowds became huge or the earliest possible dates a few hundred years ago, in the Indian context the statement is a new transformation of a more general pattern. Nor can the religious statement being made be characterized as a faddish innovation or the prophetic insight of an individual or priestly group, for no prophet has ever been involved and the priests who serve the shrine are young men obviously frightened by the crowd, which shows little interest in their priestly leadership. What is happening here is just a rather dramatic example of what must have happened over and over again in human history as units of human society went about discerning meaning for their lives by using structures they knew and generating from them transformations that met the questions of a new age. The fact that it can be done is evident from a careful reading of the religious history of humankind. The fact that the worship of Velankanni shows it can be done under the unusual pressures of a multi-traditional setting, economic change triggered by technology, and grinding social oppression and illiteracy indicates that units of human society will not easily be denied meaning and will find a way to use the structures provided to them and make an intelligible new statement even in the most challenging of circumstances.

5

Persistent Peregrination:
From Sun Dance to Catholic Pilgrimage
Among Canadian Prairie Indians

ALAN MORINIS

The cultural contents of pilgrimage centers and practices tend to be highly malleable, changing in reflection of the social and cultural trends within the field of the pilgrimage. In contrast, traditions of sacred journeying and ceremonial gathering tend to be remarkably enduring, although the ostensible purposes, end-goals, and practices undertaken show enormous variation, even within cultures and within single pilgrimages over time. This contention is borne out by tracing the persistence of pilgrimage practice through eras of social and cultural upheaval. The revival of sacred journeys of the Maoris (Chapter 12) reflects this phenomenon. The following chapter provides a classic example of this type. The Plains Indians of Canada in the nineteenth century developed an extensive ceremonial life that had as a main pillar a tradition of ritual gatherings. The colonial incursions, made especially devastating by the destruction of the buffalo herds in the early 1880s, led to the abandonment of these annual "Sun Dances". Within only a few years, however, the tribes began to gather once again, only now for a Catholic pilgrimage to a mission shrine. There are today about a dozen such shrines patronized by Plains Indians. The popularity of these pilgrimages is due in no small measure to the tradition of summer ceremonial gathering practiced until only one hundred years ago by the pagan ancestors of today's devout Catholics. Although this persistence of pilgrimage has never before been documented on the Canadian Plains, it is well known in Latin America, where (unlike in the Canadian case) contemporary Catholic shrines stand on sites of pre-Columbian sacred places.

In 1887, while on home leave in his native Brittany from his missionary station in northern Alberta, Father Jean-Marie Lestanc paid a visit to the famous shrine of Ste-Anne d'Auray. His prayers at the shrine were rewarded by a vision of Ste. Anne herself, who called on him to establish a shrine in her honor in his remote Canadian mission territory. The priest hurried back to Canada and threw himself into the construction work. The shrine he built received its first group of seventy-one pilgrims in 1889 (Drouin 1973: 52).

Father Lestanc was a member of the Oblates of Mary Immaculate, a missionary order that has established itself in western Canada and works among Indians and Metis. The first mission station west of Manitoba had been established in 1884 at a lake called Manitou Sakahigan by the Woodland Cree, in whose territory it lay. The founding priest, Father Thibault, who renamed the lake as Lac Ste.-Anne (the original meaning of the Cree name was "spirit lake," although the missionaries translated it as Devil's Lake), was not himself an Oblate, but his famous successor Father Albert Lacombe in 1855 became a novitiate of that order (cf. Hughes 1911; Breton 1955). From that date to the present Lac Ste.-Anne has been under the administration of the Oblates. It was at Lac Ste.-Anne that Father Lestanc established his promised shrine in 1887.

In the past century about fifteen Catholic shrines have been founded on the Canadian Prairies. Although both Indians and non-Indians visit these shrines on their summer celebration days, Indian pilgrims overwhelmingly predominate. Even Lac Ste.-Anne, which is visited by many non-Indians and which until 1971 reserved separate days for Indian and White pilgrims, is today much more heavily attended by Indians. In this chapter I seek reasons to account for the rise and popularity of these pilgrimages among a people that has only been Catholic for one hundred years. My contentions are two: (1) these pilgrimages were established at an historical moment when traditional Indian summer gatherings had been recently abandoned, leaving a gaping cultural void into which the new religion stepped, and (2) the new gatherings performed and continue to perform many of the social and cultural functions of the pre-missionary summer assemblies that were the high point of the social calendar among all Prairie Indian tribes. The contemporary pilgrimages are functional extensions of the traditional gatherings that had, in another cultural era, become central social events of great significance to the Plains Indian tribes. It is this transmutation of the pilgrimage traditions that I call persistent peregrination.

Pilgrimage is a practice defined by its structure—the journey to the sacred place—and not by the content of symbols, meaning, rituals, and so on, that fills in the structure. Pilgrimages tend to persist through cultural change because the structure can continue to exist while accommodating new, even radically different cultural contents. We can find examples from around the world where pilgrimages have undergone transformation with every succeeding cultural generation but have nevertheless remained popular because people continue to seek out the salving ideal that stands beyond space and time in the sacred place. What is considered "sacred" or "ideal" will change with time, but that these qualities are accessible in special locations situated beyond the sphere of everyday life—the basic belief underlying all pilgrimage systems—continues to motivate journeys to sacred places. So long as the character of God is malleable, the same sites or an enduring tradition of sacred journeying can continue to serve pilgrims' goals throughout history.

PRE-MISSIONARY SUMMER GATHERINGS

The Indians of the Plains are known to have obtained horses by the eighteenth century at the latest (Wissler 1914). This acquisition transformed subsistence foragers into extraordinarily capable buffalo hunters. An era of abundance followed, and with abundance came a florescence of culture.

All of the buffalo-hunting peoples of the Plains celebrated an elaborate annual pageant that was the high point of the social calendar. In summer the buffalo herds converged because of the abundance of pasture, and in consequence all of the dispersed bands of hunters and gatherers could come together in a full assembly of the tribe. This gathering, known in the literature as the Sun Dance, after the sun-gazing rituals performed by the Oglala Sioux, showed a good deal of ritual variation from tribe to tribe among the twenty groups that practiced the annual gathering (Wissler 1918; Spier 1921). I will deal briefly with two of the cultural groups that concern us in the next section: the Cree and the Blackfoot.

David Mandelbaum says of the Plains Cree Sun Dance: "Late in June or early July the scattered sections of a band, or even several bands, converged to the preappointed places where the ceremony was to be held. The great encampment might hold together for two weeks or even longer, if there were buffalo herds in the vicinity" (1940: 203-4). The focus of the dance was the individual who pledged to undergo austerities and often self-inflicted tortures in fulfillment of a vow. The entire event involved much prescribed ritual and could last several weeks: "This occasion was the outstanding event of the ceremonial calendar. Large encampments, often of several bands, gathered in June or July to participate. It was a time for a great spurt of social activity; other dances were held; gambling and games went on continually; it was the ideal period for courtship" (Mandelbaum 1940: 265).

Other reports on the Cree Sun Dance are similar (e.g., Skinner 1914). Pliny Goddard cites a report concerning the Cree in Saskatchewan: "The sun dance marks the yearly gathering of people whom the exigencies of life compel to spend the fall and winter in isolation, and it is looked forward to as such. The young make and the old renew acquaintances, and it is a general holiday" (1919: 307).

Of the Sun Dance among the Blackfoot, John McLean says, "The most important sacred festival of the Blackfeet is the Sun-Dance" (1887-1888: 231). He goes on to describe the religious rituals that took place in the mid-summer gatherings of an estimated 2,000 people that he observed.

Clark Wissler also comments on the importance of the Sun Dance to the Blackfoot. "In winter," he observes, "the tribes scattered out, usually two to five bands in a camp, often miles apart" (1918: 268). At the approach of summer, messengers would go out to tell the bands where the summer gathering would be held, and with the coming of summer they would assemble in one large camp circle: "The camp circle is intimately associated with the sun dance" (268). Wissler concludes, "The sun dance was for the Blackfoot a true tribal festival, or demonstration of ceremonial functions, in which practically every important ritual owner and organization had a place" (229).

George Dorsey predicted in 1910 that "with the disappearance of tribal organizations and tribal interests, there is no doubt of the ultimate doom of the Sun Dance" (1910: 649-52). Dorsey did not foresee the enduring strength of tribal identity, which has kept the Sun Dance alive into the present (cf. Dusenberry 1962; Liberty 1980). Nor did he anticipate the transmutation of the summer tribal gathering into an intertribal pilgrimage, in reflection of a new pan-Indian identity, involving Christian elements and a new set of Indian interests beyond the tribal.

CATHOLIC PILGRIMAGES OF THE PRAIRIE TRIBES

Little research has been done on the Catholic shrines that are dotted across the Canadian Prairies. In 1983 I attended the largest and longest of these gatherings, at Lac Ste.-Anne.[1] Data on other pilgrimages, although scanty, are available and were examined in the archives of the Oblate Fathers in Edmonton.[2] I will concentrate almost exclusively on the case of Lac Ste.-Anne. Map 1 shows the names and locations of the twelve most important of the contemporary Prairie Indian pilgrimages.

The pilgrimage to Lac Ste.-Anne was founded in 1889 at a time when the Indian tribes of the Plains were under great physical and cultural stress. The preceding decade had seen the complete extermination of the buffalo herds that had been the central pillar of the peoples' way of life (1877-1880), the encroachment of the railways and White settlers, epidemics (one outbreak of smallpox around this time caused over 3,000 deaths in a population estimated to be 26,000), the signing of the treaties (1876 and 1877), the Riel uprising and subsequent suppression (1885), along with other wars and skirmishes, and the devastation bred or at least exacerbated by the increasing flow of the alcohol trade. These simultaneous pressures brought the culture of the Indian tribes to the edge of total collapse, a situation in which any and all support was welcome. The missionary fathers, who had been working among the Plains Indians since the 1840s and who had already achieved a good measure of support from the tribes and their leaders, loomed large as a steadfast group of friends on whom the Indians could lean. The priests had been doctoring, teaching, preaching, marrying, and burying the Indians for forty years before they were called upon to be allies at a time of near-total devastation.

The mission at Lac Ste.-Anne, established in 1844, was the first mission west of Manitoba. At the time of the founding of the pilgrimage it had begun to go into eclipse, but the centre was reinvigorated by the new attraction of the shrine. The

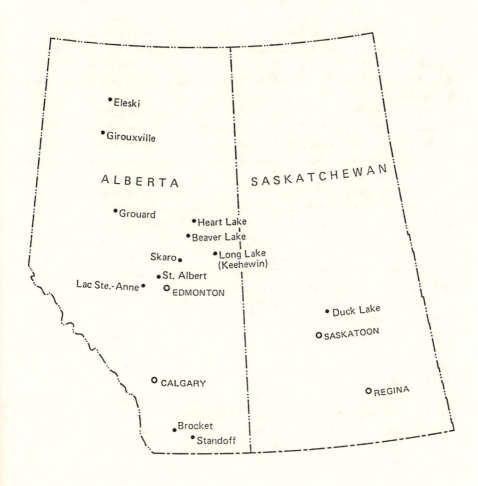

MAP 1: Indian Pilgrimages on the Canadian Prairies.

official story of the origin of the shrine, as mentioned above, tells of an instruction given by Ste. Anne in a vision had by a missionary. The pilgrims themselves tell different stories. The most common tale of the origin of the shrine that I was told during the 1983 pilgrimage was that in the 1880s a tremendous grass fire swept the Prairies and drove people and animals to flight. When the fleeing people reached the mission station at Lac Ste.-Anne, the priest led them in prayer, and subsequently rain fell, extinguishing the fire. It is said that rain is expected during the pilgrimage and is welcome.

The first pilgrimage, in 1889, attracted 71 pilgrims. By 1891 over 400 pilgrims attended. Numbers reached 1,200 in 1906, 4,000 in 1927, and 20,000 in 1982. A relic of Ste. Anne was obtained in 1896, and after this was destroyed in a fire in 1928, another was obtained. There are presently two. The large, modern shrine building was constructed in 1979.

The shrine building is the focal point of the physical arrangements at Lac Ste.-Anne. It is a large structure, open on three sides, with seating for 3,000. The closed side protects the altar and a large statue of Ste. Anne and her daughter Mary. A rustic quality has been given by building the facing and back of the altar of split logs. To each side of the altar hang banners depicting Indian images such as a tipi and pipe, bearing slogans such as "God Sent His Son to Pitch His Tent With Us" and "I Long for God as a Deer Longs for Cool Water."

The shrine is encircled by small huts, each depicting a scene from Christ's ascent to the Crucifixion. During the days of the pilgrimage priests sit and hear confession in these huts. On the last night, a procession is made of this Way of the Cross. A statue of Ste. Anne stands near the front gate to the shrine territory. Many pilgrims arriving or departing stop at this statue, touch one hand to its feet, lower their heads, and pray silently.

The remainder of the mission land is hay-field, leading down to the lakeside. This hay is cut just before the pilgrimage, and for a period of a week before the event, early travelers are arriving and pitching camp in the fields. Old photos of the pilgrimage show tipis, tents, and wagons. Today's encampment is of trailers, recreational vehicles, campers, and tents.

The largest contingent of Indians at the gathering is Cree from Saskatchewan, Alberta, the Northwest Territories, and the northern American states. Next in number are the Chipewyan, followed by the Blackfoot and Dogrib. Although the shrine is located immediately adjacent to the territory and reserves of the Stoney, these people do not attend the pilgrimage because they were missionized by Protestants. In 1983 confession was heard in English, French, Cree, and Chipewyan, and sermons were preached in these languages plus Blackfoot. The Dogrib people from the northern center of Fort Rae have been attending the pilgrimage only for the last few years, and their language is not used in public ceremonies. Other Catholic tribes, such as the Blood and the Peigan, were few at Lac Ste.-Anne because of the occurrence of a pilgrimage at Brocket, Alberta, closer to their reserves. There may, as well, be some legacy of the traditional hostilities that plagued relations between the Cree and members of the Blackfoot Confederacy.

The ritual of the pilgrimage is structured to represent a version of the human life cycle, over a twenty-four hour period. Although pilgrims have been arriving for a week previously and have been camped in large numbers on Sunday and Monday, the ritual of the pilgrimage begins Tuesday afternoon. Previous to this point there have only been mass in the shrine and the blessing of objects by priests. On Tuesday afternoon the pilgrimage proper is initiated by a local bishop who leads a procession down to the lake for a blessing of the waters. In his sermon he invokes the many practical and symbolic roles played by water, but he stresses the role of water in baptism. He calls upon the gathered crowd to renew its vows of baptism and begins the pilgrimage with an invocation of a new spiritual birth.

In small groups people, fully clothed, wade into the lake. Some go in only to a shallow depth, but others walk out along the gently sloping lake bed to reach a submerged rock, which is believed to have imprinted on it the footprints of Ste. Anne. The more devout or those wanting a special intercession from Ste. Anne submerge up to the neck and remain in the water for up to half an hour. On the shore men and women chant the hymn to Ste. Anne in Cree and set a meditative mood for the immersion. As this mood passes, bathers begin to return to shore, bringing with them bottles that have been filled with the blessed lake water and reedy lake grass that will be kept and burned as needed, to invoke this powerful moment of the pilgrimage.

Lac Ste.-Anne's shrine has developed a reputation for miraculous cures. At least thirty such cures have been recorded in the *Codex Historicus* (Drouin 1973: 89-91). Bathing in the lake is considered to be an especially efficacious means to bring about a miraculous cure, and so many of the bathers who go deepest and remain longest, especially those congregated around Ste. Anne's underwater rock, are in need of curing. One young man I observed had been brought from Horse Lake, Saskatchewan, to bathe in the hopes of being cured of paralysis that he had suffered in a snowmobiling accident the previous winter.

It would seem that bathing fully clothed, as the pilgrims do, serves to distinguish this act of ritual immersion from ordinary playful or functional uses of water. Many symbolic interpretations could be ventured to explain the attraction of bathing in clothes at this ceremony, but since none was provided by participants themselves, these interpretations would be only speculative.

Wednesday there are regular masses in the shrine, as well as special benedictions for the sick. On the front wall of the shrine hang several canes and crutches made of hand-hewn tree branches and reportedly left behind by healed pilgrims. The collection of canes and crutches is reported to have been much larger, but many were destroyed in the fire of 1928.

With the setting of the sun comes the next special event, the procession of the Way of the Cross. A priest leads a crowd of several thousand on a re-creation of the final journey of Christ to his Crucifixion. At each station, the event is told and a moral concerning steadfastness, effort, generosity, and other Christian virtues is extracted. The procession completes the stations, then proceeds to the cemetery, where the final sermon—on death and the return to God, in His "Happy Hunting Ground," the priest said—is delivered. As the final streaks of light fade into the darkness of night, the pilgrimage closes. It has led participants from a symbolic rebirth through re-baptism, through a microcosmic lifespan in re-creation of the journey of Christ, to a final resting of the body in the graveyard and the risen soul in heaven.

In 1983 the later part of this last night was given over to a Tea Dance, held around a fire just beyond the circle of light cast by the shrine. The drums were beaten and songs were sung by the least acculturated of the Indians—the Dogribs—but participants included members of all the attending tribes. As well, a number of younger priests, who are not averse to participating in Indian ceremonies such as the pipe initiation and the sweat lodge, joined in the early morning shuffling circle of dancers.

Throughout the pilgrimage it was plain that the two traditions represented—the Catholic and the Plains Indian—were two streams that at points converged, at others merged, and at still others diverged. The bathing in the lake, for example, is a point of convergence, since it brings together some pre-missionary aspects of Indian culture with Catholic symbolism. The bathing in the lake is easily assimilated to the Catholic baptism, but the fact that this lake was known as "Spirit Lake" before being renamed by the missionaries suggests that it was held in some reverence in the pre-contact period. Contemporary informants, including some of the priests, hold this view. Convergence is also to be noted in the practice of collecting lake grass, a modification of the traditionally valued sweet grass, during the ritual of re-baptism.

Another point of convergence took place during the Tea Dance. Although during the blessing of the lake the Catholic tradition ruled dominant, the Tea Dance saw the Indian tradition dominant and the priests joining in. The new generation of missionary priests is not averse to participating in Indian cultural events, even of a religious kind, that previous generations of priests would have branded heathen and tried to stamp out. Many of these so-called "buckskin priests" have adopted moccasins and beaded hide jackets and even tanned hide shawls as part of their ritual vestments. One priest attending the pilgrimage wore blue jeans, moccasins, and a buckskin jacket, regularly attended the sweat lodge in his territory, and had recently taken initiation as a pipeholder in the local religious society.

Points of merger were to be seen during the mass. Here Catholic and Indian traditions had merged to create a distinct, synthetic Plains Indian Catholicism in which the two traditions were inextricably intermingled. In sermons, the terms God and Manitou were used interchangeably. From my discussions with both priests and pilgrims I got the impression that the object of the evident devotion of the pilgrims was neither the White man's God nor Manitou but, rather, a single entity with whom they felt comfortable, who was supreme, and who was thus both God and Manitou.

A major point of divergence was to be seen in the conceptions held about the gathering. As evidenced in their sermons, the priests saw this ceremonial as a religious pilgrimage in the Catholic mold. There was much talk about morality, salvation, and the extraordinary benefits to be reaped from having visited a shrine in a year Pope John Paul II had declared a Holy Year. It was obvious when one looked at the crowd, however, that the gathering was at least multipurpose and that, undoubtedly for some, it was not at all religious. Besides the rituals associated with the pilgrimage to the shrine, the following activities and functions were significant aspects of the assembly:

Social interaction For many pilgrims, a primary focus of the gathering was the opportunity to meet with family and friends who might not be encountered at any other time of the year. Even while mass was in progress, many campsites were full of people and their visitors, discussing every aspect of life. Although some young people were evidently devout, many others were completely oblivious to the religious nature of the pilgrimage. For them the occasion was an opportunity for courting, sporting, and social displays.

Trading The gathering was attended by a trader. Pilgrims expected him to be there and brought with them tanned hides and furs to sell. In addition, behind the shrine and over a small stream that separated church land from private property, a fairly large marketplace had been set up for the duration of the pilgrimage. Small, decorative jewelry, pocket-knives, hats, and especially very cheap, used clothing were for sale, along with the odds and ends of a garage or rummage sale.

Information exchange Conversation was constant, and so the gathering created an opportunity for an update on current information of all kinds. Important topics ranged from jobs and income tax to life passages (who died and who was born) and community politics. Considering that the Indian communities are scattered over the large territories of the Prairies, a major gathering will be an occasion for the exchange of all sorts of important personal and social information.

Relaxation/holiday Many of the visitors were regularly employed and had scheduled their annual holidays to be able to attend the pilgrimage. This recreational aspect of the gathering was itself a feature of the social interaction, trading, and information exchange that took place.

These functions of the pilgrimage gathering are, in large measure, reminiscent of the functions performed among the Plains tribes by the annual Sun Dance assemblies. In pilgrimage we find the persistence of the tradition of gathering, as relics and saints have become heir to the Sun Dance poles and lodges as the focus for the personal and social activities of the mid-summer meetings. Although some of the functions of the Sun Dance gatherings have been assumed by secular pow-wows, as pointed out by Koozma Tarasoff (1980: 22), the religious core of the pilgrimages makes them the more logical inheritor of the Sun Dance tradition. Pilgrimages can perform the social functions but also provide the religious and spiritual aspects that were an integral part of the Sun Dances. It is probable that pow-wows are now more popular among Protestant Indians, although there is no reason the social aspects of pow-wows should not appeal to Catholic Indians as well.

At Lac Ste.-Anne, Alberta (photo by Gary Fiegehan)

PERSISTENT PEREGRINATION

In an early article on the remarkable recurrence of what he called ceremonialism among North American Indian tribes, R. H. Lowie reached the conclusion that the ostensible reasons for ceremonies, such as the Kwakiutl potlatch and the Plains Sun Dance, have little connection to the ultimate purpose of the rites. He concluded that ceremony itself, rather than its manifest purpose, such as success in battle or initiation, is the raison d'etre of the events: "We regard its very performance as self-sufficient, as gratifying certain specific non-utilitarian demands of the community. View it not as a primitive religion, or as a primitive attempt to coerce the forces of nature, but as a free show, and the mystification ceases: ceremonialism is recognized as existing for ceremonialism's sake" (1915: 255-56).

This conclusion is overly reductionist, but it does point to the fact that in the Plains cultural area, between groups and within the same group at different eras, great variety was permitted in the composition of ritual gatherings. While the ostensible purpose for gathering should not be dismissed so easily and totally as Lowie makes out, among Plains Indian tribes ceremonial gathering itself was a recurrent social practice in which the content varied considerably to reflect the needs and influences of the particular culture at that moment in its development. Gathering itself was an important feature of the cultural tradition; it was the focal point in the annual cycle of assembly and dispersion that dominated the life pattern of the Plains tribes.

The extermination of the buffalo, combined with the encroaching population and increasingly restrictive regulations of the Europeans (such as pass laws), brought about the temporary end of gathering in the late nineteenth century and so eliminated the crucial hinge of the annual ritual and social cycles. This change opened up a gap in the psycho-cultural environment, the magnitude of which is difficult to conceive, and the dislocation, anxiety, and suffering that inevitably followed the demise of this pillar of the social universe are difficult to imagine. When the opportunity soon arose again—now for a mid-summer Catholic pilgrimage—there was little hesitation to seize the chance. True, the ostensible purpose for gathering was at odds with the Sun Dance or other traditional ceremonials, but times had changed once again, and the acceptance of a new ceremonial content to the gatherings did not present a major obstacle to participation.

Since the Prairie Indians have adopted the practice of pilgrimage, these annual gatherings have taken over from the Sun Dance the role of the focal social assembly, where many non-ritual social functions take place. Of special note is the fact that the pilgrimages, like the Sun Dance gatherings before them, are the meeting-places for a dispersed population and so are the stage for all manners of highly valued social interaction. Without minimizing the importance of the mass and the other Catholic performances at Lac Ste.-Anne, it was clear that chitchat, gossip, romancing, complaining, instructing, and other sorts of everyday social communication took up a great deal of the pilgrims' time and were surely an important aspect of the pilgrimage, as they had been of the Sun Dances. The importance of this function of the gathering is underlined when we remember that it was likely only on this occasion of all the year that families, friends, and acquaintances would rendezvous from their remote reserves and settlements scattered over the vast territory of the Prairies. Clearly there has been cultural change since the days of the Sun Dance, but there is structural continuity as well.

A major difference to be noted between pre-missionary and post-missionary summer gatherings is that the former were almost exclusively tribal and the latter are mostly intertribal. Goddard (1919: 305) notes that the Cree Sun Dance he observed in the early twentieth century was attended by representatives of other tribes, but this was no longer the traditional situation. Already in this case, and even more so in the intertribal Catholic pilgrimages, the constitution of the assembly has changed to reflect the new identity and interests of contemporary Canadian Indians. Exclusively tribal identity has been complemented by a broader concept of pan-Indian identity, within which tribal boundaries still have some—reduced—importance. These boundaries are reinforced by linguistic and cultural differences but are crosscut by other allegiances, such as the ties to the church. Pilgrimages today can be tribal—as in the case of the pilgrimage to the shrine at Standoff, which is exclusively patronized by the Blood—but tend, under the influence of the church, to be intertribal. Here we find that the composition of the assemblage has altered to reflect changing personal and group allegiances, but once again these changes have not disturbed the continuity of the tradition of the mid-summer social gathering.

In some important ways the cultural content of Prairie pilgrimages is similar to what went on in the Sun Dances. Both lay stress on the importance of vows undertaken by individual participants. As is typical of Catholic pilgrimages, many pilgrims come to the shrine to initiate or fulfill vows to Ste. Anne, as intercessor with her grandson Jesus. Although this practice is a common feature of the Catholic tradition, it was also a central feature of the Sun Dance. Mandelbaum notes, "The dance was initiated in fulfillment of a vow" (1940: 265). During my visit to Lac Ste.-Anne I encountered a woman who had walked all the way to the shrine from her home reserve in Saskatchewan province in fulfillment of a promise made to Ste. Anne when her son was very ill.

Both Sun Dance and pilgrimage are concerned with rain, as evidenced in the most commonly heard legend of the origin of the Lac Ste.-Anne pilgrimage as told by the pilgrims themselves and noted as well in the ethnographic record on the Sun Dance. Goddard, writing about the Sun Dance of the Alberta Cree, remarks, "It seems to be held in part for the purpose of inducing rain" (1919: 306). Mandelbaum says of the Cree Sun Dance: "Prayers for rain were a salient feature of every Sun dance. The pledger continually exhorted his supernaturals to bring on a storm and used every magical device in his power to secure that result" (1940: 270).

There are also cases of continuity in ritual performances. For example, many pilgrims to Lac Ste.-Anne brought objects that they wanted to have blessed by the priests. Besides rosaries and other standard Catholic paraphernalia, pilgrims had wild herbs and traditional medicines for blessing. It was a common feature of the Sun Dance, too, that objects would be brought to receive the blessing of the person undertaking the vow of austerity.

While these manifest continuities from pre- to post-missionary summer gatherings should not be dismissed (it has, after all, been only one hundred years since the first pilgrimages were founded), it is at the level of social functions that the greatest and, to my mind, most significant continuity is to be found.

The case of Prairie Indian pilgrimages is not an isolated instance of persistent peregrination. Catholic missionaries in Latin America and India have taken over indigenous shrines, which they converted to Catholic shrines and to which people continued to come. A similar transformation can be noted in the case of the Arabian tribes that adopted Islam and, with it, pilgrimage to Mecca, which they had been visiting as a sacred place in pre-Islamic times.

It seems that the institution of pilgrimage has a great capacity to endure through the upheavals and shifts of cultural change. The reason, I suggest, lies in the structure of pilgrimage. Although it appears at first sight that the most significant aspect of a pilgrimage is the shrine deity that draws the crowds to the centre, in most cases the character of this deity is malleable. People journey to a place that enshrines some trace of a cultural ideal, usually the greatest ideal, styled God. If the ideological construction of this ideal is malleable, then the ideal will continually change to reflect changing culture, and the pilgrimage will remain popular. Pilgrimage shrines that are conceptually inflexible will retain favor so long as the ideals they house are popular and likely for some time thereafter because traditions die hard (they may even become identified as sites where the ideal past is to be encountered), but eventually they are likely to fade in public esteem as they fall out of step with current ideals and values. It could be said that it is to forestall decline that the gods of the centers are left open to reinterpretation, and because this does happen commonly, pilgrimages tend to be highly persistent practices.

In historical perspective it is clear that an enduring pilgrimage tradition emphasizes the structure of the performance over the contents. At any given moment, the specific contents of the pilgrimage institution, as constituted at that time, will undoubtedly be uppermost in the minds of participants, but it is the persistence of journeying to, and gathering at, shrines, rather than the changing characters of their occupants, that accounts for the endurance of a pilgrimage tradition, over time and through successive eras of cultural change. The stress in understanding pilgrimage then falls on ritual journeys and gatherings rather than on the sacred place itself.

This emphasis is especially pertinent in the case of Plains Indian ritual gatherings, since the actual locations of the Catholic pilgrimages do not coincide with Sun Dance sites (which themselves shifted from year to year). This variation, along with the radical changes brought about by the missionary colonization of Plains Indian culture, has not destroyed the underlying cultural template for ritual journeys and gatherings, which continue to be practiced with altering content into the present. Peregrination is the essence of pilgrimage. In this case peregrination persists through the sweeping transformations that have refashioned Plains Indian culture over the last century because the personal and group satisfactions gained from sacred journeys and ritual gatherings are largely independent of the ideational content of the institutions.

NOTES

1. This field trip was made possible by a travel grant from the Canadian Plains Research Centre, Regina, Saskatchewan. I express my gratitude for this support.

2. I would like to express my thanks to Father E. O. Drouin, O.M.I., Archivist of the Oblates in Edmonton, for his invaluable assistance and guidance in this research. My appreciation and thanks go as well to Fr. P.-A. Hudon and Fr. J. M. Lizee for their time and cooperation.

6

Pilgrimage and Heresy: The Transformation of Faith at a Shrine in Wisconsin

PETER W. WOOD

Pilgrimage is too often thought of as a feature of orthodox religious practice. Some of the better-known sacred places are, indeed, centers where the central truths of their cultus are celebrated. But in a society without a monolithic religious tradition or where religious diversity and dissent are tolerated, it is expected that the character of pilgrimage places and practices will reflect this cultural heterogeneity. Such is the situation for Catholicism in the plural religious context of North America. The following case study concerns a pilgrimage center established and maintained in the state of Wisconsin by a heretical Catholic sect known by the improbable name of "For My God and My Country Incorporated". What is revealed is that patterns of pilgrimage in American Catholicism are mostly borrowed from Europe and that this derivative tradition does not adequately serve religious needs that arise from the distinctly American context. The Wisconsin shrine may be branded as heretical by the orthodox church, but in some ways it is a pilgrimage place more appropriate to American Catholicism than are other sacred centers modeled on European shrines.

In a more general vein, this study reveals the powerful role pilgrimage can play in forging solidarity within a social group. Whatever ideals the group may celebrate, these central truths can be enshrined at a certain place where the faithful can ritually validate their identity with the group and its cosmology. Pilgrimage is an effective means for creating and reinforcing social identities, group bonds, and collective ideologies. This dimension of sacred journeying is one (although only one) important reason pilgrimage has been so popular a cultural practice since the dawn of the human era.

Pilgrimage is often conceived as a reflex of religious orthodoxy or a traditionalist practice that occurs in the context of, and reinforces conservative respect for, religious authorities. The case I present here of the Queen of the Holy Rosary, Mediatrix of Peace Shrine in rural Wisconsin, shows that pilgrimage can also be implicated in heresy, defiance of church authority, and the alteration and replacement of one faith by another.

To some extent, the process I will be describing conforms to a type of modern Catholic pilgrimage delineated by Victor and Edith Turner (1978, 1981). It involves apparitions of the Virgin Mary without child, intervening on her own behalf in human affairs to warn of impending catastrophe if mankind does not repent its involvement in modern sybaritic life-styles and godless business and political enterprises. The Turners' model of the "post-industrial Marian pilgrimage," however, does not anticipate the institution's becoming a formula of exit from the Catholic faith. Rather, they pose it as a sometimes extreme but still loyal form of intra-Catholic millenarianism. The Queen of the Holy Rosary, Mediatrix of Peace Shrine, I will argue, shows something else: the adaptation of a specifically European pilgrimage idea to the process of recruitment to, and confirmation in, a heterodox sect.

Between 1978 and 1981, I made five visits to this shrine and the community of about 500 "shrine people" who had then made their homes there. For a total of just under eight months, I lived in the adjacent non-shrine village of Necedah, Wisconsin (population 800), and conducted open-ended interviews on shrine history with resident shrine people, visitors, and villagers. The shrine community at that time was a crucible of religious controversy, its leaders denying their excommunication from the Roman Catholic Church, then professing their allegiance to another body, the American National Catholic Church, Roman Catholic Ultrajectine. Factions within the shrine movement fought bitterly over access to the movement's founder, the over seventy-year-old, self-professed prophet, Mary Ann Van Hoof (1909-1984);[1] and at least five other rival or satellite groups disputed Mary Ann's legitimacy and vied for the attention of the disaffected. Meanwhile, the villagers of Necedah saw the whole shrine movement as the intrusion of a fanatical cult into their previously peaceful community and recognized that the shrine people had grown into a formidable political presence. The number of shrine people was large enough potentially to control the school board and to cast decisive votes in township elections. The half of the village population that were ordinary Roman Catholics unaffiliated with the shrine felt a special grievance against the shrine's peremptory religious style. Shrine people, in turn, considered local non-shrine Catholics to be among their most distressing enemies.

One might doubt that these conditions would be conducive to the development of a pilgrimage center, but, during this period, the shrine drew from 20,000 to 30,000 pilgrims a year, almost all of whom were Roman Catholics who knowingly defied their church's attempt to discourage visits to this site. The shrine, in brief, was an isolated, rural religious movement, consumed in bitter rivalries both within itself and with its neighbors, promoting "heretical" doctrines, and yet persisting as the center for a stable, if small-scale, Catholic pilgrimage.

In this chapter, I attend to one of the contexts in which this pilgrimage can be understood. Because the shrine is both isolated and autonomous, it has had the opportunity to develop a rich sui generis symbolic system. Through this system, it has worked (sometimes odd) transformations on other traditions. The case history of this shrine makes clear that pilgrimage can function as a form of religious recruitment and conversion in the derivation of a new religion. Before turning to the manner in which the shrine accomplishes this transformation, however, I will note two other interpretive contexts.

First, the shrine pilgrimage can be seen as a significant variation on an international pattern. The Turners' description of the "modern" or "post-Tridentine Catholic" pilgrimage accurately captures a number of the shrine's characteristics:

1. a "highly devotional tone and fervent personal piety", which form "an important part of the system of apologetics deployed against advancing secularization" (Turner and Turner 1978: 18),

2. an "anti-modern" tone, "since they usually begin with an apparition, or vision, and they assert miracles do happen" (19),

3. "an implicit critique of the lifestyle characteristic of the encompassing social structure" (38),

4. "a general call to all humankind to repent and be saved" (209),

5. apparitions of the Virgin, who gives messages "connected with lower-middle-class interests" in which "both big business and international socialism are condemned as major causes of humankind's sins" (209), and

6. "warnings of dire calamities to be visited on mankind if it does not repent a kind of Catholic millenarianism" (149).

But in its ambiguous schism with the institutional Catholic Church, the shrine departs from the Turners' pattern.

Second, the Queen of the Holy Rosary, Mediatrix of Peace Shrine pilgrimage takes place in a "pilgrimage system" (as opposed, in the Turners' language, to a "process")—a pilgrimage system encompassing other Catholic pilgrimage sites in the United States and Canada. As of this writing, there are no scholarly works and very few sources of any sort, even in devotional literature, that deal collectively or comparatively with these sites, but in speaking with pilgrims and in visiting the sites themselves, one finds that individual shrines are part of a network. There are a few common themes that characterize the whole system, such as the focus on the Virgin Mary. There are also a few complementary themes, such as the ethnic specializations of many of the shrines. And there is a unifying force in the practice of numerous pilgrims who are familiar with and visit one shrine after another in turn.

Since this North American Catholic pilgrimage system (which may or may not include Mexico) has not been the subject of any formal study, I venture a few tentative generalizations that bear on the nature of the Necedah pilgrimage:

1. Legitimated Catholic places of pilgrimage in the United States and Canada are of three types: first, shrines that commemorate other shrines, mostly in Europe, such as the shrines at Fatima, La Salette, and Czestochowa; second, shrines that commemorate figures from the history of Catholicism in the Americas, such as the Shrine of the North American Martyrs at Auriesville, New York; and third, shrines by decree, such as the National Shrine of the Immaculate Conception in Washington, D.C., and the National Shrine of Our Lady of Victory in Lackawanna, New York, which usually commemorate the Virgin Mary under one of her many official titles. The *1988 Catholic Almanac* gives an incomplete list of seventy-eight shrines in the United States and four in Canada. Among the U.S shrines, twenty overtly refer to shrines elsewhere. There are four Fatima shrines, and two shrines each dedicated to Our Lady of Guadalupe, Our Lady of Lourdes, Our Lady of La Salette, the Infant of Prague, and Our Lady of Czestochowa. Thirty-one are primarily Marian shrines.[2]

2. The illegitimate shrines are all centered on persons who are alleged to have had visions of the Virgin Mary or Jesus. There are currently no apparitional shrines in the United States with official church approval.[3] The only legitimate shrine that appears to be founded in a miracle story (but not an apparition) is the Shrine of St. Anne de Beaupre in Quebec, which references the miraculous cure of the cripple Louis Guimont at its founding in 1658.

3. Both legitimate and illegitimate shrines are closely articulated with ethnic divisions among Catholics. Some shrines, such as the National Shrine of Our Lady of Czestochowa in Doylestown, Pennsylvania, figure as a nearly exclusive center for a single ethnic group. Others attempt to attract a multi-ethnic sponsorship.

The Shrine of the North American Martyrs, for example, has a Lebanese Day, a Hungarian Day, a Hispanic Day, an Italian Day, and so on. A more extensive characterization of this system might emphasize the diminution of interest in the pilgrimages and shrines by the mainstream church, the low status of pilgrimages in an implicit hierarchy of devotional forms, the location of pilgrimage sites near tourist and recreational areas, and the arrogation of control of pilgrimage sites to religious orders at some remove from the control of local dioceses. Catholic pilgrimage in North America is a system that has, for the most part, fallen beneath the full attention, approval, and control of the church and is thereby available to those who would reconstruct and reinterpret it for unorthodox ends.

THE NECEDAH PILGRIMAGE

In his 1973 essay, "The Center Out There: Pilgrim's Goal," (republished as "Pilgrimages as Social Processes," 1974) Victor Turner commented: "I am at present inclined to favor the view that a pilgrimage's best chance of survival is when it imparts to religious orthodoxy a renewed vitality, rather than when it asserts against an established system a set of heterodox opinions and unprecedented styles of religious and symbolic action. In this latter situation one finds sects, heresies, and millenarian movements, but not pilgrimage centers" (1973: 229; 1974: 227). Turner made this assertion despite his familiarity with Ralph della Cava's work on the Brazilian town of Joaseiro, which is a strikingly successful pilgrimage center based on "an alleged miracle whose authenticity was sternly denied by the official representatives of the Catholic Church, both in Brazil and Rome" (226). Turner's suggestion that the durability of a pilgrimage rests on its religious orthodoxy is modified in his and his wife's later writings (Turner and Turner 1978; Turner 1981), but his earlier view does, in fact, have some merit. Millenarian movements and pilgrimage centers may not be mutually exclusive forms of organizing religious experience, but they do tend in antithetical directions. The empirical coincidence of the two forms is rare or at least rarely reported. Pilgrimage is usually a ritual respite within an encompassing social order. Millenarianism is or is most often conceived to be a convulsion against such order in favor of an entirely new one.

The shrine at Necedah combines a pilgrimage process not only with a millenarianism but also with religious processes that are better identified as heresies and sectarianism. The heresies are doctrinal points that the shrine attempts to promote within the Catholic faith, despite both the official condemnation of those points by church authorities and the apparent contradiction between those points and other well-established Catholic dogmas. Sectarianism, on the other hand, is apparent in the shrine's admission of its own clergy under the rubric of the American National Catholic Church, Roman Catholic Ultrajectine. The commingling of these four orientations (pilgrimage, millenarianism, heresy, and sectarianism) is perhaps a topological anomaly, but it is very much part of the character of this somewhat inchoate and thematically acquisitive movement. The key to much of the shrine's organization and belief is the prophet's vision of a new human society constructed out of the radical transposition of the shrine's own local organization onto the macrocosms of American society and, in some sense, the whole universe. It is never entirely clear whether this transposition is to be an empirical event or whether it is to be understood in some other more metaphorical or allegorical way. This elasticity, of course, is one of the factors that enables the shrine to sustain a pilgrimage process in a context that also includes formal heresies and millenarian impulses. From the Turners' (I think correct) analysis, this combination is rife with both ideological and structural tensions and is perhaps inherently unstable. The Necedah shrine has sustained it, however, for close to forty years. That success deserves closer attention.

The shrine's yoking of pilgrimage to millenarian, sectarian, and heretical tendencies is effected by several means: by ambiguities that enable novice participants to regard their experiences within a framework of orthodox devotion even while the terms of orthodoxy are being called into question; by strict contextualization of elements that might otherwise clash; by allowing certain discontinuities to pass unnoticed; and, above all, by situating any possibility of resolving the implicit tensions and contradictions in the ongoing experience of pilgrims. Pilgrims who come to the shrine and employ the metaphors and self-descriptive language of *pilgrimage* are sometimes led to the rather different metaphors and self-descriptive language of *exodus*. The transformation is complex and happens only occasionally, but it happens often enough to have sustained this movement since 1950.

In view of the shrine's own attempt to maintain the institution of pilgrimage as a seemingly distinct component of the movement, it is fairly easy to extract an outline of the pilgrimage from the shrine's more sect-like, heretical, and millenarian aspects. I will offer such an outline and then show how the narrative structure imposed on this pilgrimage by the shrine leads some pilgrims from a position of rebellion within their church to a position of adherence to an imaginary counter-church.

Shrine pilgrimages—which is the word shrine people use to describe them—are journeys undertaken by outsiders, non-shrine residents, to visit the Queen of the Holy Rosary, Mediatrix of Peace Shrine. This shrine comprises about two and one-half acres of flat sandy land, a circuit of eleven (sometimes twelve) statues or groups of statues arranged in religious tableaux, and, apart from this main circuit, the "Sacred Spot" (site of many of the apparitions); two more tableaux, one showing Michael the Archangel holding Satan at bay, the other depicting the "choice" between nuclear war and Christian family piety; and a full-scale replica of part of Mary Ann Van Hoof's former house (which burned in 1956). Many pilgrims see more of the shrine community than this outdoor assemblage, but the statues, the house, and especially the Sacred Spot are the designated sacra that the pilgrims have supposedly sought and are, in any case, directed to.

Almost all of the pilgrims are white midwesterners, practicing Catholics, raised in the church, resident in midwestern metropolitan areas such as Milwaukee, Chicago, Rockford, Minneapolis, St. Paul, or St. Louis. A plurality, I estimate around 85 percent, are third-generation or more ethnic German-Americans, with the remainder mostly ethnic Polish or Irish and a notably small number of ethnic Italians. Most are from skilled labor and petit bourgeois occupations ranging from automobile mechanics, electricians, and stone masons to real estate brokers, grocers, and druggists. On special pilgrimage days, however, it is not hard to find less prosperous farmers, unskilled factory and construction workers, and a few pilgrims who appear to be almost indigent. Likewise, there are some participants from the professions. Thus, geographical provenance and ethnicity combined with Roman Catholicism give the pilgrims a common identity, but there is enough diversity of class to warrant the idea that, as many shrine people put it: "The shrine is open to everybody. All kinds of people come here and are welcome."

Shrine pilgrimages can occur throughout the year as individuals have time and see fit. There are, however, ten official occasions, called Anniversary Days, on which pilgrimages are especially encouraged. On these days chartered buses bring in hundreds of pilgrims (local affiliates of For My God and My Country, Incorporated arrange the charters, as do less organized groups of sub-rosa adherents in distance dioceses), in addition to others who arrive by car. On the most important dates, August 15 and October 7, the total gathering of pilgrims is between 2,000 and 3,000. An ordinary day, not marked by an announced Vigil, by contrast, brings only about twenty visitors, many of whom see themselves as tourists or skeptics rather than as pilgrims. The Anniversary Days are April 7 (Anniversary of Good Friday, 1950); May 28 (Anniversary of Pentecost Sunday, 1950); May 29, May 30, and June 4

(Anniversary of Trinity Sunday, 1950); June 16 (Anniversary of the Sacred Heart, 1950); August 15, October 7, November 12, and Trinity Sunday (whenever it occurs according to the church calendar). In addition to these occasions, the shrine celebrates fifty-two other Vigils, which are announced on a publicly available calendar and which are also propitious times for shrine pilgrimages. A few Vigils occur each month, with the greatest concentrations in June (seven), July (seven), and September (seven). An average Vigil draws about fifty pilgrims.

The elision of these pilgrimages into other religious processes can best be observed by considering the sequence of perceptions, involvements, and confrontations between private and shared experience that define the special character of the Necedah shrine. The Necedah pilgrimage can be regarded, like any pilgrimage, as a journey, but unlike many such journeys, the shrine pilgrimage includes an implicit teaching that the pilgrim should cancel his return trip.

INITIAL ORIENTATIONS

Visitors to Necedah are often apprehensive. Their feelings show in furtive gestures, in their shying away from casual conversation, and in their occasional gruffness in commerce with the townspeople. When they reach the shrine, the pilgrims' defensive facade usually begins to fall and to be replaced with its opposite, an inordinate relief and exaggerated trust in the fellowship of shrine people. Ironically, at this point they encounter the shrine's own defensive barriers, most notably the deep suspicion that shrine people have of anyone from "outside." The pilgrim approaches ready for sanctuary and offering ingenuous trust in the motives of his hosts and is met with either bland reserve or inquisitorial hostility. I observed this emotional subtext both as a resident in the town and as a frequent visitor on the shrine grounds. Often I would meet first-time visitors at the shrine who would, unsolicited, confess how they had worried in approaching Necedah, how the last stages of their journeys had been "almost frightening," and what tremendous relief they felt to be at this "peaceful place."

This apprehensiveness could, following Turner, be glossed as the pilgrim's response to several kinds of liminality. Most of the pilgrims have traveled from an urban to a rural setting. This particular rural setting, as it happens, is rife with cultural markers that declare that those who pass its threshold are entering into wilderness. The pilgrims may or may not be consciously receptive to this theme, but they at least know something about the ambivalent reputation of their destination. I have heard Necedah referred to both as "the asshole of Juneau County" and as "one of the most beautiful places I have ever seen." In more temperate form, both reputations are abroad, and it is hard to imagine that anyone who had taken the trouble to find Necedah would not also have come across its two-sided fame as a haven for religious eccentricity and cultural backwardness and as an unspoiled corner of the continent worthy of the religiously devout.

The shrine's first act of potential intervention in the lives of pilgrims is to offer them a resolution of these contradictory reports. The wilderness/countryside is split into two parts by the shrine. The negative potential, including the hints of violence and hedonistic ease that are parts of the American idea of wilderness, is assigned to the forests and hamlets that surround the shrine. The positive potential in the idea of wilderness, the sense that it is a place where pristine conditions allow both real human freedom and the possibility of building a new society, is assigned to the shrine. The shrine, in other words, addresses the pilgrim's liminality in an attempt to clarify its nature and resolve it in a fashion complimentary to the shrine's own presence in these sparsely populated mid-Wisconsin tracts.

The advocacy of this interpretation, of course, blends with the context. Shrine people make frequent use of the terms and symbols of wilderness, but they are not didactic about it and certainly not aware that it rests as much on distinctions they have created as it does on external properties of their environment. The persuasion they offer is embedded in the temporal sequence of experiences that are put before the pilgrim:

1. visual contrasts between the shrine's external and internal landscapes,

2. reminders, both iconographic and ritually enacted, about the boundary of the shrine community, surrounded by an impinging and dangerous wilderness,

3. significant and slightly disturbing variations on familiar forms of Catholic visual symbolism, and

4. finally, a verbal depiction of the shrine as an "Island" in the midst of a decaying and probably doomed country.

This sequence is not forced on unsympathetic visitors. The effectiveness of each step depends on the pilgrim's prepossession of certain knowledge and the inclinations with which he begins the process. To understand what shrine people mean when they talk about the Island and what consequences this idea has within the shrine devotional system, one must begin with the interests and motivations of the pilgrims.

Pilgrims approaching the shrine already know that it is a place mired in scandal and ecclesiastical controversy. The widely disseminated view of the church is that the shrine is both morally offensive and spiritually dangerous. To this view, shrine people reply that the church can forbid nothing that is not against faith or morals, and the shrine is against neither. Nonetheless, the primary reality for pilgrims is not the shrine's rationalization but the church's stricture. A pilgrimage to the shrine is a venture into a place known for ecclesiastical defiance. The pilgrim's visit to the shrine grounds is an act of complicity with that defiance.

The Catholics who are most often willing to take that step are the out-of-favor and not well-organized "traditionalists"—the name they most frequently use for themselves—who see the contemporary order of the Catholic church as the result of the church's domination by liberal, ecumenically-minded modernists. Traditionalists, as reported, for example, in the Turners' survey (1978), have an affinity with the apparitional pilgrimage sites that have come into being since the early nineteenth century. They lend their support to these shrines' universalistic calls for mankind to repent and to their threats of calamity if mankind does not. Their assertions of their preference for an uncompromising style of worship and rigorous piety often isolate them within their own parishes, and the church provides them few other contexts in which they can pursue these interests. Before coming to Necedah, some have been members of the Blue Army devotees of Our Lady of Fatima, while others have participated in efforts to distribute scapulars or joined renegade congregations that continue the Latin Tridentine Mass.

Thus, when shrine people inveigh against the dilution of traditional forms of worship and invent circuitous ways to continue these practices (such as the shrine's "Perpetual Adoration of the Blessed Sacrament" and its "Constant Vigil of Prayer"), they act within a recognizable, if not already familiar context for some of the pilgrims. The official church positions on Latin Mass, communion in the hand, and St. Michael's prayer for the Defense of the Church, for example, continue to disappoint these pilgrims. They see the shrine's stand as similar to their own, and, at least initially, they treat the shrine as one of the underground traditionalist alternatives to the mainstream church. This assessment is not entirely accurate, since the shrine is much further from the mainstream church than they have perceived, but it agrees with one of the shrine's own views of its position. The pilgrim's initial willingness to defy church authorities by visiting the shrine is, therefore, framed by skepticism toward the devotional practices of the contemporary church and by a thirst for what is remembered as a more elevated and spiritually-demanding set of requirements.

Once a pilgrim has come to the shrine, the shrine itself offers a second, slightly more complex justification for such a visit. Shrine people explain that the publicly announced positions of the church are really disguises for the church's true theological positions. If the Necedah shrine is denounced by the bishops, it is really to test the fortitude of the shrine's followers. If sacramental wine is said to be the transubstantiated blood of Christ, it is to hide the profounder truth that it is really the blood of both Christ and Mary. The outwardly acknowledged church doctrines are no more than foils for the knowledge of the more enlightened who collectively constitute the "Hidden Church." It is easy to see how such logic leads to heresy, but it is equally easy to see that it permits a Catholic to continue to identify himself as an orthodox member of the church long after his beliefs have substantially departed from either creedal orthodoxy or practical church norms.

The difference between a temporarily out-of-favor doctrine and an absolutely heretical belief is not always clear, especially to a heterodox believer. The steps from orthodoxy to heterodoxy can, in fact, look like buttresses put up to keep the faith from collapsing.

In any case, these two initial motives—the pilgrim's search for an affirmation of practices he thinks the church has wrongly discarded and the shrine's intimation that the church's opposition is a false front—are somewhat contradictory. The first admits the authority of the church hierarchy but challenges its conclusions. The second circumvents the authority and goes on to elaborate an independent theology. Much of the shrine's religious system, in fact, turns on the effort to transform one motive into the other, to turn the rebellious pilgrim into a shrine person. The process through which this transformation happens includes the education of the pilgrim about shrine doctrines and the enculturation of the pilgrim into the shrine community, but the most crucial component is providing the pilgrim with a deep and resonant religious experience, along with a few basic clues about how that experience can be made to make sense. Pilgrimages perhaps only rarely result in the quality of experience that might lend itself to such elaboration, but we can still observe the conditions that are meant to encourage it and the aids that the shrine provides to pilgrims to help them interpret it. The resolution of the Wisconsin wilderness into two types of anti-civilization is the first step in this process. The second is the identification of Necedah as a Holy Land.

ENTERING THE SHRINE

Necedah is approachable on main roads from four directions. The shrine has posted signs for itself, however, only on the road from the east, which passes directly behind the shrine grounds. One sign notes, "Shrine ahead." The other, at the turnoff for the shrine, says "Queen of the Holy Rosary, Mediatrix of Peace Shrine" in gold letters on a blue field, surrounded by a painting of a rosary. The only other religious marker visible to the casual observer is a now derelict waystation several miles east of the shrine that commemorates a woman's vision of Jesus on that site.

In its outward announcement of itself, the Necedah shrine is understated and underanticipated. Instead of being surrounded by a series of lesser shrines that announce the approach of a holy center and allow the pilgrim a gradual build-up of devotional feelings (the pattern the Turners, among others, describe for European shrines), the Necedah shrine almost hides from view, challenges the pilgrim to find it, and presents not a climax of gradually intensified feelings but a shock of recognition and some sense of surprise at the incongruity between the shrine and its setting.

Pilgrims often get lost. When a pilgrim does find the shrine, he parks in a sandy lot and walks toward a cluster of rough-hewn stone buildings. Necedah is in low-lying, swampy country. During most of the pilgrimage season, the air is thick with mosquitoes. Directly adjacent to the shrine, on an artificial embankment, run the tracks of the Chicago Northwestern Railroad. The atmosphere is prosaic. I frequently saw pilgrims smothering their nervous laughter.

The entrance to the shrine is marked by two arcade arches with the name of the shrine again in gold and blue letters. Below the arches, the entrance is closed with white wooden gates, beside which there is a narrower passage with a sign instructing pilgrim women to show proper respect by dressing "Mary-like." If a woman arrives wearing slacks or a skirt above her knees, she is directed by this sign to put on one of the blue wrap-around skirts available at the information booth. At this point there seems to be a profusion of signs. One directs the pilgrim to be silent in certain areas. Others give quotations from Mary Ann's messages. Some are brief explanations of symbols or projects. Suddenly, from out of the pathless, desolate, and seemingly unstructured environment, the pilgrim is in the midst of walls, fences, dress codes, immaculately kept lawns and gardens, and a precisely laid out sequence of devotional apparatus. Well before anyone at the shrine says a word, the fundamental message is clear: the shrine is an island of peaceful order in a world of disorder and meaninglessness. The absence of directional signs and the occasional misdirection suffered by the pilgrim help to foster this sense of reorientation.

THE SHRINE GROUNDS

The shrine grounds are divided into two parts enclosed by separate fences. We have just approached the threshold of the first part. It comprises ten or eleven groups of statues, most of them arranged in tableaux behind glass. The other part comprises the Sacred Spot (Mary Ann's usual site for apparitions, the focal point of Vigils), the replica of part of her former house, and one more tableau containing the statue of Michael vanquishing Satan. This second area also contains an excavation for the House of Prayer, which the shrine has had under construction for several years. Pilgrims, frequently escorted by a shrine guide, are encouraged to walk the circuit within the area containing most of the statues. The Sacred Spot and its environs, however, can be seen by a pilgrim only from a distance. Pilgrims are encouraged to approach the perimeter wall, where they can kneel and pray. Conversations with the shrine guide are encouraged in the former area, but silence is enjoined in the public areas closest to the Sacred Spot. The shrines represent visions that Mary Ann has already had; the Sacred Spot is where her regularly scheduled meetings with the Virgin still take place. The two parts of the shrine are thus asymmetrical and complementary. The circuit of shrines literally invites the pilgrim in and educates him to what the shrine as a whole is about. It offers the pilgrim the opportunity to ask questions, display skepticism, and pray without necessarily committing himself to any part of the shrine theological scheme. The Sacred Spot, by contrast, assumes that the pilgrim knows the shrine's basic theology and demands a degree of respect for that theology bordering on assent. By ostentatiously excluding the pilgrim while allowing shrine people entry, the Sacred Spot becomes not a vehicle for knowledge about the shrine but an embodiment of the shrine community's boundary. Once I entered the enclosure around the Sacred Spot in the presence of several shrine people. One of them told me that she thought my being there meant that I was now fully part of the community. Since many pilgrims visit the shrine on Anniversary Days, they witness a dramatization of the relation between the two parts of the shrine grounds. The main event of these days is the appearance of Mary Ann, who walks from the Replica (of her house) to the Sacred Spot, goes into trance, and speaks (or mumbles) both sides of a conversation with the Virgin Mary and sometimes other "Celestials." Before this event, however, there are fairly extensive ritual preparations. The detail that dramatizes the relation between the individual shrines and the Sacred Spot is a procession in which a palanquin carrying a doll-size St. Anne is carried from the St. Anne shrine all around the circuit of shrines, out the front gate, and up to the entrance of the Sacred Spot. At that point, only the shrine people who carry the crucifix and the palanquin and who have led the procession are allowed to pass through the gate into the sanctuary of the Sacred Spot. The pilgrims who have joined in the procession and sung hymns along the way are left standing outside.

THE ISLAND

If a pilgrim arrives at the shrine on a day other than an Anniversary Day, he is met by a shrine guide who offers to walk the circuit of shrines with him and explain the history of the shrine. I knew several of the shrine guides well and accompanied them often as they took pilgrims around. Some guides were more likely than others to mention the Island by name on their tours, but all of them were very familiar with the idea and passed on most of its content. Some days we would sit in the shrine information booth at the entrance to the shrine and wait for pilgrims, and, as other shrine workers came and went—reporting on the artificial flower arrangements in one shrine and stopping by to pray at the Sacred Spot after a day's labor on the St. Joseph's Home for Unwanted Men or at the Seven Sorrows of Our Sorrowful Mother Infants' Home—we would speculate on the exact boundaries of the Island and what might happen to those left outside.

The Island is not a literal island; it is an interamnian plain. Its boundaries are fixed in the east, the south, and the west by the Wisconsin River and its tributary, the Yellow River, which flows into the Wisconsin seven miles south of the shrine. To the north, however, the Island melds into the Wisconsin forest, which, far from constituting an exact boundary, is, in shrine thought, an image of the boundless. Some of Mary Ann's visions evoke the possibility of communist hordes sweeping down from Canada through this forest. No shrine person thinks the Island goes on forever. Some suggest that the "thirty-mile zone of protection" the Virgin has granted to Mary Ann must mark its northern limit. I have elsewhere argued that this geographical indeterminateness represents the shrine's desire to leave open a connection to the outside world, while it resists relations with its actual neighbors (Wood 1988: 40).

The Island is as much a moral construct as it is a place. It is the area that will be spared the "white fire" of what Mary Ann calls the "Chastisement," the conflagration that God will visit on the whole world for mankind's sins. From the people on the Island God will select the survivors. One revelation depicts the Angel Gabriel arriving in a flying saucer to spirit the shrine's Inner Circle to safety inside the North Pole. Such revelations, however, are entrusted only to members of the Inner Circle themselves, not to novice pilgrims.

Although a shrine guide might not mention the Island by name to a pilgrim, the guide would indicate some of the reasons the Queen of the Holy Rosary, Mediatrix of Peace Shrine was unlike any other. These reasons include the observation that, in all of Christianity, Necedah is the only place of Marian apparition where the Virgin promised to make regular apparitions on a fixed schedule as long as the visionary remained alive. For over thirty years, the Virgin had kept to her schedule, and hundreds of other Celestials, more than had ever appeared anywhere else, had also come to Mary Ann with messages. No other spot of apparition, the guides would explain, had been blessed with such a variety of miracles—and here there would ensue a long comparison of Necedah with shrines all over the world. By the same logic, no shrine had had to suffer as many trials as Necedah, nor had any been subject to such slander. The burden was to be withstood, however, because Holy Mother had made her wishes known and "those who carry out her wishes will receive many graces." One wish was that this shrine be built, and since then, the shrine people had been building it by hand with all donated materials.

Some shrine guides would go further and discuss the impending Chastisement, the pitiful efforts of Holy Mother to hold back the arm of her Son, raised now to strike a wrathful blow on sinful mankind. The Virgin could be assisted in her efforts to delay this blow by the prayers of supplicants, especially by recitations of the rosary. The delay, in any case, would be short. Prayers offered up would do more good for the person offering them than for doomed humanity. Some guides liked to recall that, in her early messages, the Virgin had said that if it took the church as long to approve Necedah as it had taken to approve Fatima, it would be too late to save the world. Fatima's approval came after thirty years, and, the guide would conclude, since Mary Ann's first visions, over thirty years had already passed.

Only a few shrine people were able to construct a formal theory out of these apocalyptic intimations. The theories that were put forward, moreover, did not seem to attract as much public interest as the constant rumors about miracles, unreleased prophecies, and events in the outside world so horrendous that they had to be signs that the end was coming soon. The shrine was in what Kenelm Burridge calls a "millenarian situation," but it had not invested too deeply in any single millenarian creed. The closest that the majority of shrine people had come to such a creed was their general view that the "Marian Age" of the Catholic church was coming to a close and that Necedah represented its final fulfillment and culmination. That is why, shrine people would say, the Virgin had reenacted all the miracles of all her previous apparitions in Necedah.

The good works promoted by the shrine were not expected to accomplish much toward their overt ends. Abortion would continue despite the shrine's campaign against it. Immoral television programs and advertisements would not be eliminated by the "Let's Clean Up T.V. Campaign." The "International Conspiracy of the Grand Masters" would corrupt still more governments and offices of the church despite the perfectly clear warnings coming from Necedah. Shrine people resisted these evils not because they were confident of a worldly victory over them, but because they were obedient to the wishes of Holy Mother. To some extent, shrine people could be heartened by their own failure in these projects, since it meant that the Chastisement was all the more imminent. This last thought would never have been openly acknowledged, but it could be heard in the furtive gratification of shrine people as they prompted pilgrims to tell them how bad things were in the parishes, communities, and schools away from the Island.

VISIONS

A receptive pilgrim always talked about the sorry state of his church back home and the church in general, and the guide always talked about a few of the specific "favors" she had been granted since coming to the shrine. The most important "favor" would be a "sign" given by heaven to the shrine person to signify God's desire to have that person working for the cause in Necedah. Signs of this sort usually occurred on the shrine grounds amid the circuit of lesser shrines—the same context, if not the exact spot, where the guide was relating all this material to the pilgrim. This practice of giving "testimonials" (For My God and My Country, Incorporated, gathered and published two volumes of *Testimonials of Pilgrims*) amounted to a very explicit set of clues to the pilgrim on how to initiate a mystical experience appropriate to the Necedah shrine and what to make of it if and when it happened.

Among the more frequently reported signs are movements by a statue of the Virgin or gestures by a statue such as a loving gaze or a smile directed to the pilgrim. Another category of signs consists of rosaries that turn from their original materials into gold. Another consists of unnatural rays of light that come out of the sky to illuminate objects on the shrine grounds, especially the Sacred Ash Trees beside the Sacred Spot. Sometimes a panorama of celestial figures appears in the clouds. Sometimes a pilgrim catches a glimpse of an unearthly/divine form, perhaps that of an angel. A photograph might be developed to reveal a profile of Jesus or Mary in the bushes. A few people catch whiffs of heavenly perfumes, and a few others hear celestial music.

There were also signs that it would be better not to have. The Virgin was not supposed to show herself to anyone but Mary Ann, and no one but Mary Ann was supposed to have verbal communication with the Virgin or any of the itinerant saints. The occasional pilgrim or mystic who claimed to have seen the Virgin or to have heard her voice received a frosty response from shrine people. Some of the shrine's satellite groups are led by these rival visionaries. Several ex-shrine people related to me their visions of demons swarming over the shrine grounds. They speculated that many of the visions associated with the shrine were illusions of infernal origin, intended to mislead and ensnare the unwary.

Having a vision of the acceptable type or noticing an event that can be assimilated to the category of the miraculous, such as a rosary chain changing colors, is an extremely important experience within the shrine community. It is not exactly a formal prerequisite of entrance into the community, but there are few shrine people who do not claim to have had the "privilege." Visions are the boundary markers par excellence between the sympathetic pilgrim and the neophyte, committed believer.

Other Catholic shrines do not deny the possibility of a pilgrim's encountering the miraculous on their precincts, and the church uses "authenticated" miracles as one of its most important tests in deciding if an apparition is valid. Few shrines, however, go so far as to encourage the idea that a miracle or sign is likely or that it is a relatively common occurrence. Similarly, the typical miracle of most Catholic shrines is a physical healing of those with inoperable disabilities. The Necedah shrine makes extraordinarily few claims for miraculous healings. Shrine miracles are nearly always "out there," events external to the observer, to which the observer is but a private witness or one of a party of witnesses.

The pilgrim is introduced to this pattern from the moment he arrives at the shrine. It is somewhat more difficult to say what happens if a pilgrim's first visit occurs on the great pilgrimage Anniversary Days, but my general experience was that the same type of communication took place, only intensified by the pilgrims many contacts with shrine people and more experienced pilgrims saying the same things. More experienced pilgrims were frequently more fervent expositors of the shrine's vision pattern than even the resident shrine people.

THE CIRCUIT OF SHRINES

The last component of the pilgrim's experience at the shrine is what he actually sees as he walks the shrine grounds. An elliptical path runs past the information booth at the entrance and leads counterclockwise to the statues of Joan of Arc and St. Anne, each in a stone grotto with a glass front. Adjacent to these shrines stands the most prominent shrine on the grounds, a Crucifixion scene. Facing it are three open-air statues—Christ standing on a globe, flanked by George Washington and Abraham Lincoln. At the northern end of the path, hidden around a corner, another grotto contains a "Way to Calvary Shrine," with stonework extended on the other side to permit a "Nativity Shrine," which is set up each Christmas. It is covered in the interim with a series of paintings depicting the Virgin. Further along the north side of the circuit is a "Holy Family Shrine," showing Jesus as a prepubescent boy at home with Mary and Joseph, and next is a "Way to Peace Shrine," which is a complicated melange with a statue of Mary Ann Van Hoof, whose back is turned to the viewer as she receives from Joan of Arc and St. Theresa a "heavenly painting" depicting one of her earlier visions.

At the northwest corner of the shrine grounds, the pilgrim comes to the "Mother Cabrini Shrine." Next, turning back toward the entrance, there is a pair of large (and emphatically heterodox) shrines: the "Last Supper Shrine" and the "First Mass Shrine." They depict Jesus and the Apostles at two sequential occasions, in two different rooms of the same building. In Catholic theology, the Last Supper and the First Mass are synonymous, but it has been revealed to Mary Ann that they were different events. Finally, back near the entrance, the pilgrim comes to a shrine to St. Francis of Assisi, the eponymous saint of the Necedah parish, a statue that dates to the time when Mary Ann was on better terms with the local church.

Each of these statues and all of the grottoes are arranged, so it is said, according to Mary Ann's precise instructions. The layout of the grounds was ordained by the Virgin, the dimensions of the individual grottoes were dictated in visions, and the statues were worked and reworked by professional sculptors under Mary Ann's supervision. As pilgrims tour the grounds, the guides tell them this information and go on to explain particular visual details. Thus, there is a strong warrant for interpreting these displays as something other than conventional Catholic iconography. They are, in fact, promoted not as conventional images at all but as the sculpted equivalents of eyewitness accounts, based on visions and on Mary Ann's celestial time-travel. Details such as the way Christ's feet are crossed in the Crucifixion are cited as historical accuracies that can be seen nowhere else in the world.

One theme of the pilgrim's tour is, therefore, "authenticity." The Queen of the Holy Rosary, Mediatrix of Peace Shrine is no imitation of European shrines or overseas advocate of their mystical authenticity. Rather, it is a real place of apparition in its own right. The individual shrines do not defer to others' versions but record paradigmatic Christian events in a fresh and original manner that is said to supersede and be more accurate than depictions elsewhere. A point that is made in several of the grottoes is that Catholic tradition has erred in the manner it has depicted a saint's clothing, gestures, or religious attitudes.

Located off-center in the circular layout of grottoes and having the most dramatic aspect of all the statues is the shrine's Crucifixion scene. It is a life-size Jesus, surrounded by a mourning Virgin, Mary Magdalene, an Apostle, and the "other" Mary, all enclosed in an octagonal glass case. The riveting figure is Jesus, lacerated over every inch of his flesh, with internal organs protruding, and, in the midst of his gore, turning a gangrenous yellow and purple. The tableau is fixed in blue spotlights.

Pilgrims react strongly to this figure. Some are revolted; others, exhilarated. Shrine guides explain how Mary Ann had the sculptors redo the flesh because it was insufficiently mutilated. The four other figures in the scene are depicted in spotlessly clean biblical garb and posed in attitudes of simpering delicacy. The effect is ghastly, but the idea that this shrine is "unlike" other shrines is certainly sustained. Part of the message is that the shrine's version of Catholicism refuses to accede to an unbloodied accommodationist style of religion. It is not afraid of extremes. Another part of the message is that shrine religion glorifies the symbolism of Christian suffering. There is a hint here of the martyrology to come. Yet another part of the implicit meaning lies in the shrine's extrapolation of certain ideas about masculinity and femininity.

The sexual theme is suggested throughout the various grottoes. The figures, whether they represent males or females, have limpid, idealized expressions with no trace of human feeling—no anger, no happiness, no desire—only placid and static contentment. There are three exceptions: Jesus on the cross, Judas slinking away from the table in the First Communion Shrine, and Satan held to the ground by St. Michael's spear in St. Michael's Shrine. These three exceptions were notably the statues both pilgrims and shrine people were most apt to discuss, and all three represent vanquished males. Like much traditional Catholic thinking, the shrine usually seems hostile to human sexuality. There is another level in shrine thought, however, that has something to do with the inversion of traditional sex roles, with women as a source of power, organization, and proper sexual initiative and men as deserving punishment for "bad" sexuality.

These and other complex themes are elaborated in the symbolism of the shrine grounds, but not in a manner that is readily available to the conscious introspection of pilgrims. Elsewhere (Wood 1986: 696-791), I have attempted a more thorough exegesis of the semiotic complexities of the shrine grounds, but if pilgrims approach those meanings at all, it is only after the deepening experience of repeated visits.

THE SACRED SPOT

The Sacred Spot is, among other things, a condensation of all the events and realities that make the shrine a place of utmost religious importance to Mary Ann Van Hoof's followers. When questioned about it, most shrine people agree that the Virgin could appear to Mary Ann on any site and that Mary Ann has, in fact, met the Virgin in other places. The Sacred Spot, nevertheless, has a preeminence in the emergent shrine religion, both as the holiest sacrum to those already in the community and as the obtainable goal of the truly devout pilgrim. Among the elements that comprise its significance are its links to the now mythic beginnings of the movement; its cosmic position as a point of contact among the heavenly order, the shrine order, and the outside world; and its internal structure, which images the structure of the shrine community.

To take each of these in turn, the shrine movement began in a series of widely publicized public visions in the spring and summer of 1950. *Life* magazine and *Newsweek*, for example, sent reporters to cover Mary Ann's August 15, 1950, vision, an occasion that drew a crowd estimated between 80,000 and 100,000 people. Mary Ann claimed that her visions had begun in the autumn of 1949 but that the original ones had been inside her house. On the last of these indoor visions, the Virgin had promised that their next meeting would be outside "when the flowers bloom." Later the Virgin appeared in the ash trees as Mary Ann was digging in her garden, and from that point, in the spring of 1950, Mary Ann was able to attract a core of loyal adherents and a rapidly expanding pool of less committed but sympathetic supporters. The Virgin's final appearance in 1950 occurred on October 7, and she left with the promise to return on all the anniversaries of her previous visits and on Trinity Sundays. The Sacred Spot thus became the site of the Virgin's principal rendezvous with Mary Ann, as well as the epochal reminder of the great events and the now unimaginable crowds of the movement's beginnings. Since the mythic paradigm has the original visions occurring indoors and only subsequently moving to the garden and since this movement is reenacted at each Anniversary Day, we should probably also think of the Sacred Spot as standing for the public nature of the apparitions and the Virgin's desire to address a wider audience. Certainly, inside/outside oppositions appear in great number in shrine symbolism.

Second, the Sacred Spot is seen by shrine people as divinely chosen for reasons no ordinary person can really know. Some shrine people are willing to guess. They point out that the shrine is conveniently close to where many people live but still far enough away to be unspoiled. I never met anyone who would offer a more exact explanation why this spot, in this particular copse, was chosen. But if the selection is a mystery, its consequences are not.

At this place, "Celestials" regularly approach a worthy human being, a "future saint." Mary Ann, in turn, has acquired a following of resident shrine people who comprise a community that works to carry out the Celestials' will. In so doing, the community has facilitated the development of a pilgrimage that regularly brings the apparitions and the messages to the attention of the outside world. In this sense, the Sacred Spot becomes a point of articulation among heaven, the shrine, and the world.

Finally, we should observe the way in which the shrine has organized the appurtenances of the Sacred Spot. The Spot is marked as a rectangular section containing a flat marble cross. At its four corners small granite headstones bear the names of individuals who were of special significance to Mary Ann, including her deceased first husband and her first "Spiritual Protector," Henry Swan. Another, larger granite marker sits at the foot of the Sacred Spot with Mary Ann's own name on it. These markers look exactly like gravestones in the nearby shrine cemetery, with each person's name, date of birth, and date of death (except for Mary Ann), but the actual graves are elsewhere. Around these cenotaphs there are several glass-enclosed candles and a collection of potted as well as artificial flowers. To the east of the Sacred Spot stands a structure consisting of two pillars, trellises, and a small arch bearing the name of the shrine and looking like a miniature version of the entrance to the shrine grounds. Directly in front of the Sacred Spot (to its north) is a wooden kneeler that Mary Ann uses during her visions. Behind the Sacred Spot (to its south) in a walled enclave stand the four Sacred Ash Trees. The wall behind these trees opens out on the other side to form a cement kneeler for the pilgrims. Embedded in the center of this kneeler is a small marble cross cut from the same piece of marble that sits on the Sacred Spot. Many pilgrims kiss it. On the opposite side of the Sacred Spot, twenty yards north, lies the excavation for the House of Prayer. In between, a roofed platform is sometimes set up for use by the shrine's clergy and members of the Inner Circle.

This spatial scheme accords with various distinctions within the shrine community between categories with greater and lesser degrees of access to Mary Ann's prophetic knowledge. Pilgrims, perhaps, have a vague idea of the competition within the community and the proliferation of titles that Mary Ann has bestowed on her favorites (Personal Secretary, Protector, Advocate, and Chosen One, for example), but the distinction that is most obvious is the separation of pilgrims who must remain outside the sanctuary of the Sacred Spot and shrine people who can go in.

The Sacred Spot puts the two kinds of followers at appropriate relative distances from the font of prophetic knowledge. Mary Ann kneels directly in front of the Sacred Spot, with her Protector and her Advocate at hand (to protect her from attempts by the Grand Masters to assassinate her). Other members of the Inner Circle sit back on the platform or stand off to one side. The lowest ranks of shrine people are left beyond the wall with the pilgrims, and the overflow of pilgrims watches from a distance on the shrine grounds.

CONCLUSION

The Turners are not alone in considering contemporary Catholic pilgrimage to be a conservative institution, one with a strong, anti-modern tone and one in which the participants are unlikely to see themselves as agents of a radical break from tradition. Shrine people themselves endorse this view.

One of the shrine's most explicit formulations of its purpose is its nostalgic call for "unity between church, school, and family." The efforts to preserve or, in some cases, to reactivate devotional forms that the church has suppressed or abandoned are seen by most of the participants as helping to shore up domestic virtues that have been jeopardized by modern life. Pilgrimage to the shrine is seen and felt to be an affirmation of traditional Catholic values that have been eroded by many forces, the negligence of the church being but one.

The shrine, however, builds on this last dissatisfaction. It offers pilgrims a journey back to symbols and simple pieties they think they remember, but it also adds and alters elements and shifts contexts. The shrine pilgrimage thus becomes an unsettling combination of the familiar, the unfamiliar, and the defamiliarized. The pilgrim is encouraged to wander rather freely in this environment crowded with potent religious symbols. It is a pilgrimage of questions, not answers. The shrine's explanations and Mary Ann's didactic pronouncements are neither thoughtful nor profound, but the experience of visiting the shrine can and does touch a level of deep religious feeling in some pilgrims. The key question that is prompted by this experience is, Why should the church be so opposed to Necedah?

Once they ask this question, pilgrims are well on their way to a closer reconsideration of their role in the church, a reconsideration that leads some into deeper involvement in the perplexities of shrine religion. The Christian formula for pilgrimage seems, in the case of the shrine, to require but very little adjustment to produce an end very different from the reaffirmation of orthodoxy that Turner sees as its principal destiny. This heretical shrine is able to build on the established traditions of pilgrimage to promote religious dissent and disaffection without any obvious departure from the orthodox pattern. Perhaps Necedah is exceptional in this regard, but it may also be useful to consider the degree to which other pilgrimage centers contain (or fail to contain) forces that, left to their own devices as Necedah has been, might have developed into full-fledged heterodoxies.

On the basis of these observations, we might also draw a few other conclusions about North American Catholic pilgrimage. The example of Necedah suggests that Catholic pilgrimage, at least in the United States, draws heavily on a European model but differs from it in a few respects. Just as European shrines often embody relics from the tombs of saints in the Holy Land, many American shrines embody second-order relics that have been taken from European shrines. If medieval European shrines were "proto-national" centers, in Turner's phrase, American shrines are post-national reminders of ethnic origins.[4] Somehow, in its trans-Atlantic movement, the idea of the shrine changed. Pilgrimage devotion slipped in popular acceptance as well as status, and the extant system of shrines and pilgrimages in the

United States subsumed a different set of cultural and religious priorities. The shrine at Necedah speaks most clearly to a New World demand for homegrown saints and miracles, exemplars of a felt authenticity and originality that the legitimate but frankly derivative shrines miscarry. In this sense, Necedah is a Catholic version of the vision of a new Jerusalem that has animated American sects throughout American history.

NOTES

1. Mrs. Van Hoof died in the spring of 1984. The movement founded by her has survived a subsequent reorganization and the shrine continues as a pilgrimage center. This chapter is written in the historical present of 1978-1981.

2. Further information about a few North American shrines can be found in *The New Catholic Encyclopedia* (1967). See, for example, T. J. Grady on the National Shrine of the Immaculate Conception. In the late 1950s and early 1960s, *Our Lady's Digest* published an annual "Summer Guide to Shrines of Our Lady in the United States and Canada," which was an incomplete list of shrines officially recognized by the church, as is the more recent list in the *Catholic Almanac*. The shrine at Necedah has been discussed by Michael Carroll (1985, 1986) and by Thomas Kselman and Steven Avella (1986). A more extensive examination of the points discussed in this chapter appears in Wood (1987).

3. The officially recognized Catholic apparitional shrines are described in John Delaney (1961). Bernard Billet (1973) discusses several Marian visions not, or not yet, recognized by the church, including Necedah. There have been a large number of publications from devotional presses since 1984 that deal with the contemporary apparitions in Medjugore, Yugoslavia, which is fast becoming a major European pilgrimage center.

4. Christian pilgrimage processes seem to articulate with nationalist aspirations and the ideas of regional identity in two quite different ways. As Robert Hertz's study of an annual pilgrimage in the Italian Graian Alps showed (1983), at least in the European context, pilgrimages can evoke and sustain symbolically rich and possibly ancient ideas about a geographical place. On the other hand, as Kselman and Avella's analysis of the Cold War ideology implicated in the Necedah shrine shows, a shrine can also express claims of communal and national identity that have little, if anything, to do with the specific site, other than its inclusion within a vastly larger territory. This latter form of nationalist association seems to be more characteristic of the whole class of Cold War shrines in Europe as well as the United States (see, for example, Christian 1984).

7

Pilgrimages in the Caribbean: A Comparison of Cases from Haiti and Trinidad

STEPHEN D. GLAZIER

In this chapter we see how variant pilgrimage patterns can be, even within a single region. The Baptists of Trinidad have evolved a system of sacred journeying that differs in almost every way from traditions of pilgrimage characteristic of the Catholics of Haiti. Professor Glazier accounts for the differences by relating pilgrimage patterns to broader historical and cultural trends within these two societies. Trinidad and Haiti have known very different secular histories and have very different cultures. That these distinctions have a direct bearing on pilgrimage patterns clearly demonstrates the fact that pilgrimage patterns tend to be strongly influenced by the dominant sociocultural forces playing in an era.

Pilgrimage is conventionally defined as the journey to a sacred place, but there are instances in which travel with no specific destination is still conceived and labeled as a pilgrimage. Thus in addition to journeys to sacred places, pilgrimages can take the form of sacred journeys. In my Caribbean research I encountered both journeys to sacred places and sacred journeys. For the purposes of analysis, I treat these as two ideal types of religious travel: "open pilgrimages" and "closed pilgrimages." A major difference between these two types is that in open pilgrimages the destination is not so important. Individuals of various religious backgrounds participate in open pilgrimages, while closed pilgrimages are largely restricted to members of a particular faith.

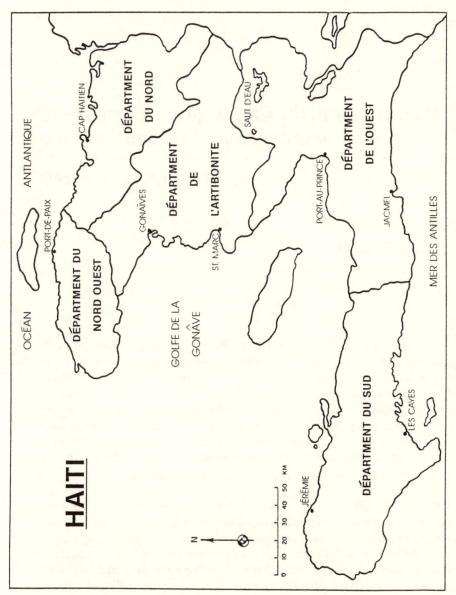

Map of the Republic of Haiti

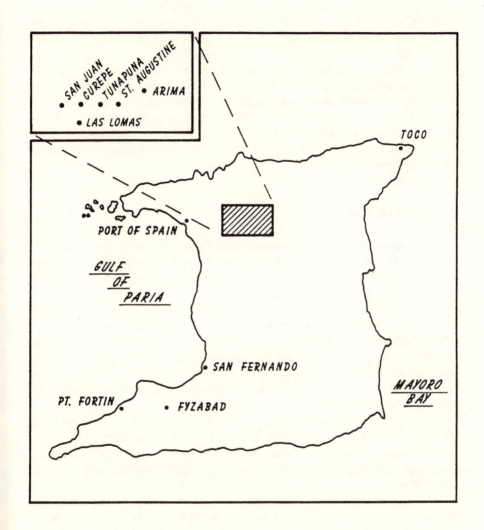

SAN JUAN
CUREPE
TUNAPUNA
ST. AUGUSTINE
● ARIMA
● LAS LOMAS

TOCO

PORT OF SPAIN

GULF
OF
PARIA

SAN FERNANDO

MAYORO
BAY

PT. FORTIN
FYZABAD

Closed pilgrimages—or pilgrimages without fixed destinations—have rarely been discussed in the literature. Such pilgrimages do not conform to most Western conceptions of the institution and they do not fit the structuralist typology developed by Victor and Edith Turner (1978). There is no question, however, that members of the religious groups involved do regard the travel as a type of pilgrimage behavior. Caribbean informants who were well aware of pilgrimage behavior at Mecca, Lourdes, and elsewhere persist in classifying their closed journeys as pilgrimages despite many differences between their own behavior and those behaviors tradition- ally associated with pilgrimages.

I will illustrate and compare open and closed pilgrimages and draw examples from the annual pilgrimages to Saut d'Eau in Haiti and religious journeys sponsored by an Afro-Caribbean cult group, the Spiritual Baptists of Trinidad (see Maps).[1] Differences of pilgrimage type reflect differences between Haiti and the islands of the British West Indies with respect to attitudes toward the land, mobility of the gods, and national sentiments. Of the above, I believe that attitudes toward the land are the most significant.

SAUT D'EAU, HAITI

Pilgrimages to Saut d'Eau are similar to pilgrimages to other religious centers in Europe and South America. The shrine at Saut d'Eau, like most pilgrimage centers, is considered to be a place of hierophany—a center of spiritual energy—and has been described extensively in the literature, beginning with Jean Price-Mars (1928: 168-77), Melville Herskovits (1937: 285-589), and Alfred Metraux (1959: 329-33) and continuing with the more recent contributions of Leslie Desmangles (1975), Michel Laguerre (n.d.; 1989: 82-100), and Harold Desil (1967), an area resident who wrote a thesis on his village for the Haitian Bureau of Ethnography. Pilgrims representing a variety of religious traditions journey to the village throughout the year, but the three major influxes occur on September 24, Holy Week, and July 16, the anniversary of the apparition.

Saut d'Eau has been an important pilgrimage site in Haiti for over 130 years. In 1842 a great earthquake devastated Cap-Haitian, the second-largest city on the island, and also provoked the formation of a majestic waterfall at this site. Prior to this event, Saut d'Eau was a small, unknown district, a part of the rural section of Canot River.

The fall itself is but one of many sacred spots in the vicinity. Among these spots, the most important are a church built in honor of the Virgin and located at the entrance to the town; Nan Palmes, where the Virgin is first said to have appeared in 1848; and St. John's Wood, the site of more recent apparitions of the Virgin and an apparition of John the Baptist. Miracles are associated with all these places. In 1932, for example, a cyclone at Nan Palmes tore down trees and homes but is said not to have harmed worshipers who had gathered at this sacred spot.

At Nan Palmes, St. John's Wood, and Saut d'Eau, pilgrims wash themselves, tie bands around trees, and take soil for use in various medicines. Participants do not differentiate between Christian and *vodun* practices, and many outside observers have noted that it is difficult to see where folk Christianity ends and *vodun* beings (cf. Laguerre 1980). One must first become a Catholic to be allowed to participate in *vodun* rites, and a pilgrimage to Saut d'Eau is a common requirement for initiation into the *vodun* hierarchy.[2]

For the pilgrim, Saut d'Eau is considered to be a place to renew relations with the Virgin and, for many pilgrims, with the *vodun* deities as well. The religion of the pilgrim, as Victor Turner (1974a), Turner and Turner (1978), and Daniel Gross (1971) have noted, is a religion of vows and promises. Pilgrims come to Saut d'Eau with specific goals in mind. They want to make a bargain with the Virgin, the *vodun* gods, or both and expect that the gods will uphold their ends of the bargain. If the gods do not deliver, the pilgrim is not obliged to keep his or her vows. The journey to Saut d'Eau in itself, whether by pirate taxi, bus, or horse, is considered to be a part of the bargain, and many go to Saut d'Eau at tremendous personal sacrifice. Often, an entire family cannot afford to make the journey, and so they send one family member as a representative.

During much of the year Saut d'Eau is a small village of about 1,800 persons who make their living as agriculturalists and petty entrepreneurs. This situation changes considerably during the months preceding pilgrimage. Like other pilgrimages, this pilgrimage seems to create its own economic "field," and a number of area residents obtain direct material benefits by hosting pilgrims. As in other small villages in Haiti, there are no hotels to accommodate the 10,000 to 20,000 pilgrims who annually visit the site, and residents rent rooms to pilgrims at high prices. Enterprising residents also construct temporary shacks to rent to vendors, who are mostly from Port-au-Prince. The church at Saut d'Eau does not keep a shop for pilgrims to buy religious articles. This function is taken over by vendors (*maden sara*), who sell candles, medals, girdles, rosaries, chromolithographs of Catholic saints, candies, and bread, as well as voodoo paraphernalia, to pilgrims. Professional gamblers assemble nightly in the vicinity of the church and wait for pilgrims who have attended novena. As Laguerre (1989: 92) observes, prostitutes from Port-au-Prince do a brisk business as well. It may be, as Shelagh O'Rourke (personal communication) points out, that Port-au-Prince entrepreneurs make most of the money; however, any money that remains in Saut d'Eau is money that would not have been made if Saut d'Eau were not a pilgrimage site.

Annual pilgrimages also give rise to exchange agreements between area residents and residents of the capital. Common exchanges involve children from Saut d'Eau who are sent to live at Port-au-Prince, ostensibly because there are more educational opportunities there. Many of these children, in fact, may end up as household servants. Residents of Saut d'Eau, in turn, guarantee Port-au-Prince residents a place to stay during the annual pilgrimage. These exchanges may continue for many years (as children grow older, they are replaced by younger sons or daughters) and are perceived to be beneficial to both parties.

TRINIDAD

The religious journeys of Trinidad's Spiritual Baptists contrast markedly with the behavior of pilgrims to Saut d'Eau. The most obvious differences are that only fellow Baptists are allowed to participate in these religious journeys (the reason I call them closed pilgrimages) and that Baptist travels involve much more institutional organization. All Baptist pilgrims travel together to the site, and Baptists charter buses for the event months in advance. Baptist pilgrimage sites are much more flexible than are Haitian sites, and sometimes pilgrims buy tickets and get on the bus without knowing beforehand what their destination will be. Since there are no recognized Baptist shrines, buses go to the other Spiritual Baptist churches or, less frequently, to waterfalls or the beach. In all cases there is a degree of uncertainty. Even when one buys a pilgrimage ticket with the destination printed at the top, the destination may be changed without notice.

Baptist pilgrims are not supposed to be concerned about pilgrimage sites. They are concerned not with where they are going but with who organized the trip. In my field experience I found that powerful Baptist leaders have little trouble filling their buses, while less powerful leaders may experience considerable difficulty in filling their buses.

While Baptist pilgrimages provide an important way for one assembly to meet another and "extend the togetherness of the faith in every country or city" (Thomas 1987: 50), they are primarily fund-raising activities. They are used by individual church leaders to pay church debts and to purchase ritual items. Over the past ten years the most common use for pilgrimage profits has been the purchase of amplifiers, loudspeakers, and microphones—items that are quite expensive in Trinidad and serve as a form of conspicuous consumption. Church leaders are judged on the basis of their acquisitions and are expected to build prosperous-looking churches. In addition, successful leaders are expected to sponsor missionary activities to Venezuela, Guyana, New York City, and Toronto—one of the few instances of a Third World religion's sending missionaries to the United States and Canada (Glazier 1988: 75-78).

The church leader who charters the bus is allowed to keep all profits for his church. Host churches, on the other hand, receive few financial benefits from pilgrimages. There is some prestige in being chosen as a pilgrimage site, but most Baptists state that pilgrimages are a nuisance for the hosts, who must prepare their churches and clean them afterward.

Few excuses, if any, are acceptable to decline host duties. Even if two churches are coming on the same day, arrangements are made so that both visiting churches may worship together, or one church comes in the morning, while the other comes in the afternoon. Weddings, baptisms, and other church rites must be rescheduled so as to accommodate sponsoring churches. In some cases even funerals must be rescheduled.

According to Baptist etiquette, there is little a host church can do to avoid becoming a pilgrimage site. Sponsoring churches send a delegate, usually a lower-

Spiritual Baptist pilgrimage

ranking member, to announce the pilgrimage at the host church. These an-
nouncements are made toward the end of services and are followed by a period of
mandatory silence. There is, therefore, no opportunity for churches to decline host
duties. Guests, in effect, invite themselves.

Pilgrimage tickets sell for between four and ten dollars, depending on the distance
to be traveled. Host churches, by and large, are chosen for their inaccessibility to the
sponsoring church. Sponsors seek sites not easily visited by church members, and
their ultimate goal, rarely attained, is to sponsor a pilgrimage to a church that no one
in their congregation has been to before. Distant churches are most desirable as
pilgrimage sites for another reason. Leaders constantly compete with one another
for followers, with the most intense competition between leaders of neighboring
churches. If it can be avoided, leaders would prefer not to allow their followers to
have too much contact with area rivals. Distant churches pose less of a threat in that
regard. In most cases, it would be impractical for members of the sponsoring church
to commute so far for regular worship. Leaders, thus, do not have to be overly
concerned about leaders within the host church "convicting" and/or stealing their
followers.

The degree of advance planning necessary for a successful pilgrimage venture
belies local Trinidadian assertions that Spiritual Baptist leaders are incapable of
rational economic activity, and most pilgrimages make over 100 percent profit for

their sponsors. All aspects of pilgrimage behavior are calculated months before the activity itself takes place. Tickets are professionally printed at least three months in advance, and many leaders will not charter a bus before enough tickets have been presold to break even. Pilgrimages may be canceled at any time prior to departure, and refunds must be specifically requested. Loyal church members are not expected to request a refund in these circumstances; therefore, leaders usually succeed in obtaining enough money to pay printing costs, even when the proposed pilgrimage does not actually take place.

Purchase of pilgrimage tickets is related to other church activities, especially a ritual known as the mourning ceremony, which is believed to determine one's rank in the church hierarchy. The Spiritual Baptist religion is highly stratified. There are twenty-one separate ranks (See Figure 1), and with each rank are associated specific duties and privileges. Most church members are highly motivated to rise in this hierarchy.

Figure 1 Hierarchy of Merit, Mt. Tabor Spiritual Baptist Church

Rank	
10	Judge
9	Inspector
8	Commander
7	Warrior
6	Teacher-Pointer
5	Captain-Prover-Diver
4	Hunter-Mother-Star Gazer-Leader
3	Surveyor-Shepherd-Postman-Watchman
2	Water Fetcher-Carrier
1	Sister-Brother

In the mourning ceremony (cf. Simpson 1970; Henney 1974; Sargant 1974; Ward and Beaubrun 1979; Taylor 1986) individuals receive visions and dreams that earlier researchers suggested reveal one's "true" rank in the faith. In my studies of the religion (Glazier 1980, 1982, 1983, 1985b) I found that visions per se are not important determinants of church rank and that what is most important is interpretation of visions by church leaders. There is no correspondence between a particular vision and a particular church rank, and two individuals, as happened several times during my fieldwork, may claim to have received identical visions in the mourning ceremony but later be assigned very different ranks by church leaders.

Leaders tend to reward their most loyal followers with high rank while less loyal followers are not so rewarded. One mark of loyalty, according to church leaders, is the purchase of pilgrimage tickets. Upwardly mobile Baptists are expected to purchase multiple tickets, and leaders tend to keep track of who has and who has not purchased tickets. Some leaders maintain records of ticket sales going back ten years or more.

Like pilgrims to Saut d'Eau, Baptist pilgrims also feel that they are entering into an unspoken agreement or contract, but instead of an agreement with the gods, they are entering into an agreement with their church leader. While Haitian pilgrims journey to Saut d'Eau for personal reasons (to get a job, obtain a promotion, be cured), Baptist pilgrims are more politically motivated. They participate in pilgrimages so they can rise in the church hierarchy. Purchase of pilgrimage tickets provides the Baptist with an opportunity to demonstrate commitment to his or her church leader.

The Baptists recognize many gods, but their gods are not associated with any particular locations. Baptist gods are incredibly mobile, and it is believed that as long as a leader is powerful, the gods, too, will be present at worship. Baptists say that the journey is the pilgrimage and that wherever they go becomes holy ground. A busload of the faithful is a "moving hierophany."

I do not know of any pilgrimage site in Trinidad that is similar to Saut d'Eau in Haiti; nor am I aware of any such sites on Grenada, Dominica, St. Vincent, or St. Kitts. C. J. M. R. Gullick (1981: 9), in his survey, also reached this conclusion.

The above cannot be explained entirely in terms of Protestant-Catholic differences.[3] It would be very easy to conclude that open pilgrimages are not common in the British West Indies because the islands are officially Protestant, but the issue is much more complex. Many islands of the British West Indies have been strongly influenced by Catholicism. Trinidad is one such island. Trinidad was a Spanish colony for about 300 years; in addition, in the 1700s there was a large influx of French Catholic planters from St. Dominique, Martinique, and Guadalupe. With over 300,000 communicants, the Roman Catholic church is still a dominant religion on the island. The point is that Trinidad Catholics—and Protestants—sometimes participate in open pilgrimages, *but to do so they must leave Trinidad.* In fact, some of my informants in Trinidad have made pilgrimages to Saut d'Eau in Haiti, the Dominican Republic, Europe, Canada, the United States, and Latin America.

DISCUSSION

There is something in the British West Indian historical experience and mind-set that does not make these people receptive to open pilgrimages. Differences between Haiti and Trinidad in this regard may reflect differences in the ways that members of these respective societies conceive of the land. Haitians conceive of the land as an extension of personal identity, while Trinidadians lack such a conception. Haitian land is said to be the home of the ancestors and the *loa* (cf. Murray 1980: 301). It is invested with sacred value.

Only Haitians are permitted to buy land in Haiti, and while this policy may simply reflect the government's desire to avoid possible domination by foreign investors, the policy is favored by the people because the land, or some land, is sacred to them.

Such a concept is not common among residents of the British West Indies. West Indians recognize the existence of sacred ground at Mecca, Lourdes, or Saut d'Eau, but they do not recognize the existence of sacred ground on their own islands.

British West Indian land becomes valuable when outsiders consider it to be valuable; for example, certain parcels of land have value for the production of materials for export, like sugar, asphalt, pitch, or oil. Some land in Trinidad is so valuable that it is sold by the centare (10.76 square feet), but it is valued primarily as a commodity to be exploited. Anyone can buy land in Trinidad, and defacement is not considered to be a religious problem. San Fernando Hill, a former Spiritual Baptist pilgrimage site and long a holy site for South American Indian groups such as the Warao (Wilbert 1977), has literally been chopped away by mining interests. Baptists, however, do not view the destruction of their site on San Fernando Hill in religious terms. As one informant stated, "We was vexed, but we moves on."

Haitians, on the other hand, view the destruction of religious sites in religious terms. No one is permitted to put up a building that might detract from the holy shrine at Saut d'Eau. Haitians also tell of a priest who cut down one of the trees in which the Virgin was said to have appeared. According to legend, the priest died almost immediately thereafter. Later, a U.S. marine is said to have tampered with the Haitian shrine, and he, too, fell ill and died. No one, it is believed, should tamper with holy places.

These notions contrast with my Trinidad experience. In Point Fortin, a Baptist leader willingly relinquished his church's property when speculators thought that there might be oil in the area. The leader boasted about how much money he had been given and bragged that now he could build a bigger church than a rival leader who had not given up his land rights. A Haitian *houngun*, on the other hand, would never give up his congregation's property (Leslie G. Desmangles, personal communication).

While Baptist leaders derive no special power from their association with a particular church or region of Trinidad, *vodun* priests derive much of their power from their association with a particular ceremonial center. Every *vodun* leader is inextricably linked with a specific geographical location, and this association is important even when a *vodun* priest leaves Haiti. Both *vodun* priests and Spiritual Baptist leaders serve congregants outside the Caribbean, especially in New York City, Miami, and Toronto. In the Haitian case, the priest serves as an ambassador for his local (Haitian) congregation. He represents, in descending order of importance, his center, his village, his region, and his nation. In the Baptist case, the leader is not seen as an ambassador for his Trinidad church. When a Spiritual Baptist leader directs ceremonies outside Trinidad, he represents himself. It is even possible, but not likely, that a man could become a highly respected Spiritual Baptist leader in the United States or Canada without ever having set foot in the Caribbean. It should be noted, however, that most Baptist leaders in the United States do make the journey to Trinidad or St. Vincent to participate in mourning ceremonies—not to mourn in the West Indies per se, but to mourn under a particular Baptist leader there.

It has often been the case that British West Indians seek recognition from outside their own region. New York Spiritual Baptists, for example, may not be impressed that their leader has come all the way from Trinidad, but Trinidadian Baptists will be impressed that their leader was recognized in New York City. This attitude may stem from the colonial experience. Colonials were taught that all good things come from the metropole, and it would be interesting in this regard to compare Haitian attitudes with those of the citizens of Martinique or Guadalupe.

Both Trinidadians and Haitians are extremely mobile people. There are almost as many Trinidadians and Haitians living outside their respective countries as there are living in them. Haitians living in New York, however, are much more likely to think themselves Haitians who happen to live elsewhere (even if they have lived in New York for the last twenty years), while Trinidadians living in New York think themselves New Yorkers. They say that they are from Trinidad but not of Trinidad. For Trinidadians, who feel that they must obtain recognition from outside Trinidad, this distinction is important. The late prime minister of Trinidad and Tobago, Dr. Eric Williams, embodied this ideal. He was born in Trinidad but was educated at Oxford and taught at Howard University. He was from Trinidad—that is, he was born there—but he was not of Trinidad—he was recognized in England and the United States. Another illustration of this ideal is provided by the writer V. S. Naipaul, who was born in Trinidad but has lived in London for most of his adult life. Naipaul, too, maintains the distinction between being from Trinidad and being of Trinidad. He cringes each time he is introduced as a "Trinidadian novelist." I doubt that a Haitian-born novelist would so react.

To summarize, I have sought to distinguish two pilgrimage types in the Caribbean: (1) open pilgrimages, such as the annual pilgrimage to Saut d'Eau in Haiti, and (2) closed pilgrimages, such as the journeys sponsored by Trinidad's Spiritual Baptists. Examples of both types may be found throughout the Caribbean region, but on each island a particular type dominates. Seventh-Day Adventists of St. Vincent and Trinidad, for example, sponsor closed pilgrimages, although they do not label them as such. Pentecostals in St. Vincent, Trinidad, and Barbados also sponsor similar religious journeys, as do Shangoists in Grenada. It may be fruitful to follow up on the lead suggested by the Baptists and investigate other church-related trips as if they were full-fledged pilgrimages. If nothing else, researchers should explore the economic importance of such travels for the churches involved. In the Baptist case, pilgrimage was found to be the economic mainstay.

Pilgrimages to Saut d'Eau fit well within Turner's (1972) discussion of ritual topography, while Baptist pilgrimages do not (cf. Turner, 1974a, 1986). When Spiritual Baptists travel toward a pilgrimage site, for example, the route does not become increasingly invested with sacred value. It is not clear in the Baptist case exactly when the "real" pilgrimage takes place. Is it on the journey or at the site?

In the Haitian context participants represent a variety of religious traditions from all over the island, while in Trinidad most participants are Baptists who belong to the same church. In the Haitian context the pilgrimage site is believed to be sacred, while in Trinidad it makes little difference to participants where a pilgrimage is held. Baptists are concerned with the identity of the organizer of a particular pilgrimage rather than its location. In the Haitian context pilgrimages generate their own socioeconomic "fields." Material benefits flow directly to the people of Saut d'Eau as residents provide pilgrims with food and shelter. In Trinidad material benefits flow directly to the Baptist leader who arranged transportation to the site. Few benefits, if any, accrue to hosts in this context.

Differences in Caribbean pilgrimage types may reflect attitudes toward the land, mobility of the gods, and national sentiments. These factors are very much interrelated, but I believe that attitudes toward the land are the key factor. In countries where land is viewed as a commodity, pilgrimage sites may be flexible, and in countries where some land is held to be sacred, there may be considerably less flexibility.

Nationalism is also a factor. In 1844 the Dominican Republic proclaimed independence, and Haitians suddenly found themselves cut off from their traditional shrine, Nuestra Senora de Altagracia del Higuey. Saut d'Eau became important at this time because, as Laguerre (n.d.) points out, Haitians could not bear to be without a national shrine. Trinidadians, on the other hand, do not seem to feel the need for a national shrine. Trinidadians have a national festival—Carnival—but, like their pilgrimages, their festival lacks a center. Carnival is not one fête but many fêtes held at many different locations. If there is a center, it is the reviewing stand where the best bands and costumes are chosen, but the exact location of this stand, as might be expected, changes from year to year.

NOTES

An earlier version of this paper was presented at the conference "Pilgrimage: The Human Quest", held at the University of Pittsburgh, May 14-17, 1981. I wish to thank N. Ross Crumrine, Alan Morinis, William D'Antonio , Vincent Crapanzano, and Seth Leacock for helpful comments and suggestions on earlier drafts.

Participant observation among Trinidad's Spiritual Baptists was conducted during the summers of 1976, 1977, 1978, 1979, 1982, 1986, and 1990. Data on Saut d'Eau are taken from published reports and personal interviews with two anthropologists who conducted fieldwork in the area: Leslie G. Desmangles and Shelagh O'Rourke.

1. Trinidad's Spiritual Baptists are part of an international religious movement with congregations in Tobago, St. Vincent, Grenada, Venezuela, Guyana, and New York City. I estimate that there are about 10,000 members of the religion in Trinidad. Membership is predominantly black and cuts across social and economic lines.

An increasing number of wealthy East Indians and Creoles have become involved in the religion (Glazier 1983: 84-86), and the Spiritual Baptists have become more and more visible in Trinidadian society. They have been featured in newspaper articles; have been the topic of seven senior theses at University of the West Indies over the past eight years; have published their own histories; have been the subject of an internationally acclaimed novel, *The Wine of Astonishment*, by Earl Lovelace; and have been incorporated into popular music: "Socca Baptist" (1980) by Blue Boy (Austin Lyons) and "Bahia Gyal" (1989) by David Rudder. While Blue Boy's treatment of the faith was clearly derisive ("What to them suppose to be spiritual; to me it was just like bacchanal"), Rudder's "Bahia Gyal" cites the Baptists as an example of the pan-African spirit and emphasizes the similarities between Spiritual Baptist "adoption" ("groaning in the spirit") and Somba rhythms in Brazil.

2. Relations between *vodunists* and Roman Catholicism are difficult to sort out. During the sixty years following Haiti's independence, Roman Catholicism had almost no impact on *vodun* (Davis 1988: 36). During this century the church has periodically surfaced as an opponent of "pagan" *vodun*. Desmangles (1979) has argued that while Catholic iconographic elements and votive objects were adopted into *vodun*, it is misleading to describe contemporary *vodun* as a syncretism of African traditions and Catholic ritual. The two religions, he contends, coexist even today in a juxtaposition that has not fused one with the other. A similar pattern has been noted for Afro-American religions and Christianity in Trinidad (Glazier 1985b).

3. Protestant-Catholic differences are no longer clear-cut. Protestantism—especially Pentecostalism—is very strong in Haiti (Conway 1980), but Haitian Protestants also make the journey to Saut d'Eau. See David Martin (1990: 128-33) and Stoll (1990: 113) for a discussion of the increasing influence of Protestantism in Haiti and throughout the Caribbean.

8

Pilgrim Narratives of Jerusalem and the Holy Land: A Study in Ideological Distortion

GLENN BOWMAN

Glenn Bowman's chapter provides a detailed look at how the magnetic image of one of the world's oldest and most important sacred places (Jerusalem) is transmitted through its pilgrimage field. In some cases the transmission is accurate, but much more commonly it depicts a distorted image of the sacred place that fits with the ideological preconceptions of believers and with the pragmatic agendas of the propagators more than with the known facts. In this chapter we can also find a clear illustration of the phenomenon James Preston discusses as the spiritual magnetism of sacred places.

Throughout the Middle Ages Christian pilgrims played a major role in keeping open the way between Europe and the wider world. They traveled by land and sea to visit the holy places of Jerusalem and Palestine and left records of those travels to inform others of what they had seen and to publicize the sacred potency of the Holy Land. Even before 333 A.D., when the anonymous author of the *Itinerarium Burdigalense*—the first extant example of the genre of pilgrim narratives—traveled approximately 3,400 miles overland from western Gaul to Jerusalem,[1] pilgrims were being drawn to the city the emperor Constantine had renamed and developed as the preeminent Christian domain.[2] They went to visit the sites of biblical incidents, with early pilgrims attending nearly exclusively to Old Testament sites and later pilgrims seeking out the proliferating monuments to events directly associated with the lives of Christ and his disciples.[3]

The incentives for the long and dangerous journey to Palestine were manifold and changed considerably from period to period. Prayer and the seeking of salvation were certainly common elements, but relic collecting (by purchase or theft), penance and punishment, trade, and mere curiosity played significant parts in the practice of pilgrimage.[4] Research into pilgrim motives and expectations is, however, fraught with difficulty; the voices of the greater mass of pilgrims have been silenced by time, and those few we hear preserved in the pages of the 496 texts still extant from the period A.D. 333 to A.D. 1500 (Rohricht 1890) are in large part those of a political and clerical elite, which can hardly be seen as representative. The implication that these texts cannot be used as direct sources for reconstructing the moods and expectations with which most pilgrims approached the holiest sites of Christianity should not put off the cultural analyst. Texts about the Holy Land produced by a cultural elite and widely distributed throughout the stations of Christian civilization had a considerable effect on how persons not of those hegemonic groups conceived of the holy places and their significance. I suggest that the various images of Jerusalem and the holy places proffered by these pilgrimage narratives communicated the central values of powerful elites to a wider audience and in so doing helped to constitute a lexicon adopted by the popular imagination.[5] These texts linked the structures through which political power was exercised in the late classical and medieval periods to the sacred landscapes of the Holy Land in a way that lent sacral legitimacy to the apparatus of secular power while simultaneously rendering credible and familiar the mythical domain in which Jesus walked and the prophets preached.

The framework provided here for the investigation of European pilgrim narratives might be productively extended to incorporate different but analogous modes of practice and representation, but I will not attempt a direct comparative link between medieval Christian Jerusalem pilgrimage and pilgrimages operating in other contexts (local and national European pilgrimages) or other cultures (the Islamic *hajj*, Jewish *aliya*, Buddhist *pravrajya*, Hindu *tirtha-yatra* and so on).[6] Jerusalem pilgrimage—especially the Catholic form—is exceptional in being presented and proclaimed through the medium of an extensive genre of first- and second-person pilgrim narratives, and the subject of this investigation is the nature of those narratives, not of the pilgrimage itself.[7]

The Holy Land, viewed through the thousands of pages left to posterity by the real and putative pilgrims of 1,200 years, appears both fantastically protean and strangely fixed. Epiphanius and Arculf, two seventh-century pilgrims, describe the Dead Sea and its environs in radically different ways. What is important in Epiphanius's *The Holy City and the Holy Places* are the biblical referents that can be localized there: "To the South of the cave [of John the Baptist], about two miles away, stands the Wife of Lot, a pillar of salt, who is looking back. To her east is a hole emitting smoke and from the hole comes a voice saying, 'Woe to Sodom.' Rumour has it that this is the chimney of Hades, where the prisoners are" (xii:1-6 in Wilkinson 1977: 121).

Sodom's salt in Arculf's *The Holy Places* belongs to an economy that is distinctly not one of salvation:

> When the waves of the Dead Sea are licked up by big storms, a great deal of salt is brought to the shores around. This is most useful when the sun's heat has made it sufficiently dry, both to the people who live in the neighbourhood, and also to countries a long way off. This salt is different from some which is found on a mountain in Sicily, for if you take some of the rock from that hill and taste it, it is the saltiest salt. This has its own name, "the Salt of the Earth." Thus there are different names for "Salt of the Sea" and "Salt of the Earth." Holy Arculf informed us about this 'Salt of the Earth' which comes from the mountain of Sicily. He spent several days there, and found it really was the saltiest salt, having tasted it by sight, touch and taste. He informed us also about the salt of the Dead Sea, and said that he had tested it in the same three ways (II:xviii in Ibid: 107).

Epiphanius the Monk and Arculf (who was a bishop from Gaul, according to Adomnan, his scribe) were both clerics who traveled to the Holy Land in the same century to see largely the same holy places, but the descriptions provoked in each by the locales differ widely. Epiphanius's discourse on the Dead Sea is informed by a logic of scriptural reference and, ultimately, one of soteriology while that of Arculf seems initially naturalistic and finally mercantile. Yet, as the two pilgrims' descriptions of Bethlehem illustrate, there are, as well, notable continuities. Epiphanius writes:

> To the South of the Holy City is Holy Bethlehem where Christ was born. The church, "The Most Holy Mother of God," is exceedingly large, and below the altar is the Cave (the double one). In the eastern part Christ was born, and on the west is the holy Manger: the two caves are together, and they are decorated with gold and with paintings of what happened. And to the north of the cave is the well which was not dug. And in the water of that well is the Star that journeyed with the Magi (IV.1.1-10 in Wilkinson 1977: 117).

Adomnan, following Arculf, relates:

> In the corner of this city on the extreme east is a natural half-cave. The innermost part of it is called the Lord's Manger, in which the Mother laid her son when he was born. But what is said to have been the actual place of the Lord's Birth is near the Manger, but closer to the entrance. This Bethlehem Cave of the Lord's Manger has been adorned all over its inner surface with precious marble, in honour of the Saviour. Above the stone room, belonging to this half-cave, and the particular place where the Lord is said to have been born, has been built a Church of Saint Mary of generous size. I must mention briefly a Rock outside the wall. Onto it was emptied from over the top of the wall the vessel which contained the water in which the little body of the Lord was first washed. When the water from this holy washing was poured over the wall, it found its way onto a rock below, and into a sort of natural channel. Thus this was filled with water on the day when the Lord was born, and from that day to this, through a period of many centuries, it has remained full of very pure liquid, never less nor more ever since our Lord performed this miracle on the day of his birth. A prophet wrote a verse about this: "Who brought forth water from the rock" [Psalm 78.1.6], and Paul the Apostle too, "But that rock was Christ" [I

Corinthians 10.4] who against nature brought forth from the hardest rock the water to console his thirsty people in the desert. It was the same "power and wisdom of God" [I Corinthians 1.24] which brought forth water from this rock in Bethlehem, and keeps its pool always full of liquid. Our friend Arculf looked at it with his own eyes, and washed his face in it (2.1-3.4 in Wilkinson 1977: 104).

Both men describe not only the dual structure of the cave, half sanctified by the birth and half by the manger, but also the magnificence of the cave's decoration and the greatness of the church built over it. They furthermore both attend to the rupture of the natural order initiated by Christ's coming and signal that rupture with their descriptions of the miracles relating to the well "which was not dug."

The texts of Arculf and Epiphanius, like those of the hundreds of other late classical and medieval pilgrims who narrated their travels to the Holy Land, are made up of two sets of elements. One is a series of excursuses, prompted by things or events experienced during their travels through the holy places, that interject into descriptions of the holy places personal accounts and meditations presenting the particular experiences and reflections of travelers in ways that can seem to the reader to have little, if anything, to do with the Holy Land. The other is the description of the holy sites themselves and the events—and beliefs—the narrators associate with those places. In this mixing of contemporary, often idiosyncratic experiences with the archetypal landscapes of the holy places, pilgrim narratives are similar to the Xhosa *ntsomi* (oral narratives) described by Harold Scheub:

The Xhosa ntsomi is a performing art which has, as its dynamic mainspring, a core-cliche (a song, chant, or saying) which is, during a performance, developed, expanded, detailed and dramatized. Interlocking images and details tie the major expansible images together, along with looser constructions such as transitional images and details. The performer fulfills two essential functions during her performance—one, as a medium, connecting the past to the present by externalizing the core-images of the inherited tradition; and two, as an artist, going beyond the mere communication of core-images, and giving those images a fresh, contemporary and vibrant form (1975: 3-4, 99).

Although the "expansible images" of the pilgrimage narrative tradition (the set pieces describing the holy sites) differ from those of the *ntsomi* by being extra-textual (ostensibly pointing to sites and objects in the empirical world), it is a central contention of this chapter that that "outside world" is itself constructed within the narrative tradition. Thus, throughout the period here being discussed, the texts purport to describe a distant terrain (Palestine and its peripheries) while, in fact, using that terrain only as a pretext for presenting images of the holy places already deeply inscribed in the popular imagination. The verisimilitude of the texts arises not from naturalistic description but from convincing rehearsals of the accepted sites and their biblical referents. Hence it is not all that important that the narrator goes on a journey to the holy places or that the places are described in ways that exactly echo earlier descriptions; what is important is that the narratives associate the holy places with the biblical mythology so central to the Christian cultures of the period.

Thus the Bordeaux Pilgrim writes, "Twenty-eight miles from there [Sychar] on the left of the road to Jerusalem is the village called Bethar, and a mile from there is the place where Jacob slept on his way from Mesopotamia, and the almond tree is there, and he saw a vision, and an angel wrestled with him" (1973: 155). Mandeville, a famous armchair traveler of the fourteenth century, reports that Bethel is a rock located within the confines of the Holy Sepulcher and alludes to it as the place where Jacob was "slepynge whan he saugh the aungeles gon up and doun by a ladder and there an aungel helde Jacon stille and turned his name and cleped him Israel" (1967: 63 [Book XI,ll.18-19, 21-22]). Mandeville's Bethel is also the place where the Jews kept the Ark, where David saw the angel and his bloody sword, where Zacharie was told of the coming of his son John the Baptist, where Mary learned the Psalter and Christ was circumcised, where St. Symeon received Jesus into the Temple, where Christ forgave the woman taken in adultery, and where the rock itself split in two in order to hide Jesus from the Jews who would have stoned him (63 [XI,1.22-XI, 1.3]).[8] The Bordeaux Pilgrim, whose text plays a role in the setting up of Palestine as the Holy Land, accordingly makes an effort both to establish the place as a "mythscape"—a repository of Christian sacrality—and to stress simultaneously that it is part of a real world that he has experienced and others can experience; in the passage cited above not only are the biblical referents pertaining to Bethel invoked but the place is unequivocally located along a road the pilgrim has himself traveled. Mandeville, who writes 1,000 years after the Bordeaux Pilgrim, is not so concerned to emphasize the continuity between the Holy Land and the world of his contemporaries; by 1357 no one in Europe doubts that Palestine is the Holy Land, and it suffices for a writer simply to rehearse a litany of holy events associated with that land to whet the desires of a massive audience to hear more—no matter how fanciful—of that mythscape.[9]

I have mentioned the above divergences and convergences to illustrate both the amazing lability and the constraining framework of pilgrims' representations of the landscape of the Holy Land. The guidebooks and itineraries are not simply referents pointing unobtrusively toward historical incidents and specific locations but are, instead, parts of an elaborate, intertextual discourse in which the journey to the Holy Land serves as an occasion for theology, economics, folklore, politics, and sheer fantasy to converse with one another. I do not deny that some of our writers were actual pilgrims who suffered the arduous journey to Palestine and back before writing or relating their travels.[10] I am, instead, suggesting that before we attempt to link any of the pilgrim writings to an empirical world—that of the medieval Levant—or to the actual practice of Christian pilgrims, we ought to study the tales themselves: how they are organized, what presuppositions underlie their assertions, what they focus on and what they disregard, and to what extent they talk to and of each other rather than of a world outside the *scriptoria*.

The narratives pertaining to the Holy Land are not unlike the lore surrounding the figure of St. Besse, on which Robert Hertz wrote in 1913. Hertz, commenting on the several bodies of mutually contradictory traditions that had grown up around the figure of the mythological saint (one set popular and perpetuated in the Alpine villages, the other clerical and promulgated by the hierophants of the plains cathedral city of Ivrea), wrote:

> [one] popular tradition is no more or less true than the other. From the moment that all the essential elements of the cult find themselves transposed to an ideological level which suits the intelligence and the emotions of the believers, it does not matter that the two legends contradict each other or diverge; they are equally legitimate for the different milieus which accept them. The historical personality of St. Besse seems very problematical and uncertain, since even in the small society of his earliest devotees, two disparate traditions have been able to survive down to our own time. Neither of these tell us anything about the real identity of the hero which they have in common; but both shed a sharp light on the habits of thought and on the psychology of the profoundly different social groups in which they were elaborated (1983: 76, 79).

The lore surrounding the saint, like the traditions encompassing the Holy Land, not only constitutes its own object but does so according to the needs and perceptions of the people who promote it. With this idea in mind, we find ourselves reading texts on the Holy Land not to discover the literal lineaments of that land but to uncover the concerns, both cultural and personal, of those who wrote them and those for whom they wrote them.

Pilgrim texts were written with certain implicit strategies—religious, political, mercantile—to affect certain audiences. In this respect they are like historical writings that reveal the lay of a land not immediately present to their audiences. Haydn White, attacking the idea that historians objectively re-present past occurrences, writes: "historical explanations are for the most part based on the acceptance of certain commonplaces which (the author) shares with certain groups of readers. The "logic" of his discourse is not a logic at all, but simply the rhetorical techniques available to him for exploiting the implications of these commonplaces for explanatory purposes in his discourse" (1978: 23).

Such "commonplaces," which can also be called "ideological elements," reorganize the past or the distant to accord with the structure of what is present. In pilgrim narratives they form a cultural geography that presents as real domains that have their primary existence in ideology. If we, as students of pilgrimage, fail to place the strategies and the rhetorics informing the texts in the social and political contexts that motivate them and, instead, treat the material presented in these texts as empirical data providing "real" evidence of medieval pilgrimage practice, we will find ourselves in the unenviable position of travelers pointing what they believe is a telescope toward their destination and discussing with growing excitement the vibrant colors and strange shapes the kaleidoscope presents to their eyes.

This warning may seem unnecessary; students of these materials are aware the Christian descriptions of Palestine and the Middle East play a bit fast and loose with the facts. C. Raymond Beazley, writing at the turn of the century, noted that "the religious feeling, which drove men from such great distances, closed their senses to much of human life, to most things that lay not exactly in the path of their devotion"

(1897: 12). Donald Howard, in 1980, claims that "the distinction between fact and fiction isn't in this case a strong one. Travel itself is 'imaginative': travels are fictions to the extent that the traveller sees what he wants or expects to see, which is often what he has read" (1980: 10). Even Eucherius, writing to his co-presbyter Faustus in the early fifth century, recognized that a Christian carries a good deal of ideological baggage on voyages to foreign lands. He supplements his collection of Christian observances of Jerusalem and Judaea with a long descriptive quotation taken from the writings of the Jewish historian Josephus, which closes with: "Such is the opinion of Josephus. I decided to introduce him at this point for the sake of this account, so that those who prefer to take pains in seeking the truth may rely on a Jewish account of Jewish geography" (Wilkinson 1977: 55). The recognition that pilgrimage texts distort their subjects should lead, however, to more than just cautious skepticism in scholars trying to reconstruct pilgrim practice or map the contours of the medieval East. These texts are much more than dubious chartings of passages through foreign terrains. They are systematic reformulations of otherness and as such are guides not to the Palestine pilgrimage but to the topography of popular medieval ideology.

We have, in the extant pilgrimage texts, a library of nearly 500 works, which cover, irregularly, the 1,200 years between the beginning of the fourth and the end of the fifteenth centuries. Such a wealth of any genre is exceedingly rare, but the pilgrimage texts are made all the more valuable by having been written to appeal to wide audiences throughout several distinct historical periods (the declining years of the Roman Empire, the long period of collapsing central government and developing feudalism, the late medieval centuries of increasing trade, rapid urbanization and growing nationalism). They are excellent guides to the changing configurations of the beliefs of the European Christian community because they deal with a symbolic landscape central to those beliefs. Pilgrimage narratives, when considered as ideological devices, reveal a dual function. On the one hand, they serve to render the strangeness of the East familiar to a people who know it solely through the symbols and parables of scriptural religion. On the other, they bring the powerful and supportive emotions generated in the minds of their audience by images of sacred places into association with political and ecclesiastical authority structures: "ultimate sacred propositions are periodically reaffirmed and sanctify sentences directly important in the regulation of society. The sacred thus escapes from strictly religious contexts, and sentences concerning economic arrangements, political authorities, and other social conventions may, in fact very likely will, be sanctified" (Rappaport 1973: 409).

PILGRIM NARRATIVE AS TRANSLATION AND APPROPRIATION

Frederick Jameson describes the classic travel narrative as a "process of transformation whereby the object given, the hitherto unexplored landscape—Nature—is worked over until it can be dissolved and assimilated by the older value systems of some more properly European superego—in other words, Culture" (1977: 16).

Pilgrims familiarized the alien territories their texts traversed by constantly "riveting" the landscape of Palestine to the mythical ground of Christian scriptures. Leo Spitzer, analyzing the rhetoric of Egeria's *Travels*, expresses this union of text and place with a learned pun: "The eye of the pilgrim wanders incessantly from the Biblical *locus* [i.e. passage] to the *locus* [locality] in Palestine" (1949: 239). With Egeria the consequence of this mode of vision is that only what can be translated into the familiar language of the Bible is noted and all else is rendered invisible by the narrator: "Since the significance of the places seen by Aetheria, the *id est*, as it were, is alone important, we cannot expect to find nature described for its own sake; formation of terrain interests her only insofar as it can be illuminated by the Scriptures" (244). Even in later texts, where curiosities merit mention for their novelty, the net of Christian interpretation is still used to draw the unfamiliar into the reader's ken. Thus Friar Simon Fitzsimons, a fifteenth-century pilgrim, describes bananas as being "signed with the sign of the crucified, for when they are cut across there appears in them most clearly the image of the crucified as on a cross extended."[11]

Pilgrimage texts are some of our earliest travel narratives, and they, like the later examples discussed by Jameson, make familiar the strange, but Jerusalem and the Holy Land were not an "unexplored landscape" unresistingly assimilable to the "older value systems" of European culture. The monuments of two and a half millennia of eastern culture faced pilgrims who came from lands whose works seemed barbaric in contrast. Yet Palestine, according to Christian interpretation of the Judaic Old and New Testaments, was sacred ground and a legacy from the Son of God to his European worshipers. Figural exegesis demanded that the events in Old Testament history be rendered as no more than prefigurations of events in the life of Christ and the history of the Christian people. This kind of interpretational imperialism lent itself easily to both a textual and a literal usurpation of the Jews' history and holy sites. "Jerusalem was treated as the legitimate spoils of a Christian-Roman victory over the Jews, whose entire heritage—including the Temple—accordingly passed into the hands of the Christians" (Nibley 1971: 1570). Such "imperialism" was not restricted to the properties of the Jews. The Constantinian program of church building was, as John Wilkinson points out, an "abolition of pre-Christian sanctuaries which had been occupying the sites" (1977: 35). After the destruction of Jerusalem by Roman legions in A.D. 135, the site of Christ's Crucifixion and Resurrection was covered with a temple to Venus. Constantine, 200 years later, wished to efface all signs of religious alterity from the city he planned to enshrine as a monument to Christianity:

> He could not consent to see the sacred spot thus buried, through the devices of his adversaries, under every kind of impurity and abandoned to forgetfulness and neglect. As soon, then, as his commands were issued, these engines of deceit were cast down from their proud eminence to the very ground, and the dwelling places of error, with the status and the evil spirits which they represented, were overthrown and utterly destroyed. He gave further orders that the materials of what was thus destroyed, both stone and timber,

should be removed and thrown as far from the spot as possible. Fired with holy ardor, he directed that the ground itself should be dug up to a considerable depth, and the soil which had been polluted by the foul impurities of demon worship transported to a far distant place (Eusebius 1890: 525-526 [III, xxvi, xxvii]).

The Jewish Temple, destroyed by Roman legions under Titus in A.D. 70, was left in ruins throughout the long rule of Christian Rome as proof that God had abandoned the Jews and transferred his allegiance to the Christians and their state. Thus, just as the Old Testament was read by Christians as a Christian text relating "as through a glass darkly" the coming of Christ and the future of Christianity, so, too, the city of Jerusalem was reconfigured when it fell into Christian hands to accord with the image of Jerusalem promoted by Christian religious literature. Alterity was elided.

The Jerusalem of the pilgrims was a new and eminently Christian city. Eusebius, Constantine's biographer and Bishop of Caesarea, wrote in the *Vita Constantini*:

On the very spot which witnessed the Saviour's sufferings, a new Jerusalem was constructed, over against the one so celebrated of old which, since the foul stain of guilt brought upon it by the murder of the Lord, had experienced the last extremity of desolation, the effect of divine judgement upon its impious people. It was opposite this city that the emperor now began to rear a monument to the Saviour's victory over death, with rich and lavish magnificence. And it may be that this was that second and new Jerusalem spoken of in the predictions of the prophets (1890: 529 [III, xxxviii]).

That "New Jerusalem" was nearly celestial, and the putting on of its proper form as a Christian monument was enacted according to a metaphorical logic that castigated all that was not a celebration of Christ as waste and desecration. Arculf, immediately before talking of the disappearance of the Jewish Temple, discusses a rain that cleans the "revolting dung" left by animals off the streets of the city. He calls the rain a "baptism" contrived by the "Eternal Father who will not permit it [Jerusalem] long to remain filthy, but speedily cleanses it in honour of his Only Son, since the holy places of his Holy Cross and Resurrection are contained within the circuit of its walls" (Wilkinson 1977: 95). Such Christian "cleansing" manifested itself as well in textual glee about the disappearance of a Jewish landscape—the early sixth-century Breviarus reads "From there you come to the Temple built by Solomon, but there is nothing left there apart from a single cave" (Wilkinson 1977: 61 [A:6])—and in policies that legitimated the expulsion, and occasional massacre, of Jews who attempted to resettle the city they, too, considered holy.

Arculf further mentions that over the "ruined remains" of the Temple the Saracens had built a mosque (Wilkinson 1977: 95 [I.i]). The Muslim conquest of Palestine and Islamic people's involvement in the Holy Places did not, for various reasons, trouble local Christians, European pilgrims, or Western ecclesiastics until nearly the time of the Crusades. Their hatred of Judaism had devolved largely from an appropriative reading of Scripture and was not, therefore, transferable to a faith not mentioned in the Bible. Furthermore, the Western church had been growing cooler and cooler toward the designs and dogma of the Byzantine government which ruled Palestine until the Muslim conquest of 636 (a coolness that would later be exacerbated by the iconoclastic policies adopted by the Byzantine state in 726). The Muslim invasion ended Byzantine interference in the religious policies of Palestine and gave resident Christians an autonomy they had not previously known by forming them into *millets*—protected religious communities ruled over by the Christian patriarch and responsible only to the Muslim caliphs.[12] Taxes were lower than when under Constantinople, order was better kept and trade was improved. Pilgrimage flourished during the Islamic occupation (A.D. 636-1071): "the Moslem authorities, whether Abbasid, Ikshid, or Fatimid, seldom caused difficulties, but, rather, welcomed the travellers for the wealth that they brought into the province" (Runciman I 1971: 44).

The rift between Eastern and Western Christianities made for strange pairings. By the late eighth century, the continuous pressure Byzantium imposed upon Islam led the Caliph Harun al-Rashid to seek alliance with Charlemagne, king of the Gauls and soon-to-be emperor of the Holy Roman Empire. Charles was given "a nominal and undefined Carolingian protectorate of a spiritual or religious character over Jerusalem and the community of eastern Christians."[13] Despite the insubstantiality of the Carolingian position, it gave the Franks the sense that they, rather than the Byzantines, were the legitimate protectors of, and rightful heirs to, the Holy Places of Palestine (see Runciman 1935). The Western church, rather than being threatened by Islam, received from the non-Christian rulers greater access to, and control of, the sacred sites of Jerusalem and the Holy Land than it had ever enjoyed while Palestine was under the rule of its co-religionists in Constantinople. Consequently, until the closing years of the eleventh century, the vituperative and bellicose language its devotees had directed at the Jews was never used in reference to the Saracens; prior to the time of the Crusades all that surfaced was a low murmur of dissatisfaction with bureaucratic interference and the capitation tax levied on pilgrims.[14]

The rhetoric of appropriation still lay at hand, however, and merely awaited the development of a situation conducive to its displacement onto Islam. The eleventh-century organization of the Catholic Church into the ultimate spiritual and lay authority in the West led to the promotion of the idea of Holy War as warfare fought in support of the church's interests.[15] The concept was field tested against the Norman invaders of southern Italy in 1053 and again, more successfully, against the Muslim occupiers of Spain in 1063. When Turkish incursions into the East blocked the overland pilgrim routes and effectively sealed Palestine to pilgrims, the language of pilgrimage was transformed by papal usage into a language of war. Gregory VII and his successor, Urban II, both fostered the "medieval interpretation of the Crusades [as] a pilgrimage or 'passagium' conducted to the Holy Places beyond the sea for the remission of sins" (Atiya 1962: 17). Gregory called for armed pilgrimages to Jerusalem in a letter to Henry IV in 1074, but he died before he could extend to militant pilgrims his policy of absolving those who died for the Cross (46). Urban at Clermont in 1095 channeled into the paths of Holy War those who wanted to follow that Cross; in the *Anonymi Gesta Francorum et aliorum Hierosolymitanorum* he is quoted as saying "if anyone desired to follow the Lord zealously, with a pure heart and mind, and wished faithfully to bear the cross after Him, he would no longer hesitate to take up the way to the Holy Sepulchre" (quoted in Krey 1921: 28). Robert the Monk, another chronicler of the Clermont speech, in his *Hierosolymitana Expeditio*, quotes the pope's statement of the ends toward which militant pilgrimage was directed:

> Let the Holy Sepulchre of the Lord, our Saviour, which is possessed by unclean nations, especially move you, and likewise the holy places, which are now treated with ignominy and irreverently polluted with filthiness. Let none of your possessions detain you, no solicitude for your family affairs, since this land which you inhabit, shut in on all sides by the sea and surrounded by mountain peaks, is too narrow for your large population; nor does it abound in wealth; and it furnishes scarcely food enough for its cultivators. Hence it is that you murder and devour one another, that you wage war, and that frequently you perish by mutual wounds. Let therefore hatred depart from among you, let your quarrels end, let wars cease, and let all dissensions and controversies slumber. Enter upon the road to the Holy Sepulchre; wrest that land from the wicked race, and subject it to yourselves. That land which, as the Scripture says, "floweth with milk and honey" was given by God into the possession of the children of Israel. Accordingly, undertake this journey for the remission of your sins, with the assurance of the imperishable glory of the kingdom of heaven (quoted in Krey 1921: 31, 32).

Urban's call for a militant pilgrimage was quickly answered by the lords and knights of Western Europe who, cut off from land by its scarcity and by the growing popularity of primogeniture, wanted to carve kingdoms and fiefdoms out of the East (Bloch 1962: 203-08). Their history is one of betrayals and massacres. The pages of William of Tyre's *A History of Deeds Beyond the Sea* are filled with vivid descriptions of the ways the Crusaders took custody of the places they were to guard: "the pilgrims reached the city most carefully and boldly killed the citizens. They penetrated into the most retired and out-of-the-way places and broke open the most private apartments of the foe. At the entrance of each house, as it was taken, the victor hung up his shield and his arms, as a sign to all who approached not to pause there by that place as [it was] already in possession of another" (William of Tyre I 1941: 372).

The liberators of Jerusalem (for that is the city of which William speaks) were even more awesome than was the city itself after its liberation: "It was not alone the spectacle of headless bodies and mutilated limbs strewn in all directions that roused horror in all who looked upon them. Still more dreadful was it to gaze upon the victors themselves, dripping with blood from head to foot, an ominous sight which brought terror to all who met them" (ibid.).

The Crusades, in which the pilgrims' language of appropriation found voice in military action, reveal the ease with which the legitimizing power of the sacred could be extended to cover any sort of behavior. Raymond of Aguilers, after describing "the city filled with corpses and blood" in the *Historia Francorum qui ceperunt*

Jerusalem (c. A.D. 1102), declares: "This day will be famous in all future ages, for it turned our labors and sorrows into joy and exultation; this day, I say, marks the justification of all Christianity, the humiliation of paganism, and the renewal of our faith. 'This is the day which the Lord hath made, let us rejoice and be glad in it,' for on this day the Lord revealed Himself to His people and blessed them" (Krey 1921: 261).

The use of pilgrimage rhetoric for expansionist exhortation was common throughout the following centuries. Mandeville, following form, writes, "If we be the right children of Christ we ought to demand the heritage that our Father left us and do it out of heathen men's hands" (Mandeville 1967: 2). Bertrandon de la Brocquiere (traveled 1432-1433) considered his guidebook to be as much for military expeditions as for religious travelers. He opens with, "I have fairly written out this account of my short travels in order that if any king or Christian prince would wish to make the conquest of Jerusalem and lead thither an army overland they may be acquainted with all the towns, cities, regions, countries, rivers, mountains and passes" (1968: 283).

PILGRIM NARRATIVES AS CHARTERS FOR DOMINANT SOCIAL STRUCTURES

The imperialist logic manifest in pilgrim narratives is not the only aspect of colonization in which the texts partake. They also function as means whereby the Roman church lays claim to the minds of European Christians. Pilgrims were witnesses to the *realia* of Christian history, and that history provided legitimation for a social order in which clerics and kings lorded it over persons whose access to divine power was mediated by church and state (Duby 1980). Pilgrim narratives testified to this witnessing and provided those persons who lacked either the wealth or the patronage to make the journey themselves with vicarious experience of the holy places. Felix Fabri writes of his departure for Palestine, "As I sat on my horse all the brethren flocked round me and eagerly begged me to take careful note of all the holy places I saw and to write an account of them and bring it to them so that they also, in mind if not in body, might enjoy the pleasure of visiting the holy places" (1893: 58).

The pilgrim's devotion to Christ and the places of his ministry provided a model for the dedication of the lower strata to a religion that commanded that they accept their suffering and submission in hopes of future reward.[16] Valerius, in the seventh century, writes of Egeria to his fellow monks at Vierzo: "While she sought healing for her own soul, she gave us an example of following God which is marvellously profitable for many. Here she refused rest, that she might with constancy attain to eternal glory and bear the palm of victory. Here she inflicted material burdens on her earthly body, that she might present herself irreproachable, a lover of heaven, to heaven's Lord" (Wilkinson 1973: 177-78).

Jerusalem and its environs provided a paradigm of salvation to both pilgrims and those whose pilgrimages were at second hand. The Holy Land lay miles and months (even years) to the south and east,[17] but it also lay as a goal in the minds of all Christians. Palestine was sacred ground, and in Jerusalem, its symbolic center, were both the axis of the world and, as Photius wrote in the ninth-century *Amphilochai*, "the source of our immortality" (Wilkinson 1977: 146). Pilgrims oftimes believed that their literal imitation of Christ, effected through walking in his footprints, would carry them along his spiritual path to heaven. Rodulf Glaber in the *History of His Own Time* (A.D. 1044) recounts the story of a man dying in Jerusalem who called out to Christ, "I believe that as I have followed thee in the body in order to reach this place, so my soul, unscathed and joyful, is going to follow thee into Paradise" (Wilkinson 1977: 147). The Holy City provided "contact with the biblical past and with heaven itself, of which Jerusalem was believed to be a physical fragment" (Nibley 1972: 1571). Its continually reiterated presence at the heart of sermons, songs, lore, and all the other ideological vehicles of medieval Europe[18] transformed the real city into a figure of paradise: "In the minds of simple folk the idea of the earthly Jerusalem became so confused with and transfused by that of the Heavenly Jerusalem that the Palestinian city seemed itself a miraculous realm, abounding both in spiritual and in material blessings" (Cohn 1970: 44-45).

The confusion of the literal and the symbolic that compounded Jerusalem in Palestine with the City of Heaven provided emperors, kings, lords, popes, and priests with a means of manipulating the population of the late classical and medieval periods. If the Holy Land was the sacred ground that housed the promises and powers of bestowing salvation, then the persons and institutions providing access to that realm shared in the power and the glory of its divinity. Constantine's exploitation of the Holy Land and its sites as a means of linking the machinations of his policies with the economy of salvation was probably the initial impetus of Jerusalem pilgrimage (Kee 1982; Hunt 1982: 6-49). Charlemagne validated his claim to emperorship of the Holy Roman Empire by becoming lord, protector, and benefactor of the Christian pilgrims in the Holy Land.[19] The Latin kingdoms "Outremer" were wrenched from the hands of the Turks and Muslims for the benefit of adventurer aristocrats by peasants and soldiers driven to fight and die by papal propagation of the fear that their sacred grounds were being closed off and desecrated by infidels.

Royal patronage of Jerusalem and Palestine forged a strong bond in popular imagination between sacred power and secular might. Secular power, while incarnate in historical individuals, can transcend the limits of space and time by affiliating itself with the sacred.[20] The aura of eternality bestowed on the Holy Land by its participation in the sacred history of Christianity was shared in by secular rulers who glorified the holy places and kept the pilgrim roads clear. Constantine, in a complex rhetorical movement of self-effacement that effects an equation of divine and imperial intent, illustrates how his glorification of the site of Christ's entombment in fact enables him to participate in divine grandeur: "I have no greater care than how I may best adorn with a splendid structure that sacred spot, which, under Divine direction, I have disencumbered as it were of the heavy weight of foul idol worship; a spot which has been accounted holy from the beginning in God's judgement, but which now appears holier still" (Eusebius 1890, 528 [III.xxx]).

The churches that Constantine built to commemorate God's victory in Constantine's consolidation of the Christian empire were mentioned so often in pilgrimage narratives that the glory of God and the glory of the archetypal emperor of the Christian lands were entwined throughout the centuries. The "Basilica of Constantine" or the "Church of St. Constantine" was built over the site of Christ's martyrdom, and the title referring to the emperor's name soon ousted the original title, the "Martyrium," which evoked Christ's sacrifice (cf. Wilkinson 1977: 175). Arculf, possibly reflecting the changes in governance that had occurred since the Fall of Rome, refers to it as "the Basilica built with great magnificence by King Constantine" (Wilkinson 1977: 97 [I.6]).

Charlemagne's contributions to the sacred landscape gained him renown as well. Bernard the Monk, writing in A.D. 870, more than half a century after Charlemagne's death, praises the Christian emperor in the first sentences about Jerusalem in *A Journey to the Holy Places and Babylon*: "We reached the holy city of Jerusalem, where we stayed in the hospice of the Most Glorious Emperor Charles. All those who come to Jerusalem for reasons of devotion and who speak the Roman language are given hospitality there. Beside it there is a church in honour of St. Mary, and thanks to the emperor it has a splendid library, and twelve mansions with fields, vineyards, and a garden in the valley of Jehosophat" (Wilkinson 1977: 142).

Two sentences later he refers to the place where Christ's Cross was found (allegedly by Constantine's mother Helena[21]) as the "Basilica of Constantine." The mythology linking secular power with sacred ground proliferates throughout the Middle Ages; folk tradition legitimates the power of the legendary King Arthur by having him go on pilgrimage to Jerusalem (see Runciman 1969b: 77), the Crusade propagandists frequently refer to Charlemagne's pilgrimage to the Holy Land (on which he never went),[22] and Mandeville, in a rather perverse rendition of the ceremony of investiture, has Charlemagne receive the foreskin of Christ from an angel in the Church of the Holy Sepulchre (Mandeville 1967: 61).

In his *Archaeology of Knowledge* Foucault discusses "the origin, that promise of the return, by which we avoid the difference of our present" (quoted in White 1979: 83), with reference to the way talking of original moments and the "being" of humanity constituted in those moments enable the speaker to elide historicity and the ways practices and the passage of time change the character both of humankind and of the world in which it resides. Narratives laying out pilgrimage to Jerusalem proved that the way to the reality of a sacred past was still open to those living in the present and by doing so affirmed that the moral and redemptive order promulgated by contemporary readings of biblical materials were in fact established in that past. This cancelation of history is graphically revealed in narratives about the Holy Land. In a letter to Marcella, Jerome speaks of how "as often as we enter [the Lord's Sepulcher] we see the Saviour in His grave clothes and if we linger we see again the angel sitting at His feet and the napkin folded at His head" (Jerome 1893: 62 [XLVI]) and, in another letter outlining the pilgrimage of an acolyte, Paula, through the holy places, relates:

She declared in my hearing that by the eyes of faith she could see [in Bethlehem's Grotto of the Saviour] the Infant Lord, wrapped in swaddling-clothes, wailing in the Manger, the Magi adoring, the star shining above, the Virgin mother, the careful nursing, the shepherds coming by night that they might see the Word which had been made, and might even then declare the beginning of the Evangelist John, "In the beginning was the Word, and the Word was made flesh" (Jerome 1896:7).

The typical descriptive device of contiguity in these narratives repeatedly unites events of the pilgrims' present with events out of sacred history as though nothing, much less hundreds or thousands of years, stands between the moments. This mythical mode of presentation, in which the past is tied to the present by bonds of eternity, sanctifies those activities and those authorities which in the present reveal and conserve the fonts of the divine past. As long as the church could lay claim to the heritage of the Holy Land and the aristocracy could protect that heritage, they could command the allegiance of those who believed that the promise of their salvation resided in Palestine.

CONCLUSION: THE UNRAVELING OF DISCOURSE

The structures that lent coherence to medieval society and its ideologies were predicated on an agrarian mode of production in which the mass of the population produced crops under the spiritual protection of the clerisy and the physical might of the nobility. The range of experience was restricted, and voyages to the Holy Land—whether literal or vicarious—simply proved that God's hand and his providence ordered and guarded his realms. Pilgrimages were meant to confirm faith and not to provide grounds for curiosity.

In the later Middle Ages, however, acceleration in the circulation of goods, shifts in the pattern of demographic concentrations, and changes in the tenor of social expectations led to a mythology-subverting transformation of social forms and collective representations. The growing influence of the monetary economy of the mercantile towns and the cosmopolitanism of their merchants contributed to the decay of the sense of a limited, static, mythic world. The Crusades, which brought the pilgrims of God into intensive administrative contact with real cultural otherness (and the wealth of the cities of the East), fostered a new perception of travel. The Church, by marketing indulgences and relics, had already shown that the Holy Land had economic, as well as spiritual, value. That perception blossomed as pilgrims and Crusaders discovered that the economies of the East could be made to provide much more than spiritual currency. The intensive production of pilgrimage narratives in the fourteenth and fifteenth centuries (according to Rohricht [1890], there are 93 extant European pilgrim texts from the fourteenth century and 280 from the fifteenth century) was generated by an intense curiosity about the ways of life and the opportunities for trade that lay in the alien worlds outside the cultural boundaries of Europe. Pilgrims like Felix Fabri and Bernard von Breydenbach were fascinated with the peoples and products of the non-Christian East, and their attitudes differed greatly from those of pilgrims like Egeria who prided themselves in having no contact with heathen natives.

A new sensibility based on exchange and heterogeneity begins to inform all aspects of European life in the later medieval period (cf. Holmes 1975; Miskimin 1975; Leff 1976; Hilton 1978), and that change has very visible effects on the literature of pilgrimage. A mythical system that had linked an organic society to its validating origins in the Holy Land fragmented into a multitude of discourses—on trade, other cultures, science, languages, and the exotic. With that fragmentation pilgrimage narrative became just one of a multitude of meditations on the spaces beyond the bounds of Europe and came to serve a much more limited audience than it had in the heyday of medieval pilgrimaging. Jonathan Sumption, rather disparagingly, claims that with the later medieval period, pilgrimage proper was the domain of "poor fools and old women" (Sumption 1975: 123). For others, who would map the world out of which modernity developed, Jerusalem became no more than a way station on the road to locales in which true value lay. Marco Polo, whose *Travels* (first published in 1300) stands as one of the first monuments to modern travel writing, goes to Jerusalem not to sanctify his soul but to satisfy the demands of a non-Christian patron, the Great Khan Kubilai, whose backing offers Marco Polo access to wealth and power. He visits Jerusalem to pick up an item necessary for his trading in the Far East, and his description of the Holy Land is subordinated to the quest for that object:

The Great Khan directed the brothers to bring oil from the lamp that burns above the sepulchre of God in Jerusalem. They went straight to Acre, where they met the legate. They asked his leave to go to Jerusalem to get the oil from the lamp at Christ's sepulchre which the Great Khan had requested. This being granted, they went from Acre to Jerusalem and got the oil. Then, returning to the legate at Jerusalem, they said to him: "Sir, we wish to go back to the Great Khan, because we have delayed too long" (Marco Polo 1958: 36, 38).

Within the economy of Marco Polo, miraculous oil from the Tomb of God is no more than another element in the circuit of exchange that will eventually enable him to return to Venice as a rich man. The *Travels* offers no meditation on what to so many had been the center of the world and the source of all salvation; its hero is too anxious to get to the edge of the known world where real value can be found.

I have argued in this chapter that the visions of pilgrims, as presented in the massive body of their writings, provide a glass through which we can see the transformations of European beliefs and perceptions as clearly, if not more so, than we can see the landscape of Jerusalem and the Holy Land. The terrain that gives shape to these texts is made up of the designs of prelates and politicians, the desires of monks and merchants, and the slow movements of patterns of production and trade. Jerusalem provided the pilgrim writers with a way of talking about Europe, and in their writings we find not so much the historical Holy City as Europe cast in the image of Jerusalem.

NOTES

1. Mileage computed from internal evidence in the *Itinerarium Burdigalense* (Bordeaux Pilgrim 1896).

2. Hadrian had renamed Jerusalem Aelia Capitolina in A.D. 135 after suppressing the Jewish uprising led by Bar Kochba and destroying the city. It was known by that name until A.D. 325, when Constantine renamed it Jerusalem and made it the showpiece of a "grand policy of church building in the eastern part of the empire" (Wilkinson 1973: 10). Wilkinson claims that pilgrims began to come to Palestine after Constantine had built up the Holy Land and that earlier travelers, like Melito of Sardis (A.D. 160) and Alexander of Cappadocia (A.D. 216) (see Eusebius 1965: IV.26, p. 188, VI.11, p. 250), were naturally interpreted as pilgrims after pilgrimage became the model (Wilkinson 1973: 10).

3. *Egeria's Travels*, an incomplete pilgrim narrative dated between 381 and 384 opens with the phrase—repeated throughout the text—"biblical sites were pointed out" (Wilkinson 1973: 91). Spitzer demonstrates that an exclusive focus on the scriptural facets of the Holy Land characterizes Egeria's text (Spitzer 1949) and this core concern with biblical sites continues to inform pilgrimage texts throughout the ages. The terrain itself, however, shifts both in the places attended to and their references. Beazley asserts with regard to early pilgrim narratives that "most of the legendary sites are connected with Jewish history and the Temple rather than with the life of Christ and the Holy Sepulchre" (Beazley 1897: 58). Nonetheless, the will of pilgrims and local residents (often foreign priests and monks who settled in the area) to provide concrete "witness" to every biblical episode and character led to the "invention" of an extensive landscape that, more and more, included sites associated with New Testament passages. Writing of sites presented on fourth-century itineraries, Wilkinson asserts that "almost three-quarters of these sites were arbitrarily selected to become the foci of pilgrimage" (1977: 38); by 1187 the Crusaders had added another twenty-nine biblical sites to the fourth-century maps, of which "twenty-five were probably fanciful" (39), as well as another five that were attached to extra-biblical stories, such as those about the place in Bethlehem where the trees bow down at Christmas and the rock on which Christ wrote "Our Father" (ibid.).

4. Sumption's *Pilgrimage: An Image of Medieval Religion* (1975) is a rich, if somewhat unstructured, collation of primary and secondary data on the several forms of medieval pilgrimage. Readers will benefit from reading it with reference to the more schematic *Pilgrimage Yesterday and Today: Why? Where? How?* by J. G. Davies (1988). F. E. Peters's *Jerusalem: The Holy City in the Eyes of Chroniclers, Visitors, Pilgrims and Prophets from the Days of Abraham to the Beginnings of Modern Times* (1985) collects a wide range of writings on Jerusalem to give a strong sense of the textuality of the site. Peter Walker's *Holy City, Holy Places: Christian Attitudes to Jerusalem and the Holy Land in the Fourth Century* (1990) inquires into the origins of Christianity's particular approaches to the holy city. My "The Mirror of God: The Image of the Holy Land in the Pilgrimages of the Various Christianities" (Bowman 1991) approaches the interaction of pilgrims' expectations from the city and the practice of their pilgrimages. Peters's *Jerusalem and Mecca: The Typology of the Holy City in the Near East* (1986) gives a strong sense of how the city is organized on the ground to respond to the expectations of visitors, as does I. W. J. Hopkins's *Jerusalem: A*

Study in Urban Geography (1970). Relic collecting is discussed in Patrick Geary's *Furta Sacra: Thefts of Relics in the Central Middle Ages* (1978) and in Marie Gauthier's *Highways of the Faith: Relics and Reliquaries from Jerusalem to Compostella* (1983). Collecting gained immense impetus from the demand by the second Council of Nicea in A.D. 787 that all consecrated churches have relics. U. Berliere (1890), E. van Cauwenberghe (1922), and C. Vogel (1963) are standard texts on the development of penitential pilgrimage. Trade and pilgrimage have not to date received due academic attention. Trade (by several other names) was important, however; Bishop Willibald came close to being detected smuggling balsam while returning from Jerusalem to Constantinople. His biographer, a monk named Hugeburc, compounds what we would see as separate discourses when claiming, "If they had found anything they would at once have punished and made martyrs of them" (Willibald 1895: 28). Edith and Victor Turner suggest that pilgrimages played a generative role in the development of modern trade; they write that pilgrimages "may very well have helped to create the communications networks that later made mercantile and industrial capitalism a viable national and international system" (Turner and Turner 1978: 232; cf. Turner 1974a: 188). Giles Constable (1976) and Christian Zacher (1976) rehearse the long-running debate between those who argued that pilgrimage was spiritually beneficial and those who contended it was a futile exercise in curiosity.

5. See Antonio Gramsci (1971; especially 3-43) on the links between culture and the aspirations of a social class or group to rule an entire society, as well as Louis Althusser's discussion of "ideological state apparatuses", "repressive state apparatuses", and the role of the church in the maintenance of state power in the Middle Ages (Althusser 1971: 143-49, 165-70).

6. There have been numerous studies of the world's pilgrimages, but most have operated from descriptive rather than analytical bases. Recent anthropological exceptions are William Christian (1972), Alan Morinis (1984), and John Eade and Michael Sallnow (1991). Morinis offers a critical summary of sociological theories of pilgrimage (11-30; 321-65). Although Dean MacCannell's *The Tourist: A New Theory of the Leisure Class* (1976) focuses on the development and significance of tourism, his theory of "siting" is of use to the anthropology of pilgrimage.

7. Elite traditions that use pilgrimage as a means of legitimating the rule of their representatives will, of course, mention pilgrimages in their pronouncements—thus, the advocacy of Buddhist pilgrimage in the *Edicts of Asoka*, Muhammad's declaration of the *hajj* as the Fifth Pillar of Islam, the Deuteronomic insistence on the *aliya*, and so on. Bodies of texts relating travels of pilgrims to and through holy places are rare. Aziz Atiya (1962: 47) notes with some bewilderment that there are no records of pilgrimages from Byzantium to the Holy Land, although there certainly were Byzantine pilgrims. Islamic travelers pass through the holy cities of the faith, but only as sights on a larger tour; the travelers' writings are not pilgrim narratives. The Chinese missionary Huen-Tsiang left a popular record (translated into folk tradition as *Monkey*) of his seventh-century journey to Buddhist holy places in India, but the work seems more a legitimation of his role as missionary to the Chinese than a pilgrim narrative. Judaic itineraries and pilgrim narratives began with the record of the *aliya* of the ninth-century Rabbi Ahimraz the Elder of Venose (Italy), but such pilgrimages were, because of Christian anti-Semitism, infrequent until after 1187, when Saladin reopened Palestine to the Jews (see Peters 1986: 137, 144, 224 on Christian maintenance of Hadrian's second-century ban on the presence of Jews in Jerusalem). Jewish pilgrimage narratives did not spring up with pilgrimages as did the Christian texts, and this fact leads one to believe that they may have evolved under the influence of the Christian tradition.

8. John Wilkinson, in the gazeteer of his *Jerusalem Pilgrims*, notes that the village of Bethel disappeared from maps after 600 and that subsequently the name floated from place to place. It was attributed to a village near Bethlehem in 1106, to another near Sechem in 1130, and, as we have seen, to a rock within the walls of the *Holy of Holies* itself in 1357 (Wilkinson 1977: 151).

9. M. C. Seymour, editor of the 1967 edition of *Mandeville's Travels*, writes:

The book was immediately successful. Approximately 250 manuscripts survive to attest to its tremendous popularity. Within a hundred years it had been translated, often many times, into Latin, English, High and Low German, Danish, Czech, Italian, Spanish, and even Irish: it had been abridged and epitomized for widely differing audiences, and even turned into an English metrical romance; and in almost every part of Europe successive editions began to appear as soon as printing presses were set up (Seymour 1967: xiii).

10. The shadows of other narratives that frequently fall over individual pilgrims' texts suggest that many or most pilgrims knew the writings of their fellow travelers before they set out or set down their own. Fabri, after returning from his first pilgrimage and before embarking on his second, applied himself to reading the writings of other pilgrims: "I read with care everything on this subject which came into my hands; moreover I collected all the stories of the pilgrimage of the crusaders, the tracts written by pilgrims and descriptions of the Holy Land, and read them with care; and the more I read the more my trouble increased, because by reading the accounts of others I learned how imperfect, superficial, irregular and confused my own pilgrimage had been" (Fabri 1893: 50). Mandeville immersed himself so well in the sea of narrative that he never felt the necessity of gaining experience in any literal sea. Seymour writes that *"Mandeville's Travels* is a compilation at second-hand of other men's travels and contains a sufficient number of inaccuracies and inconsistencies to make it extremely improbable that its author ever left his native Europe" (Seymour 1967: xiv). Nonetheless, we can assume that most pilgrimage narrators actually did make the journey. Henry Savage (1977) and E. D. Hunt (1982: especially 50-82) extrapolate from pilgrim narratives to offer detailed descriptions of the pilgrimage journey itself.

11. Fitzsimons 1948: 22; see also Edwin Ardener (1989: 145) on the description of coconuts in John Lowes's *Road to Xanadu* (Lowes 1927: 314).

12. See John Joseph, *Muslim Christian Relations and Inter-Christian Rivalries in the Middle East* (1983); Steven Runciman, *The Historic Role of the Christian Arabs of Palestine* (1969a); and Kamel Abu-Jaber, "The Millet System in the Nineteenth Century Ottoman Empire" (1967). Amnon Cohen critically examines the category of the *millet* in *Jewish Life Under Islam* (1984).

13. Atiya 1962: 37; see also Wilkinson 1977: 11-12 on the myths and realities of Charlemagne's relations with Jerusalem and its Muslim rulers.

14. Willibald's *Hodoeporicon* (1895) provides illustrations of some of the problems that could beset a Christian pilgrim traveling in the mid-eighth century. Bernard the Monk's late ninth-century narrative (Wilkinson 1977: 141-45) is filled with details of the expenses entailed and difficulties encountered when traveling under Muslim rule.

15. For the eleventh-century development of the church, see Sir Richard Southern (1970: 34-44). On holy war, see Runciman (1971, Vol. 1: 83-105).

16. See here Max Weber's model of the relations between the religious conceptions of elite and underprivileged groups (1978).

17. See Wilkinson (1977: 19) for the times spent in travel by various pilgrims.

18. Burchard of Mount Sion writes in his *Itinerary* of 1280 that all men should wish to free the Holy Land from the Saracens "for what hour is there of the day or night all the year round wherein every devout Christian doth not by singing, reading, chanting, preaching and meditating, read what hath been done or written in this land and in its cities and holy places" (1895-1896: 4).

19. "It was the prestige of ruling Jerusalem that warranted the change in Charlemagne's title from king to emperor" (Nibley 1972: 1576). See also Atiya (1962: 37).

20. The state already has a transcendent quality similar to that of religion. Balandier, following Marx, writes that "state power and religious power are similar in their essence due to the fact that the state is situated (or appears to be) beyond real life, in a sphere whose distance is reminiscent of that of God or the gods. It triumphs over civil society in the same way as religion conquers the profane world" (Balandier 1970: 100). Meyer Fortes and E. Evans-Pritchard suggest that the linking of religious symbols with the structure of the state imbues the machinery of secular power with sacred force: "Sacred symbols, which reflect the social system, endow it with mystical values which evoke acceptance of the social order that goes far beyond the obedience exacted by the secular sanction of force. The social system is, as it were, removed to a mystical plane where it figures as a system of sacred values beyond criticism or revision" (1940: 17-18; cf. Rappaport 1973). Ernst Kantorowicz suggests that the ruler, by associating himself with such sacred symbols, endows himself with their power and perpetuity: the nimbus of the emperor "indicated the bearer and executive of perpetual power derived from God and made the Emperor the incarnation of some kind of 'prototype' which, being immortal, was *sanctus*, regardless of the personal character, or even the sex, of its constituent" (1957: 80). Sabine MacCormack discusses the late classical ceremony of "Adventus" in which direct links were forged by religious symbols between emperors and divinities (MacCormack 1972).

21. The legend of the emperor's mother's discovery of the three crosses is both ancient and tenacious. It did not, however, appear until sixty years after her death (cf. Hunt 1982: 28; Wilkinson 1977: 175) and is not mentioned in Eusebius's detailed description of the Holy Sepulchre and its site (*Life of Contantine* III.xxxviii [Eusebius 1890]). Wilkinson suggests the story originated in "an attempt to account for the existence of the relics purporting to be the Wood of the Cross in terms of events which took place in the already well-known buildings erected by Constantine" (Wilkinson 1977: 175).

22. See Norman Cohn (1970: 71-73), Wilkinson (1977: 12), and Runciman (1969b: 77). Propagandists couched the Crusades in a terminology so suited to contemporary social structures that the Crusades appear as "the complete feudalization of Christianity by an ancient chivalric tradition, with Jesus as a liege lord whose injuries must be avenged and whose stronghold must be liberated" (Nibley 1972: 1572).

9

Pilgrimage and Its Influence
on West African Islam

JAMES STEEL THAYER

This chapter is a case study that focuses on one of the functions of pilgrimage. In fact, pilgrimage has the capacity to perform many functions simultaneously. It can satisfy a personal, spiritual longing or a practical need, while at the same time enhancing social integration or serving as a stage for cultural diffusion. This chapter clearly documents the powerful impact the pilgrimage to Mecca has had on society and culture in one of the farther-flung regions of the Muslim world—West Africa. From the twelfth century to the recent past, pilgrims to Mecca were the main conduit through which the trends and influences playing at the center of the Muslim world reached this periphery. Although the role played by pilgrims and pilgrimage varied in different eras, the reader can see how effective the institution of pilgrimage has been in shaping significant aspects of the Muslim universe. It is a short step to extrapolate to more general conclusions, because what Professor Thayer documents in detail about West African Islam is, in one form or another, true for all places where pilgrimage is accorded a significant role in the culture. Sacred places are revered; the knowledge, both spiritual or theological and mundane or practical, gained there is highly valued. The returned pilgrim bears with him the traces of the most treasured ideals of his society. The ideas and influence he delivers to his local social group bear the stamp of divine legitimacy. It is no wonder pilgrimage has been so commonly a source of social and cultural change (and reinforcement) and has been so vigorously opposed by powers whose interests it would not serve. Sacred places—peripheral, otherworldly, remote—are anything but irrelevant to the main currents of social life flowing through the bazaars and government houses in the midst of worldly empires.

Islam is a religion that encourages and even requires certain forms of wandering or travel. The best known is the *hajj*, the pilgrimage to Mecca that takes place every year and is required of every Muslim once in his life if he is financially and physically capable of it.

The Islamic pilgrimage is a religious practice central to Islam but has its origin in pre-Islamic Arabia. The city of Mecca and its environs (especially the plain of 'Arafat) had served as the sites of shrines and pilgrimage long before the lifetime of Muhammad the Prophet (c.A.D. 570-632). During the traditional month of pilgrimage in pre-Islamic times, many different tribal groups came from all over the Arabian peninsula to participate in religious rituals in the western part of the peninsula (called the Hijaz). This assemblage was possible only if these warlike and often feuding tribes could come and go in peace, so the month of pilgrimage (along with the months preceding and following it) was a month of peace. Warring, feuding, and violence were proscribed during this time, and no weapons could be carried in the pilgrimage territory. In addition to the religious activities of the Hijaz, large fairs were associated with the pilgrimages, and merchants from all over the peninsula assembled to sell their wares to the pilgrims in Mecca.

The pilgrimage was continued in an altered state under the leadership of Muhammad. Muhammad himself, after the submission of Mecca to his rule and to the religion of Islam (A.D. 628), purified the Meccan shrines of their pagan elements and consecrated the sites to Allah, the one true God of Islam. Many of the ancient customs were banned, and other pre-Islamic rituals and peregrinations were given new Islamic interpretations. For example, the *Ka'ba* was now interpreted as the structure built by Abraham. The Prophet led the pilgrimage several times, thus publicly instituting and validating the rituals of the Islamic pilgrimage for all time. The genius of the institution of the *hajj* can be seen not only in the fact that it occurs at a specific time every year but also in the fact that the ritual actions of the pilgrims, from the donning of the pilgrim robes to the final circumambulations of the *Ka'ba*, are carefully laid down and specified from the life of the founder himself. This exactness provides a rich sense of historical continuity and a concrete expression of the unity of Muslims the world over.

The *hajj* is one of the so-called five pillars of Islam (the others being the confession of faith, fasting during the month of Ramadan, prayer, and alms-giving). The *hajj*, because of the personal sacrifice and traditional difficulty involved in making the journey, has always been regarded as an honor and the high point in the life of any Muslim who succeeds in this venture. Any Muslim who has made the *hajj* has the right to bear the title *hajji* (pilgrim). In many parts of the Muslim world, the departure to, and return from, the pilgrimage are marked by special services and celebrations by the pilgrim's family and community.

One aspect of the importance of the *hajj* is reflected in the numbers of people who participate. Before the modern era of widespread air travel, the numbers of pilgrims were usually in the tens of thousands. Besides the arduous and often lengthy journey to Mecca, epidemics among the pilgrims often reduced their number and discouraged others from undertaking the *hajj*. Today, however, with better conditions and organization, over a million Muslims travel every year to Saudi Arabia to participate in the annual pilgrimage.

The spiritual and intellectual impact of the *hajj* is realized in different ways. Through participation in the pilgrimage rituals, the pilgrim increases his piety or devotion to God and his fidelity to the teachings and practices of Islam. Further, by coming into contact with Muslims from all over the world, his sense of participation in, and belonging to, the *'ummah* (community of the faithful) is increased and strengthened. In some cases the pilgrim may be fired with zeal to preach Islam in his native country, which might be noted for the imperfection of the practice of Islam or the half-hearted commitment of the believers.

The thesis of this chapter deals with the impact of the *hajj* for the Muslims who made the pilgrimage to Mecca from West Africa. Islam was brought to West Africa by means of the Arab and Berber traders who came south across the Sahara Desert from North Africa. The new religion became the cult of the royal and noble classes, and from the twelfth century onward there are records of Muslims (both rich nobles and their Muslim *'ulama*, scholars) making the pilgrimage to Mecca. Except for these pilgrims, there was almost no contact between the great centers of Islam in Egypt, Arabia, and the Middle East with the territories of the Western Sudan, separated as they were by that sea of sand, the Sahara Desert, a desert approximately the size of the continental United States. These pilgrims served throughout history as the vehicles for communicating the ethos and teachings of the Arabian and North African theological, spiritual, and reform movements. Because of their prestige as pilgrims and their strong relationship to the secular powers, these pilgrims were in a position to institute religious reforms in West African societies on their return from the *hajj*. With the loss of political cohesion in the savannah area after 1591, the relationship of the pilgrim to the general society was altered. The function of pilgrims was altered once again during the era of the *jihads*[1] (1700-1885) and the colonial era. A further, significant change in the role of the pilgrim has occurred during the modern, post-colonial era. In other words, the pilgrimage and the pilgrim have served different functions for West African Islam over time, and this chapter investigates these different functions and the reasons for them.

Because of the time depth involved, this chapter is necessarily historical in nature. To many people it still comes as something of a surprise to learn that the history of many peoples in sub-Saharan Africa can be traced to the tenth or eleventh centuries. Arab historians took a lively interest in West Africa, and the writings of al-Bakri, ibn Battuta, and others provide a rich and informative narrative. In time, some African Muslims became fluent in Arabic, and their writings, such as those of the schools at Timbuktu or of the *jihadist* Uthman dan Fodio, provide insights into the nature of Islam throughout the centuries. My own field research among the Susu people of Sierra Leone and Guinea focused on problems of religion and social organization, but the recent increase in the number of people making the pilgrimage to Mecca drew my attention to the whole subject of the pilgrimage, particularly to its forms and influence in West Africa.

The interest in pilgrimage as a theoretical problem has been increasing in recent times. Victor Turner (1979) and others (Geertz 1968; Eickelman and Piscatori 1990) have greatly expanded our understanding of pilgrimage, particularly with regard to its symbolic dimensions and the ways in which its rituals and symbols affect and transform the pilgrim. While fully appreciating the contributions of writers like Turner, I have a somewhat different emphasis. In researching this chapter, I saw clearly that, beyond whatever effects the pilgrimage may have had on individuals, it had far-reaching consequences for the Muslim societies of West Africa. Inasmuch as pilgrims came into prolonged contact with Arabic society in Egypt and Arabia, they were influenced sufficiently by developments in Arabian Islamic society, thought, or spirituality that many of them sought to reform West African Islam to make it conform more closely to the Arabian model. The pilgrimage, then, served primarily a didactic or reformative function within the context of West African Islam, and the reader is invited to compare and contrast the evidence and conclusions of this chapter with other ethnographic or historical examples of pilgrimage, either within Islam or within other religious traditions.

West Africa, unlike North Africa or East Africa, is isolated from the Middle East. There was an unbroken line of conquest that united Arabia with North Africa, from Egypt to Morocco and up into Spain. Even with initial difficulties from the fickle Berbers and political differences with the indigenous peoples (Cooley 1972: Chapters 1, 2), Islam took root among these people as Christianity, apparently, never did. More significantly, there was a slow "arabization" of the peoples and cultures of North Africa. Not only did many of the native peoples adopt Arabic as their native language (including the Moors—who speak the Hassani dialect of Arabic—as far west and south as Mauritania), but some Arab tribes contributed to this cultural transformation by actual immigration into North Africa and the Sahara—Arab tribes migrated as far south as southern Chad,[2] and parts of Algeria, Tunis, Libya, Morocco, and the northern part of the present-day Republic of the Sudan have substantial populations of Arabs.

In East Africa, the situation was slightly different. Because of the existence of Christian Nubian kingdoms until the fourteenth century, the expansion of Islam southward (overland) from Egypt was blocked (Trimingham 1964: 37). The Arabs, however, had a navy and a sizable merchant marine fleet, and exploration, trade, and settlement soon began to take place from Somalia all the way south to Tanzania and Madagascar. For various reasons, Islam did not spread inland but remained the religion of the coastal peoples. Arab and Persian traders plied their trade up and down the coast. Occasionally traders would settle and marry native women and live the rest of their lives in one of these trading ports (this hybrid race along the coast was called in the local dialect *Swahili*, coastal dwellers), but they were in no sense cut off from Arabia and Persia. Ships traveled to and fro constantly, and even when these Afro-Arab settlements coalesced into city-states in the eighteenth and nineteenth centuries, just as often as not they requested their rulers to come from Arabia or Persia (Trimingham 1964: 52).

In any study of the spread of Islam, the influence of traders as missionaries of Islam is crucial, from the earliest days up to the present. Any number of well-known authors (Trimingham 1962 and 1964; Kaba 1974; Levtzion 1980) have pointed out the influence that Muslim traders have had in the spread of Islam throughout West Africa, principally through the influence they exerted on (and often through alliances subsequently formed with) the local ruling houses. With regard to this chapter, it is clear that pilgrimage would hardly have been possible without the routes and caravans of traders. My contention, however, is that, during much of the history of Islam in West Africa, the pilgrims themselves, by virtue of their royal or religious status, transmitted from Egypt and Arabia much of the thought, spirituality, or spirit of reform that they learned during their travels or their stay in the Middle East. While traders may have been the carriers of popular Islam, these pilgrims—kings or nobles or religious savants—were often those who were strongly impressed by the example or reforms of Islam in its "pure" form, that is, as found among Muslims in the Holy Places. Further, because of the pilgrims' high social status, they were able to bring about changes in Islamic belief and practice in their homelands in ways that traders never could.

The history of Islam in West Africa is entirely different from that in other parts of Africa because of the great sea of sand that separates North Africa from the Sudan.[3] The Sahara is one of the world's largest and most awesome deserts. Even with pack animals like camels, well-adapted to the climate, it has been estimated that the trip from northern Nigeria to the nearest seaport on the Mediterranean took from seventy to ninety days (Boahen 1963: 356), and this estimate assumes that there were no calamities such as sickness among the animals or humans. There has always been a high mortality rate among those who travel the Sahara. For Africans, the great fluctuations in temperature between the heat of the day and the cold of the night often brought on fever or cough. Also, the unpredictable and fierce sandstorms of the Sahara have literally buried caravans. Besides these dangers, many people and even whole caravans perished because well-known water holes and oases dried up periodically and unpredictably (Boahen 1963: 354-55).

In spite of these hazards and hardships, trade between North Africa and West Africa has been going on at least since 1000 B.C. (Boahen 1963: 350-51). With the introduction of the camel into the region around the beginning of the Christian era, trade to and from North Africa increased steadily, reaching its height from the eleventh to the sixteenth centuries (Boahen 1963: 349-50). Gold, ivory, slaves, salt, dyes, and kola nuts were taken from the Sudan. Indeed, by the fourteenth century ibn Khaldun reports that in one caravan 12,000 camels went forth from Cairo and were bound for the kingdom of Mali in West Africa (Trimingham 1962: 72).

In the latter part of the seventh century of the Christian era, the Arab Muslims had brought all of the Maghrib under their domination. Within a short time Arab and Berber Muslims also took over the caravan trade from the Maghrib to the Sudan. Because the traders were few in number, they did not effect much in the way of islamization of the Sudanese. In 1076, however, the Muslim Almoravids of Morocco subdued the kingdom of Ghana (not to be confused with the present state of Ghana, but rather a kingdom in the Senegal-Mauritania region). Two things are noteworthy of this conquest. The first is that when the Almoravids arrived in the capital of Ghana, they found that Islam was already present there as the religion of the traders (Trimingham 1962: 27-28, also 31, 53). In fact, reserved for the Muslims was a quarter of the city, complete with mosque, *madrasa* (school), and *imams* (prayer leaders). The second fact is that the royal family of Ghana, along with some of the nobles, accepted Islam at the time of the conquest. In Ghana and in succeeding empires members of the ruling class came to embrace Islam as their own religion (although, in their official capacity, they often had to perform other non-Islamic rites, such as rites of veneration for the royal ancestors), but Islam did not become the religion of the masses. Specialists were trained who ran the schools and observed the Islamic rituals, but besides this "clerical" class and the nobility, Islam did not make much of an impact on the religious beliefs or practices of the masses (Works 1976: 6).

This elitist character of West African Islam continued into the following centuries, and the pattern of Islamic allegiance and practice was followed by the empire of Mali, which succeeded Ghana as the principal power of West Africa in the thirteenth and fourteenth centuries. J. Spencer Trimingham quotes ibn Khaldun, who writes, "The first of their Mali kings to join Islam was Baramandana who made the pilgrimage, an example followed by his successors" (1962: 62). The most famous Malian ruler to make the pilgrimage was Mansa Musa, who went to Mecca in 1324 with a retinue of 6,000 slaves, servants, and followers. According to historical sources and contemporary accounts, he was fabulously rich, carrying with him so much gold that when his party arrived in Cairo, they created a fiscal crisis by flooding the market and thus devaluing the price of gold throughout the city. The Egyptian merchants were quick to seize the advantage, however, and inflated their prices so that the Africans spent more than even they could afford. Mansa Musa and his retinue ran up large debts, and on the return trip they were accompanied by a good number of merchants who went with them to collect on the king's debts from him back in Mali. On his return trip Mansa Musa also brought with him Arab poets and adventurers (Trimingham 1962: 65). In addition, this pilgrimage apparently involved serious discussions for Mansa Musa, for he learned in Cairo that Islam does not allow the taking of free Muslim women as concubines. His pilgrimage took almost three years to complete, and it is noteworthy that Arabs were interested enough in this remote area of the Islamic world that a good number of writers and adventurers accompanied Mansa Musa back to his kingdom. Besides Baramandana and Mansa Musa, two other emperors of Mali made the *hajj*—Mansa Ule (reigned c. 1260-1270) and Sakura (reigned c.1290-1300). The latter was murdered on his return from Arabia.

The early period of Islam in West Africa culminated with the rise of the Songhay Empire (1493-1591). As in Mali, one of the emperors, Askiya Muhammad, made a pilgrimage well-known to Arab chroniclers. The founder of the Songhay Askiya dynasty (*askiya* is a title), Muhammad Ture ibn Abu Bakr, went to Mecca accompanied by a large number of important people from the administrative and scholarly "classes" of his empire, gave 1,000 gold dinars as alms in the holy city, and built a hostel for African pilgrims (Trimingham 1962: 98). It might be mentioned that he was not the only West African monarch to build hostels for his countrymen on pilgrimage. One monarch of the kingdom of Kanem-Bornu (in the northern Nigeria-southern Chad region) built, as early as 1242, a Maliki *madrasa*-hotel in Cairo for the comfort and instruction of Kanembu pilgrims (Trimingham 1962: 115).

There is every indication that these pilgrims, although a mere trickle of the population of West Africa, came into contact with important and influential Muslims in Arabia and Egypt. Muhammad Ture ibn Abu Bakr, mentioned above, is said to have met and talked with prominent reformers in Mecca such as Abd al-Rahman al-Suyuti and al-Majhili; this latter savant initiated one pilgrim, 'Umar ibn al'Bakka'i of the Kunta tribe, who was to become, in Trimingham's words, "the propagator of Qadiriyya in the Sahel" (Trimingham 1962: 98n).[4] He himself is said to have met with the caliph and to have been installed as caliph(?) (*'amil?* *wakil?*) of Songhay by the sharif of Mecca, but this story is highly suspect (al-Naqar 1972: 21-25). On the basis of his conversations with the jurist al-Siyuti, he instituted reforms regarding slaving within the empire after he returned to West Africa. Indeed, Sufism spread rapidly into the Sudanic region because of the pilgrims and the traders who came from the Maghrib. Many Sufis, in the pre-Wahhabi period,[5] chose to settle in Mecca or Medina, and they undoubtedly came into contact with many West African pilgrims. "The mystics have spiritualized the *hajj*, and spoken of the importance of the 'inner pilgrimage,' but most of them have performed this duty not only once, but many times. Some of them lived for a certain period in the sacred environment, so that Mecca was always a center where scholars from every part of the Islamic world would meet" (Schimmel n.d.: 155). It must be remembered that the people who went on the *hajj* in this early period were nobility and royalty, but the religious class that served them as scholars and *imams* also accompanied them on the pilgrimage, and this latter group was particularly sensitive to the intellectual and spiritual currents flowing through the Islamic world, and these people, with their royal patrons, were most often the agents of religious revivalistic or reform movement in their native lands (Levtzion 1979: 84). Many of the early royal pilgrims were among the most enthusiastic reformers. In 1048, Yahya b. Ibrahim recruited the Maliki scholar Abdullahi b. Yasin to instruct his people in the true religion. His rigorous instruction was not well received by Yahya b. Ibrahim's people, the Juddala, but the point here is that reform was prompted and facilitated by the combined forces of pilgrim kings and scholars (Levtzion 1979: 91).

Besides the religious activity in central West Africa (i.e., the empires of Ghana, Mali, and Songhay), the areas of Kanem-Bornu, territories loosely bordering what is now Lake Chad, were very active Muslim centers. The earliest recorded pilgrimage is that of *Mai* (a royal title) Dunama b. Umme, who between 1098 and 1150 made the pilgrimage two times and died while making his third. Over the next four centuries over twenty kings or *mai* made the pilgrimage from Kanem-Bornu to

Arabia. One of the kings of Kanem-Bornu, Idris ibn Ali, did a great deal to further Islam in his kingdom and not only built a pilgrim hostel in Mecca for his countrymen but also instituted *shari'a* and *shari'a* courts in his native land. His learning was not entirely spiritual and theological, however, for we learn that on his pilgrimage to Mecca, c.1575, he "discovered the value of firearms. He imported Turkish musketeers. Another innovation was his employment of Arab camelry" (Trimingham 1962: 122). My point here is to show that the Maghrib and the Hijaz were the focal points in the dissemination of different kinds of innovations and reforms from the Islamic heartland and that the pilgrims from the western Sudan were the agents of their dissemination. In fact, they were probably the only carriers of such ideas to the Western Sudan (although we must not overlook the influence of traders) and were, because of their high status or relation to royalty, the very agents capable of implementing change in West Africa.[6]

In 1591 Morocco sacked the capital of the Songhay empire and brought it to an end. In retrospect, this event marks the end of the first, early period of Islam and the beginning of what I shall call the middle period of Islam in West Africa, a period of decline and stagnation. To recapitulate the main features of the early period, Islam in the Sudan was characterized by its isolation from other centers of the Islamic world because of geographical factors, by its non-Arabic character, and by its confinement to the ruling elite and a clerical class. In spite of these factors, the royal and clerical pilgrims to Mecca established hostels in the Maghrib and the Hijaz and met many Muslim religious leaders whose ideas and reforms they took back with them and instituted among Muslims in their homelands.

What caused the decline of Islam in the ensuing era? Several factors can be noted, each of which had some effect. A. Adu Boahen (1963: 350) points out that political conditions in the Sudan deteriorated after the fall of Songhay. The Sudanic region was rent asunder by wars, and no central power came forward to assert itself in the midst of this chaos. With the region in a continual state of flux and unrest, the trade routes that had connected the Sudan with the Maghrib were disrupted. After all, much of the glory of the empires of Ghana, Mali, and Songhay had had its basis in the fact that these empires all served as the centers of trade routes. The empires not only were the beneficiaries of these trade routes but provided security for the caravans against bandits and opposing armies. Now there was no central authority capable of providing such security, and the trade routes dwindled and the caravans were greatly reduced in number. This last fact bears directly on pilgrimage, for many nobles and clerics accompanied trade caravans through the Sahara, not only because the traders knew the route and the oases but also because there was safety in numbers against thieves or marauders. Besides these advantages, the existence of a caravan meant that the pilgrim was spared the cost of raising a retinue to serve as his personal guard. Also, Boahen points out that the loose federation of tribes generally known as the Bambara, who had always resisted islamization and were generally hostile to Islamic kingdoms, now held sway over much of the Sudan, with no Islamic power to counteract their aggression (Boahen 1963: 350-51).

Another reason for the decline of the caravan trade was the increase of the coastal trade. The Portuguese had first appeared along the coast toward the middle of the fifteenth century, and by the sixteenth century, English, Portuguese, Spanish, Dutch, and French ships were dropping anchor off the coast and negotiating with local Africans for gold, ivory, indigo, and, most importantly, slaves. Trade that had formerly gone inland to the great trading centers in the Sudan now turned away from the savannah regions and headed, instead, to the coast. It might be added, parenthetically, that the American Indian indirectly participated in a population explosion in West Africa, for many of the traders introduced New World foodstuffs into the tropical forest areas of West Africa and made those areas much more attractive for permanent settlement. Among other things, yams, maize, sweet potatoes, mangoes, beans, cassava, pineapples, tomatoes, and new forms of peppers were introduced here, creating a plentiful food supply and enticing savannah peoples to this tropical region. All of the above reasons contributed to the general decline of Islam in West Africa.

It must not be thought, however, that Islam died out at this time. To the contrary, it continued to exist, but it lacked the political base necessary for expansion, and its ties with the Islamic fatherland in Egypt and Arabia grew more and more tenuous as fewer and fewer pilgrims made the pilgrimage because of the dangers involved, to say nothing of the time and expense.

J. S. Birks makes the point that Muslim savants of this period also concocted theological formulations that denigrated the *hajj* and sometimes even claimed that it was not one of the five pillars of the faith (Birks 1978: 10). Too much, however, can be made of this theological polemic against the necessity of the *hajj*—after all, few people could read such works, and the traditional Muslim reverence for the *hajj* had certainly taken hold among the Muslims in West Africa, particularly under the influence of the Maliki school of Muslim law, which states unequivocally that it is the duty of all Muslims in good health and of proper age to make the pilgrimage to Mecca.

Furthermore, as M. Hiskett makes clear, there were centers of Islamic learning and piety that did continue in this age. Indeed, his article relating to the state of learning among the Fulani before the era of the *jihads* shows that, while the quantity of Arabic scholarship may have been small, the quality of the works of these Muslim Fulani savants was often of a high caliber. The schools continued to exist, even expand—it was the political basis of the Islamic societies that had disappeared. Other aspects of the religion continued as before. Hiskett makes the point that wandering, learned men contributed, even in this age, to the propagation of Islam and that their peregrinations were directly linked to the *hajj*: "The teaching of religious sciences was in the hands of a number of famous scholars. Sometimes these teachers were peripatetic; at other times they taught in the mosques and the schools. The peripatetic system was bound up with the pilgrimage, for the teacher passed up and down the country on his way to and from the East; and with him went his students" (1957: 573-74).

The era of the *jihads*, which started around the end of the eighteenth century, marks a significant change in the nature and form of Islam in West Africa and can be said to initiate the modern period of Islam in West Africa. There is every reason to believe that the *jihadist* reformers, both those from Futa Toro (in northern Senegal) and those from the Hausa states (in northern Nigeria), were influenced either directly or indirectly by the pilgrimage to Mecca. One of the *jihadist* leaders, a well-known reformer and Sufi, was Al-Haji 'Umar ibn Said (known more popularly as Al-Haji 'Umar Tal), who had made the pilgrimage to Mecca (1827-1830) and in Mecca or Egypt was initiated into the Tijaniyya order of Sufism. In fact, much of his subsequent activity in the western Sudan has been ascribed to his desire to overcome the influence of the Qadiriyya brotherhood (Trimingham 1962: 181); however, another famous *jihadist*, Uthman dan Fodio, had as his teacher Al-Haji Jibril ibn 'Umar, a well-known pilgrim and reformer who had spent many years in the Middle East (Levtzion 1980: 84). Other *jihadist* pilgrims deserve mention. Muhammad al-Min al Kanimi, ruler of Bornu from 1808 to 1837, made the pilgrimage before becoming ruler and later was a leader, with Uthman dan Fodio, of the *jihads* in this eastern section of West Africa. A later figure, named Muhammad al-Amin al-Sarakole, a ruler in Senegal, also made the pilgrimage and was a follower of Al-Haji 'Umar Tal and a member of the Tijaniyya. He led a short-lived *jihad* in 1885 but was defeated and killed in 1887.

The *jihads* were widespread from 1780 to 1890 throughout the entire Sudan. Although the focus in this chapter is on the western Sudan, it must not be forgotten that the Mahdist movement in the eastern Sudan (in what is today the Republic of the Sudan) in the 1880s was also an example of a *jihad*, so one can rightly say that all of the Sudan experienced this form of religious and political upheaval.

The causes of the *jihad* are difficult to determine. Hiskett seems to give primacy to religious revivalism inspired, in part, by the ferment that was moving the whole Islamic world. The eighteenth and nineteenth centuries were the time of the Sufi revival, and the founding of the influential Sanusi brotherhood had repercussions all through the Sudan. Also, the *tariqa* (Sufi orders) known as Rashidiyya and Amirghaniyya were formed at this time under the influence of the general "neo-Sufi revival" (Rahman 1966: 206-7) and had great influence in North and Sudanic Africa. Further, the Wahhabi movement, founded in the eighteenth century, began at this time to exert influence beyond Arabia, especially via the pilgrims (Kaba 1974: 48).[7] There may certainly have been other factors that contributed to the rise of the *jihads*. Hiskett, although he favors the more religiously oriented explanations, does concede that the *jihadic* conflicts did often pit different classes and occupations on opposite sides of the conflict. For example, Al-Haji 'Umar Tal's movement attracted many escaped slaves who flocked to his cause, and the Tijaniyya brotherhood in West Africa (which Al-Haji 'Umar Tal espoused) became allied with the poorer classes in open opposition to the more aristocratic Qadiriyya brotherhood. Finally, many of the *jihads* involved different classes in opposition throughout these wars: nomads versus peasants, slaves versus enslavers, commoners versus aristocrats, and provincials versus urban intellectuals (Hiskett 1977: 166-67). Thus, under the influence of a pilgrim reformer like Al-Haji 'Umar Tal, the *jihad* was not simply a method for spreading Islam or the Tijaniyya brotherhood but the means for the most rapid and far-reaching reordering of society and social life in general that West Africa had ever before witnessed.

The consequences of the *jihads* were enormous. Not only were ruling families, classes, and states upset over the western Sudan, but Islam was enjoined on the native population as it had never been before. For the first time since it was introduced into West Africa in the tenth century, Islam was not simply the cult of the noble or clerical classes but now became, through the medium of the *jihad*, a mass religion. Islam was purified of many pagan elements that had been heretofore permitted, particularly in the Futa Toro, Futa Jallon, and Kanem-Bornu-Hausa regions, and millions of the indigenous peoples were converted to Islam. Islamic institutions and schools, the Arabic language, and the daily practice of the religion spread to almost all parts of the western Sudan.

As pointed out above, in the period prior to the time of the *jihads* the number of people going on pilgrimage had declined, a fact attributable both to the decline of Islam itself and to the decline of the caravan trade, a decline justified by new revisionist tendencies in West African Muslim theology that denigrated the *hajj*. With the revival and spread of Islam through the medium of the *jihads*, however, the institution of the *hajj* was slow to assert or reestablish itself.

The question of why the pilgrimage to Mecca did not also revive in popularity along with the revival of Islam is a difficult one. To begin with, travel conditions throughout the region were still unsettled and precarious. Not only was the western Sudan in chaos because of the *jihads* that periodically swept over large areas, but North Africa itself was experiencing a great deal of trouble and interference from European powers. At the beginning of the nineteenth century, Europeans began occupying areas along the coast of Africa, usually under the pretext of pacifying the Barbary pirates or of protecting their commercial interests. From Egypt to Morocco, Christian Europeans were making their economic and political presence felt in a way that proved most unsettling to the traditional economic and political patterns of the area. Given the rise of trade along the African coast and the turbulence in the northern countries along the Maghrib, caravan trade almost ceased to exist. Route after route closed because of the impossibility of making a profit and because of the danger involved in such expeditions. This abandonment of the caravan routes further discouraged would-be pilgrims from making the dangerous and arduous journey.

There was also a theological reason, which, like the theological reasoning of the pre-*jihadic* era, provided even normally pious Muslims with a perfectly acceptable excuse for not going on the *hajj*, namely, that waging the *jihad* was more efficacious in God's eyes than the *hajj*. Birks makes the following comment: "The *jihad* did not oust the view of abstention from pilgrimage prevailing in West Africa and, in fact, devalued the *hajj* still further: the deed of the Holy War gave heavenly rewards equal to, if not greater than, those accruing from a visit to the Holy Places" (1978: 11). As Lansine Kaba (1974: 47) points out, there had long been an equivalence in West African Muslim thought between the *hajj* and the *jihad*, whereby it was reckoned that the sufferings and privations of the *hajj* were equivalent to the *jihad*, a striving in the way or cause of Allah.

The pilgrimage, however, certainly did not cease altogether at this time. In fact, in comparison with the pre-*jihadic* period, the number of pilgrims increased somewhat. As the desert routes closed, more and more pilgrims made the trek across the savannah from west to east and went from the area of northern Nigeria eastward to the Red Sea through southern Chad and through the northern part of what is now the country of Sudan. Birks makes the point that those who went on the pilgrimage were not the kings or nobility of yesteryear but were, rather, "religious extremists" (1978: 11). What Birks means by this phrase is unclear, but what is clear is that the *jihads* did not stop the movement of pilgrims to Mecca. The *jihadists* did not promote or encourage the use of the traditional trans-Saharan routes of pilgrimage, and because of the incorporation of many peoples as practicing Muslims, the *jihads* did have the effect of altering the types of pilgrims who now went to Mecca.

As in times past, the movement of pilgrims, even during this difficult period, facilitated the dissemination of Islamic learning from the Hijaz to West Africa. Ivor Wilks notes that in the eighteenth and early nineteenth centuries the number of pilgrims from the eastern Guinea-northern Ivory Coast increased considerably and that the Dyula towns (i.e., of the Muslim people he was studying) were prosperous enough to support many teachers "[whose] passage to and from the Hijaz would create an intellectual climate within which learning could flourish" (1978: 176). As mentioned above, some of the *jihadists* themselves, notably Al-Haji 'Umar Tal in 1827, went on the pilgrimage and returned from that experience profoundly affected by what they had seen and heard in the Holy Places.

One work from this period has recently been translated from Arabic and narrates the pilgrimage of a Moor from Mauritania who set off for the Hijaz in 1838, the middle of the *jihadic* era. The work, which has the charming title of *The Pilgrimage of Ahmed, Son of the Little Bird of Paradise*, is a journal of the pilgrim's progress through North Africa and Arabia. Being a Moor, Ahmed spoke the Hassani dialect of Arabic and thus had an immense advantage over many of his Sudanese fellow Muslims who did not speak Arabic as their mother tongue. He was both a pious and a learned man (and apparently quite rich, because on his return from Arabia he founded and endowed a *zawiya* in Fez). On his way to Arabia he passed through Fez (where he swore allegiance to Mawlay 'Abd al-Rahman, a Moroccan *shaykh* and a *sharif*, d. 1859) and Marakesh and went by sea from Morocco to Egypt. His journey was interrupted repeatedly by the French, who by now controlled the area and placed travelers in quarantine as a matter of course to control cholera and other diseases; the fact that the French thought that diseases were caused and controlled through natural means rather than through the power of God alone, noted Ahmed rather sourly, just proves that they are *kaffar* (pagan). He entered Alexandria, where he visited shrines and local *shaykhs*. After the fast during Ramadan he proceeded to Cairo, where he again visited the shrines of dead saints and talked with the scholars, *qadi*, and *mufti* in that city. Having made the pilgrimage, he made his way homeward through many of the same towns, and also visited Tripoli, Tunis "the verdant" (he skipped Algiers "because it was in the hands of the Christians"), and Gibraltar, before returning to Morocco. He was well received everywhere, even by the

Christian authorities in Gibraltar, and stayed for long periods of time with each of his hosts, various *shaykhs* and *muftis*. Since he was a scholar, many of his hosts gave him books (he returned with over 400 books, all acquired on his travels, either as gifts or by purchase—and in the days before many Arabic books were produced by movable type). In all, the pilgrimage took just about six years. My point here is that Ahmed's account was probably fairly typical for many pilgrims at that time and a typical pattern of pilgrimage experienced by Africans for centuries. Not only did he deepen his faith, but he came into close and intimate contact with these cognoscenti of the Islamic world, a familiarity with them and their works that he would otherwise never have had in his out-of-the-way homeland in Mauritania. Through the pilgrimage and the contacts he made throughout North Africa and the Middle East, his intellectual and spiritual world was greatly expanded, and although the journal ends with his return to his homeland, we may assume that his tribal group and his students became the immediate beneficiaries of this *'ilm* (knowledge).

But all of West Africa was in a great state of flux. Not only were the *jihads* raging through the area at this time (the first half of the nineteenth century), but European powers were establishing permanent colonial bases where, before, there had been only trading posts or coastal enclaves. By the extension of their influence or through military means, the European powers slowly encroached on the African continent throughout the second half of the nineteenth century. Although the whole of West Africa was not pacified from the colonial point of view until almost the beginning of the Great War, by the 1880s the Europeans were confident enough of their general hegemony and respective spheres of influence that an amicable agreement could be reached at the Conference of Berlin in 1884 concerning the partition of the continent.

With regard to Islam, colonialism had several immediate and far-reaching consequences. First of all, it stopped the *jihads*. Samori, Al-Haji 'Umar Tal, and their followers were all discouraged from continuing the *jihads*, and their empires were dismantled. In a sense, then, the natural evolution of Islamic history in this area was halted. With the imposition of the colonial Pax, however, Islam spread more rapidly than ever, far faster than it had even under the impetus of the *jihads*. Muslim traders and clerics in the colonized areas had access to territories and peoples that were once closed or off-limits to them. Movement across West Africa was freer than ever, particularly into the forest zone along the coast, and as Muslims came to settle there, they made converts in greater and greater numbers. Another reason for the increase of Islam may also be laid to the fact that Muslims no longer came among "pagan" peoples as *jihadists* or as slave traders but as missionaries and as fellow Africans. People like the Bambara, who had resisted Islam for centuries, now converted rapidly in great numbers. Lastly, Africans may have felt drawn to Islam at this time as a covert protest against European domination—Islam offered literacy, a historical tradition, and a world religion that could confound European notions of African "primitiveness" and that served as a rebuke to the hordes of white missionaries swarming throughout the colonies of West Africa.

The *hajj* continued to draw increasing numbers to Mecca, albeit along slightly different routes. The colonial era witnessed the complete demise of the trans-Saharan caravan trade. The coastal cities were now the trading centers (as well as serving as the capital cities for colonial administration), and all commerce went south and west toward the coast. Birks points out that more and more desert routes were closed so that by 1911 the route from Mauritania to Fez was closed due to lack of traders (1978: 13) (along which pilgrims like Ahmed and many others had gone to Mecca, via Fez, where they could venerate the tomb of al-Tijani, founder of the Tijaniyya brotherhood). The French were so alarmed at the decrease in caravan trade (and the imminent pauperization of the Bedouins) that they forbade the transport of salt by lorries; that is, they insisted that it be transported by camel to the coastal cities. Pilgrims, then, were left with no alternative but to cross the continent from west to east along the savannah and proceed on to the Hijaz by crossing the Red Sea in boats. The British, trying to ingratiate themselves with the Muslim population under their control, sponsored pilgrimages for the members of the Muslim nobility.

All in all, the colonial powers left Islam to itself during this period. While the French were in some ways hostile to Islam (they expected that the more advanced natives would adopt Catholicism as a matter of course), the British were quite supportive of Islam, permitted *shari'a* courts in northern Nigeria to continue to rule on matters pertaining to family law in cases involving Muslims, and forbade Christian missionaries from establishing mission stations in these Muslim territories. Among Africans, the colonial presence brought about a situation in which it became a title of distinction to be called a Muslim, and many formerly oppressed classes in African society realized a new status by becoming Muslim. Elliott Skinner writing at the end of the colonial era, notes: "Today there are obvious rewards for those Mossi who embrace Islam; besides such tangible ones as getting wives and children, there are intangible ones of upward social mobility and greater prestige. It is important to note that most liberated slaves and serfs are now Moslems. Formerly these non-Mossi had low status, but today those who have been to Mecca bear such proud titles as Hadji" (1958: 1108).

With the withdrawal of the colonial powers and the coming of independence, African peoples and states entered a new era. The consequences for Islam were no less momentous than they had been during the three previous eras. Although it is still too early to discern all the forms and features of Islam in post-independence Africa, it is possible to say that the new states are very conscious of Islam and of the Muslim populations within their borders, although, no matter how strong Islam may be, it does not prevent states from trying to manipulate Islamic institutions and peoples in such ways as to promote the interests of the secular powers. In other words, many of the new African states attempt to pacify and please their Muslim subjects and to manipulate them through good and even favored treatment in much the same way that the colonial powers before them had used Islam and Muslims to their advantage. Among other things, many states encourage the Muslim majorities within their borders. Not only does this action bring a certain stability to the government, but it encourages an inter-ethnic solidarity among disparate peoples within one nation-state. Even radical socialists, such as Ahmed Sekou Toure, president of Guinea, committed their countries to a brand of socialism that they consider to be compatible with, or supportive of, a vision of Islamic socialism or an Islamic society.

One concrete way in which states show their support of Islam and their Islamic populations is to support pilgrimage flights to Mecca. Guinea, Nigeria, and Senegal all subsidize air travel to and from Jidda for those who wish to go during the month of pilgrimage. One result of this policy has been that many thousands can go to Mecca who in the past would have lacked the means or the stamina to make this demanding trip. In 1978, 135,326 pilgrims made the pilgrimage from black (non-Arab) Africa, of whom all but 47 arrived by air. From Senegal, 4,825 pilgrims went to Mecca, all but 7 of whom went by air. From Mauritania, 1,084 went on the *hajj*, and all but 8 went by air (Kingdom of Saudi Arabia, *Statistical Yearbook* 1978).

Besides the fact that many more people now go on the pilgrimage, I believe that air travel on these subsidized flights has even more profound consequences for Islam in West Africa. These trips to and from Jidda encompass a time span between two and four weeks (depending on the day the pilgrim departs from his homeland and the day that he is put aboard the plane for the return trip after the pilgrimage). The pilgrim disembarks in Jidda and, after processing by the Saudi government, is shuttled to Mecca to begin the pilgrimage, after which he is brought back to Jidda to be taken home. Without too much thought, one can see how different this type of pilgrimage is from the one made by Ahmed over 150 years ago. Not only does this pilgrimage not take six years, but the intimate contacts that Ahmed made with scholars, *shaykhs*, *mufti*, and *qadi* in the Hijaz and North Africa are entirely absent. In days gone by, pilgrims lingered in the Holy Places and often made lesser pilgrimages to Medina and Jerusalem, besides living in the Holy Places and meeting their fellow Muslims from all over the world. Ahmed relates that, after the pilgrimage itself, he visited the graves of 'Aisha and Khadijah, wives of the Prophet, besides visiting Medina "the illumined" and praying in the Mosque of the Prophet. Such lesser pilgrimages in the Hijaz made a profound impression upon him, as did all the shrines of saints (as well as living teachers) he visited in Cairo, Alexandria, Tunis, and Fez. In short, what was once a pious peregrination through the sacred places of Islam has now been reduced to a shuttle flight from a West African entrepot to Jidda with just enough time to perform the pilgrimage rites before being shunted onto a return flight to West Africa.

As we have seen throughout this chapter, the pilgrimage to Mecca has provided Muslims in West Africa with contact with the heartland of Islam for 1,000 years, and the great revival and reform movements of the Islamic world were brought back and incorporated into West African Islam through the medium of pilgrims. In short, the function of the pilgrimage was pedagogical as well as pious, and this pedagogical aspect or function is the one that has been lost under the present circumstances. In the eighteenth century the influence of the Wahhabi movement had been felt by many of the pilgrims who had lingered in the Hijaz and had been influenced or instructed by the Wahhabi *'ulama*; in turn, they had gone back to West Africa with a burning desire to reform Islam. Today, however, such influences and pedagogy would be lost on pilgrims who do not remain in Arabia long enough to perfect their spoken Arabic and who must subdue their educational and pious interests to the exigencies of airline schedules.

The centers of Islam, however, have not relinquished their self-imposed duty to foster and propagate Islam. To the contrary. But it is no longer the pilgrimage or the pilgrim who is the focus or medium of propaganda. No longer do pilgrims return to the western Sudan with a newfound familiarity with Islamic trends or thought that they gleaned from Saudi Arabia, nor do pilgrims inspire the reform movements in the Western Sudan as they once did. The pedagogical function of the pilgrimage has ceased to exist among the pilgrims from West Africa (and from many other parts of the world).

Instead, as Tareq Ismael and others have pointed out, in the post-colonial period various Islamic countries have taken upon themselves the duty of propagating Islam south of the Sahara by different means. The leader in this field was Egypt, and its effort was initiated after Nasser's coup. Shortly after Nasser became president of Egypt, he, along with King Saud of Arabia and Ghulan Muhammed of Pakistan, established Egypt's leadership in Muslim affairs in Africa (Ismael 1971: 147-48). More specifically, the educational institutions of Egypt were used to promote Islamic religion and Arabic culture south of the Sahara. In the law of the Reorganization of Al-Azhar University, one of the oldest in the Islamic world, it states that Al-Azhar "carries the burden of Islamic missions to all nations and works to expose the truth of Islam" (Ismael 1971: 149). The rector of that university, Sheik Hassan Ma'amun, declared that "the most prominent role of Al-Azhar is the international call to Islam, its propagation of the Holy Koran, the Arabic language and religious jurisprudence among people who do not speak the language of the Holy Book" (Ismael 1971: 151). Under the direction of Nasser, Egypt greatly increased its commitment to educating students at Al-Azhar and at secular universities. In 1952-1953, the last year of the old regime, 15,000 Egyptian pounds were expended for scholarships for foreign students. By 1963-1964, this sum had risen to 375,000 Egyptian pounds (Ismael 1971: 151). Saudi Arabia also expanded its number of foreign students, and although the records of Libya are not open to the public, I would guess that Colonel Qadaffi's expenditure for foreign students to study Islam in Libya far exceeds Saudi Arabia's and Egypt's earlier contributions.

Besides encouraging students to come to Egypt to study, Al-Azhar established in 1963 Islamic Arab missions throughout Africa. These were complexes consisting of grammar and secondary schools, a mosque, and a small infirmary run by qualified 'ulama from Al-Azhar. In other words, Egypt under Nasser undertook an ambitious program of missionary activity throughout sub-Saharan Africa. In interviews I conducted with various leaders of the Sierra Leone Muslim Brotherhood, it was reported to me that during the sixties several hundred Egyptian teachers came to teach in the Brotherhood schools throughout Sierra Leone (note that this Muslim Brotherhood has no relation to the militant Egyptian organization but is, rather, an educational and missionary society founded by Sierra Leone. At the present time there are about a dozen Egyptian teachers still in Sierra Leone.[8]

Thus, while the convenience of modern transportation has effectively ruined the pilgrimage as a vehicle for teaching pilgrims about the nature of Islam in the Middle

East, this function has been taken over, with the help of oil money and an increased consciousness of the *dar al-Islam,* by the countries of Saudi Arabia, Egypt, and Libya. Because of the need to limit the scope of this chapter, I have not even mentioned the educational activities of such movements as the Ahmadiyyah movement,[9] but they are of increasing importance in their role of informing Islamic consciousness in West Africa, Asia, and the Caribbean. For almost 1,000 years the pilgrim transmitted currents of Islamic teaching, spiritual life, legal interpretation, and reform from Egypt and Arabia back to West Africa. What was once the function of pilgrims returning from the *hajj*—to teach, to institute reforms, to spread Islam throughout West Africa—has now been taken over by foreign Muslim missionaries or by African Muslim students who have returned from their formal studies in Egypt, Arabia, or North Africa.

In conclusion, I think that it is now clear that the *hajj* has served different functions in the life of West African Muslims. Its primary function, which occupied the place of paramount importance until the modern era, was the diffusion or dissemination of Islam from its intellectual and spiritual capitals in North Africa and the Middle East back to West Africa. Because the pilgrimage was, in effect, a migration of an elite, they were capable of reorganizing their society and religious practices so that they conformed to what they had learned or seen on pilgrimage. For much of the history of West Africa, the pilgrimage was the medium by which these African Muslim elites (both clerical and aristocratic) were informed of movements and developments in the *dar al-Islam,* and they, in turn, were the media for the dissemination of such ideas throughout West Africa.

It is significant that the post-colonial era has greatly changed the nature and function of the Islamic pilgrimage for West Africa. No longer is the *hajj* restricted to aristocrats and their cleric escorts. Masses of West Africans are flown to and from Jidda and spend only the month of pilgrimage in Arabia. Clearly, the mode of transportation and the almost unseemly haste with which the Saudi government processes the pilgrims in, through, and out of the country have also radically changed the experience and importance of pilgrimage for West African Islam. What was once the great source of education and inspiration for Islam in the western Sudan has been replaced by the education of Muslim students in North Africa and Near Eastern countries. I would predict that these young students will be the agents of the dissemination of Islamic thought and practice as the pilgrims once were in West Africa.

In general, the *hajj* in the context of West African Islam can be seen as a vehicle for the diffusion of religious and cultural concepts and practices. Thus, while the pilgrimage always served a religious end for those who participated in it, because of the knowledge, books, Sufi initiation, or whatever else they acquired in the Holy Places, the pilgrims themselves served as the conduit through which these were spread throughout West Africa. Thus, the emphasis in this chapter has been on the pedagogical function of pilgrimage in the spread of religion and culture. One crucial factor in this study of pilgrimage is the participation of elites. West African Islamic elites made the pilgrimage to Mecca for a variety of reasons, most of them probably rooted in their Muslim piety, but the pilgrimage itself greatly enhanced their status and prestige. In addition, as mentioned before, because of their aristocratic status, whatever may have inspired them in the Hijaz might be instituted in their homelands. The migration of elites via pilgrimage can be seen in historical perspective as the thread that has tied together the Islamic world north and south of the Sahara. Without it West African Islam would have had a very different history and character.

Finally, I would like to suggest that the discussion of the *hajj* presented in this chapter may be of some interest in the wider context of the anthropology of pilgrimage. Perhaps the most interesting point in that light might refer to the functions that the *hajj* has played over time. Although it served originally as the means for the diffusion of Islamic religion and culture, it now serves different, more individual functions. Yet the *hajj* continues, its popularity unabated. The institution has persevered regardless of the function it has served or serves, collectively or individually. To be sure, the attraction of the *hajj* may ultimately lie beyond any social benefits that accrue to the participants. It may rest instead in the fundamental religious sensibility of the pilgrims, who sing as they approach the Sacred Mosque at the start of the *hajj*: "I am here, O God, I am here; at Thy command, I am here."

NOTES

1. *Jihad*, derived from the Arabic word meaning to strive for, means, in its religious context, to strive or struggle for the cause of God and Islam. Although *jihad* can be interpreted in moral, political, or economic terms, it has most frequently been understood as a military campaign waged to defend the borders of the *dar al-Islam* or to propagate Islam among unbelievers who refuse to accept it.

2. These were the Shuwa Arabs of the southern Chad-northern Nigeria region.

3. The word *Sudan* in this sense is not to be understood as the modern Republic of the Sudan but rather to the area south of the Sahara and, unless otherwise noted, to the area north of the tropical forest zone. Primarily, in this chapter the word will be used to mean sub-Saharan West Africa.

4. Qadiriyya is one of the largest of the Sufi brotherhoods (*tariqa*) in Africa.

5. The Wahhabi movement was founded in Arabia by Muhammad ibn Abdul Wahhab (1703-1787). This is a reform movement, puritanical in the sense that it attempted to remove all innovations after the third century of Islam from Muslim belief and practice. The movement was extremely anti-Sufi, and Wahhab's polemics were aimed at the cult of the saints and all that that implied (mentioning the name of a saint in prayer, asking the saint to intercede on behalf of the suppliant, making vows to the saint in return for favors, and making pilgrimages to the tombs of saints). Wahhabism became the reigning orthodoxy on the Arabian peninsula (under the patronage of the royal house of Sa'ud), and Sufi shrines were destroyed and their practices outlawed (cf. *Shorter Encyclopedia of Islam*, 1953: 618).

6. An observer might well point out that historical records focus on the powerful and wealthy, not on the common people. While it certainly is true that historiography is traditionally elitist in its focus, I do not feel that the emphasis is misplaced in the study of West African Islam. The aristocratic class was the Muslim population during much of this period (witness the mass conversions that occurred only after the *jihads*). Also, because of the expense

involved, it would be highly unlikely that commoners could afford to make the pilgrimage to Mecca, unless as a servant or companion to a noble patron.

7. Also, G. S. Rentz (1969: 283) writes, "In Africa the great *jihads* of the nineteenth century, led by Uthman dan Fodio, Al-Haji 'Umar Tal, and others, were marked by striking similarities to their Arabian counterparts [i.e., the Wahhabis]."

8. This information is from my research in Sierra Leone, 1979-1980.

9. A good discussion of the Ahmadiyyah movement in West Africa can be found in H. J. Fisher, *Ahmadiyyah: A Study in Contemporary Islam on the West African Coast.*

10

Specialists in Miraculous Action: Some Shrines in Shiraz

ANNE H. BETTERIDGE

This chapter describes the specialized characters of various shrines in the Iranian city of Shiraz and relates these individual reputations to pilgrims' motives for undertaking sacred journeys. What we see is true of many places besides Iran: different needs or desires cause pilgrims to call upon different shrines. As both an outcome and a cause of this situation, each shrine develops its own body of legend and lore to account for its specialized character and capability. The differentiation of shrines by reputation and the consequent resort to different shrines by different pilgrims (or the same pilgrims under different circumstances) are the factors that permit the sharing or overlapping of pilgrimage fields by a variety of sacred places within a limited region, as occurs in many parts of the world.

Victor Turner was not alone in regarding pilgrimage centers as thresholds, although he was a pioneer in analyzing pilgrimage as a liminal activity. As he phrased it:

A pilgrimage center, from the standpoint of the believing actor, also represents a threshold, a place and moment "in and out of time," and such an actor—as the evidence of many pilgrims of many religions attests—hopes to have there direct experience of the sacred, invisible or supernatural order, either in the material aspect of miraculous healing or in the immaterial aspect of inward transformation of spirit or personality (1974: 197).

In Iran, Shi'i Muslim shrines are referred to as thresholds. The most important shrine in the country, site of the eighth Imam's tomb in Masshad, is formally entitled *"Astan-e Qods-e Razavi"*—"the threshold of holiness of Riza." The most popular shrine in the city of Shiraz is simply called *"Asunih,"* a colloquial pronunciation of the diminutive form of "Astan"—"threshold." It is also the place in Shiraz where miracles are thought most likely to occur. On such thresholds conventional relations of cause and effect are suspended: supernatural powers may be brought to bear on problems that do not yield to conventional forms of redress or where conventional means are not within the reach of troubled individuals. Here I am concerned with the ways in which divine power is thought to work through the shrines of Shiraz.

Shi'a Muslims in Iran recognize two kinds of miracles. The first, and more obviously miraculous, are rare and earthshaking miracles—*mu'jizat* (singular, *mu'jizih*). These impressive miracles are worked by prophets and are expressly intended to prove the legitimacy of a prophet's claim as representative of divinity. *Kiramat* (s. *kiramat*) are more modest miracles. Unlike the grander *mu'jizat*, *kiramat* occur with some frequency and may, in fact, appear notably lacking in miraculous qualities to the uninitiated. Asked to give an example of *kiramat*, a Shirazi woman told me of a rainy morning when she stood in a torrential downpour, was soaked to the skin and was unable to get a taxi. It was not until she requested the assistance of Imam Riza that a taxi stopped for her. She reckoned the taxi's arrival as a miracle and attributed it to the Imam's influence.

Kiramat are less momentous miracles than the more exceptional *mu'jizat*, but each occurrence of a *kiramat* does mark a departure from the ordinary. In terms of religious history, *mu'jizat* are more consequential miracles; in terms of individual lives it is the occurrence of *kiramat* that renews personal faith.

As one gentleman told me, a *kiramat* "solves a problem": it is just such assistance that men and women need to ease their daily lives. This chapter deals with the occurrence of minor miracles—*kiramat*—at the shrines of Shiraz.

I will begin by providing a brief introduction to Shi'i doctrine. Shi'i beliefs constitute the background in terms of which miraculous action makes sense. The background sketched, I proceed to the miracle-working specialties attributed to some shrines in Shiraz.

Although the Sunni sect predominates in the Islamic world overall, Shi'ism is the dominant form of the religion in Iran and claims some 90 percent of the population as its adherents. Shi'i Islam[1] is distinguished by a belief in the imamate (*imamat*), the doctrine that divinely appointed leaders, or Imams, exist who are uniquely able to guide human society and interpret the law revealed by the Prophet Muhammad. Sunnis maintain that the Islamic community was responsible for selecting the Prophet's successors, who would govern according to Islamic law but not be responsible for spiritual guidance. Members of various Shi'i sects differ as to the exact number and identity of the Imams they acknowledge, but the majority recognize a succession of twelve Imams, beginning with 'Ali ibn Abi Talib, cousin and son-in-law of the Prophet. The twelfth Imam, born in 868, disappeared from human sight but continues to influence the world of men. He is expected to reappear as a messiah when God wills and to institute a reign of justice on earth.[2] The Shi'i understanding of religious authority has definite consequences for the way the identity of saints buried at shrines and their abilities as intercessors and miracle-workers are perceived: shrine sites are usually the burial places of Imams or their relatives.

The distinctions between Shi'i and Sunni Islam as popularly conceived and practiced become evident in a comparison of saintly figures in the two worlds. Seyyed Hossein Nasr has commented that the function served by saints for the Sunni is served by the Imams and their descendants (*imamzadihs*) for the Shi'a and that "this essential identity can be 'existentially' experienced in the presence of barakah of the tombs of Sufi saints on the one hand and of the Imams and their descendants on the other, although the particular perfume of each can be recognized" (1966: 175).

Information provided in the anthropological literature on saints in North Africa suggests that *imamzadihs* and North African saints share many qualities (Eickelman 1976: 160). Both are approached as intercessors because of their privileged position in relation to God. Saints in North Africa and *imamzadihs* share the ability to perform miracles (*kiramat*) which shore up popular faith in their high rank (Gilsenan 1973: 20). In both instances, descent from holy figures is often combined with the ability to work wonders.

Not all Muslims perceive saintliness in the same way, however. As Dale Eickelman has noted, holy men and saintly figures do exist throughout the Muslim world, but "this is not to say that they all play similar social or cultural roles. They decidedly do not. But everywhere they popularly represent an implicitly hierarchical conception of the relations between man and God" (1976: 10). In each region the configuration of the hierarchy extending from man to God is based on local conceptions of the sacred and the way in which it is manifested.

Although Nasr chooses to emphasize the similarity between the Sunni and the Shi'a, the "particular perfume" of each is distinct. A priest answered my question about the distinction by saying that there is very little difference between the two sects anymore. The only serious point of disagreement he noted is the Shi'i doctrine of imamate, but this one issue makes a world of difference in the popular practice of religion. The privileged position of the Imams is reflected in the role played by their deceased descendants, *imamzadihs*, who serve as important local links to divinity for the Shi'a.

The difference in belief results in dissimilar roles played by the living descendants of saints in each society. The *seyyed* complex that has grown up around saints in Morocco gives an important role to their living patrilineal descendants. Living relations of one deceased Moroccan saint serve as mediators for tribesmen who enlist their services in return for assorted offerings (Eickelman 1976: 162-70). No such position as mediators in society is given to living descendants of Imams, although *seyyeds* (descendants of the Prophet) should be treated with respect. In Iran *seyyeds* are not thouqht to have a special relationship with enshrined *imamzadihs*; believers communicate directly with entombed representatives of the Imams. Also, while a man may achieve sainthood during his lifetime in North Africa (Gilsenan 1973: 44), in Iran he must be dead and buried to merit saintly status.

The comparison becomes more difficult when one considers that there have been important Sufi (Islamic mystic) leaders in Iran and that they are referred to as *awliya* (singular, *vali*), a term used to describe saints in North Africa (Eickelman 1976: 159). For the Shi'a, 'Ali, the first Imam, is the archetypical *vali* and is referred to as *vali ollah* (literally "friend of God"). The *awliya* in Iran are respected and particularly revered by members of Sufi orders. Their role, however, is eclipsed by the omnipresence of *imamzadih*s and the intermediary role *imamzadih*s play for many Shi'a. It has been suggested that the development of Sufism, or Islamic mysticism, was a response to "ossification on a ritual, intellectual, emotional and social level" in Islam (Gilsenan 1973: 10). For the Shi'a, however, this function has been performed to a large extent by the great affection for the family of the Prophet, including the Imams, as reflected in Shi'i doctrine and ritual. This situation appears to be related to the lesser importance of Sufi orders in the Shi'i world.

The *hajj*, or pilgrimage to Mecca, is of paramount religious importance to both Sunni and Shi'a (see Farmayan and Daniel 1990), but visits to shrines, particularly those of the Shi'i Imams and their descendants—*imamzadih*s—are of great significance in the daily lives of Shi'a Muslims. A great deal of attention and affection is given to the Imams in the popular performance of Shi'ism. The strong emphasis placed on revered individuals is reflected in the identification of a holy place and the person who is associated with it. The word *imamzadih* is used to refer both to a shrine where a descendant of an Imam is buried and to the actual descendant. Thus, when visiting a shrine, a pilgrim is usually paying a personal visit to an esteemed individual.[3] Other sorts of pilgrimage places exist in Iran, such as sacred trees, wells, and footprints, but even these are often identified with a holy person who may have visited or in some other way affected the spot. In any event, the tombs of *imamzadih*s are common shrine sites in Iran. This chapter focuses on *imamzadih*s in the city of Shiraz.

Shiraz is centrally located in the southwestern province of Fars, of which it is the capital. At the time of my research—December 1974 to November 1976, with continued residence in Iran into January 1979—Shiraz had a population of approximately 500,000. The city is an active commercial center and boasts of a university, several hospitals, an air force base, and theological schools. Numerous *imamzadih*s, 83 of which I have visited, are scattered throughout the city; more are discovered as building projects go forward and new burial places are unearthed. Most of the shrines are located within the boundaries of what was once the city wall; the area remains distinct as the old city of Shiraz.

Shiraz's major shrines attract visitors from beyond Shiraz, many from outlying rural areas. Visiting is an important social activity in Iran; one is bound to visit senior and important members of one's family. Many Shi'a feel the same obligation toward the Imams and their relations. Ahmad ibn Musa, popularly known as Shah Chiragh, is the elder brother of the eighth Imam, Riza, and the ranking member of the family of the Imams in southern Iran. Most visitors to Shiraz feel obliged to pay their respects to Shah Chiragh by visiting his tomb, and many come expressly to do so.

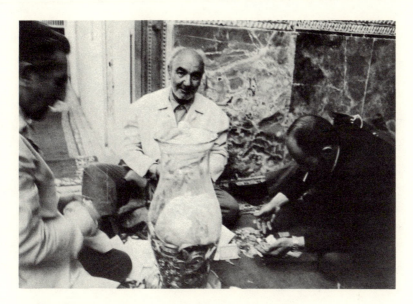

At Shah Chiragh

At Shah Chiragh

Shah Chiragh

Only two shrines in Iran are more important than Shah Chiragh, the tomb of the eighth Imam in Masshad and that of his sister, Ma'sumih, in Qum. Middle-level shrines are locally popular and may draw some visitors from the immediate environs of Shiraz. Small back street shrines are frequented primarily by Shirazis, especially those who live near them.

In all these cases it is fair to call visitors to the shrines pilgrims. The word for "pilgrim" in Persian, *za'ir*, also means "visitor," underscoring the personal nature of pilgrimage in Iran. Pilgrims' visits may be brief and involve little travel, but they are characterized by the same attitudes and rituals, albeit abbreviated, as are visits to major shrines and are described in the same terms. While it is true that pilgrimages to Masshad and Shi'i holy places in Iraq confer more prestige than visits to local shrines, local representatives of the Imams' families are due the same respect and hold out the same possibility of assistance as their more illustrious relations. Only the pilgrimage to Mecca is differently regarded for being religiously obligatory (*vajib*), rather than simply recommended (*mustahhab*), as is pilgrimage to other shrines. There are those who contend that many shrines in Shiraz are of dubious origin and that pilgrimage to them is of questionable value. Nonetheless, the same people aver that their favorite *imamzadih*s are above reproach, a fact often proved by the occurrence of miracles at the shrines.

Generally speaking, *ziarat*, or pilgrimage, in Shiraz is performed with tangible purposes in mind. Yet, although tangible purposes may dominate, visitors to Shiraz's shrines often set out with mixed motives. They may perform in the hope that they will be the beneficiaries of divine favor in some palpable way, but they comment that the experience of *ziarat* is comforting (*taskin*) and "heart-opening" (*dilbaz*) in and of itself.[4] Time and again I met people who, when distraught and unable to discuss problems with relatives and friends, would visit *imamzadih*s to find calm and comfort. Older women no longer able to get about easily often envied me the time I spent visiting shrines. They saw the process of pilgrimage itself as socially and spiritually rewarding.[5] Making a pilgrimage also brings the pilgrim religious merit (*savab*). Still, I was reminded that performing *ziarat* could not outweigh major sins, such as murder, and would not markedly alter one's position in the sight of God. In cases where major difficulties were encountered, people wished to make the *hajj* to seek forgiveness or spiritual strength; local pilgrimage was not felt equal to the task. I will confine myself here to a discussion of the palpable rewards sought by Shirazi pilgrims, though such favors may be sought in concert with spiritual goals in actual practice.

*Imamzadih*s, by virtue of their association with the Imams, are thought able to work miracles (*kiramat*)—events that cannot be caused by human abilities or natural agency. *Kiramat* do not occur haphazardly, although it may appear so to someone whose petition goes unanswered. I was told that pilgrims may request favors that are not ultimately in their best interests, and so particular boons may not be granted. An *imamzadih* may entertain any sort of request, and no problem is too petty for his or her consideration. I have encountered petitions ranging from the desire to die in the near future, suicide being sinful, to a young woman's formal request that her moustache be removed.

Certain shrines in Shiraz are perceived as having specialties in miraculous action. As a result, each pilgrim in search of divine assistance is presented with an array of shrines and saints to be consulted, depending upon how he or she defines the problem at hand. This situation is not unique to the shrines of Shiraz or to the Muslim world[6]; however, the specialization of shrines has not, to my knowledge, been discussed in the literature on pilgrimage. Further, in attending to the ways in which men and women approach pilgrimage and attempt to realize their desires through it, popular conceptions of divine power and the relationship between man and God are elucidated. In each place where shrines exist, the rationale behind their existence will depend on the local conception of what is sacred. In Shi'i Iran this understanding is intimately bound up with the feeling held for Imams and their kin. Through observing the closeness of the relationship between pilgrims and those to whom they pay their respects at the shrines, the eminently personal nature of the pilgrimage process in Iran becomes evident. The pilgrimage process is personal in two ways: first, as the acting out of a relationship between individuals—one regarded as nearer to God than the other—and second, because the performance of *ziarat* is an individual matter, answering private needs.

I will describe here the system of specialization that exists among Shiraz's shrines and consider how some of them have come to be regarded as peculiarly able to deal with specific types of predicaments. I will also discuss how Shirazis attempt to put the special talents of *imamzadih*s to work through the making of vows.

I should note at the outset that shrines having distinct talents are in the minority.

Of the *imamzadih*s I visited in Shiraz, 13 percent had obvious miracle-working specialties. These shrines, however, are noteworthy for being among the more popular places of pilgrimage in Shiraz as well as being of manageable size for research purposes. Beginning with them, one can establish a base of knowledge and understanding. Activities occurring at these shrines and attitudes held about them make up something of a microcosm of what is taking place at larger, unspecialized places of pilgrimage and are a more full-blown expression of what is involved at smaller, neglected shrines where it may be difficult to discern what, if anything, is happening. By starting with well-known and popular middle-level shrines, neither overwhelming nor seemingly inconsequential, one can begin to understand the forces at work in pilgrimage in Iran and later bring these understandings to bear when approaching more complicated pilgrimage sites.

Tile work at Imamzadih-yi Ibrahim

THE SYSTEM OF SPECIALIZATION

The system of specialization of Shiraz's shrines is recognized by Shirazis and thought to be part of the natural order of things. A man known simply as "Masshadi," a friend of a shrine custodian, took it upon himself to explain the variety of *imamzadih*s to me. As he leaned against the doorjamb of the shrine and drew his cloak about him, he lectured to me slowly in sonorous tones. In his estimation, the differences among the *imamzadih*s are comparable to those among ranks in the army: each position carries with it certain duties. Apart from this diversity, the *imamzadih*s are alike in that "each of them, in one way or another, must work miracles." It is not stretching the point to speak of a system of specialization existing among the city's shrines. The distribution of duties is in line with the conception of Shi'i holy figures making up a society among themselves, parallel to, and able to influence, human society. The collectivity of *imamzadih*s is characterized by its own kin relationships and social networks.[7]

Having a specialty in miracle working appears to depend on one of two factors or a combination of the two: first, facts relating to the private life of the *imamzadih*, such as his or her personality and life history, and second, the exact nature of an *imamzadih*'s relationship to an Imam or other revered individual. Noting a correspondence between a petitioner's plight and his or her own or that of an illustrious ancestor, an *imamzadih* may be favorably inclined to respond to a pilgrim's request. The *imamzadih* may then intercede on the pilgrim's behalf.

The bases for *imamzadih*s' specialties are illustrated in the following discussion of specific shrines. The shrines mentioned are well-known and often visited in Shiraz, there being no doubt as to their miraculous powers or particular inclinations.

Problems encountered at various stages of life can be taken to certain shrines in Shiraz with the hope of resolution. Female *imamzadih*s are, not surprisingly, receptive to the petitions of women and girls who visit their tombs. One of the most troubling events for girls, traditionally, is marriage; finding a good husband is a major concern of young women, and they seek help in their search at local shrines. In these cases, the personal background of the *imamzadih*s inclines them to respond to the girls' requests.

Bibi Khiyr ul Nisa

Two shrines in Shiraz are said to mark the graves of unmarried women, and their sympathies lie with girls and women in similar straits. I was assured that appeal to these shrines will soon result in a proposal of marriage. At Abish Khatun the custodian, or *mutavalli*, is a woman; she informed me that trusteeship of the shrine has been in her family for seven generations and has always been held by a woman. She went on to point out, "She is a girl [i.e., unmarried] herself," and she fondly patted the grillwork around Abish Khatun's grave as she spoke. The shrine has worked other kinds of miracles but is best known for *bakht gusha*, or "opening luck," used in reference to bringing about marriage for a girl.

Girls hoping to be married also visit Bibi Dukhtaran. At that shrine the *mutavalli*, an elderly man, recounted the case of one woman who had come to the shrine with several of her daughters. "The mother wanted one to marry. The girl's father bothered her and she would be better off married. Two or three months ago that was. Next thing I knew, they brought some sweets for me: the girl had married. I don't say it happens and is effective, people do." He also told me that a goodly number of older women visit the shrine after they have been divorced and want to find new husbands.

Following marriage the next problematic situation confronting women is pregnancy. It is extremely important that a woman be able to bear children, especially sons; two shrines in Shiraz are known for their abilities in this regard. The shrine of Shah Qiys is best known for help in bringing about conception. In this instance it is the *imamzadih*'s relation to an Imam that determines the shrine's specialty, rather than any popular understanding of the *imamzadih*'s personality. Shah Qiys is known as a son of Imam Riza; consequently, parenthood takes precedence as the dominant theme, drawing pilgrims to the shrine. The importance of Imam Riza's role in fostering miracles at the shrine is made clear by a chant recited by women who visit Shah Qiys: "Shah Qiys of Riza, grant my wish. Oh Imam Riza, grant my wish."

Once the pregnancy is under way, the wish for health and an uncomplicated childbirth comes to the fore. These issues are dealt with by Siyyid Abdullah. Women visit the shrine in the ninth month of their pregnancy (*mah-i khudishun*, "their own month") to assure an easy delivery. In my discussions about *imamzadihs* with women who lived near the Shahzadih Mansur shrine, Siyyid Abdullah was mentioned. Mention of his name prompted one woman to ask her pregnant neighbor, "Have you vowed your belly?" (*kumit nazr kardi?*). The neighbor replied that she had not as yet but certainly would. The women had no doubts that going to Siyyid Abdullah would guarantee an easy birth. When I asked why that shrine, rather than any other, is effective, the pregnant woman replied simply, "It just works."

Later, on a visit to Siyyid Abdullah, I talked to a man who works at the shrine. He went into great detail extolling the virtues of the shrine and pointed out things pilgrims had brought when their requests were answered as proof of the *imamzadih*'s power. According to him, if women are healthy and go to the shrine, they will have no further need for a doctor. The delivery will be made without difficulty, and the child will be a boy. I asked if he knew why the shrine was particularly helpful to pregnant women. He answered that Siyyid Abdullah had been among the many

Siyyid Abdullah

relatives of the eighth Imam, who hid in Shiraz after Imam Riza was murdered in Tus. When Siyyid Abdullah's hiding place was discovered, he was martyred; his pregnant wife was killed along with him, and she, too, is buried at the shrine. Understandably, the *imamzadih* is unusually responsive to the entreaties of pregnant women.

I discussed what I had heard with Mrs. Tasviri, a woman who regards herself as rational and is little given to the performance of pilgrimage on a regular basis. She doubted the truth of the explanation I had been given at the shrine. When she was pregnant with her first child, the women in her family urged her to pay a visit to Siyyid Abdullah. She stubbornly refused until her husband persuaded her to make the trip. He gave her a "scientific" explanation for the practice, which she repeated to me:

In those days pregnant women just sat at home. They didn't go out at all, barely budged. This is dangerous: a woman, especially toward the end of her pregnancy, should have some exercise. If all she does is sit, the chances are greater that she will run into trouble—bleeding; perhaps the baby will die. By insisting that pregnant women, especially in the ninth month, walk to the *imamzadih*, it was certain that they would get some exercise.

Some women did not live very far from the *imamzadih*, centrally located on a narrow alley near Bazar-i Vakil, but others had to walk a long distance. Mrs. Tasviri laughed as she recalled the numbers of women who have given birth on the doorstep of the shrine.

The series of points of view about the *imamzadih* illustrates the variety of ways in which people regard *ziarat* and shrine specialization. Similar ranges of explanation could be cited for other shrines. Some believers know the bare facts of the system and take them for granted, others are acquainted with elaborate legends about the shrine, and a few adduce quasi-scientific explanations for pilgrimage customs. Yet in each case, the people are involved in the system of pilgrimage; their different ways of understanding it all support the pattern of *ziarat* as it exists in Shiraz.

Should a child fall sick or suffer an accident, Siyyid 'Ala ul din Husain is the most likely *imamzadih* to provide assistance. His tender age at his death provides the primary reason for his specialty in working miracles. The custodian of Imamzadih-yi Zanjiri related the story of the boy's death to me as follows:

> He was thirteen years old and hid in a tree. At night he came down to pray—it was all so no one would see him. The daughter of the man who owned the land where he was hiding got up to wash for prayer. She saw him, light radiating from his face, and ran away. The *siyyid* went back up into the tree. The girl's family became worried and began to look for her. Someone said he had seen a boy with her, that the boy must have taken their daughter. They began to search for him. At night, when he climbed down to pray, they saw him. They cut him, hacked him apart with shovels and pick-axes. After that the girl, poor thing, came back and explained what had happened. When she understood that they had killed the young *siyyid*, she died of grief. Her father was very sad; he gave everything he had to Siyyid 'Ala ul din Husain.

Details of the story vary slightly according to who tells it, but all are in agreement that the *imamzadih* was very young when brutally murdered in a garden in the south of Shiraz.

On account of his youth, the *siyyid* is said to be very soft-hearted and quick to grant the requests of pilgrims to his tomb. In fact, Siyyid 'Ala ul din Husain is one of the most popular shrines in Shiraz and said to be the most likely to grant requests. Although one can present any type of request to the young *siyyid* and have good reason to hope that he will answer it, he is known for one type of cure in particular. Since Siyyid 'Ala ul din Husain died as a boy, he is very sympathetic to the problems of children. His shrine is renowned as a place where children's diseases are cured.

Not all shrines having specialties address themselves to difficulties characteristic of particular stages of life. Some problems can occur at any point, and a few shrines cater to pilgrims at just such impasses. In the case that follows, the shrine's ability is due less to the personality of the resident *imamzadih* than to his genealogical connection to a saintly personage.

Imamzadih-yi Zanjiri is known as a place where pilgrims seeking cures for diseases may hope to find help. The shrine custodian attested that food served at the shrine has cured the sick, both children and adults. She informed me that some enthusiastic visitors take the food home for members of their families and on occasion send it abroad. The *imamzadih* is a descendant of the fourth Imam, often referred to as *bimar*, "the sick." The fourth Imam is best remembered for the illness that prevented his participation in the Battle of Kerbela, in which his father—the third Imam, Husain—was killed. Accordingly, illness has become the particular province of his descendant.

The importance of an *imamzadih*'s genealogical ties and his personality unite in determining the nature of his specialty at Siyyid Taj ul din-i Gharib. The *siyyid* is known for his personality and is said to have inherited it from his forefather, 'Abbas, half-brother of Imam Husain. The *imamzadih* serves as a court of first appeal in the swearing of oaths. Hazrat-i 'Abbas inherited the qualities of wrath and bravery from his father 'Ali, the first Imam. 'Abbas, in turn, passed these traits on to his descendants. Taj ul din-i Gharib defends himself quickly, just as he defended religion and the rights of others when he was alive. He was described to me as the least patient *imamzadih* in Shiraz; he has a fierce temper and should not be underestimated. Anyone who takes his name in vain and swears a false oath at his shrine will be severely punished. Those who are capable of telling barefaced lies in the police station or courthouse may break down and tell the truth when confronted with the threat of the *imamzadih*'s power. The *mutavalli* informed me that some fifteen years back a man had sworn a false oath at the shrine. As he left the *imamzadih*, he was suddenly stricken with severe pain in the stomach and fell dead in the shrine courtyard.

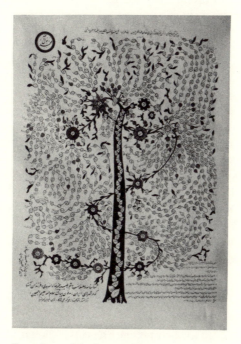

Genealogy of the *imamzadihs*

Times are changing; the *mutavalli* explained that we are living in an age of deceit. People are more ready to lie nowadays, and it takes the *imamzadih* longer to punish offenders. Nonetheless, there is no doubt that those who lie will suffer the consequences of their misdeeds sooner or later in the form of financial loss, sickness, or death.

Not all shrines have narrowly defined talents. If little is known of an *imamzadih*'s background or personality, it is most unlikely that he or she will develop a reputation for expertise in one area. Other shrines are so powerful that they defy restriction to special abilities. For example, Shah Chiragh, as the highest ranking *imamzadih* in Shiraz, is above specialization. He is a generalist among miracle workers, and all sorts of problems are taken to him for resolution. The same gentleman who compared the division of labor among *imamzadihs* to military organization described Shah Chiragh as having the paramount position of *bab ul havayij*, "the gate of needs," in Shiraz.[8]

Still, there are a number of *imamzadihs* who fall somewhere between their little-known fellows and their extremely powerful kin. They are intimately known, their personal inclinations and talents a matter of public knowledge. These middle-range *imamzadihs* are felt to be more easily approached than their more powerful and forbidding relatives. *Imamzadihs* of this kind tend to favor pilgrims whose pleas involve situations of importance to the *imamzadihs* themselves or to the Imams to whom they are related. The *imamzadihs*, like other men and women, have their own histories, abilities, and tastes. They are felt to favor the requests that are most touching, and these are popularly understood to be the requests of those pilgrims whose situations are in some way analogous to circumstances in the *imamzadihs*' lives or in the lives of their revered forbears. The mutual understanding that can exist between an *imamzadih* and a troubled individual generates a sympathy that, it is felt, can be put to work for the unhappy petitioner.

Even those shrines with particular spheres of competence may be approached by people with other kinds of problems. Theoretically, all *imamzadihs*, as relations of the Imams, can serve as channels of divine power and deal with any kind of request. The fact is simply that certain shrines are regarded as more likely places to seek particular sorts of favors. The shrines are different not in kind, but in degree. None of their abilities is mutually exclusive, and a prospective visitor to a shrine may select for himself or herself the most appropriate, congenial and convenient place to which to appeal. Generally speaking, pilgrims do recognize both a hierarchy of resort— some places having shown themselves to be more powerful than others—and a system of specialization among shrines. With these things in mind, men and women do their best to assure positive responses to their entreaties.

MAKING VOWS

Once the *imamzadih* to whom to present a request is chosen, a pilgrim must decide how best to phrase his or her appeal. Although a plea may be simply expressed, requests often take the form of vows (*nuzur*; singular, *nazr*). Briefly, making a vow involves the statement of a request, followed by a promise of what the petitioner will do in return should the plea be granted. The quid pro quo style that characterizes much of social interaction is felt to be an effective way to deal with an Imam or *imamzadih* as well. The process of vow making—like the appreciation of *imamzadihs*' specialities—is founded on popular understanding of the Imams, their descendants, and their relation to the Shi'i faithful. Vows are calculated to prompt the desired response by being structured in a way deemed likely to appeal to the Imam or *imamzadih* addressed. Here I will describe the process of vow making in general and proceed to a description of specific vows made at some shrines in Shiraz.

At a shrine the statement of a vow may be made orally or in written form or be represented by a shred of cloth or piece of string tied to the tomb grating or window. Fastening this cloth or string is referred to as *dakhil bastan*, or "binding the request for help." It is a concrete representation of the petition. One woman instructed me in how to go about it: "First you declare your intention [*niyyat mikunid*], then tie it. If your wish [*murad*] is granted, then you bring what you vowed; you leave the cloth tied on. For example, if you want to get a degree, say, 'I'll tie it; let me get the degree, and I'll give 'x'.'" In an extreme case, someone who is seriously ill may bind himself or herself to the grating around the tomb at the shrine and entrust himself or herself to the care of the Imam or *imamzadih*. The tying is not just a binding of the saint to pay attention to a request but the initiation of a two-way transaction as well, binding the petitioner to the saint as well. As with most social bonds, it works two ways. If the saint answers the petition, the pilgrim is then bound to provide what has been promised.

dakhil bastan

A vow may also be symbolized by a safety pin fastened to the tomb grating or pinned to the green cloth spread over it. A padlock attached to the grating will serve the same purpose. These things represent the closed luck of the suppliant. Fastening a shred of cloth, a safety pin, or a padlock to the tomb is a figurative statement of an impasse in the pilgrim's life, a symbol of the "knotty" problem confronting the petitioner. These tokens of vows can be seen in local shrines throughout Iran and testify to the prevalence and persistence of the custom. When a vow is successfully completed, some people in Shiraz go to the shrine in question and unlock their padlocks, then toss the keys and lock inside the tomb enclosure. This action is a concrete sign that the problem symbolized by the lock has been solved and that the relationship initiated by the act of locking has come to an end.

Unlike formally enjoined rites, vows, once initiated, need not be carried through to completion. At the time a vow is declared, it is conditional. It will be fulfilled provided that specified conditions are met; if they are not, the previously stated promise is null and void. A suppliant stating a vow will usually specify a time limit during which the desired favor should be granted and thus maintains some personal control over the process. Should the vowing process not lead to successful resolution of a problem, one is not left with a large debt, as would be the case in dealing with secular professionals such as doctors and lawyers.[9]

Should the desired state of affairs come into being, a believer is bound to keep his or her promise. I was advised by a woman experienced in the making of vows: "When I make a vow, I must certainly pay it, and it must be whatever I specified, be it sponsoring a sermon in memory of the Imams [rauzih], reciting a series of greetings to the Prophet, giving a sum of money to the poor, whatever. It is obligatory according to religious law [vajib-i shar'i]. If you don't fulfill it, it's a sin, the same as not doing daily prayers."

The process of vow making is then potentially twofold. The first stage consists of appealing to a holy person for a particular favor and promising a specified gift in return; however, the granting of the vow is out of the petitioner's hands. Only should this occur is the second phase, performance of the act or presentation of the thing promised, performed.

In some vows, as I came to know them in Shiraz, the individual making the vow implies a comparison between his or her circumstances and those of the holy individual being addressed; the comparison is reflected in the form of the vow. This comparison is often made at shrines that are seen as having special talents in miracle working. It is hoped that the analogy will be compelling and persuade the Imam or imamzadih to intercede with God on the petitioner's behalf. The comparison may be symbolized at the outset of the vow, in its fulfillment, or at both points.

At the shrine of Shah Qiys, son of Imam Riza, a woman wishing to bear a child may make a small cradle of fabric and place a tiny bundle of cloth in it to represent the child she desires. If her request is answered, the nazri, or thing presented in fulfillment of the vow, is shir birinj, a kind of rice pudding. Shir birinj is commonly vowed in circumstances involving infants, who are referred to as shirkhurha, "milk-drinkers." The shir birinj represents the woman's relationship to her newborn baby. In offering the pudding at the shrine, a woman is able to celebrate her answered vow with others who share her *nazri*.

The curing talent attributed to Siyyid 'Ala ul din Husain is reflected in the *nazri* traditionally presented at the shrine, *sufrih-yi Hazrat-i Ruqiyyih*. *Ruqiyyih* was the youngest daughter of the third *Shi'i Imam*, Husain. Following the Battle of Kerbela in which her father was slain, Ruqiyyih and the other survivors were led away to Damascus by the Umayyad troops. In describing the *sufrih*, cloth on which food is placed, and the sermon, or *rauzih*, recited over it, one Shirazi woman told me the story of Ruqiyyih as it would be recounted in the sermon:

> She wanted to see her father. They said she didn't understand the difference between the living and the dead, so they brought her father's severed head to her, covered with a cloth. At first she thought they were bringing her dinner, and she said that she didn't want anything to eat. When she understood that it wasn't dinner, she drew the cloth aside. As soon as she saw her father's head, she died. It is said that she was three years old.

The *sufrih* spread in her name takes a very simple form in Shiraz.[10] Several things are arranged on a cloth spread on the ground at the shrine. Four small candles are placed on a mud brick, one on each corner, and lit. The brick is included as a symbol of the ruins at Damascus where members of the Imam's family were kept. More specifically, some say that a brick served as Ruqiyyih's pillow when she was in captivity, and so the brick is placed on the *sufrih* in memory of her suffering. The only foods set on the *sufrih* are bread and dates. Thorns may also be added to represent the thorns over which the survivors of the Battle of Kerbela walked barefoot as they were taken to Damascus.

Vowing to spread *sufrih-yi Hazrat-i Ruqiyyih* is said to be especially efficacious when requesting cures of children's diseases, although it may be vowed in other instances. It is poignantly fitting that the *sufrih* and *rauzih* commemorating the death of Hazrat-i Ruqiyyih be presented at the shrine of the young murdered *siyyid*, 'Ala ul din Husain, and to mark the cure of an ailing child.

In vowing to give this particular combination of foods at the shrine, the petitioner compares the plight of the afflicted child for whom the vow is made to that of Siyyid 'Ala ul din Husain and Hazrat-i Ruqiyyih. Each is young and a victim of tragic circumstance.

Others seeking cures may vow to distribute *ash-i sabzi* at the tomb of Imamzadih-yi Zanjiri, descendant of the fourth Imam. *Ash-i sabzi* is a thick soup traditionally vowed in the name of the fourth Imam and need not be given out at the shrine. Imamzadih-yi Zanjiri serves as the Imam's local representative, and his shrine provides the place where successful vows to the fourth Imam may be celebrated. Many women participate in a large celebration of this kind, which is held annually at the shrine on the anniversary of the death of Zain ul 'Abed din, the fourth Imam. Women combine mourning for the Imam with the celebration of requests he has answered during the previous year; the observance serves as a testament to the Imam's power and his descendant's role as a channel for his miracle-working talents.

The juxtaposition of spatial, temporal, and culinary references to the Imam adds to the force of the ritual and its effect on the assembled women.

As mentioned earlier, some saints are regarded as generalists in miracle working; the vows that celebrate their talents are often nonspecific as well. A vow dedicated to the third Imam, Husain, involves paying visits to many of Shiraz's shrines. Imam Husain has an exalted position among Shi'i saints and is omnipotent in the realm of miracle working. Accordingly, *nazr-i Imam Husain* may be vowed in the event of any sort of predicament. Just as the vow is not particularized, so its performance is not restricted to a single shrine site. This vow is still performed, although less commonly than in the past.

If a person chooses to make this vow and his or her request is answered, the successful petitioner must walk barefoot through Shiraz on the eve of 'Ashura, the day when the third Imam was martyred. The custodian of Siyyid Taj ul din-i Gharib's shrine is well-versed in Shirazi pilgrimage practices. According to him, some of the people performing this vow also fast. Most important is that they control themselves:

> They are barefoot because on the field of Kerbela the people were barefoot. They say it is forbidden [*haram*] to wear shoes. They go with candles to all the *imamzadihs*. They go from Shah Chiragh to Siyyid Mir Akhar to Asunih [Siyyid 'Ala ul din Husain] to here to 'Ali ibn Hamzih, Qadamgah—all on foot. Even if they have cars, they walk. That night it is forbidden to go anywhere in a car, to laugh, or to make love. They pay respect.

The route people traverse is known as *chihil u yik minbar*, "forty-one stepped pulpits." It is supposed to include visits to forty-one holy places throughout the city. A woman describing the custom to me said that people stop in at places that are *aujaghdan*, literally, "having a hearth," in this context meaning "blessed." Among the places included in the route she mentioned are numerous shrines and some private homes.

On the eve of 'Ashura people fulfill this vow by, in some ways, reenacting the sufferings of Imam Husain and his family on the field of Kerbela. Rather than presenting something in consequence of the vow, they perform it. They share in the hardship of the holy family and in so doing energize their faith. The landscape of Shiraz, so well known to them in everyday life, is invested with spiritual meaning on this occasion. Participation in sacred history enriches the lives of those who walk barefoot through the city and serves as thanks to Imam Husain for assisting them in their time of need.

CONCLUSION

Through the declaration of a vow, a believer attempts to forge an alliance with an Imam or *imamzadih* and to state his or her case in such a way that it will compel a favorable response. If a favor is granted, the officially recognized correspondence between the holy personage and the believer may be celebrated publicly at the relevant shrine. Once the relationship is firmly established, a Shi'a may feel a certain kinship with the Imam or *imamzadih* who has proved helpful. He or she may then continue to appeal to that saint in the future and further strengthen the bond between them. The bond may last a lifetime.

Attention to the pilgrimage process, including vowing patterns, reveals a great deal about the pilgrims and their understanding of divinity as it is manifested locally. The specialties that exist in miracle-working indicate areas of great concern to pilgrims and about which men and women often feel uncertain or powerless. In appealing to the *imamzadih*s, pilgrims are able to lose some sense of their power-lessness, find comfort, and strengthen their faith. The very act of appealing to a particular saint offers hope, which may otherwise be in short supply.

In the process of vowing and the occurrence of miracles that may result, men and women come to see that divine powers are at work in the world, may influence personal lives, and are neither remote nor unyielding. The Imams and their descendants are approached as individuals; they are contacted as men and women who have experienced difficulties similar to those that plague pilgrims to their shrines. As a result of their own experience of tragedy, saints may be both sympathetic and helpful. The saints' individuality is reflected in their miraculous specializations. Religion is personalized at the shrines, which are regarded with deep respect and affection.

Pilgrimage shares the liminal quality characteristic of rites of passage (Turner 1974a: 182). Like a participant in the tribal initiation ceremonies described by Victor Turner (1967), a pilgrim becomes separated from the mundane world of his daily life and enters a sacred realm. The pilgrim is subsequently able to return to his social involvements renewed and the better for the experience. An important feature of liminality is its creative potential. During the liminal period ordinary social definitions and rules are suspended, and there is "a certain freedom to juggle with the factors of existence" (Turner 1967: 108).

At Shi'i shrines in Iran, the potential is sometimes realized through the occurrence of miracles. At other times a request for assistance, phrased as a vow, serves to transfer an earthly problem to the divine realm for readjustment. The petitioner is able to reinterpret his or her own experience in the light of divine cause and effect. A negative response on the part of a saint may be interpreted as a sign that suffering should be borne or that another saint should be consulted. In either case, the difficulty is no longer lacking in structure or meaning and the distraught petitioner is comforted or encouraged. Miracles for Iranian Shi'a, as for the members of an Egyptian Sufi brotherhood studied by Michael Gilsenan, "break the everyday routine and pattern of things by showing the unseen but 'true' form that lies beneath. They offer a reminder, a basic marker of the 'real' essence of the universe" (1982: 79).

The process of *ziarat* to the shrines of Shiraz and the making of vows affirm to believing Shi'a that divinity is not unapproachable. The divine is rendered palpable, accessible, and something of which to be fond, not simply in awe. By its repeated enactment, local pilgrimage reinforces belief in the Imams, their descendants, and their miracle-working powers. Further, the emotional bonds of believers to the saints they revere are strengthened through the process of local pilgrimage. The Imams' humanity is emphasized through sharing their suffering and their divinity is accentuated through experiencing their ability as intercessors. In and of themselves, local pilgrimage and vows made at the shrines of Shiraz express in everyday life the nature, form, and intimate quality of the sustaining relationship that Shi'i Islam establishes between the Imams and the community of believers.

NOTES

1. For further information on Shi'i Islam see Tabataba'i 1975, Chittick 1981, and Momen 1985.

2. A detailed consideration of the idea of the messiah in Shi'i Islam is provided in A. A. Sachedina's *Islamic Messianism: The Idea of the Mahdi in Twelver Shi'ism.*

3. The *hajj* may also be referred to as *ziarat-i khanih-yi khoda,* "visit to the house of God." It is, however, clear that this is a visit to a place rather than to a person. The *hajj* is the merit pilgrimage par excellence in Islam (see Bhardwaj 1973: 169), although the decision of when to make the *hajj* is dependent on facts having to do with the pilgrim's personal life.

4. This is true of pilgrimages in general. As Victor Turner has put it, a pilgrim hopes for "direct experience of the sacred, invisible, or supernatural order. He hopes for miracles and transformations, either of soul or body." (Turner 1974a: 197).

5. The close relationship that exists between women and shrines in Shiraz is discussed in Betteridge 1981.

6. For mention of specialization among shrines in other locales, see Christian 1972: 85, 87, 88, 119; Crapanzano 1973: 170; Eickelman 1976: 162; Mernissi 1977: 108.

7. While doing research at the Endowments Organization in Shiraz, I learned that the

Monthly accounting at Shah Chiragh

imamzadihs, like other Iranians, receive loans from their relatives. At that time Imam Riza had made a sizable loan to help his older brother, Shah Chiragh. The money was to help pay for costly refurbishing of the shrine complex. The popular and wealthy shrine of Qadamgah, where 'Abbas is reputed to have cured a child, loaned 30,000 tuman in 1975 (worth approximately $4,285) to Taj ul din-i Gharib, a descendant of 'Abbas, for renovation of his shrine building. The loan was being repaid in monthly installments of 1,000 tuman without interest.

8. This comprehensive title is usually reserved for Hazrat-i 'Abbas, half brother of Imam Husain and a very popular figure in Shi'i hagiography.

9. See Mernissi 1977 for a comparison of attitudes toward resorting to saints and medical professionals by women in Morocco.

10. A somewhat more elaborate version of *sufrih-yi Hazrat-i Ruqiyyih* is described as occurring in *Khurasan*. See Ibrahim Shukurzadih 1346. *'Agayid va rusum-i 'amih-yi mardum-i khurasan. Intisharat-i bunyad-i farhang-i iran* "23," pp. 43-54.

11

Sanctification Overland: The Creation of a Thai Buddhist Pilgrimage Center

JAMES B. PRUESS

Professor Preston has pointed out that the sacred place exerts what he calls "spiritual magnetism," a force that draws people out of their everyday orbits to journey to the pilgrimage center. The spiritual magnetism of a center is often represented in the culture as a great, mysterious force, but whence does it arise? This question is the focus of the following case study. The history of the founding of a Thai Buddhist pilgrimage center is traced from the point of inception through completion. The central problem faced and overcome by the shrine founders is where and how to obtain some artifact that could act as the dynamo that would generate spiritual magnetism for the new center. In the end it is decided to take a fragment of the sacred imprints of the Buddha's footprints from another shrine.

This process of dividing and transporting sacred objects has echoes throughout not only the Buddhist but also Hindu, Christian, and Muslim worlds. The bodies and possessions of saints tend to suffer innumerable such divisions. The holy relic embodies in the flesh the revered ideals that the shrine represents, but never as the full manifestation of the ideal; it is but a trace that expresses the mystery in which it participates only in an oblique or diminutive form. The tiny shard of bone, the sliver of wood, or the dust from a rock generates magnetism and so attracts pilgrims, in part because these relics symbolize an ideal, but the greater attraction in their presence lies in the very fact that they are so token and incomplete. They are but a trace, and only the active participation of pilgrims converts the trace into the ideal it stands for. This conversion occurs within the pilgrims themselves. The relic calls out to the living to become the saint, the hero, or the realized one in the course of their pilgrimage and so to manifest the ideal in themselves, and the pilgrims have answered and continue to answer this magnetic appeal wherever the culture—like Thai Buddhism—proposes that there are extraordinary but possible ideals to be achieved.

In this chapter, I describe and analyze a unique kind of Theravada Buddhist pilgrimage experience.[1] This particular pilgrimage (which occurred in May 1972) was not typical of the hundreds of journeys undertaken annually in contemporary Thailand by people who travel to well-known sacred places to secure happiness and future well-being through making merit (*tham bun*) (Pruess 1974, 1976a). First, the ultimate destination of the pilgrimage was a small, remote shrine whose existence was scarcely known outside of the region in which it was located. Second, the specific objective of the pilgrimage was the capture of this local shrine's sanctity or sacred power and its transfer to a second site over 300 kilometers away. Third, the pilgrims were previously unrelated individuals or groups from diverse socioeconomic backgrounds and places of residence. Fourth, the organizer and leader of the pilgrimage was a person whose religious role and reputation were beginning to attract considerable public attention. Fifth, the last stage of the pilgrimage itself was characterized by uncertainty and unpredictability, as most of the pilgrims did not know the exact location of their destination.

I begin by describing the objectives of the pilgrimage, the participants, the journey to the site, and the events that occurred there. Then I discuss the outcome of the pilgrimage in terms of its major objective, the transfer of sanctity. Finally, I consider the pilgrimage and its results as (1) an example of the transfer of imputed sanctity from one place to another, (2) an activity that is associated with charismatic monks, and (3) a meritorious enterprise that enlists the participation of persons from different local communities, regions, and socioeconomic backgrounds.

THE OBJECTIVE: THE DEVELOPMENT OF A SACRED CENTER

Prominent government officials and members of the clergy ask a venerable monk, with many years of experience in the monastic order, to lend his prestige to a meritorious project, the creation and development of a sacred center that will benefit the inhabitants of an economically depressed region. The center will satisfy the devotional needs of nearby local communities and attract merit-seeking Buddhists throughout the area. In addition to facilities for religious education and meditation, there will be visual representations of Buddhist themes and symbols as an environment for devotional pursuits. The monk agrees to provide inspiration and direction for the enterprise because it is an opportunity to assist the laity in their quest for merit and to leave an enduring, imaginative legacy upon the rural landscape of his native region.

Monks and political leaders have always been important for the establishment of sacred places since the time of the Buddha Gotama. According to the Theravada Buddhist tradition, the first pilgrimage sites were the four sacred places in India and Nepal associated with events in the Buddha's life (birth, Enlightenment, first sermon, demise), as mentioned by the Buddha himself and recorded in a canonical text, the *Maha-Parinibbana Suttanta* (Rhys Davids [trans.] 1900: V: 16-28). In addition, there were the repositories (*stupa, dagaba*) that would enclose the remains of the Buddha after his cremation. As Buddhism spread throughout the Indian subcontinent and into other parts of Asia, new sacred places appeared for the devotions of converts who frequently resided at a considerable distance from the four holy sites mentioned by the Buddha.[2] The sites for these new shrines were sanctified by the presence of symbolic objects or "reminders" of the Buddha: the alleged relics (remnants of the Buddha after his cremation) and their repositories, his personal belongings, the alleged "descendants" of the Bo tree (Ficus religiosa) under which the Buddha achieved enlightenment, "Buddha's footprints" (impressions in rock surfaces), "Buddha's shadows" (outlines of the Buddha on rock inside caves or on hillsides), Pali inscriptions proclaiming the basic teachings of the Buddha (the Four Noble Truths), seats from which the Buddha supposedly preached sermons, and (by the first century) images of the Buddha himself. With the exception of the personal belongings, examples of these objects have been discovered and can still be seen in contemporary Thailand.[3]

The presence of these symbolic objects by themselves, however, was not always sufficient to convince devotees of the sanctity of the sites. For many sites there were claims that the Buddha Gotama himself had actually visited the spot during his lifetime. These claims appeared in myths that were designed to "explain" the origins of sacred places to legitimate their special sanctity. In addition, many of these myths represented the introduction of Theravada Buddhism into the area by describing the Buddha Gotama's own alleged sojourn there. For example, in the Buddhist tradition of northern Thailand, there is the belief (recorded in a number of shrine myths) that the Buddha, shortly before his demise, made an extended journey through the region for the purpose of "showing mercy toward all creatures" (Sanguan 1965: 466-67). During the course of the journey, the Buddha preached sermons, made converts, and left "footprints" as mementos or promised the supernatural appearance of relics at certain places after his cremation. This belief in the Buddha Gotama's actual visit to a region beyond the borders of his native land is found in the shrine chronicles of other Asian Theravada Buddhist traditions (Jayawickrama 1971; Pruess 1976b). Furthermore, some myths assert that the Buddhas of previous eras had made similar visits and had been moved to leave appropriate mementos behind.

In Thailand, as elsewhere in Theravada Buddhist Asia, both the clergy and their royal patrons were instrumental in the establishment of sacred shrines as functioning institutions for pilgrims. While the available historical and epigraphical evidence on this matter is far from clear, it seems that monks may have brought with them from India or Ceylon alleged Buddha relics for enshrinement at specific sites as part of their mission activities of propagation or "purification." In addition, one may assume that, along with the doctrinal knowledge expressed in the Pali scriptures, the monks transmitted the lore concerning Buddha relics, footprints, and stories of the "Buddha's visits" (Damrong 1971: 173-74). They were certainly responsible for the composition of shrine chronicles that incorporated and elaborated such tales. Finally, monks were present at the places themselves and provided ritual services to pilgrims and local devotees.

Kings, the most powerful and influential of the laity, undertook the construction and repair of repositories, sanctuaries, and other structures at sacred sites. They were also responsible for the material support of the resident clergy at the shrines. These actions were expected, indeed required, of any ruler who aspired to the ideal of the "virtuous Buddhist monarch." The establishment and support of sacred places (and frequent veneration of their sacred objects) provided opportunities for kings to accumulate merit for themselves, demonstrate their piety, and legitimate their rightness to rule. Many Buddhists believed that a well-kept shrine and its well-fed clergy ensured the prosperity of the kingdom and its inhabitants.

These factors, then, have been important for the establishment of the famous and frequently visited pilgrimage centers in contemporary Thailand: the discovery, arrival, or creation of a sacred object; its enshrinement at a particular site; the construction of sanctuaries and other buildings; the invention of a myth that proclaims the sanctity of the place by reference to the actual Buddha or his disciples; and royal pilgrimage. While there is considerable variance between shrine chronicles and other available evidence concerning a shrine's antiquity, there is little doubt that a number of sacred places in Thailand have been functioning pilgrimage centers for hundreds of years. For example, the Shrine of the That Phanom Relic in northeastern Thailand probably dates from the 10th century or earlier, while the shrine chronicle states that the reliquary was built shortly after the Buddha Gotama's demise. The sanctity of the place has been confirmed by the actual visits there by Gotama and his three predecessors, each in their respective eras (Pruess 1976b: 18-28). Sacred places have come into being within the past one hundred years as well and are still being created at present, when gigantic Buddha images are under construction in rural areas. Symbolic objects have sometimes been brought to Thailand for enshrinement at a specific site; for example, in 1981 the Supreme Patriarch of the Theravada Buddhist monastic order in Bangladesh presented a "hair relic" of the Buddha for enshrinement at newly-built Wat Thamma Mongkhon in Bangkok. Or, as happened in northeastern Thailand in 1951, a Buddha image or casket containing a relic might have been discovered in a cave or other remote place and later enshrined at a nearby settlement.

We are concerned here with two other sacred places of relatively recent origin, one a functioning but minor devotional center for a little over fifty years, the second a product of the late 1960s. The sanctity of the former (located in northern Thailand) was activated through the discovery of rock impressions that local people believed to be footprints of the Buddha Gotama and his three immediate predecessors. The development of the latter (situated in northeastern Thailand) has, for the most part, necessitated the creation of Buddha images and other symbols of the tradition, including reproductions of the four Buddhas' footprints. In both cases, monks with reputations and followings were important for the transformation of these sites into functioning shrine centers.

THE SACRED COMPLEX

Wat Phra That Naung Sam Meun is situated at a remote, sparsely populated spot that many years ago had been the precincts of an ancient city.[4] This city had probably been the capital of an outlying principality of Lawo or Lopburi, a flourishing minor empire of the eleventh and twelfth centuries. It later fell under Khmer dominion and was eventually, for unknown reasons, abandoned to crumble into ruin. Besides a number of building foundations, only two structures remain of the city's past glory. The first is an alleged tomb of one of the rulers. The second (and most prominent) is a repository thirty-five meters high, built of red brick, said to enshrine the relic of an unspecified *arahant* (potential Buddha). The monument had stood for years amidst the scrub growth in splendid neglect, the most recent repairs (according to a dilapidated stone inscription) sponsored by the Lao ruler Cao Anu in the early nineteenth century.

The site of the ancient city was the official property of the Thai government, although inhabitants of nearby villages had been allowed to farm portions of it. The monument itself attracted the interest of provincial government officials and ecclesiastics who, in the early 1960s, wished to establish a temple-monastery and shrine at the site. After cultivating contacts with monastic and lay patrons in the upper reaches of the Bangkok-based national bureaucracies, the provincial authorities were gratified when the Department of Religious Affairs (a branch of the Ministry of Education) granted permission for the establishment of the new temple-monastery. The national government designated one-sixth of the land as official temple property, and by 1963 buildings and Buddha images were under construction and a resident monastic community was being recruited.

It seems that the planners of the project wished to develop a sacred complex where Buddhists from both within and beyond the immediate locality could worship, make merit, and become exposed to the Buddha's teachings as mediated by a resident monastic community and depicted in a variety of symbolic structures and objects at the site. In time there would be a school for local monks and novices and meditation facilities for clergy and laity. In addition to the anticipated spiritual consequences of the center's presence, there might also be indirect economic benefits for the inhabitants of a district where poor soils and uncertain weather combined to make local agriculture a difficult and unrewarding activity.

The sponsors of the project recommended as abbot of the new temple-monastery an elderly monk, Luang Phau Si That, who was highly regarded by clergy and laity alike because of the piety of his behavior, his lifelong devotion to the practice of meditation, and his reputed supernatural abilities. The sponsors may have assumed that this charismatic presence would be a magnet for donations and large numbers of pilgrims. A high-ranking government official, long an admirer of the monk, supported the recommendation, and the various levels of the monastic hierarchy acted upon it.

The venerable monk, however, who was residing in a forest hermitage, declined the honor. According to one of his disciples, the monk (at that time in his sixties) had never shown interest in becoming a "civil service cleric" (*phra kharachakan*), having all his life refused ecclesiastical titles, names, and administrative positions, however minor. He preferred to be addressed by the vernacular honorific *luang phau* ("venerable father") and to be regarded as an ordinary person pursuing the essentially monastic goal of individual salvation. His forty-five year career as a monk, however, was scarcely typical. In the first place, Luang Phau Si That had evinced a strong interest in the practice of insight meditation (*wipatsanna kammathan*) and during his early years as a monk sought out teachers at those places where this activity was encouraged. Second, he adopted the mode of life most suitable to the performance of insight meditation. During the first half of his monastic career, he either resided in remote forest monastic retreats in northeastern Thailand or else engaged in the wandering life of a *phra thudong* (from Pali *dhutanga*: "ascetic practice"), a monk who temporarily renounces sedentary living. During the decade prior to World War II he traveled widely throughout mainland Southeast Asia, covered territory by foot, usually alone or in the company of other monks, avoided all large settlements except those where Buddhist shrines were located, and settled into monasteries only during the three-month "rainy season retreat." These years of mobility were interrupted by short stays at monasteries in northeastern Thailand, where Luang Phau was already, without conscious intent, beginning to attract the attentions of both clergy and laity. One of the ironies of the Theravada Buddhist monastic career is that the monk bent upon world renunciation can never completely escape the attentions and needs of the laity in the world. The more insistently the monk seeks to withdraw to the relative isolation of the forest hermitage or the rigors of lonely travel at society's margins, the more attractive he becomes for the laity, who interpret this behavior as a sign of great merit.

Luang Phau seems to have perceived this paradox. His monastic career in the 1940s and 1950s definitely shifted toward the life-style of the town dweller. He resided in a series of urban monasteries in northeastern Thailand and in the national capital. His activities as a meditation master in these monasteries brought him into contact with monks from all ranks of the *Sangha* (Buddhist order) and attracted the regard of influential laity. For example, the prime minister invited him to preach at his home several times and wished to become a lay disciple. At the same time, his esteem among villagers of the northeastern region remained undiminished. Many of them believed, for example, that Luang Phau was an *arahant* (one who had already achieved Enlightenment, lacking only the supramundane characteristics of a Buddha) or would be reborn as one in the next life. Attributed to him was a supernatural prowess that resulted from many years of meditation. He was able to cover great physical distances in short periods of time (a reasonable assumption considering his history of prodigious travel) and was allegedly responsible for miraculous cures through the exercise of indigenous medical arts. At one time he could correctly predict the winning number of the National Lottery, until a deity warned him to desist.

While Luang Phau refused the office of abbot, he did agree to reside at the temple-monastery of Wat Phra That Naung Sam Meun and to provide assistance and moral support in the development of a sacred place. During his travels in northern Thailand, he had spent several months at the forest hermitage of the renowned charismatic monk, Khru Ba Si Wichai (about whom I will say more later on). He was impressed with this monk's efforts to publicize and restore neglected sacred places in northern Thailand, and considered such activity to be meritorious service for the laity. Assuming this role upon settling down at Wat Phra That Naung Sam Meun, he became the chief planner and architect of the project. He exercised a free hand in the conception and layout of the shrine precincts, selecting the kinds of structures, images, and sacred objects that would symbolically express important themes in the Theravada Buddhist tradition. Among these objects were the representations of the footprints of the four Buddhas.

PILGRIM'S OBJECT: THE FOOTPRINT RELICS

The veneration of the Buddha's footprint is an ancient custom in Buddhist societies. As a visible sign of the impression of the Buddha-person upon the mundane world, the footprint also symbolizes his birth, his "setting forth" in the world.[5] In Thailand there are a number of impressions in the surface of rocks that people believe to be "genuine" footprints of the Buddha Gotama. The best-known example is enshrined at Wat Phra Phuttha Bat, north of Bangkok. According to myth, during an actual visit to the region the Buddha Gotama left this impression as a memento to a hermit whom he had converted to Buddhism (Bidyalankavara 1954: 40-41). In addition to this specimen, there are a number of other rock impressions that are locally venerated as Buddha's footprints, especially in northern Thailand.

Temple-monasteries and shrines may include among their decorative religious iconography representations of the Buddha's footprint (*phra bat camlaung*, "holy footprint copy") that have been produced by Thai artisans. The chief identifying feature of such a representation is frequently an image of a wheel (signifying the Dhamma or teachings) upon the sole of the foot, one of the thirty-two extraordinary physical characteristics of all Buddhas. Luang Phau specified this design for the construction of four footprint "copies," one each for the Buddha Gotama and his three predecessors, Kokusandha, Konakomana, and Kassapa.[6] These objects, intended for veneration by pilgrims, were to be placed upon the circumference of a knoll located in the precincts of the temple-monastery.

These artisans' products were strictly representations. No myth would claim that the four Buddhas had actually visited the site. The presence of these objects around the edge of the knoll, one at each of the four cardinal directions, would be sufficient to remind people that four Enlightened ones had set foot in this world. Luang Phau, however, felt that a further heightened sanctity was needed. He recalled that during his travels in northern Thailand around forty years ago, he had stopped at a remote forest shrine to venerate footprints of the four Buddhas. Local inhabitants believed these rock impressions were genuine. The monk conceived the idea of a pilgrimage to this site to transfer some of the sacred essence of these authentic impressions to the representations that were soon to become prominent features at the new temple-monastery.

While the footprint replicas were under construction in early 1972, Luang Phau contacted one of his disciples, a young monk who was teaching at Wat Phra That Chom Thong, an important shrine in northern Thailand. To refresh his memory, he requested information about the precise location of the Four Buddhas' Footprints. The forthcoming journey was publicized among the monastic communities and their congregations in the vicinity of Wat Phra That Naung Sam Meun. The pilgrimage was scheduled for the latter part of May, to coincide with the major Buddhist holiday of *Visakha Buja*, which commemorates the birth, death, and enlightenment of the Buddha Gotama.

Briefly, the purposes of the pilgrimage were as follows: (1) to obtain rock samples from each of the four "genuine" Buddha footprints and transfer them to the footprint replicas at Wat Phra That Naung Sam Meun; (2) to venerate the four "genuine" footprints and present monks' requisites as an offering to the resident monastic community at the shrine; and (3) to view and venerate the celebrated Buddha relic at Wat Phra That Chom Thong, at which place the party of pilgrims would be joined by Luang Phau's young associate and several other interested persons.

THE PILGRIMAGE: THE CAPTURE OF SACRED POWER

Most pilgrimage groups in contemporary Thailand are homogeneous in their composition. They are made up of members of a village or urban temple-monastery congregation, or else formed on the basis of shared occupation, employment, or membership in some sort of formal organization. The group of pilgrims who journeyed to northern Thailand in May 1972, however, was composed of several aggregates of laity from different villages and towns that coalesced around a core of previously acquainted clergy. These monks, who were disciples, students, or friends of Luang Phau, publicized the pilgrimage among the members of their respective temple-monastery congregations. The largest lay aggregate to attach itself to the central core comprised both female and male residents of the two farming villages located closest to Wat Phra That Naung Sam Meun. In addition, there were smaller groups of men and women from two nearby district towns and the provincial capital. None of the members of these lay aggregates was acquainted with members of the others prior to the journey. Among the thirty-five members of the party, only twelve wore the saffron robe, women outnumbered men, and there were more middle-aged and elderly than other age groups. Three teenage novices were the only juveniles in the party; there were no small children.

The group traveled over 500 kilometers to Wat Phra That Chom Thong in northern Thailand. They rode in their chartered bus without a single lengthy stop along the way. To save time and money, Luang Phau and the lay organizers wanted to reach both Wat Phra That Chom Thong and the Four Buddhas' Footprints on the same day, May 27, which in 1972 was *Visakha Buja*, the most auspicious Buddhist holy day in the annual cycle. Because of the exhaustion of Luang Phau and some of the older pilgrims, however, the party decided to spend the afternoon and evening of May 27 at the former shrine and visit the latter on the following day.

The Shrine of the Chom Thong Relic is unique in that the alleged Buddha relic enshrined there is visible to the naked eye rather than embedded in a brick repository. During the daytime hours of the dry season, the relic is displayed inside a glass chalice covered with a perforated gold lid. Members of our group of pilgrims joined the hundreds of devotees from the locality (who were visiting the shrine on the final day of the annual festival then in progress) in making merit by "bathing the relic," or pouring perfumed water into the chalice. Unlike the proceedings on the following day at the Buddhas' Footprints, however, this ritual was performed individually and did not involve all members of the group assembled together and led in worship by a monk.

Six people joined the party as it departed for the Four Buddhas' Footprints the next morning. Three of them were natives of Chaiyaphum province, where Wat Phra That Naung Sam Meun is located. They were employed in Chom Thong district at the time as monastic school teacher, public school teacher, and agricultural extension worker. In addition, there were two residents of the town, a teacher and a watch repairman, neither of whom had ever visited the Buddhas' Footprints before. Finally, I was invited to accompany the pilgrims from Wat Phra That Chom Thong, where I was doing field research at the time.

One of the monks assured me that the trip to the shrine and back would last only five or six hours at the most; however, the actual event proved otherwise. None of the members of the party knew the exact location of the sacred place and how to get there. Only Luang Phau had been there before, but he had approached the shrine over forty years ago on foot from the west, from Burma, not by road from the southeast. Thus, during the entire morning of May 28, the pilgrims proceeded erratically on a series of rutted dirt roads, halted at crossroads to ask directions, hesitated at forks along the way, and made false turns and switchbacks. As the elevation increased, the roads became worse, and the pilgrims had to abandon their eighty-passenger motor coach and travel in the second vehicle on the journey, a 1.5-ton truck that had been donated to Wat Phra That Naung Sam Meun by a retired rice miller who was driving it on this pilgrimage. An hour later, a washout in the narrowing mountain road and the driver's nervousness (or inebriation, as some of the pilgrims claimed) brought this vehicle also to a standstill. At this point, the physical unity of the pilgrim group dissolved into segments that closely resembled its original constituent parts. Thus, the impatient Chom Thong contingent began hiking the last five or six kilometers to the shrine on their own, while the others settled down for a leisurely lunch. After the meal, the urbanites, the younger monks and novices, and some of the villagers resumed the journey on foot, while Luang Phau and the older pilgrims returned to a nearby village to hire an oxcart and driver to transport them the rest of the way. By 3:30 P.M., all of the members of the party, in twos and threes and half-dozens, had made their way to the village where the Shrine of the Four Buddhas' Footprints is located.

I must pause here for a brief consideration of these sacred objects. The four impressions of the Buddhas' footprints cover the top of a cement platform that is approximately 3.1 meters long and 2 meters wide and is covered by a pavilion to shelter the objects and devotees from sun and rain. The impressions are not super-imposed one on top of the other but assume a pattern in which the largest footprint (of the first Buddha, Kokusandha) covers the entire surface, with two smaller impressions (attributed to Konakomana and Kassapa) in the upper left and a slightly larger mark in the lower right-hand corner that was left by the Buddha Gotama.

According to local accounts, a hunter who belonged to one of the non-Thai ethnic groups in the region (probably a Karen) accidentally discovered these impressions over one hundred years ago. He had entered the valley several times previously but had been unable to kill or capture any of the game there. He informed lowland Thai monks about the footprint impressions in their natural state. Other devotees came to venerate the sacred objects and make merit by attaching gold leaf to them (the presentation of "wealth" to symbols of Buddhas).

The Four Buddhas' Footprints remained in this condition until 1929, when the famous northern Thai monk, Khru Ba Si Wichai, visited them. He noticed that the features of the footprint impressions were slowly being obscured by the accretion of gold leaf that nobody had troubled to remove. The monk arranged for laborers to cover the impressions and the rock outcrop with a thin layer of cement, from which the gold leaf could be more easily detached. The pavilion was erected around the platform. Soon afterward, the village of Thai-speaking farmers and gatherers of wild tea plants and its temple-monastery was established near the sacred objects. The shrine itself, however, because of its remoteness from main population centers and lack of publicity, attracted devotees mainly from the neighboring lowland district, with scarcely a single visitor from outside the northern region.

Unlike the famous Buddha's Footprint at Wat Phra Phuttha Bat, these impressions have not yet become the subject of a story that attributes their presence to actual visits by the four Buddhas. This lack of a myth may be the reason a local authority on northern Thai shrines claims that these impressions are not genuine (Sanguan 1965: 70). Several of the pilgrims in our group, however, did not agree with this opinion. Why, they asked, would someone come to this remote spot for the purpose of forging footprints in such impermeable stone? Only Buddhas, with their superhuman qualities, would have no difficulty leaving their marks on such a hard surface. After all, weren't Buddhas also "larger than other human beings?"

The members of the pilgrim group assembled inside the meeting hall of the small temple-monastery to present monks' requisites (robes, blanket, and pillow) to the abbot, who was the only monk in residence at the time. After the brief ceremony was completed, the monks and the pilgrims climbed the steps to the platform and the

Footprints of the Four Buddhas. The laypeople applied gold leaf to the surface of the impressions and placed lighted candles and incense sticks into small, sand-filled trestles at the base of the platform. When they were finished, Luang Phau and the other monks set to work to accomplish the chief objective of the journey, the extraction of sanctity from the symbolic objects for transfer home. First, Luang Phau, prostrating himself in front of the platform, requested that the guardian deities of the shrine allow him to disturb the sanctity of the place for highly meritorious reasons. Second, he and another monk took small wads of surgical cotton and applied each to the surface of one of the footprints to attract dust and bits of detritus. Each cotton wad was then deposited inside its own separate container, a tiny enamelware urn labeled with the name of one of the four Buddhas. These four containers in turn were placed inside a wooden box for easy storage and transport. Third, another monk, using hammer and chisel, removed four flakes of rock from a portion of the platform that had not been covered with cement. These four chips were wrapped in cloth and also deposited into the wooden box. Finally, all of the monks bowed down in front of the platform and recited in Pali (the sacred language of Theravada Buddhism) words of leave-taking, which are sometimes used at the conclusion of the devotional services (*tham wat*) performed among the monks at many temple-monasteries.

The veneration of the Footprints and the extraction of their sanctity were competed by 5 P.M. under an overcast sky. All agreed that they must start back to reach the truck before nightfall. The abbot, bidding farewell to the pilgrims, pointed out to them a footpath that would shorten their walk by four or five kilometers. Thus the pilgrims, who had arrived at the shrine in discrete clusters of individuals, undertook the first stage of their return in two groups, the majority of them on the footpath, Luang Phau and the older members of the party by oxcart on the winding valley road. They were accompanied by brief showers of rain, which brought a touch of coolness in the air and turned footpath and road, in more exposed places, into slippery tracks. The pilgrims were in an animated mood and were undisturbed by mud, moisture, or the land leeches that clung to the high grass at the edge of the path. The watch repairman from Chom Thong town who had visited the Buddhas' Footprints for the first time claimed that he had never walked so far in his life and had sore leg muscles to prove it. Nevertheless, this return walk was like floating through the air, only because he had made merit by venerating the four sacred objects. Other pilgrims noted that the benefits of the pilgrimage were already making themselves apparent in the form of the refreshing showers of rain; however, the passengers in the oxcart had an unsettling experience during their descent. At a steep dip in the road, the two oxen skidded on the slippery surface and plunged suddenly forward. One elderly woman fell off the rear of the cart as the driver, with difficulty, brought the oxen and the cart to a stop against a row of trees at the bottom of the hill. The woman, although shaken, was not hurt. The happy outcome of this incident was attributed to the presence of Luang Phau in the cart, although the monk stated that it was because they had just venerated the Footprints of the Four Buddhas; the merit resulting from this act would ensure the pilgrims' safe return home.

THE OUTCOME: LEGITIMIZING WITH SANCTITY

Artisans at Wat Phra That Naung Sam Meun had completed the four replicas of the Buddhas' Footprints on June 1, 1972, just after the return of the pilgrims from northern Thailand. On the following Full Moon day (the most important of the four "Buddhist sabbath" days that occur each month) there was a special ceremony during which the Four Footprint replicas were sanctified in the manner that I describe below. Unfortunately, I was not able to attend this event; however, I visited several months later to make observations and talk to people there. Before considering the ongoing evolution of the shrine as regional center, I must briefly describe the environment and structures of Wat Phra That Naung Sam Meun.

The temple-monastery/shrine complex is located six kilometers from the nearest village; its remoteness from urban population centers almost equals that of the Shrine of the Four Buddhas' Footprints, although the terrain is flat and relatively treeless. The compound is quite large, with much open space separating the various buildings and structures. These fall into three categories. First, there are the "historic" structures that existed before the sacred place was developed: the *stupa* or reliquary which encloses the alleged relic of an unidentified *arahant*, and the tomb of the ruler who established the ancient city. Second, there are the Buddhist structures or objects designed by Luang Phau in the late 1960s and intended for the passive observation or veneration by visitors: (1) the Footprints of the Four Buddhas; (2) a seated Buddha image, twenty meters high; (3) a reclining Buddha image, forty meters long and twenty meters high; and (4) wall murals and tableaux of figures depicting the punishments of hell and the rewards of heaven. (Unfortunately, space does not allow a description of the fascinating iconography and symbolism used in some of these creations.) Finally, there are the structures used by members of the monastic community and by pilgrims or as settings for the interaction between these two groups: large pavilion for instruction and pilgrim lodging, temple meeting hall, dormitories, kitchen, barn, food stalls, and ordination hall (under construction at the time).

The Footprints of the Four Buddhas are situated at the top of a low knoll so that each points in one of the four cardinal directions. The Footprints are identical in size, shape, and design: seventy centimeters long, twenty-three centimeters wide, painted gold, with a red image of the Wheel of the Law (Dhamma) in the center of the sole. How, then, does one determine the correspondence between any of the Footprints and a particular Buddha? This identification is accomplished by a small sculptured image of an animal that is located next to each Footprint. This animal represents the last bestial incarnation of each Buddha before the human existence in which Buddhahood was achieved. Each Buddha's proper name incorporates the Pali language referent for that animal. The correspondence of Buddhas and Footprints to animal image and point of the compass is as follows:

Name of Buddha	Cardinal Direction	Animal
Kokusandha (#1)	west	chicken
Konakomana (#2)	south	serpent
Kassapa (#3)	north	turtle
Gotama (#4)	east	cow

The Footprint that symbolizes the appearance of the Buddha Gotama in the mundane world points in the most auspicious of the four cardinal directions, the east, the direction of the rising sun. In the center of the knoll is a representation of Mt. Meru, the center of the Hindu-Buddhist universe, surrounded by figurines depicting several Jataka tales.

Unlike nearly all Buddhist pilgrimage centers in Thailand, none of the established objects or structures at Wat Phra That Naung Sam Meun links the site with any presumed manifestation of the "actual" Buddha(s) in this world. No object or structure had been infused with the magical power that this manifestation would confer. Luang Phau, through the pilgrimage to the Four Buddhas' Footprints, effected a "translation" of this power from another site where (according to local belief) the four Buddhas had actually manifested themselves. The sanctity of the "actual" Footprints, in the form of detritus on cotton wads, was incorporated into the shrine complex of Wat Phra That Naung Sam Meun in the following manner. According to Luang Phau's specifications, under each of the Four Footprint replicas was a depression in the concrete platform just large enough to accommodate one of the small enamelware containers of detritus. During the ceremony on the Full Moon day of June, each container with its sacred contents was placed into the depressed area of the appropriate platforms (the container marked with Kokusandha's name at the platform on the west side of the knoll, and so on). The Footprint replicas were then positioned on top of the platforms over the containers and sealed with plaster. The sanctity and power that adhered to the "original" Footprints were thereby enshrined in direct proximity to the copies of these sacred objects.

During the period of my visit, however, there was no way for pilgrims to know that this sacred power was near at hand—they saw only four obvious, stylized Buddhas' Footprints in concrete. The abbot of the temple-monastery said that eventually there would be a stone tablet with an inscription informing visitors of the sanctity of the Four Footprints and the details of the pilgrimage. (Nobody had decided what to do with the fragments struck from the surface of the rock outcrop.) In addition, local monks were preparing a pamphlet that would include the history of the ancient city, a biography of Luang Phau, the development of the shrine, and an account of the pilgrimage. This pamphlet would be important for generating publicity, as pilgrims who received copies at the shrine might distribute them among their friends and neighbors on their return home.

Also important for a pilgrimage center's emerging reputation is its designation as a "royal temple" (*wat luang*) by the national government's Department of Religious Affairs, with the approval of the king. This status is conferred upon certain temple-monasteries that have achieved some sort of regional or national renown. In early 1972, Wat Phra That Naung Sam Meun was decreed a third-class, "ordinary" (*saman*) "royal temple," which entitled the temple-monastery to financial support from a special government fund. In addition, two practices associated with all royal temples were already in effect. First, a group of government officials from Bangkok, the nation's capital, had presented new sets of robes to the monks and novices at the end of the previous "Buddhist Lent" (Pali *vassa*, Thai *phansa*). At most rural and urban temple-monasteries, this annual presentation of robes (called *thaut kathin*) is performed by members of the temple congregation or congregations from other temples in a form of reciprocal exchange between lay temple communities. At royal temples and pilgrimage shrines in general (all of which have resident clergies), however, special groups of devotees from outside the local community sponsor this ceremony. Second, the king had sent a huge candle to the temple-monastery for the beginning of the Buddhist Lent in July 1972. This candle was lit and kept burning throughout the duration of this ninety-day period. This practice, observed at all royal temples, is a kind of present-day substitute for the annual royal pilgrimage by kings in the past.

Thus, the design of a sacred complex that visually represents Buddhist myths and symbols, the transfer and incorporation of sacred power, and the ritual and administrative links with secular, national-level authorities have contributed to the development of this budding pilgrimage center. The real attraction of the sacred place, however, seemed to be the presence of the monk whose imagination and reputation were crucial to its development. During the day of my visit, there were three groups of pilgrims from nearby provinces in northeastern Thailand: one large group of 150 people and two smaller ones of 30-35 pilgrims each. These were villagers, mostly middle-aged and elderly, about 75 percent of them women. Wat Phra That Naung Sam Meun was the only stop on the itineraries of all three groups. The stated purpose of the pilgrimage in each case was the acquisition of merit by presenting offerings (monks' requisites) to Luang Phau in return for his blessing.

Luang Phau was meeting some of the pilgrims and chatting with them under a shady tree about five minutes' walk from the temple meeting hall. He was surrounded by pilgrims, people from nearby villages (including several farmers who had gone on the pilgrimage to the Four Buddhas' Footprints), and several monks. Visitors received the following items as souvenirs of their pilgrimage: (1) a small framed photo of Luang Phau practicing meditation; (2) a medallion with Luang Phau's image on one side, the image of the *stupa* on the other; (3) a small packet of "hermit's magic medicine," medicinal powder that Luang Phau had allegedly discovered inside a cave in the hills fifty kilometers away. After conversing with the monk and receiving his blessing, pilgrims dispersed to view the various sites in the compound.

Thus, the objective of the pilgrimage to the Four Buddhas' Footprints, the translation and incorporation of sanctity, resulted in the legitimization of Wat Phra That Naung Sam Meun through indirect association with the appearance of "actual" Buddhas in the mundane world. Nevertheless, in the eyes of pilgrims, this legitimization was secondary to their devotional needs as long as these could be satisfied by ritual interaction with a charismatic monk of considerable reputation, perhaps a potential Buddha himself. The power of the designer was more potent for them than the sanctified products of his design.

CONCLUSION: "SHRINE DEVELOPMENT" AS INTEGRATIVE ENTERPRISE

In the historical religions, there are numerous instances of the translation or transfer of sacred objects from one place to another. For example, relics associated with Christ, the apostles, and early Christian saints and martyrs circulated from Rome and the Middle East to recently converted areas of northern Europe. Gift-giving, theft, and commerce were the mechanisms of relic circulation throughout medieval Europe. Once a relic entered a new community, to acquire meaning in the eyes of new believers, it had to undergo a process of authentication, largely accomplished through myth and hagiography (Geary 1986).

Similarly, in Theravada Buddhism the transfer of Buddhist relics from India to the Buddhist kingdoms of South and Southeast Asia created new pilgrimage centers that were more accessible to converts unable to travel far distances to reach older sites. The acquisition of relics also served to legitimize the power of new Buddhist rulers in these regions. Monks were often the bearers of relics as gifts from an older monastic community to a new one. In addition, invading armies would pillage shrines and seize sacred objects to secure their victory and humiliate their opponents. (Relics of the Buddha, unlike those of Christian saints, seem never to have been commodities for barter or sale.) Tales of the Buddha's visits and other miraculous events soon appeared to authenticate the sacred object for new devotees.

In the Theravada Buddhist tradition, however, there have also been instances where the object of the translation from site A to site B was not a specific image or relic but, rather, other concrete objects that were specific to, and located within, the spatial boundaries of a particular sacred place. For example, some Thai pilgrims (usually monks) have visited Bodh Gaya in India and returned with saplings of the Bo tree (the "descendant" of the tree under whose branches the Buddha achieved Enlightenment). They plant these saplings in the compounds of local temple-monasteries. I recall a similar example in which a monk from northeastern Thailand who was studying in India went on pilgrimage to the four sacred places associated with the Buddha's life and obtained samples of the soil from the shrine compounds. He later returned to his home village, where the earth samples were incorporated into the local soil at the ground-breaking ceremony for an ordination hall at the temple-monastery. In these cases, translation establishes a connection between one's own local place for merit-making and the sacred geography of the Theravada Buddhist tradition in a more concrete manner than mere reproduction of a famous sacred object or structure (the copy of a Buddha image, for example, or imitations of the Bodh Gaya *stupa* in temple architecture).

The pilgrimage to the Four Buddhas' Footprints and its outcome illustrate the second type of translation. The sacred objects were not moved (as these were nonportable), but, rather, sanctity itself was moved, in the mundane form of rock fragments and dust. This material was taken to another site and incorporated into replicas of the "original" sacred objects to "legitimize" the site through symbolic linkage with the actual Buddhas who had appeared in the world. In most cases of translation from site A to site B, the journey to site A usually takes the form of a pilgrimage whose chief benefit for the participants is the accumulation of merit. The actual transfer of sanctity is also meritorious, because it results in the widening of the field of merit-making opportunities to new groups of pilgrims who travel to the newly sanctified site B. A journey was undertaken to the "original" Buddhas' Footprints to venerate them and present monks' requisites to their caretaker, religious actions that occur in all Theravada Buddhist pilgrimages. I believe that this use of pilgrimage to tap and transfer imputed sanctity from one site to a new site (thereby generating pilgrimages to the latter) is not an unusual phenomenon in Theravada Buddhism or other historical religions and is an important side effect of the growth and expansion of those religions, especially in those areas that are located far from places directly associated with the founder of the religious tradition.

The pilgrimage to the Four Buddhas' Footprints and the subsequent transfer of sanctity also enhanced a monastic reputation, which itself became more important for the ongoing development of the new sacred place (Wat Phra That Naung Sam Meun) than the incorporation of sanctity itself. Thus we cannot ignore the crucial role of Theravada Buddhist monks in the process of pilgrimage shrine development, especially as monks are both legitimate targets for lay merit-making and transmitters of the Buddhist teaching (Dhamma). In the case of Luang Phau, he admitted that his involvement in the design and construction of a sacred complex was intended to serve the laity of his native region; however, not only was this involvement for the public, but it also brought the monk to the public as well. The sacred place became an appropriate setting, through its symbolic association with actual Buddhas, for the renowned monk to reside and receive pilgrims, some of whom may view him as a potential Buddha.[7] The activities of Luang Phau in the pilgrimage and transfer of sanctity followed the tradition of the monks who transported Buddha relics from India into Southeast Asia. As a model for these activities, however, he chose a more recent exemplar than the missionizing monks in the early days of the religion.

Khru Ba Si Wichai was a highly regarded yet controversial monk who spent most of his life in northern Thailand, the latter half in a remote forest hermitage. His career and reputation were similar to those of Luang Phau in several respects. He was well known as a virtuoso of meditation and as a forest-dwelling monk who refused official posts and titles. Yet he devoted much of his time to "public service" activities for the laity. First, he was actively concerned with the renewal or rehabilitation of various sacred shrines in northern Thailand that had either been neglected by local devotees or else were inaccessible to them. One of his accomplishments in this vein was the sponsorship of a road to the hilltop shrine of Wat Phra That Doi Suthep, now one of the most popular pilgrimage centers in the northern region. In addition, I have already mentioned his contribution to the Shrine of the Four Buddhas' Footprints. Second, he propagated the teaching of Theravada Buddhism among various ethnic minorities of the region, an activity that did not necessarily result in larger numbers of converts but did produce a following of devotees from a number of different ethnic groups. This following, along with the monk's support from his own people (the Thai speakers of the northern river valleys who call themselves *khon meuang*, "people of the locality"), made him suspect in the eyes of the Bangkok government authorities, who viewed him as a possible focal point for regional dissent.[8]

Luang Phau viewed this monk and his activities with approval. Many years ago during his travels in northern Thailand, he spent several months with Khru Ba Si Wichai at his forest hermitage, where he studied and practiced meditation. He had been impressed both by the older monk's piety and learning and by his services to the laity. Returning to his native region, Luang Phau had settled down in a remote spot after many years of roaming. Unlike Khru Ba Si Wichai, however, he did not direct his activities toward any specific ethnic groups within a particular locality but rather made himself more accessible to a more variegated constituency.

This constituency consists of those people who have chosen Luang Phau as a target for their meritorious religious action. These people can be divided into three general categories. First, there are the inhabitants of the villages that are located near Wat Phra That Naung Sam Meun. Some of these people may work on the land of the temple-monastery, visit the place for devotional purposes, or send their sons there to be ordained. Second, there are the inhabitants of northeastern Thailand as a whole (excluding the villages in the first category), who are ethnic Lao in dialect and culture and adherents of a Theravada Buddhist tradition that differs from others in Thailand chiefly in terms of the annual calendar and content of ritual. This category includes both rural and urban people, although devotees from farming villages constitute the majority of pilgrims. Third, there are the government officials and other well-to-do elites from Bangkok, who undertake pilgrimages to Wat Phra That Naung Sam Meun to present offerings to Luang Phau and the monastic community, especially during the annual *kathin* ceremony. All three categories include monks as well as laity, although the monks are paying respect to Luang Phau as a friend, teacher, and senior member of the order much more than venerating him as a source of meritorious power.[9]

The boundaries of this constituency are determined by the limits of Luang Phau's reputation—the degree and the extent to which favorable information about this monk has reached people who will want to seek him out for purposes of merit-making and veneration. This information has spread beyond his native region through two main channels. First, the network of relationships among monks, especially between masters and students and between seniors and juniors, is an important means of transmitting information about any notable member of the order. During Luang Phau's travels and study in Bangkok, he met monks from other parts of the country who informed fellow monks and laity within their own networks and communities. A second but perhaps less significant channel for information is the bureaucratic, elite network of relationships, both among Bangkok officials and between them and bureaucrats in the provinces of northeastern Thailand. There are connections between this network and monastic lines of transmission, with the nexus perhaps being the Department of Religious Affairs in the Ministry of Education, although further investigation is needed to discover the positions of these linkages.[10] A former prime minister must have relied upon such channels as a source of knowledge that influenced him to seek out Luang Phau for the purpose of patronage.

Additional pathways for information about Luang Phau will be initiated by future pilgrimage to Wat Phra That Naung Sam Meun. The publication of the biography of Luang Phau as part of the shrine guidebook and the distribution of this guidebook to pilgrims may promote his reputation among possibly wider circles of devotees, although this result depends upon the number of pilgrims who visit the shrine, where they come from, and what happens when they return home.

Thus the limits of the venerable monk's following, considered as a "religious community," are diffuse and fluid, determined by the range of his reputation and the willingness of individuals to act upon the information they receive by using him as a target for religious action. The members of his following, however, do not constitute a "cult" in the sense that they share an exclusive body of beliefs and ritual, nor are they a "sect" that carefully differentiates itself from other religious communities. As is the case among contemporary Thai Buddhists in general, these people would not restrict their religious activities to encounters with a single monk, nor would they organize their religious action with reference only to monks, who, after all, constitute only one part of the Triple Gem (along with the Buddha and the Dhamma).

Obeyesekere (1966: 22-23) observed that Theravada Buddhist pilgrimage in Sri Lanka removes pilgrims from their parochial, local domains and unites them in an integrated "moral community" of devotees at a pilgrimage center. In recent years, however, pilgrims from various localities and ethnic groups have begun to view pilgrimage to important shrines in terms of their own particular religious or political interests (Nissan 1988). In the case of the pilgrimage to the Four Buddhas' Footprints, the participants were adherents of one regional tradition ("Thai-Lao" or *Isan*) who were traveling to a remote shrine associated with the regional tradition of northern Thailand. Their major purpose was to effect a translation of sanctity for the ultimate benefit of their own local community. Yet the achievement of this goal required matter-of-fact arrangements with Theravada Buddhists from other traditions, localities, and conditions of life—brought together in a meritorious enterprise that was organized and directed by a charismatic religious figure.

This joint participation by people at different levels of the contemporary national society can be illustrated in another instance where the Footprints of the Four Buddhas were important, not as a source of transferred sanctity but as a model for replication. In late 1972, the prime minister sponsored the construction of a large reclining Buddha image at a temple-monastery in a district in southern Thailand. One local district official who had recently visited northern Thailand and had heard of but not actually seen the Footprints of the Four Buddhas arranged through members of the monastic order to have a copy of the Footprints made for installation at the southern temple-monastery. The actual manufacture of this copy took place at

Wat Phra That Chom Thong, where local artisans worked under the supervision of monks at the shrine. The copy was one-half the size of the original. The entire object (including platform) was made of cement mixed with precious gems, which had been donated by northern Thai merit-makers. Local people had also been invited to donate funds for the project, presumably to cover labor and transport costs. The names of those who gave substantial sums were recorded on a stone tablet that would be transferred to the southern temple-monastery along with the manufactured copy of the Footprints in April 1973 (by truck and train, under police guard).[11] Thus another meritorious enterprise, drawing upon manifestations of the Buddhas at one shrine in order to grace the devotional setting of another, far distant site, involved individuals at the level of the nation-state and in two widely separated regions: government officials, monks, and those laity who could afford to donate money or time to the project. Such an undertaking, facilitated by modern communications and transportation, seems to demonstrate both the ideological unity and the sociological complexity of the contemporary Thai Buddhist community.[12]

NOTES

1. The pilgrimage journey described here was an unexpected and unsought event that interrupted the routine of my fieldwork on Theravada Buddhist pilgrimage in Thailand, undertaken from September 1971 to August 1972 with the support of a Fulbright Hays Doctoral Dissertation Research Abroad Fellowship. In May 1972, I was exhausted after covering Buddhist holiday festivities at the shrine of Wat Phra That Chom Thong and gratefully accepted an invitation from Phra Maha Prawet Rattitham (one of my informants there) to join the pilgrims. This outing, however, which I treated initially as a welcome diversion, assumed significance once I learned what these pilgrims were actually intending to do.

I obtained most of the background information for this pilgrimage after the event, through conversations with Phra Maha Prawet and other Buddhist monks in Bangkok, Nong Khai, and That Phanom, as well as through interviews with monks and laity during a day's visit to the pilgrimage's place of origin in August 1972.

2. These four places are Lumbini (the birthplace of the Buddha), located in southern Nepal; Bodh Gaya (where the Buddha attained Enlightenment), located south of the city of Gaya in Bihar state, India; Sarnath (where the Buddha first preached), located north of Varanasi (Banaras), Uttar Pradesh state; and Kusinara (the place where the Buddha passed away), located near Kasia, Uttar Pradesh state.

3. The following list includes the best-known and most frequently visited pilgrimages in Thailand. Each shrine appears according to the name of the temple-monastery (*wat*) with which it is associated, the province in which it is located, and the type of sacred object that attracts pilgrims.

1. Wat Phra Pathom Cedi, Nakhon Pathom (Relic)
2. Wat Phra That Doi Suthep, Chiang Mai (Relic)
3. Wat Phra That Haripunchai, Lamphun (Relic)
4. Wat Phra That Phanom, Nakhon Phanom (Relic)

5. Wat Phra Maha That, Nakhon Sri Thammarat (Relic)
6. Wat Phra Phuttha Bat, Saraburi (Footprint)
7. Wat Phra Phuttha Chai, Saraburi (Shadow)
8. Wat Phra Sri Maha Pho, Prachinburi (Bo tree)
9. Wat Phra Thaen Dong Rang, Kanchanaburi (alleged "Deathbed")
10. Wat Phra Thaen Sila At, Uttaradit ("Holy Seat" upon which the Buddha preached a sermon)
11. Wat Phra Sri Ratanasadaram, Bangkok (Image)
12. Wat Phra Sing, Chiang Mai (Image)

While Pali inscriptions of the Four Noble Truths are found in museums and temple-monasteries, they are not objects of pilgrimage.

4. The "Temple-Monastery of the Relic [at the] Pond [of the] Thirty Thousand" gets its name from a marshy pond located in its precincts. According to a local myth, two princes (descendants of the ancient city's founder) quarreled over who should receive the right of succession. One prince called upon 30,000 deities to aid him in a battle with the other, who was assisted by some "forest people" and, with the aid of a hermit's magic, a fearsome giant. This giant so terrified the 30,000 deities that they plunged into the pond in alarm and perished.

5. According to a canonical biography of the Buddha (*Majjhima-Nikaya: Acchariya-bhu-tadhamma-Sutta*), after his birth the future Buddha Gotama took seven steps in the direction of the north.

6. Although there were twenty-four Buddhas who preceded the Buddha Gotama of the present era (*Khuddaka-Nikaya: Buddhavamsa*), in the Theravada Buddhist traditions of Thailand only the last three are mentioned with any regularity.

7. Tambiah (1984) describes and analyzes the phenomenon of forest-dwelling monks in Thailand whose charisma in the eyes of merit-seeking laity derives from their pious efforts to renounce or ignore the world. The charisma of these "forest saints" becomes accessible to the public by means of amulets or pilgrimage.

8. Keyes (1971) and Tambiah (1984: 302-4) provide more information about the political repercussions of this monk's activities.

9. Additional research is required to document these points. In these paragraphs I am only suggesting the broad outlines of the monk's community of supporters, according to the information that I obtained during the pilgrimage, my visit to Wat Phra That Naung Sam Meun, and conversations with monastic acquaintances of Luang Phau in northeastern and northern Thailand.

10. Tambiah (1976) discusses connections between bureaucratic and monastic networks.

11. I am grateful to Phra Maha Prawet Rattitham for informing me of these events.

12. The current close linkages between government and institutionalized religion in Thailand place this nation in sharp contrast to its Theravada Buddhist neighbors, such as Cambodia (Ishii 1986). During the nineteenth century, Siam (Thailand) was a strong state expanding at the expense of Cambodia, whose society was wracked by warfare and political turmoil. In the early part of the twentieth century, there was a conscious effort by the ruling elite to establish Theravada Buddhism as a "state religion" in Siam, whereas French colonial efforts to promote close ties between the monarchy and the clergy in Cambodia were frustrated by the nationalist sentiments and protests of many monks and lay Buddhists. In postcolonial Cambodia, mounting political instability was accompanied by disaffection from "establishment Buddhism" on the part of many rural people and the manipulation of Buddhist symbols and institutions by the urban elite, both of which were under way well before the civil war and revolution of the 1970s (Vickery 1984: 8-17). The Theravada Buddhist "establishment" in

Thailand (i.e., the *Sangha* bureaucracy and its lay allies), however, is confronting challenges by various Buddhist reformist movements that are supported by an upwardly mobile urban middle class (Jackson 1989).

12

Mission to Waitangi: A Maori Pilgrimage

KAREN P. SINCLAIR

This chapter documents a contemporary pilgrimage undertaken by a group of Maori, native inhabitants of New Zealand, and is an extremely useful study for making clear some of the essential generic characteristics of pilgrimage. The pilgrims visit a particular tree at which the spiritual power of the founding ancestors is supposed to have been stored. The Maori, like most Fourth World peoples, are suffering great dislocation and sociocultural distress in the present era, and so a journey to regain the hidden vital essence of the people is truly a quest for intimate communion with a culturally-validated ideal. Reconciliation with a difficult past and retrieval of the pristine, formative energy of a viable culture are the goals and the hopes of these travelers.

The important role of personal experience in pilgrimage is also brought out. While the goal of the pilgrimage concerns collective needs—essentially the regeneration of a traumatized culture—what guides the pilgrims' journey and serves as the means to reach the goal is the personal experiences of individual pilgrims, in the form of visions.

The malleability and syncretic quality of pilgrimage come out as well. In this case the ritual content of the pilgrimage is a fusion of Maori traditions and Christian processes, mixed with contemporary innovations. The journey to Waitangi is thus a fairly true representation of the state of Maori culture in the present.

The pilgrimage to Waitangi[1] was the undertaking of a rather small, select group of Maori, yet the concerns expressed and the issues addressed illuminate the position of all Maori in contemporary New Zealand society. Moreover, this pilgrimage demonstrates the persistence of Maori tradition in the face of considerable pressure to abandon the past and to conform to conventions introduced by the Pakeha[2] (New Zealanders of European, predominantly British, ancestry).

The pilgrimage described here, the third such mission, took place in September 1972. Annual journeys continued throughout most of the decade. The pilgrims were members of a religious movement, *Maramatanga*, that derives much of its meaning and symbolism from the Maori tradition of prophecy and from the members' understandings of Christianity. The pilgrimage to Waitangi was an integral part of their larger mission—to maintain vigilance over, and therefore to protect, the physical and social landscape that the Maori occupy in contemporary New Zealand.

This series of activities could quite readily be viewed as the marginal behavior of a remote group of pilgrims, yet time has vindicated these individuals and their ritual diligence. The members of *Maramatanga* continue to uphold a Maori perspective in an increasingly Pakeha world, and for this position they have won significant approval and respect within the Maori community. More importantly, the 1970s witnessed a reinvigorated Maori political presence. For 150 years, Maori and Pakeha have been at odds about the implications of Maori sovereignty and have quite frequently clashed whenever Maori attempted to express self-determination (McCreanor 1989: 39). Maori exercise of rights over land has remained a consistent issue. At present, this has moved to the forefront of New Zealand's political consciousness as the Waitangi Tribunal is faced with the adjudication of a multiplicity of Maori claims against alleged Pakeha usurpation of indigenous rights and prerogatives.

The pilgrims were, quite naturally, concerned both with themselves and with their personal sanctity. But in the course of the pilgrimage, the personal and specific yielded to more general commentary on critical aspects of the Maori condition. Over the course of this mission, individual interests were merged with, and were ultimately overshadowed by, the imperatives of the group. Pakeha values and Pakeha intrusion were examined and rejected. Waitangi proved to be an especially apt place to put forth alternative understandings of the past; this was to be an arena in which essentially religious undertakings anticipated decades of Maori political activity.

BACKGROUND

The Maori, the original Polynesian inhabitants, had been in New Zealand for almost 1,000 years before the arrival of Captain Cook in 1769. Arriving from eastern Polynesia, they adapted Polynesian culture to New Zealand's more temperate climate. Their first contacts with Europeans did not bode well. "Being forthright, most Maori struck back when the early Western visitors killed some of their fellows, thereby acquiring reputations for savagery" (Oliver 1989: 108). This inauspicious beginning deterred neither British colonists nor missionaries. By the second decade of the nineteenth century the British presence became undeniably established, as colonists eager for the opportunities denied them in England arrived in New Zealand intent on land acquisition and increased social status. Anglican and Wesleyan missionaries were soon joined by Catholics in the attempt to win Maori souls. Until the 1830s, however, Maori autonomy was maintained, as Binney illustrates: "It was a Maori world; even as the new ideas penetrated, it still followed logically that all human actions (whether by stranger or no) had consequences for those whose world it was. But by the 1830s, the two epistemologies were increasingly regarded by Maori as being in competition." (1989: 22).

Initially, Maori chiefs saw little reason to cast their lot with strangers whose power and prestige were untested. But missionaries were able to appeal to Maori interests by providing access to literacy, medical skills, and British technological innovations. New qualities of leadership, perhaps inevitably, superseded traditional prerogatives; the skill to perform in this new domain began, gradually, to eclipse notions of rank and genealogical seniority as a basis for tribal authority.

Diversity and variation marked the Maori encounter with Christianity. Such differences make it difficult to generalize Maori experience in the past and create obstacles to encapsulating it in the present.[3] The notion of "fatal impact" does not do justice to the complexity of the engagement of Maori and colonizer. Maori responded to ideas that served some purpose for them and in this way were able to maintain their dominant position well into the nineteenth century. As Marshall Sahlins (1985), among others, has pointed out, the system simply accommodated new ideas by molding them to structures already in place. This accommodation, of course, bedeviled the missionaries, who watched their work take on unexpected consequences.

In 1840 the Treaty of Waitangi (so called because of the site chosen at the northern end of the North Island) was signed, ostensibly ceding New Zealand to the British crown. There were, however, two versions of the treaty, one in Maori and one in English. From a Maori perspective, far from granting land rights to the British, the treaty actually guaranteed continuing Maori possession of land and protection of their autonomy.[4] The British, for their part, understood the Treaty as granting them colonial rights and benefits. Nevertheless, as Binney (1989: 25) points out, the Maori still held the balance of power.[5] Perhaps more importantly, Maori understood themselves to retain dominion over the land of their ancestors.

The ostensible goal of British colonial policy in New Zealand was to allow the pioneer classes, tyrannized in Britain by the aristocracy, a chance to lead egalitarian lives. By midcentury, however, it became clear that such classes came to New Zealand and in their turn tyrannized the Maori. Indeed, the colonial policy at this time was an interesting "combination of naive humanitarianism and imperialistic realpolitik [in which native welfare was advanced] through the confiscation of tribal lands and the destruction of tribal institutions" (Stocking 1987: 81). Not surprisingly, Maori resisted British hegemony, especially when they lost land at an alarming rate. By the 1860s, the differences between New Zealand's two populations had moved to the battlefield.

The land wars have been understood for the last hundred years as a Pakeha triumph, the inevitable victory of superior weaponry wielded by superior tacticians. The work of James Belich (1986) provides an important and necessary corrective. His reexamination of contemporary accounts leads him to the conclusion that the notion of unmitigated success by the colonists could be sustained only by repeated distortions and misrepresentations. Such sophistry was not deliberate. In the Victorian scheme of things Maori inferiority was axiomatic.

In Judith Binney's (1986, 1987) studies of two East Coast Maori prophets, one of whom was an active participant in the land wars, discrepancies between the written records of British settlers and the oral traditions of Maori participants again emerge. Differences in perspective and differences in the mode of transmission should allow us to anticipate divergences between Maori oral and Pakeha written accounts. Yet Pakeha versions are understood as history, while Maori representations are seen as folklore or legend. In this very critical sense, Pakehas, or colonials, have controlled history, at least the official versions. Maori narratives are transmitted and taught on *marae* (ceremonial land) throughout New Zealand.[6] But these are private, tribal understandings and cannot hope to compete with the stories that come under Pakeha dominion.

From the mid-nineteenth century to the present, a number of Maori men and women, wearing the mantle of spiritual leadership, have transformed private understandings into public discourse. These Maori prophets have repeatedly broken the silence that surrounds Maori renditions and have forced a less than enthusiastic public to take cognizance of an alternative point of view. This perspective has been most effectively rendered in a religious idiom. That should not, however, obscure what to the Maori would be the obvious political intent of these narratives. In the nineteenth century, the language of the Old Testament, summoning forth a vision of a dispossessed but Chosen People, proved to be an especially apt vehicle for the expression of Maori grievances. To the dismay of missionaries, the new introduced religion had been transformed into an instrument for dissent and rebellion.

Nineteenth-century prophets, embroiled often in personal confrontations with colonial authorities, used this imagery to express their disaffection and disillusion. They called themselves Jews, celebrated the Sabbath on Saturday, and defined themselves as Israelites, exiled from the promised land at the hands of Pharaoh. This identification allowed them to place some distance between themselves and the clearly New Testament orientation of the missionaries. More importantly, they asserted that moral right was on their side, a definite advantage in their struggle to "control the sign" (Comaroff 1985). Indeed, the interlocking frameworks of introduced and native understandings only served to emphasize the authority, or agency, of the prophets.[7] These movements did not intend to discuss the past; on the contrary, their intent was to define the present, and there can be no doubt that in this they were very successful.[8]

Te Ua Haumene, a west coast prophet whose message mobilized local Maori during the land wars of the last century, provides an example of a pattern that has persisted over the last one hundred years. As the founder of the *Pai Marire* religion, he has achieved legendary status among both Maori and Pakehas. For the former, however, he has become a hero, a voice for Maori discontent and disaffection, while for the latter, Te Ua represents a form of incoherent treachery that could be remedied only through colonial intervention.

The angel Gabriel delivered the prophetic message to a dangerously ill Te Ua. Almost immediately, he declared himself well, marshaled his followers, and commenced what proved to be his long and somewhat bloody career. Spiritual messages that impelled one to action, rescued one from the throes of sickness, or warned of impending danger were quite common in traditional Maori culture. The use of Gabriel, conceived by Christians as a messenger, is an example of how readily the two religious traditions could be molded to accommodate one another.

Although many missionaries did not support the New Zealand Company, an agency of colonization, Maori could not help but see in these men of God threats to their independence and autonomy. When war broke out, regardless of the stance adopted by the missionaries, troubling contradictions emerged. Men who had represented themselves as peaceful proved not to be so pacific when land was at stake. Battles took place on Sunday, an ostensible day of rest and goodwill. Far more troubling was the fact that two different sides, with two very different aims, were applying to the same divine source for assistance.

A new relationship with the introduced but undeniably powerful deity now seemed necessary. Maori, led by Te Ua and later by other prophets, sought to disentangle themselves from European influence. Increasingly, as the nineteenth century wore on, missionary Christianity was modified to accommodate elements of the Old Testament and the reintroduction of a specifically Maori ideology.[9] Now some Maori saw themselves not as Christians, a term used by the missionaries, but as Jews. Old Testament narratives of loss and dispossession gave meaning to the devastating Maori experiences of expropriation and subordination.

In the more than a century that has elapsed since Te Ua's death, five prophets have achieved national preeminence, while dozens of other visionaries have proliferated with more local followings. Some have advocated accommodation to the European, while others have attempted to establish self-sufficient communities that would be free of dependence on the Pakeha (see Webster 1979; Binney, Chaplin and Wallace 1979; Binney 1986; Scott 1981). In an attempt to prevent further settlement, Te Whiti, a Taranaki prophet, instructed his followers in techniques of passive resistance. Maori pacifism, however, has almost always been countered with Pakeha violence.[10] Such high-handed tactics have left a residue of bitterness and distrust that has lingered for most of the twentieth century.

In the early twentieth century, the Maori population stabilized and then increased, while several Maori distinguished themselves in the national arena. A Maori renaissance was heralded, but the effects of this were largely lost in the influenza epidemic of 1918, which registered a disproportionately high Maori mortality rate, and in the worldwide depression, where Maori suffered more devastating dislocation than did New Zealanders of European ancestry. During this time, under the leadership of such prominent individuals as Sir Apirana Ngata, Princess Te Puea, and Te Rangi Hiroa (Sir Peter Buck), Maori health became a national priority, land schemes sought to achieve economic prosperity for rural Maori, and traditional art forms were resurrected and redefined. Maori dances merged with European music to produce the action songs still heard today, old chants were organized and preserved, schoolchildren were taught *haka* (war chants), and youths were once again taught their genealogy. Nevertheless, the cultural domination of the colonists was evident. Binney writes: "But the reality was that all the manifestations of the state, even the native schools, had been imposed. The teachers attempted to set examples of 'English' modes of living and standards of dress. The curriculum bore little relevance to the daily lives of the pupils. The language in which they were now being taught was one only a few spoke at home. The distance between Maori and Pakeha was vast" (1990: 230).

Twentieth-century prophets also recast their message. No longer referring to themselves and their followers as Jews, they have come to rely, instead, on New Testament imagery. Maori selection, however, remains a critical component of their ideology. The work of the prophets, the movement from the Old into the New Testament, presents a view of New Zealand history that stresses the coherence of Maori experience. From the vantage point of the late twentieth century, the prophetic tradition has left a legacy of enduring divine favor.[11]

It has always been land that has divided Maori and Pakeha. In the nineteenth century, the loss of land came to stand for Pakeha betrayal and duplicity. In the twentieth century, calls for the return of Maori land echo Maori assertions of self-determination, identity, and autonomy.

THE MAORI IN CONTEMPORARY NEW ZEALAND

In the period immediately following World War II, Maori migrated from rural areas to seek better employment and social opportunities in the cities of New Zealand; however, for most, social advances proved elusive. Instead, Maori and other Polynesian migrants have formed an underclass with distinct characteristics, as David Pearson writes:

> Over the past forty years the rapid process of Maori urbanization, and the recruitment of migrant labour from the Pacific Islands, has followed a familiar pattern that marks the movement of migrant replacement forces from peripheral areas of low economic growth to expanding metropolitan core areas. Polynesian labour, almost exclusively unskilled and semi-skilled, and suffering the opprobrium and consequent discriminatory repercussions of a covert but widespread racism in the labour and property markets, rapidly formed a culturally and phenotypically distinctive subordinate fraction of the working class (1984: 211).

The Maori population has increased from 8 percent of the population at the beginning of the decade to over 12 percent in the 1986 census.[12] The fertility rate of the Maori population remains significantly higher than that of the non-Maori[13]; projections for the period 1981-2011 suggest that the Maori population may rise at over five times the rate of the Pakeha population (The New Zealand Population 1986: 44). Moreover, when compared to Pakehas, there is a much higher percentage of Maori under twenty five. Maori continue to have lower levels of educational attainment, higher school dropout rates, and higher crime rates than their Pakeha counterparts. A young, unskilled population—a cohort that is unlikely to find anything other than unskilled or semiskilled employment—raises troubling possibilities for the Maori and for New Zealand. Housing problems can also be anticipated, given a population typified by high levels of unemployment and a high incidence of teenage pregnancy (New Zealand Planning Council 1986: 57). Both urban and rural areas will be affected, the former because of the concentration of Maori workers and the latter because they must now accommodate returning Maori youth despite their inability to offer employment to these individuals.[14]

Today Maori activism is much more pronounced than at any time in the recent past.[15] This renewed attention to Maori arts and language has been recognized as a new Maori renaissance. The proliferation of preschool language nests around the country, *kohanga reo*, is an attempt to ensure that the Maori language is not lost. Here three- and four-year-olds are given sufficient instruction in Maori language that they often start elementary school completely bilingual. Moreover, the *Te Maori* exhibit's successful tour of the United States and its triumphant return and tour throughout New Zealand clearly increased Maori pride in their artistic heritage and led to a focus on the artistic potential of many contemporary artists.[16]

By far, the greatest index of renewed Maori activism has been the vigorous reexamination of traditional Maori land rights. Land has become a critical link between the past and the future (Greenland 1984: 86). The history of European settlement is now understood as treacherous confiscation of the Maori's most valuable asset. Indeed, the economic concerns that motivated New Zealand's development have been called into question by Maori radicals, who have asserted that this process deprived the Maori of both their land and their culture. In the continuing debate Maori spiritual links to the land are contrasted to the Pakeha's purely economic interest. More to the point, the contemporary problems of the Maori are laid at the feet of a society based on materialism and nonhumanistic values.[17]

Inevitably, the dissonance between the myth and the reality of New Zealand's ethnic situation has emerged (Levine 1987: 423). These themes, along with questions of land and resource ownership and management, are being played out in the Waitangi Tribunal. Under the Treaty of Waitangi Act, 1975, and its amendment in 1984, the tribunal, which has been hearing claims involving rights to fishing grounds and control of resources, has restructured Maori-Pakeha relations. Anthropologists and historians (see Levine 1987; Sorrenson 1987) have suggested that the treaty is being reinterpreted and Maori perspectives are, for the first time, being given a fair hearing. Inevitably, both Maori and Pakeha perceptions of the past must change as the Tribunal introduces a Maori view of history into New Zealand discourse. It is certainly significant that the pilgrims to Waitangi set themselves this task fifteen years earlier.

MARAMATANGA

The men, women, and children who journeyed to Waitangi belong to a religious movement, *Maramatanga*, whose name means "light," "enlightenment," or "knowledge." The term derives further significance from its association with a Maori prophetess, Mere Rikiriki, who called her own work *maramatanga* and who was active at the turn of the century. In the 1930s, an itinerant prophet, Mareikura, brought his gifts and his message back to his tribal area in the center of the North Island. He, like many other of his followers, had traveled about, visiting the *marae* of other religious leaders. In the course of these journeys, he came to understand his own gifts and began to define his mission.

Mareikura discovered that, like other leaders, he was able to divine the causes of personal and physical distress. His home *marae* became a focus for individuals seeking relief from a variety of afflictions. But for his descendants, his legacy is to be found in his fidelity to ringing a bell at seven o'clock in the morning and evening to summon people to prayer. That bell continues to be rung twice a day at the appointed hour; indeed, seven o'clock prayers continue to be seen as essential. Mareikura, following the work of Mere Rikiriki, felt that it was his job to *tapae*, to lay to rest the ancestral spirits that continue to move over the New Zealand landscape.[18] Therefore, from the earliest days of the movement's history, its members have taken responsibility for the ritual status of the ground they occupy. More importantly, their actions attest to the enduring importance of the past for the construction and understanding of the present.

In 1935, the direction of the movement shifted. That year, Mareikura's granddaughter Liina died at the age of fourteen. This death was an enormous blow to her family, for she had been an especially beloved child. Her parents' grief was intensified because they had already lost another child in the influenza epidemic of 1918. As her grieving relatives gathered around her coffin, Liina's spirit came back. Mareikura's daughter, Anaera, bereft and despairing, was not comforted by the spiritual return of her lost child. On the contrary, the events of that evening terrified her. She was convinced, gently by her father, more forcefully by others, to allow the child's spirit to speak.

For years Liina communicated with her family through her mother. Anaera was a reluctant medium, receiving messages while dreaming. Still asleep, she would utter the message or sing the song aloud. Others, listening intently, would write down whatever communications Anaera disclosed. Often, when she awoke, she could not recall them.

Anaera continued the work of her father and undertook, with the spiritual help of her daughter, a variety of missions. The most important of these was to Rotokura, a lake within the vicinity of the *marae* that, so the members learned through revelation, contained healing waters. Members continue to journey there on annual pilgrimages.

The responsibilities of leadership proved difficult for someone of Anaera's disposition and temperament. Shortly before her death in 1948, she fasted for a period of seven days and seven nights. At the end of that time, the channels were opened. Now, the spirits of the dead, known collectively as *wairua*, could communicate with any member of *Maramatanga* without the assistance of a human intercessor. This change reallocated responsibility and redefined leadership. Anaera and Liina no longer held a monopoly on spiritual communication.

Traditional Maori society had been stratified according to principles of genealogical seniority, rank, and gender. These were, now, to be of no account. The universal accessibility of the spiritual realm would overwhelm more mundane distinctions. This departure from traditional sources of hierarchy was to have a radical impact on relationships within the movement. Following the example of Anaera, women have continued to receive messages. Following Liina, many of the identifiable *wairua* have been female. Perhaps more significantly, the books that record songs, dreams, and other sources of revelation believed to have been sent by the *wairua* have, by and large, been kept and passed down through women. Similarly, younger members need not defer to their elders in matters of revelation. Yet members of the movement are very aware of the hierarchical classifications that describe the Maori social universe. In fact, these distinctions, based on genealogical ascendancy and principles of seniority, are characteristic landmarks in a world that is too often dominated by Pakeha conventions.

The tension between hierarchy and equality, however, is less significant than the inescapable differential of knowledge and ability among the members of the movement. Although the spiritual world and the inspiration it provides are ostensibly accessible to all members, the ability to navigate the complexities of *Maramatanga*'s ideological and ritual system is not as evenly distributed. Despite an ideology that would suggest otherwise, some individuals distinguish themselves—by the force of their personality, by their penetrating insights, by their ability to sustain contact with the *wairua*. Implicitly, these differences are recognized. They are most recognizable at times of great ritual moment, such as during pilgrimages and other missions.

For the past fifty years, members of *Maramatanga* have been in touch with the spirits of the dead. The *wairua* are seen as messengers and guardians, alerting and protecting their charges in a world marked by treachery and betrayal. As in the traditional Maori world, *wairua* use songs, chants, and dreams to communicate with the living. Individuals are obligated to share any spiritual revelation with other members of the group. Such sharing takes place at a yearly round of gatherings (each known as a *ra*) that commemorates events in the spiritual history of the movement.

On these occasions, members gather to give thanks for their good fortune, to seek spiritual assistance in the face of misfortune, and to discuss, debate, and dissect messages and dreams that have been received. Pressing problems will get an airing in these circumstances, with the advice of the group sought and given. Despite any divisions that might mar the movement, Maori hospitality is celebrated in an ambience that emphasizes unity and harmony.

For most members, the *ra* provide an opportunity to increase their spirituality. Such occasions are seen as refuges from a world that is dominated by Europeans; they are viewed as a time for replenishing the resources of the individual and of the group. It is almost with relief that people turn to the spirits and to one another to affirm the value of being Maori. Through songs and dreams the spiritual world lends support to this contention. On the days set aside for the celebration of the spiritual, the members are confident that they are working under the auspices of the *wairua* in a world temporarily untainted by the Pakeha. This round of spiritual commemorations organizes the year for members of *Maramatanga* and remains an intensely satisfying experience.

Members of *Maramatanga* are very aware of the tradition of Maori prophecy. Indeed, many of the ancestors of the current membership traveled from the *marae* of one prophet to that of another. The idiom of revelation has been deeply engraved. But because for the members of *Maramatanga* channels with the spiritual world have been opened, the legacy of Anaera is felt by all Mareikura's descendants. The members refer to themselves as "the chosen few," the *hungaruarua*, and their work is known as *tikanga*.[19] *Tikanga*, while asserting the tribal rules of rightness and correctness, speaks as well to tribal authority.

These rules define the context in which the beliefs and practices of *Maramatanga* are enacted. This code links the current membership to their immediate history, while missions and pilgrimages engender confrontations with the more distant but nevertheless potent time of the ancestors. Maori is the one language of revelation; Maori etiquette governs all ritual events. This monopoly of Maori conventions effectively precludes a Pakeha influence on any activity of great moment. On these occasions, the presence of the past is undeniable.

The contemporary members of *Maramatanga* have worked hard to retain fidelity to their past. Many of the older generation are bilingual and are painstakingly instructing their children to carry on tribal traditions, for theirs is an important tribe, one renowned for the jealousy with which it guards tribal matters. The prestige of their tribal affiliation and their notable facility in Maori concerns have often made them exemplars of the persistence of tradition in the modern world. But they also participate at all levels in the hierarchy of the Catholic church in New Zealand. Members of *Maramatanga* largely comprised the delegation to Rome that petitioned the pope for a Maori archbishopric in 1986. Today, the newly appointed Maori archbishop is frequently accompanied by the members of the movement, for they have known him since his youth as a parish priest.

Their mundane lives have certainly been touched by the employment, housing, and other difficulties that affect Maori generally as a disadvantaged group. But the spiritual guidance that they have come to expect allows them to assume an activist stance and to turn to advantage many of the liabilities of their present situation. Theirs is one of the most successful *kohanga reo*, ("language nests") in the country. Many of their young people have returned from the cities of the North Island because of their inability to find work. At present, they have been incorporated into work schemes that emphasize Maori weaving, carving, and music. Unlike many young people, they are participants in a stable community at the same time that they are also enhancing their ability to function within a Maori context. Nevertheless the pressing social problems that all Maori confront should not be minimized; Maori are still underemployed, and there is not enough suitable housing. Many movement members rely on pensions and government grants, but the dismantling of New Zealand's welfare state over the last decade has left these individuals, and others like them, especially vulnerable.

In the years preceding the missions to Waitangi, members of *Maramatanga* persisted in their concern with the ritual integrity of what they defined as a Maori domain. When the government threatened to dam a river, which would, as a result, overflow its banks in areas where the members' ancestors were buried, a pilgrimage was undertaken to a mountain that had always protected this group and that was also the source of the disputed river. The proposed dam was never built. More important, however, is the vigilance that this movement demonstrates; they see themselves as responsible for shaping and protecting the physical and spiritual landscape. Pilgrimage has allowed them to participate in this process.

During the late 1960s, members attended a *whare wananga* conducted by an important ritual specialist. This was the traditional school of learning, in which esoteric lore was imparted to chosen individuals. Although many ethnographers have maintained that this institution was no longer functioning in the twentieth century, the experience of the members of *Maramatanga* runs counter to conventional wisdom. At the least, this fact demonstrates the degree to which the Maori world has remained inaccessible to European scrutiny.

In their journeys to Waitangi, the pilgrims of *Maramatanga* have actively engaged the Maori past. Waitangi, the site where land rights were relinquished, provided an appropriate arena for a Maori reenactment and reinterpretation of history. This task could not be easy.[20] Annual pilgrimages went on for a decade and spanned the 1970s. The third pilgrimage, which I attended, took place in September 1972. The pilgrimages and the visions that inspired them address the excesses of the colonial experience. More directly, they confront the contradiction of how a treaty meant to protect the Maori left them disenfranchised. On this issue a small band of pilgrims, basing their actions on private revelation and tribal, almost parochial concerns, came face-to-face with New Zealand's destiny.

EARLY PILGRIMAGES TO WAITANGI

It was formerly a common belief in New Zealand that the ancestors of the contemporary Maori arrived in seven canoes from a legendary Hawai'iki.[21] The tribal divisions found among Maori today are held to be derived from the canoes and their landing spots at various sites on the North Island. So strong is this belief that individuals who know little of their genealogy can readily supply the name of their ancestral canoe. In the 1950s, Mareikura's son-in-law and his ward were inspired to journey to the seven canoes' landing sites, scattered throughout the North Island. At that time, they removed the *mauri* (life force) from them. One of the ostensible reasons to go to Waitangi was to return the *mauri*. (This is transmitted spiritually, not physically.)

Another member received a vision that prompted the pilgrimage at this particular time. Here, revelation provided both insight into past events and a narrative that gives a distinctly Maori turn to New Zealand's colonial history. According to this vision, in 1840, all the paramount chiefs, representing all seven canoes, arrived in Waitangi. The wisdom of signing the treaty was hotly debated. A local *tohunga* (religious leader) grew concerned that power and politics dominated a situation where such powerful chiefs were involved. The *tohunga* suggested that the *mana* of the leaders be buried in the ground, thereby freeing them to make their decision unencumbered. He then planted a *karaka* tree on top of this sacred spot. Here it would remain until claimed by a future generation. The tree, taking root in the sacred *mana* of the Maori people, would inevitably be *tapu* (ritually charged, sacrosanct).[22] For the members this revelation defined their purpose; the intention of the first mission to Waitangi in 1970 was literally to reclaim the *mana* of their ancestors and to restore the *mauri* to the people. When this purpose has been accomplished, all Maori will derive the benefit of restored power and sanctity while they themselves will be vindicated; the *wairua* have indeed given them assistance to be the *hungaruarua*, the chosen few, while their diligence and deprivation in pursuit of this goal further justify their view of themselves as spiritual workers. The motivation for the first mission was derived, then, from an amalgam of generally available New Zealand history and Maori traditions (the Treaty of Waitangi, the tradition of the seven canoes) and their own esoteric information provided by revelation. What emerges is not only a coherent construction of the past but a reasonable description of their present circumstances. A problematic treaty has left the Maori powerless, their source of strength somehow buried, almost, but not quite, accessible. Through these visions, the members of *Maramatanga* are expressing the Maori loss of their vital essence. They realize that if, somehow, they can succeed in retrieving and restoring it, they will have a potent weapon in their battle with colonial interlopers. Moreover, the selection of Waitangi as a site demonstrates the degree to which the members of *Maramatanga* speak to a tradition that depends on the dual authority of biblical discourse and Maori notions of spiritual revelation.

When they arrived in Waitangi, their first task was to approach the tree. In addition to their own knowledge of the tree's sacredness, there had been rather widespread feeling in New Zealand that the tree was ritually powerful. There was, then, naturally some trepidation as they neared it. Suddenly, one woman was seized by a desire to reach out, touch the tree, and shake its hand. To her surprise and relief, the tree responded in kind by grabbing her hand and shaking it back. The pilgrims then prayed and recited a rosary. The old and the new were not merely blended, but one was transformed into the other. For the membership of *Maramatanga*, this fusion justified their view of themselves as pivots of history. For those who witnessed and for others who heard of the event, this was strong evidence that peace had been made at last with the *karaka* tree; no longer would it inflict suffering upon unwitting trespassers. Members maintained that in the years following that initial encounter, the tree has blossomed and borne fruit. There can be no doubt that for these pilgrims their reconciliation with the tree was the beginning of a new accommodation to the past.

The second mission in 1971 continued the themes of the first; now, however, children and their emergent Maori identity were the focus. Both of the early missions attempt a reconciliation with the behavior of their ancestors. Traditional beliefs and Christianity are fused to form a coherent means of dealing with a situation that neither on its own can handle. According to another vision about the tree, members have been told that the fruits shall be eaten by subsequent generations. Explicitly, fruition and growth in the future are contrasted with the sterility and barrenness of the past. A tree rooted in the buried power of their ancestors and now transformed by Maori chants and Christian prayers is a remarkably apt image for a people who are renegotiating their past. More importantly, with each successive vision, the authority, the authorship, and the ultimate responsibility of these pilgrims for their past and for their history become more obvious.

THE THIRD PILGRIMAGE TO WAITANGI

The third pilgrimage took place in September 1972. For the members of the movement my participation was, after six months of fieldwork, only slightly disruptive. By my presence, however, I was able to act as a witness to their claims of superior spirituality. This was expressed as a value to be judged against European acquisitiveness and materialism. As the mission progressed and as spiritual messages multiplied, they were certainly able to sustain this view of themselves.

The third pilgrimage continued the task undertaken in the previous two. Here the major differences from other pilgrimage situations are evident; the same pilgrims journeyed year after year to the same sacred site, the significance of their mission known only to themselves, their goals never quite fulfilled. For many individuals and to the membership at large, each mission lacked a sense of closure. Nevertheless, there are many structural similarities with the pilgrims of other religious traditions.

Plans for the pilgrimage involved assembling at Kurapita (a pseudonym[23]) in the center of the North Island on Thursday, journeying to Auckland on Friday, and undertaking the first leg, Auckland to Waitangi, on Saturday. This schedule was essentially maintained but was altered somewhat to accommodate the sudden death of a close relative and her *tangi* (funeral ritual) in a neighboring town. All traveling was done in automobiles, several of which were at least fifteen years old and in less than perfect repair. There had been considerable dissension in the weeks preceding the pilgrimage that ultimately resulted in the decision by several members not to embark on this particular mission. Their absence, however, informed the behavior of others. To protect themselves from recriminations, the pilgrims established strict rules of conduct that were followed diligently: all the cars remained together in one convoy, prayers were said at the appropriate times of the day in the suitable places along the way, and most members fasted and refrained from smoking during the trip between Auckland and Waitangi.

Those who had decided not to go, while offering their prayers, were explicitly suspicious of the enterprise. In fact, one hour before we actually left, I was contacted by a woman who assured me she had received a spiritual message and the trip was off. By contrast, those who went had their own interpretation. They maintained that they had been subjected to a test and only a few had held fast—a notion that was to become explicit in the messages that were received in the course of the trip. Nevertheless, upon learning of car breakdowns and misunderstandings about directions and meeting places, several of those who remained behind assumed attitudes of scarcely concealed self-righteousness.

Visions started even before the first leg of the journey was under way. While in a south central town awaiting the rest of us, one woman suddenly saw a tree in her living room. An airplane hovered about its upper branches, then came to rest on the tree. As it did so, the vision disappeared. There was some discussion but a consensus was readily reached that this vision was a propitious omen, signaling the benefits that would accrue to the tree and to the pilgrimage. The tree obviously conjures up the tree at Waitangi. The pilgrims thus saw this vision as an early sign that the mission had divine approval. For the visionary, however, a more personal interpretation was proposed.[24] Her construction implied that the airplane was the Holy Spirit and the tree was a foundation, a pillar of the movement's works. For her, then, the meaning was clear: she would be a foundation and would be visited by the Holy Spirit as the mission unfolded.

In the preliminary hours several spiritual messages indicated the antipathy between the two factions of the movement. In these communications the selectness of those traveling on was reaffirmed while the others were urged to regenerate their commitment, as in the following messages received that first Thursday evening at Kurapita: "To the few who stood fast, greetings. My calling to the many only few [have] gathered. To those who [have] fallen along the wayside pick yourselves up and try again."

Other messages made explicit the goals of the pilgrimage. Public discussion was attendant upon all spiritual communication; nothing was taken for granted. In this manner individuals were able to express their most profound sentiments about their present undertaking. To assure spiritual support, there was a rather long service in the chapel; solemnity and piety marked the occasion. Spiritual messages that indicated the willingness of the *wairua* to lend assistance were especially comforting at this time. The following message, received by the same woman mentioned above, makes explicit the purpose of the pilgrimage while it alludes as well to the elect character of this group of pilgrims: "My greetings to the chosen few who held fast to my salvation. In my hands I hold the *mana* of everything that was taken away from you. I will give according to those by whose works I have bare before me. Ask and you shall receive, seek and you shall find, knock and the door shall open onto you. These are my tokens I will pledge before you."

In these early discussions many individuals were compelled to examine the impetus behind such a mission. As people stood to speak, it became clear that there was no simple reason behind this pilgrimage; motivations were varied and complex and operated on many levels. There was certainly a desire to reaffirm spiritual contacts, to make amends for the mistakes of the past, and to assure the dignity of all the Maori people. On another level, the concerns of the movement itself loomed large; they wished to continue the work and to promote, with spiritual guidance, their own definitions of Maoriness and their own version of Maori history. Finally, for most individuals, there were profoundly personal goals to be attained in their quest.

Two aspects of the forthcoming journey were emphasized. Primarily the pilgrim-age was seen as a vehicle through which members of *Maramatanga* and their children could increase their Maoriness. Then their task was to bring forth the spiritual essence and to "anchor their works." Here the essentially political dimen-sion of the pilgrimage is evident. Maori spirituality, so often contrasted with European materialism, takes on new significance. They are armed to change the world, and the instruments of this transformation are to be their restored *mauri*, *mana*, and their own understanding of Christianity. Their *mana*, submerged when Pakehas took over New Zealand, will now endow the Maori with ultimate political and moral superiority, while their Christianity will allow them to refashion the world of their ancestors. Maori, not Pakehas, will define the situation. Their mission, once achieved, will strengthen and secure the position of all Maori. They will, indeed, be anchored and steadfast in contemporary New Zealand.

The journey from Kurapita to Auckland took most of Friday night. During the trip most of the rather solemn discussions in the car centered around the missions and the spiritual aspects of the participants' lives; past songs, dreams, and people now dead were remembered. At 4 A.M. we arrived in Auckland, where we spent what remained of the night at the home of relatives who had offered their hospitality during previous pilgrimages. Other members of the family had already arrived, and discussions of the adventitious journey ahead continued. Most people did not go to sleep until 5 A.M. and then only to doze for a short time. A prayer service at 7 A.M. (a time of regular prayer for movement members) officially began the day of the pilgrimage. We departed shortly thereafter for the trip to Waitangi with five cars to our convoy, each with approximately six or seven adults and some children. One of the pilgrims had brought a reproduction of the Virgin Mary[25], which was to figure prominently in the events at Waitangi.

During the trip, which took about six hours, the cars all stayed close together, while inside the cars the people were solemn, moved by the impressiveness of their undertaking. Most were fasting, and the majority abstained from smoking. There were frequent prayers, and with the exception of the children, there was no idle chatter. When we approached Waitangi, all the cars left the road for a final prayer. As we gathered by the roadside, those members that had received messages or visions during the journey recounted them to the group. Several individuals had received *paos* (short chants) from the *wairua* (all of whom had been active during their lifetimes), while others had had visions of the Virgin Mary. In essence, all the preliminary messages prepared the pilgrims for a successful mission. The *wairua* expressed great joy at the sight of family engaged in such a holy enterprise, while the emergence of the Virgin was viewed as an especially potent omen. In addition, the frequent cloudbursts that marked the journey were interpreted as "showers of blessing." Thus, before we even reached Waitangi, a host of heavenly signs had already vindicated their resolution.

Once in Waitangi, our first stop was the church house[26], where a service was held. This followed the procedures that obtain during *ra*: individuals stood up to offer their gratitude for a safe journey and to express their hopes for a successful mission. Several men moved to the front of the church to lead the assembled congregation in prayer. In keeping with the harmony of the occasion, care was taken to ensure that both Anglicans and Catholics were given opportunities to lead the service. At this time, several people had visions or, as the following indicates, felt compelled to speak.

An elderly man who usually remained silent arose to address the members. He said the *mauri* (the critical essence) must be retrieved on this mission. He went on to contend that the early vision had made this goal clear and that the pilgrims had been unfaithful to that vision when, on previous occasions, they had returned home without it. Those present at the time agreed vigorously; many went so far as to suggest that the disputes and controversies that had disrupted their personal relationships were a direct consequence of their past failures.[27]

Another vision in the church vindicated those who had chosen to come on this pilgrimage. In this case, a woman was the recipient. In her vision, a table appeared laid out with glowing gold trinkets, and two angels were dispensing them. The message was: "Come one, come all, my dear people. To the few who stood fast. Before me I have my tokens of blessings, to each according to their work. Take these gifts and work it to my glory. Offer your thanks back to me and my heavenly father. Lucky people, you. You are bound to the glory. Nurse it. Make it work to the good of you all. Glory will rebound unto you."

From the church, we moved on to the *karaka* tree. Here the picture of Our Lady of Perpetual Succor was placed on its branches and held there by one of the children. A rosary was said (in Maori), and the people bowed their heads in prayer. At this time it was pointed out to me how the tree had grown since the original mission two years previously. The juxtaposition of the picture of the Virgin Mary and the *karaka* tree (with all its connotations of *mana* and *tapu*) was perhaps the most dramatic visual representation of the fusion of the two traditions that I witnessed. For the members, however, this was not a juxtaposition at all, but merely two aspects of a carefully merged, coherent whole. Their future depends equally on the cooperation of the Catholic pantheon, their own *wairua* helpers, and the (re)establishment of their roots in the past.

We then moved down to the beach to the flagpole and to the Treaty House, both tourist attractions.[28] Again, prayers were said at the flagpole[29] while those of us who had not attended previous missions were taken to the beach to see the original landing place of one of the seven canoes and to hear the story of the visions that had led up to the pilgrimage. After a brief tour of the Treaty House, where a copy of the original treaty is encased, we got into our cars and started back to Auckland.

When we arrived in Auckland, prayers were said for the safe completion of the trip, and a hearty meal was served. Most discussion of the mission awaited a night's sleep. That evening, however, several women dreamed of holding babies or of giving birth. As such a turn of events was biologically improbable in most of the dreamers' cases, these dreams were interpreted as a concern with rebirth, regeneration, and the emergence of a new era. In sum, about two hours were spent at Waitangi, while over thirty hours were devoted to traveling there and back. In the minds of the pilgrims, however, there could be little doubt that the outcome of the mission readily justified any discomfort or inconvenience.

Although the actual journey to the pilgrimage site had been completed, the tasks of the pilgrims were far from over. The work of the next day (Sunday) began with a service at 7 A.M. Almost immediately thereafter, a discussion of the mission was under way. The signs and symbols employed by the movement were freely and openly discussed. Chants and *haka* revealed in the pilgrimage hours permitted a discussion of many central issues and provided an opportunity to measure the movement's success. Now the goals of *Maramatanga* dominated and overshadowed the accomplishments of individuals. By concentrating on major concerns, the groups aspired to and achieved a fragile consensus. In the highly charged, liminal time of the pilgrimage, elements of the past and present were restructured into a more suitable arrangement. Unity was affirmed; continuity was asserted. The purpose of the pilgrimage was often made explicit, as in the following statement by one of the movement's most articulate spokesmen: "Some of us are ignorant of the fact that the anchor is there. The anchor has to be pulled down. The anchor on a boat is useless when left floating. But once down, it holds. Cast your line and anchor it to Waitangi." He went on to explain that the work was an octopus; all the followers were merely tentacles that must come back from time to time to nurture the main body. For the organism to survive, each tentacle must support the others. Significantly, he described the *ra* and the pilgrimage as refuges and suggested that while members might live in the world of the Pakeha, they could draw the necessary strength and sustenance only from occasions such as these. He ended his speech with a plea for unity, an appeal that must have been especially compelling to pilgrims whose mundane social world was so often rent by conflict.

The discussion lasted for about ten hours before we embarked on the journey home; however, the visions and inspirations were far from over. The trip home, starting at 5 P.M., reached its conclusion twelve hours later in the Pakipua chapel. It was punctuated by several short stops (for gasoline and prayers) and a two-hour rest at Kurapita. As we left Auckland, there was a brief shower, followed by a full rainbow, yet other indications that the pilgrims' passage had met with spiritual approval.

We arrived in Pakipua shortly after 5 A.M. and hastened directly to the chapel. Here thanksgiving was offered for our safe return and for the success of the pilgrimage. Here, too, the final vision of the mission occurred. With her head bent in prayer, one woman saw two baskets appear on the altar, one blue with a white handle, the other white with a gold handle. Both were overflowing with gold stars—yet further proof, if more be needed, of the bountifulness of their spiritual reward. Indeed, the pilgrims had been transformed from a community of exiles to a community of the triumphant. At the pilgrimage center, charged with multiple "signifiers," the past has been recaptured, their destiny once more their own. It is not surprising that this transformation occurred at Waitangi, for as Victor and Edith Turner have written:

> Thus, history, both of good and evil, God's will and man's disobedience, is conserved in the symbolism of the pilgrimage center. In a sense, all times are believed to coexist there, for the drama of salvation is the same in all ages: man's free will rejects or cooperates with God's grace, resulting in damnation or salvation. Yet the duration of an individual's life or a nation's history provides many opportunities to repent of the evil choices, time being "the mercy of eternity" as William Blake once wrote (1978: 114).

Those who journeyed to Waitangi took advantage of one of those opportunities.

CONCLUSION

The pilgrimages to Waitangi confronted a past that encompassed terrible experience for the Maori. Domination, expropriation, and subjugation have been examined in the cold light of a century and a half of colonialism. These essentially moral issues do not lend themselves to easy resolution when historic facts of defeat and despair continue to impinge upon the present. Pilgrimage becomes an appropriate vehicle to return to the past and to subject it to the scrutiny of the present. By its very liminality, pilgrimage permits the rearrangement of structure and by its very intensity provides direction for future social life (Geertz 1972, 1983; Turner 1973, 1974a; Meyerhoff 1974).

The journey to Waitangi encompasses elements of both indigenous Maori religion and Catholicism. This dualism should not be surprising. *Maramatanga* itself combines aspects of two distinct traditions while, for their part, the pilgrims are torn between commitment to tribal community and their place as an ethnic minority in an industrial, western society. In their journey to Waitangi, the pilgrims of *Maramatanga* left behind local parochial traditions. But they willfully maintained, indeed asserted, the constraints of kinship. The pilgrimage process emphasized the depth of their commitment to their families and expressed their affinity with other Maori. For them, unlike most other Christian pilgrims, salvation is a corporate, not a personal issue. The moral unit continues to be the social group; under these circumstances the individual ceases to matter. This very stance is in opposition to the dominant values of New Zealand Pakeha society. In fact, the entire pilgrimage process is a celebration of those aspects of Maori culture most valued by Maori and least valued by the larger society. Good fellowship and hospitality are exalted, but their importance lies in the contrast with Maori expectations of Pakeha behavior.

The past is both reconstructed and renegotiated; as such, it frames the way meaning is derived in the present (see Sahlins 1985). For these pilgrims, the absence of structure at Waitangi permits liberation from a profane social world and from a problematic social identity. Pilgrimage can and does arrest the inexorable process of accommodation, for only by confronting their past can the members of *Maramatanga* define themselves anew.

More than anything else, the visions that characterize *Maramatanga* reveal new possibilities. They join with other voices from the Maori tradition of prophecy in pointing out that the ground that has been regarded as immutable is, in fact, contested terrain. Such revelations inevitably raise doubts as to the way we in the West understand history, for they make clear that the stories that can be told of conquest, confiscation, and dispossession cannot be linear. Instead, they must involve divergences, returns, and missed opportunities (see Clifford 1988). This perspective on the stories is as true for Pakehas as it is for Maori, with one critical difference. Maori have often been trapped by the stories that can and have been told about them.[30] Visions and revelations not only keep faith with past Maori reliance on orality but grant authority once again to the Maori. This cannot help but be ennobling and sustaining.

The conversation between Maori and Pakeha has also been enhanced by the privileged discourse initiated in movements such as *Maramatanga*. Here the difference between Maori orality and Pakeha reliance on a text is at its most obvious. It is no accident that the text is the Treaty of Waitangi. The members of *Maramatanga*, however, motivated by private and orally transmitted revelations, respond not by legal disputation but by religious action. The Waitangi Tribunal, which ostensibly bows to Maori convention by holding its forums on *marae*, has, nevertheless, been influenced by Pakeha notions of justice and of history. The pilgrims to Waitangi know better. They realized that they had to be present at the site of battle to be effective.

In the current heady atmosphere in New Zealand, the political implications of their pilgrimages have not been lost on the members of *Maramatanga*. The interrelationship between religion and politics is neither new nor surprising; it is far from unique to the Maori case. But the lesson remains clear. Salvation and grace depend only partially upon transcendence. Ultimately, moral redemption lies in the creation, by whatever symbolic sacred means, of a positive place within the mundane social order.

NOTES

1. I have done fieldwork among the members of *Maramatanga* since 1972, and I have been in New Zealand for periods ranging from five weeks to two years. My most recent fieldwork was June-August 1991. My research and writing have been supported by a variety of sources that I gratefully acknowledge. These are a Fulbright Fellowship, a National Science Foundation Research Traineeship, and a Brown University Graduate School Fellowship. Eastern

Michigan University has provided me with summer money on several occasions, two sabbaticals, three faculty research grants, and a Josephine Nevins Keal Award. In addition, I have received support from the National Endowment for the Humanities in the form of a Travel to Collections Grant in 1987 and a Fellowship for College Teachers, 1989-1990. I would also like to acknowledge the kindness of Judith Binney in reading a draft of this chapter, though all mistakes are mine.

2. The term *Pakeha* has been accepted in New Zealand discourse to refer to New Zealanders of British or Western European ancestry. It is generally not italicized for the same reason that Maori is not italicized. These terms of reference, originally applied by an alien group, have come to be terms of distinction and definition.

3. K. R. Howe writes:

> Given the nature of Maori society and politics there could not be a single or general Maori response. Rather there were innumerable responses at different times and at different places for different reasons depending on local circumstances. In other words, all the explanations offered by various historians may be valid, if only for the area they studied, and no attempt should be made to generalize for New Zealand as a whole from particular case studies. Indeed, even within a single community, where all members were subject to the same social context, responses varied widely. This is only to be expected given the fragmented small scale individualistic and competitive nature of Maori society compared with the more stratified societies controlled by a ruling elite elsewhere in the Pacific (1984: 225).

The ancestors of the pilgrims who are the subjects of this chapter were evangelized most effectively by Richard Taylor, a Church Missionary Society missionary who worked in their ancestral area for thirty years in the middle of the nineteenth century. By the end of the century, however, Anglicans were superseded by Catholics. While *Maramatanga* is today Catholic, there is a general ecumenicism found among Maori (see Armstrong 1990) that places emphasis on common beliefs rather than on sectarian differences.

4. M. P. K. Sorrenson explains that the Maori people continue to look to the Maori version of the treaty. In this, Maori autonomy would appear to have been preserved. He writes:

> According to the preamble, he [the New Zealand governor] was to protect the Maori and their property from Europeans now colonizing the country. However the power and autonomy of the chiefs—their "rangatiratanga o o ratou whenua o ratou kainga me o ratou taonga" (their chieftainship over their lands, their homes and other treasures)—was expressly preserved in the second clause of the Treaty. To the Maori chiefs who signed the Treaty their *rangatiratanga* was far more than a guarantee of their possession of land and other properties; it was also a guarantee of their autonomy and authority, above all their mana, as chiefs; even in some recent interpretations, a guarantee of Maori sovereignty (1987: 173).

In the quite astonishing number of books and articles that have come out on this topic in 1990, New Zealand's sesquicentennial, there has been some disagreement about the intentionality of the disparity between the Maori and the English version of the treaty. Thus H. Yensen, Kevin Hague and Tim McCreanor write:

> It is not difficult to see how these differences arose. Williams was given the task of translating a treaty of cession in such a way that Maori would sign it. He had been living

among Ngapuhi in the Bay of Islands and was familiar with Maori beliefs and concerns. He would have known that the chiefs would not agree to sign away their rangatiratanga or sovereignty. Indeed, one of their principal concerns at the time was the threat to their authority posed by Pakeha lawlessness and land-grabbing.

Williams no doubt truly believed that the imposition of British rule would be beneficial for Maori, and perhaps felt that this justified deceiving them in order to obtain their signatures. The British intended to acquire sovereignty, but the Treaty drafted by Williams in Maori confirmed Maori sovereignty over their lands and possessions, and ceded only sufficient governance to control British subjects (1989: 22).

5. Binney writes:

The Treaty of Waitangi was introduced into this world. It was introduced into a society that was unquestionably primarily oral. But by 1840 there were a significant number of Maori adults reading biblical texts in Maori, and a few who, as we have seen, were writing or dictating letters in Maori. Moreover, the Treaty was not just a text, or texts. It was a series of propositions, introduced into a world where, in many parts of the country, there had already been extensive debate about admitting Pakeha into their communities and about whether or not to protect them. For in 1840 the balance of power still lay in Maori hands (1989: 25).

6. Binney has noted that oral narratives are, at least in some areas, still the major means of transmitting history. It is not so much that Maori histories are ignored; more seriously, they are lost. For Binney, the culpability, largely unwitting, rests with Western-trained historians. Thus she writes: "It is only relatively recently that Western-trained historians have come to realize that they have been perpetuating colonialist attitudes in their so-called objective histories. At the same time, these histories have served, to a considerable extent, to erase Maori memories and perceptions" (1987: 17).

7. Most commentators point out that these movements allowed Maori to "meet the challenge of European settlement on Maori terms. It represented a Maori attempt to adopt Western culture, but in a way that would not deny Maori identity" (Clark 1975: 110). There can be little doubt that for most Maori these movements provided useful means through which individuals could define themselves.

8. Christina Toren (1988) notes that most movements of this kind often appear to be defining the present but are, in fact, making statements about the past.

9. It is not clear if Maori always understood Christianity in terms of their traditional beliefs or if their failure to flourish under Christianity led them to return to their traditional ideology. Regional differences make it impossible to generalize; however, evidence supports the former interpretation.

10. Indeed, passive resistance and self-sufficient communities were almost always interpreted by settlers as opposing the will and interests of the crown. By casting prophets and their communities in essentially treasonous terms, the extreme action taken against them could be justified.

11. Not only followers of Maori prophets or their descendants feel this way. Today the tradition of Maori prophecy has become significant for all Maori.

12. It should be pointed out that the whole issue of ethnic census statistics has come under attack. Their accuracy is called into question in a population that has had some degree of intermarriage and miscegenation for almost two centuries. But more importantly, the political

implications of ethnic statistics have raised concerns. Brown, who does not share such concerns, has written:

> In addition to their reliability the relevancy and acceptability of official ethnic statistics have also been subject to increasing criticism. Some critics are opposed to the traditional form of ethnic question as it appears on the census, arguing that a biological definition is no longer relevant to the reality of ethnicity in New Zealand today. Other critics are opposed to the very existence of official ethnic statistics, arguing that the statistics are a significant contributing factor in the reproduction of racism and racial inequality (1984: 179)

13. According to 1981 census information, Maori women at age sixty had given birth on average to 6.11 children, while Pakeha women of the same age had given birth to 2.76 children. Between 1962 and 1982, however, the Maori total fertility rate fell by 63 percent, a substantial narrowing of the gap between Maori and non-Maori (*Population of New Zealand* 1986, vol. 1).

14. The New Zealand Planning Council Monitoring Group Report No. 4 wrote:

> The labour force projection for Maori has both short term and long term implications. In the short term, there will be severe pressure to find jobs for young Maori—more so even than in the early 1980s. In the longer term, unless this disadvantage is overcome the current young adult Maori population (15-24 years old) may pass through the remainder of its life cycle always severely underprivileged by comparison to its non Maori peers. Assuming subsequent smaller Maori labour force entrant cohorts finding job seeking easier, young Maori today may also be underprivileged by comparison with future Maori cohorts. This stark and highly undesirable effect of composition derived changes will affect all related areas of social policy. There will also be significant regional differences with adverse effects being most marked in those urban areas where there are significant concentration of Maori, and in rural areas where Maori have been a high percentage of the total population and where unemployed urban Maori are now returning (1986: 55).

15. For a history of Maori activism, see R. Walker 1984 and Walker 1987.

16. The success of the *kohanga reo* is often undermined by the fact that a child's parents may be unable to reinforce language learning in the home, as they speak only English. More importantly, evidence has shown that once children start school, their ability to speak Maori decreases significantly.

17. Hauraki Greenland has written:

> Thus, as a moral and political critique, the issue of land was the device by which radicals sought, on a holistic basis, to question pakeha society using its own proclaimed values. They claimed that social and economic development had led to cultural and economic "genocide"; that the empty and obsessive pursuit of material wealth had debased the communal and organic Maori way of life; and that the welfare state was in fact oppressive and hegemonic.

The stereotype of the Pakehas as predators was matched with one that emphasized the sublime traits of the Maori. Maori people retained an emotional and spiritual link with the land. Communal bonds survived, individualism was muted and kinship links formed a cushion of support. The Maori had an inherent integrity that had been eroded since contact. This honour could be redeemed, however, by a return to a pride in one's Maori identity (1984: 92-93).

18. A related endeavor is to *whakanoa*, to "make *noa*," to remove the *tapu* or sacredness and power from specific sites.

19. Marshall Sahlins refers to *tikanga* as the recurrence of events, the "eternal return." Thus he writes: "The Maori world unfolds as one eternal return, the recurrent manifestation of the same experiences. The collapse of time and happening is mediated by a third term: *tikanga*: the distinctive action of beings/things that come of their particular nature" (1985: 58-59).

20. Maori and Pakehas view missions differently. There was never any expectation that the work that had to be accomplished could be done in one mission or, for that matter, that the work of *Maramatanga* could be accomplished in one generation. The very incompleteness provided continuity from one year to the next. For Maori, continuity, rather than completion, would seem to be the more important issue.

21. This tradition has been called into question by David Simmons (1976). More recently, Allan Hanson (1989) has discussed the political implications of this belief.

22. Bradd Shore has recently worked at redefining *tapu*. He argues along with A. Hanson and L. Hanson (1983) that *tapu* is ritually powerful because it involves proximity to divine forces. He writes, "*Tapu* is a state of contact with the divine by which the particular is encompassed and bound by the general, and thereby rendered intelligible" (1989: 164).

23. Although the names used in this chapter are the Maori names of individuals most often known by their English names, the towns are pseudonyms which offer some degree of anonymity and some protection of privacy to people who very graciously shared their stories with me.

24. This particular woman manipulated symbols on a very obvious level, especially in the messages that she received at Waitangi. More than others, her interpretation of the Bible and of Catholic dogma tends to be literal rather than metaphorical. The others, as an example, seldom mention the Holy Spirit, prefer, when it is relevant, to use the Maori equivalent, and only infrequently make such direct allusions to biblical phrases. In many ways her overt handling of much of the movement's ideology was an asset to me. Although these messages occasioned some degree of skepticism from time to time, she was viewed by the others as sincere, if somewhat melodramatic.

25. This particular reproduction, given to the group during a Catholic retreat in 1962, figures prominently in chapels associated with *Maramatanga* and is often found in the homes of individuals. The formal name of this reproduction is *Our Lady of Perpetual Succor*. Originally, according to the members, the painting was done in Europe in the fifteenth century and survived, rather miraculously, the vagaries of time. Taking this reproduction along on missions, as they did at every suitable opportunity, is tantamount to taking along Our Lady. The picture is referred to as "she." It is fairly large, approximately twelve inches by twenty inches, and was often awkward to carry. These difficulties only made their determination and gravity more obvious at the same time that they demonstrated the integral part that Catholicism played in these proceedings.

26. The church was deserted since it was a Saturday afternoon. The fact that it was an Anglican church did not detract from its importance. It had been visited by the group in previous years, and everybody felt it was appropriate to stop here at this time.

27. Those who stayed home, however, took issue with this point of view. They maintained that something like this essence cannot, by its very nature, be subject to removal; it has roots (thereby making it permanent and immobile), and from these roots all Maori people benefit. They maintained that, since the other missions, each of them had derived something (one

woman, for example, said her health had remained good). In this sense, then, the mission was fulfilled three years ago. They went on to argue, quite self-righteously, that if this benefit was the purpose of the trip, then it was clear that such a pilgrimage was not now necessary. In any event, the idea of removing the *mauri* was quite unthinkable.

28. Because of its historical significance, Waitangi is a tourist attraction much like Boston or Philadelphia; important events that took place there are marked and commemorated. The original treaty has been prominently displayed in a glass showcase. Its meaning and significance are clearly different for different segments of the New Zealand population.

While the members of *Maramatanga* met tourists at all points on their journey, they kept the reasons for their undertaking entirely to themselves. Thus, for example, they did not discuss their interpretations of unfolding events when they thought they might be overheard.

29. The flagpole commemorates an act by Hone Heke, a Northland Maori who dared to question British intent when they erected a flagpole (see Sahlins 1985). In the context, this act was clearly subversive. The pilgrims to Waitangi are both aware and proud of this history. By their actions, they seek to invoke the past so that it may frame the present.

30. James Clifford (1988) makes this point about the Mashpee, a tribe of Native Americans whose position is very similar to that of the Maori.

Postscript:
Anthropology as Pilgrimage,
Anthropologist as Pilgrim

COLIN TURNBULL

We end where we began and where the study of pilgrimage must ever return—with the pilgrim. Professor Turnbull, typical pilgrim, is highly reflective in looking back on his own sacred journeys. He draws upon experiences as a pilgrim to Hindu shrines during student days in India, continues with reflections on the sacred "journeys" to the forest among the Mbuti of Africa, and ends with a consideration of the homologies among these diverse sorts of pilgrimage and the quest of anthropology. Despite the apparent world of difference between the anthropologist and the pilgrim that is the object of this chapter, only when this gap is bridged can the anthropologist hope to interpret pilgrimage in language that both makes sense to the scholarly reader and is true to the pilgrim's quest. The anthropologist who sets out to accomplish his work in this fashion joins in the pilgrim's search. Literally, this task involves a very sincere effort at participant observation, which is necessary, considering how alien to the intellectual traditions of academia are the ideational frameworks within which the typical pilgrim operates. But more metaphorically, for the anthropologist to join the pilgrim is to recognize the identity that exists between the quests of scholar, pilgrim, and all of our species who set the mountain peak as their goal. Here we find the universal fact that, at a deep level, pilgrim's quest is none other than the human quest. An appropriate place to end this volume is with a statement that echoes the title of the conference out of which this collection grew: Pilgrimage: the human quest. We have come again to the place of our beginning, only, like pilgrims, we return seasoned by the journey. Where future generations of scholars, thinkers, and pilgrims go from this point is not known. Hopefully, by this collective endeavor, a little more of the path has been charted. I can find no better words to express my own sentiments on this score than those with which Professor Turnbull ends his essay: "The quest for society is one and the same thing as the quest for the Self, which for some of us is also the quest for the Sacred that ultimately unites us all."

The contents of this volume not only tell us a great deal about pilgrimage and about various ways of looking at the phenomenon as a social institution; they also tell us a great deal about anthropology and anthropologists. Together they highlight the inescapable fact of both individual diversity and its richness. The analogy between tourism and pilgrimage that is made several times in the book tells us about both institutions and about anthropology and anthropologists. I am inclined to think that some of us are tourists, others are pilgrims, and all of us are a little of each. The diversity of approach and manner of presentation suggests that temperament should be a major consideration in fieldwork and that some anthropologists are more or less able to participate than others at certain levels, just as some are more or less skilled at objective observation than others.

The difference between the tourist and the pilgrim anthropologist shows up in the chapters, for instance, in the styles and focus on the secular and the sacred. The tourist tends to emphasize the social (if not corporate) and secular nature of the quest. To be a pilgrim suggests that the nature of the quest is sacred and supposes a capacity for subjective involvement and concern with beauty and love, with those very human qualities that most of us admire and respect yet are generally expected to shun in our academic treatment of human society. But just as tourism is every bit as valid a human experience as is pilgrimage and just as vital for our understanding of human society, so are both approaches to anthropology. The scientific approach of objective detachment, analytical and impersonal, focused primarily on group behavior and concerned mainly with the secular, is no more and no less valid than the humanistic approach that allows for subjectivity and involvement and that takes cognizance of such intractable human forces as emotion, belief, and faith at an individual level and direct concern with the sacred. Few of us are capable of both skills; some of us with great ability in the one approach are singularly inept in the other. Unless we pretend to infallibility, there is no cause for concern, and the present volume suggests that there is much ahead for anthropology if we respect and appreciate each other, each being content with our own approach and skills, for then together we can open up whole new fields for investigation leading to a deeper and more significant understanding of human society and human behavior than we have been able to arrive at up to now.

Indeed, one of the first topics raised here is the fact that pilgrimage, of such vital and obvious social significance, has until recently been almost totally neglected by anthropologists. To try to dismiss it as an institution of largely historical importance is obviously false, for while the grand days of pilgrimage seem to lie in the past, that impression is partly because of how we have defined it, and equally false is its apparent absence in so many small-scale societies. The institution is alive and well today, if on a different scale and with different social significance, as we see in the many contributions presented here.

Some of the reasons pilgrimage has been neglected as a field of study have been suggested here, including our lack of ease with process, with what cannot readily be subjected to the holistic framework, and with what involves so intensely the human and individual experience. I suggest that we have tended to avoid, in our study of religious systems, what is central to all religion: the power of Faith, the sense of the Sacred, the perception of Spirit.

In just the same way that it is not comfortable or seemingly appropriate, in "polite" society, to discuss God in the living room, so among polite anthropologists it is too often considered improper and inappropriate, if not irrelevant, to discuss Spirit and Faith, Beauty and Goodness, which are dismissed as though they had no substantive reality or application. It is still less acceptable to attempt to capture such qualities and report on them from the point of view of personal experience (our own or that of others) in the societies we study. In short, we choose to ignore, if not deny, the very reality of human emotions as a force in human society and a factor in social organization. This volume may provide a stimulus for a new direction in our fieldwork and in our writing, for even though the topic is sacred journeys, there are few attempts to convey any sense of the Sacred.

Any anthropological study of pilgrimage is going to be seriously deficient if it does not deal with the power of the Sacred to attract the individual and transform him from one condition of being into another, for this process of sacralization is directly comparable with, and significant for, our understanding of the process of socialization. We are too often so fascinated by the tidiness of structure (and anti-structure) and so bent upon the scientific analysis of empirical fact and its reduction to theory and system, that we tend to overlook the less tangible but nonetheless real fact of process, which is just as legitimate as a subject for study. Indeed, if we are to branch out from our study of system to a study of process, why should we not also investigate the socializing fact of human aspiration as manifest in the process of pilgrimage? If we do so, then, among other things, we will find even stronger ground for comparing tourism with pilgrimage, for tourists are just as likely to be motivated and guided by aspiration as are pilgrims and may well be just as susceptible to inspiration.

Since the anthropologist would, in keeping with his own cherished ideals, not make any value judgment that might elevate the pilgrim above the tourist or lend support to the popular concept of the one as being a religious fanatic and the other as a mindless hedonist, I hope that it is without offense that I suggest that some anthropologists might usefully be classified as primarily either tourists or pilgrims, for there is no question that just as both tourism and pilgrimage center around a quest, so does anthropology. Pilgrim and tourist (and anthropologist) alike are bent on self-satisfaction. Both pilgrim and tourist are seekers, though the quest of the one is as ostensibly sacred as that of the other is secular. Similarly, there is perhaps a vital difference in the quest of the two kinds of anthropologists, those who see it as one of the humanities and those who derive more profit and satisfaction from seeing it as a science. As with pilgrimage and tourism, there is considerable overlapping, but what is lacking by comparison is a comparable clarity of objectives. However different our approaches and techniques and focus of interest, the two approaches surely belong to each other, for in the practical aspects of undertaking a search for the Sacred, the pilgrim not only must deal with the profane but, in dealing with it, finds his quest for the Sacred sharpened and strengthened. So the tourist in his quest for secular perfection often has to confront the Sacred, and this brush with holiness serves to heighten his achievement of pleasure and secular satisfaction, almost by sanctifying it. The ideal tourist resort is, after all, not for nothing often conceived and advertised as "paradise."

While anthropologists have conventionally tended to focus on the empirical realities of the ethnographic context and have devoted themselves to the system revealed therein—to organization and structure—and have sought to explain the phenomenon of social organization in theoretical terms, in the course of their essentially secular quest and their use of strictly scientific method, they have necessarily come up against such realities as myth, belief, and that most intractable phenomenon of all (because, in essence, it is suprarational), faith. While they have successfully integrated such phenomena into their theories and their perception of system, the realities are subordinated to the system. Similarly the anthropologist who, like the pilgrim, is more avowedly concerned with the socializing force of concepts such as truth, goodness, beauty, and God and who feels that such concepts outweigh as social forces those of reciprocity, symbiosis, structure, deep structure and anti-structure necessarily has to take the system into consideration. For the one the system is the goal; for the other the system is merely the way to the Sacred. Perhaps the difference is between those who are fascinated by knowledge and those who feel more attracted to understanding.

Without pursuing this imperfect analogy further, I look now only at two popular and frequently mentioned foci of interest: the fact of travel and the mode of travel. These have been well explored in all the preceding chapters, but I am curious to discover what profit might be gained by further exploration with more of a focus on the process of sacralization involved in pilgrimage, corresponding perhaps to the process of socialization involved in tourism. The point having been made of a possible analogy between the two processes, if not the two institutions, I restrict myself to pilgrimage.

While travel has been dealt with, for instance, and proper importance attached to the fact that whereas on some pilgrimages the journey is of secondary importance to arrival at the shrine, and on other pilgrimages the journey itself is what is sacred (and may, in consequence, be circumscribed by numerous prescriptions and pro-scriptions), not much has been said about the profanity often accruing in the first instance to travel and then at the shrine. Virtually no attention has been given to travel other than physical. Our focus in anthropology has been so heavily on the physical, material, social, structural, and functional aspects of travel (in both pil-grimage and tourism) that we are in danger of not taking fully enough into consideration the rational, intellectual, and, above all, spiritual considerations that also go to make pilgrimage all that it is. This under-emphasis applies, I think, to many other anthropological studies as well, and of course the question has been raised as to whether or not anthropologists, social or otherwise, should face or are equipped to face such considerations. Indeed, one of the many contributions this volume makes is that it raises this very issue, for it is clear that pilgrimage is far more than a mere structural happening, event, or theory. It often profoundly affects the spiritual self-perceptions and aspirations of individuals involved as both hosts and guests (to use the excellent title of that book by V. L. Smith), as well as the structure of the societies and communities involved. If we are truly dedicated to our holistic approach, then I cannot see how we can escape the reality of holism, which demands that we investigate many areas beyond those that are presently within the generally accepted province of anthropology. Even our most solid and conventional works by our most conservative scholars involve forays by those scholars into highly special-ized fields as disparate as gynecology and geology, economics and theology, history and agriculture. The ever-lengthening string of anthropological subdivisions testifies to the eclecticism that is a necessary corollary of holism. Yet none of us pretends to have qualified as scholars in all such fields; most are content to do our best by consulting with specialists in such other scholarly fields as cross our path. I can see no logic, then, that can justify our exclusion of realms that could be said to be more properly the province of philosophy or theology. On the contrary, when we do not even make the attempt to extend our inquiry into such realms, while recognizing our limitations, we have deliberately mutilated the holistic portrayal we pretend to present. When we do not consider the undeniable fact of human aspiration and we refuse to examine it in all its depth at the individual level, we do more than mutilate the concept of pilgrimage; we amputate one its most vital (and socially significant) members.

In any truly holistic consideration of either pilgrimage or tourism, their consid-eration as intellectual and/or spiritual journeys to sacred ideals, if not to the Sacred itself, is surely as important as the mere consideration of journeys to sacred places. Such internal pilgrimage may precede physical pilgrimage, proceed from it, accom-pany it, or achieve the same ends without any physical movement. If there is no such internal process, then the outer appearance of pilgrimage does not deserve the name; it is mere travel and is lacking the socially vital power of transformation that only the internal process can effect. To the extent that pilgrimage is a personal experience, as well as being an important part of the social fabric, we cannot fully understand either the outer or the inner journey in isolation. If we make the attempt, then we are as superficial in our studies as the tourist is so often (and often wrongly) accused of being in his travels. The exercise will not be worthless, but it will lack the fullness and richness that are the potential of our discipline.

This consideration applies to both the fact of travel and the mode of travel. While thorough ethnographic description is, as always, the first prerequisite and a sound analytical framework the second, we should have an equally rigorous description of the personal aspirations of pilgrims and a thorough understanding of the nature and source of their inspiration. We have to go still further, for while inspiration and aspiration may be related to religious belief (and thus part of a structured system of religious practice) and be sacred rather than secular, they may also, or alternatively, be related to religious faith and therefore be spiritual rather than intellectual. Again, they are personal, and, far from being a part of a given social system in the sense of being determined by it, by being apart from it they may thereby have the power to transcend the divisions often created by such systems. The very resistance at various points in their history of organized and generally exclusive churches to pilgrimage and their attempts to control or dominate it at other times are surely a measure of the power of faith to break free from the confines of belief, the power of the individual to move from one social system to another or to transcend sociality itself.

If religious belief is difficult enough for the anthropologist to deal with adequately, religious faith by its very nonrational nature seems to present even greater obstacles. Perhaps the matter of temperament comes in here, for the only way that I can see by which we can effectively tackle faith is for the fieldworker to be willing to sacrifice his academic self and perhaps his personal, moral, and "religious" self and, through this self-sacrifice, open himself to total, unfettered participation in the process of spiritual quest and subject himself as nearly as possible to the same conditions in time and space to which the other pilgrims are subjected. However intensive the intellectual preparation for such a venture, in itself it is not enough. The degree to which we can project our own resultant experience upon that of the other pilgrims is, of course, questionable; but we can at least follow the model, as part of our participant technique, of those other pilgrims, some of whom make such projections, or seek to compare experiences, while others are content with their personal experience and prefer to keep it private. The one preference or the other may be manifest in the chosen mode of travel—in company or alone—but the experience itself may determine a change of preference. All these facts will be revealed only by total participation.

I will illustrate this viewpoint by reference to the well-known pilgrimages in the Himalayas, to the various sources of the Ganga and Jumna rivers, in which I have twice participated at an interval of thirty years. It says something about this ancient pilgrimage that on each occasion I sought merely to observe as an academic "tourist" but was ultimately compelled to participate as a pilgrim. Here follows a description of the Jumnotri, Gangotri, Badrinath *yatra* (pilgrimage) as made in 1950 and again in 1980, but I avoid comparison (however instructive) so as to focus on both the mode of travel and its significance in terms of the sacred quest and also the fact of travel. I examine the question of sequence, the way in which individuals, including myself, have to make a decision as to which of the various shrines to visit; I myself was compelled to exclude Amarnath and Kedarnath because of illness on the first attempt and the approach of winter on the second. The same issue of choice faced fellow pilgrims, but what we compared were "feelings" rather than "reasons" for our individual choice, since each of us, after all, had our own uniquely personal Sacred in mind and chose the sequence that led us progressively through various stages to the stage that, for us, would represent the ultimate. I will also examine the mode of travel (taxi, bus, foot), the point of origin (where does the journey begin to be sacred: at home, once one reaches Rishikesh, or further on at Uttarkashi?), and the way in which the journey itself may become sacred. A brief conclusion reflects thoughts on the subjective technique as a valid tool for revealing new truths of anthropological significance.

For instance, over thirty years ago as a graduate from Oxford in Modern Greats, a kind of elite version of General Studies, with a heavy concentration in politics and philosophy, I went to India on a purely intellectual quest (I thought), therefore in no way a pilgrimage in the meaning I choose to insist upon. For purposes of clarity and to help distinguish the processes of pilgrimage and tourism, the term *pilgrimage* is restricted to forms of quest involving the concept of Spirit or supernatural.

I did not go straight to Banaras Hindu University but stayed with an orthodox Hindu family in Baroda until the university year began. I then commenced my studies toward a doctorate in the Department of Indian Religion and Philosophy and was slightly disturbed to find religion included in the departmental title. It was not long before a series of "accidents" involving two of the other few foreigners at the university brought me to a Hindu *asram* in the city and into the presence of one of India's great religious teachers, Anandamayi. There the sacred journey began. I did not make a conscious decision, but within a few days something compelled me to pack my bags and accept Anandamayi's invitation to live at the *asram* while continuing with my studies at the university, a condition made quite explicit. I was able to preserve my self-image of being engaged on an entirely secular, intellectual quest.

As part of my studies it was evident from all that I saw at the *asram* (including the visits of a number of prominent scholars and philosophers) that pilgrimage was a religious phenomenon that I would have to investigate. I was encouraged by my sponsor, J. K. Birla, the university, and Anandamayi to join the great pilgrimage to Kailas/Manasarovar in outer Tibet. The pilgrimage was to start from Birla House, in Delhi, in recognition of Sri J. K. Birla, who not only made it financially possible for participants but personally encouraged many other students, like myself, to undertake the long, difficult, and sometimes dangerous journey. He recognized the secularity of my interests and commented that this, too, was within the Hindu tradition and that it might turn out otherwise.

Given that secular orientation, then, when the opportunity came, I joined two very secular Hindu friends from Oxford days on the pilgrimage to Jumnotri, Gangotri, and Badrinath, before going on to Kailasa. I was surprised that, as English as they were in their education and their outlook, they were interested in any pilgrimage, but they assured by that for them it was just to be a hiking vacation and a chance to see more of their homeland, of which they knew so little. They fell in with my plan to join the Kailasa group by making the direct approach from either Gangotri or Badrinath. Experienced climbers warned me of the hazards, but when one, who was a Hindu, said that, of course, it was possible "if it was God's will," that assurance was enough for me. He and another provided all the technical information necessary, and in the early summer the three of us set off from Bombay, via Delhi and

Mussoorie, and traveled that far by plane, train, and bus. From Mussoorie we struck across country on foot with four Gurkha guides who doubled as porters, the seven of us carrying more or less equal loads of sixty pounds each.

The mood of the others changed the very instant we left Mussoorie and set foot on the rough trail leading toward Jumnotri, the source of the sacred Jumna River. My own mood changed, perhaps similarly, since we all shared a common tradition of a British public school and Oxford or Cambridge. My mood brought on an increasing distance from my two friends, at times amounting almost to hostility. For one thing the older brother, although born in India, knew so little Hindi he had constantly to refer to a dictionary, while I could speak the language without aid, fluently but badly. The younger brother, whom I knew better, spoke none. Given that India's independence was barely two years old, certain tensions were inevitable, but there was much more to our discomfort than that. I had already been in India almost as long as the older brother and longer than the younger but found myself embarrassed when I found that because they showed no reverence for the little shrines we passed on the way, I sometimes felt compelled to do so, however secretly. I had as yet not even heard of anthropology, yet I was disturbed when I found that my curiosity about the villages through which we occasionally passed and my inclination to stay and meet some of the people were not shared. Each night we camped out in the open, and even then I heard sounds that the others did not. Consequently, while they often remarked on the beauty of the scenery, I found that it was precisely when it was most beautiful or when the sounds or smells were most evocative and enriching that I kept most to myself. The journey itself had begun to be sacred, and Jumnotri remained a mere physical place where I would be able to observe Hindu religion and philosophy in action.

By the time we got to the pilgrim center of Hanuman Chatti, the Gurkhas, as if sharing our mutual disenchantment with each other, had taken to leaving what there was of a trail and followed the most direct and precipitous route possible, even adding some of our load to theirs to make that possible. The increased discomfort and difficulty gave me some pleasure because they made me appreciate the countryside in a new and exciting way, such as by tasting the earth when I stumbled and fell face down, by smelling the rocky wall of a ledge or the presence of animal life other than our own, by touching familiar things with tired feet and tired hands and recognizing how little I knew them, and by discovering my increasing distaste for the canned and dried foods we had brought with us in such absurd quantity. Although I tasted the food of our Nepali guides only by smelling its aroma, I found it much more nourishing and began to eat less of our own, a fact that some might find significant in light of my subsequent bout of hepatitis but that to me has a totally different and deeper significance.

When we sighted the infant Jumna far below in the densely forested gorge, in which Hanuman Chatti lay concealed, my friends decided on the spot that they were not going to make the journey up to the source of the river but would wait for me while resting up at the *dharmasala* (pilgrims' rest house) we knew to be there. Sensing that we had already parted company in terms of our unspoken, truer quests,

I was content when the Gurkhas took my load and told me how to cut off to the Jumnotri trail, which I followed alone, with brash self-confidence and unwise haste. Once, however, I reached the trail, which was deserted, I slowed down not because I was fatigued but because here was a totally new experience. In fact the trail was not deserted at all. All along the way were little shrines and cairns marking the passing of earlier pilgrims and telling their story as clearly as if they were talking. I thought of Dr. B. L. Atreya, the supervisor of my doctoral dissertation at Banaras Hindu University, but found myself certain that he would approve such nonacademic feelings. I felt that Anandamayi and J. K. Birla would be angry at me for my departure from my earlier plan to join the Kailasa pilgrimage at Delhi and decided to cut Badrinath out of the schedule and strike out for Kailasa from Gangotri, a thought that any experienced mountaineer would have laughed at, given my inexperience, but at which one old man I met did not laugh at all, saying that he had once done it and that if it was right for me, then I would do it too. His qualification of "rightness" escaped me at the time.

The final approach to Jumnotri included the traverse of a sheer cliff-face far above the tiny torrent that seemed to be a mile below, but the very real terror I felt at one point when I thought I was sure to fall impelled me forward rather than backward, as though there was something I had to reach and would reach—because it was "right," because it was "a sacred place"? There was no intellectual judgment made or rational decision to go forward rather than do the sensible thing and go back, given the fact that there was nobody to help me if I got into trouble. Yet the impulse was as strong as any physical push forward could have been or has been in my life. Could that have been a spiritual impulse? It was certainly something quite new to me, and I was rational enough to feel embarrassed at such nonacademic feelings while feeling a new excitement and a degree of conviction in rightness of action that I think I had never previously known.

Here I must abbreviate the narrative, for I want to juxtapose this with what happened some thirty years later when I faced that same cliff ledge separating me from apparently the same goal, Jumnotri. On the first occasion, having negotiated the traverse and crossed the river by a footbridge, I found the site to be as I had read and been told about it. There was a small temple, which I virtually ignored since nothing was going on inside it. The hot springs interested me more because of their unexpectedness. Some pilgrims were there, cooking their food in what seemed to be a pit of boiling water steaming out of the rocks. I was politely shown how to cook the rice and small pieces of potato that the Gurkhas had given me for the occasion, but by then my brush with the Sacred had passed, and I merely picked at the food, before it was thoroughly cooked. After a little sightseeing, I decided that there was nothing further here to help me with my dissertation so I might as well begin the return trip down to Hanuman Chatti and continue the trek to Gangotri and Kailasa. The secular, once again, had taken over.

I reached Hanuman Chatti the following night and found that my friends far from wanting to stay longer to rest up, as they had planned, were ready to leave at dawn. There is a long route that nearly all pilgrims take, but directly above Hanuman Chatti there is a direct route over a high, snow-and ice-filled pass. Since my friends were as ignorant as I and they were already wanting to cut this expedition as short as possible, they agreed to take the short route. I quickly found myself far ahead, reveling in my increasing conviction that for me, at least, the best still lay ahead. The two brothers kept as close as possible, but they were slowed by stopping to help each other as they slid and stumbled. The Gurkhas brought up a sensible rear.

So I was once again alone when I had my next brush with the Sacred. I crossed over the pass well ahead of the others and found a rocky overhang in which I could shelter from the storm that had sprung up and where the snow was less deep and soft. I looked down toward the Ganges valley and over to where Gangotri lay but felt no elation. I tried to see if the mountains that lay between me and the glacier that led from Gaumukh, beyond Gangotri, into Tibet and Kailasa were visible, but by now the swirling snow was a blizzard obscuring everything. I gave a passing thought to my friends, presumably still struggling up the steep, snow-filled gorge behind me and promptly felt sick. I at first blamed my friends, whom I had deserted in more ways than one. Not exactly a spiritual experience, the recognition that I was sick, very sick, indeed, did give rise to my next confrontation with the Sacred. Rather than be concerned about my condition, which was something obviously far more than mere exhaustion or the mild nausea to be expected by some at such heights, I felt an extraordinary pleasure and satisfaction. I had arrived, and it no longer mattered what happened. I was totally, absolutely content with everything as it was, whatever that might be. Consequently, when my two friends came puffing around the corner and told me what an inconsiderate fool I had been and asked why I was wasting time sitting there when I should have been finding a way down the dangerous slope below in the gathering snowstorm, I was again content to find myself alone in a quest that had become so sacred that it seemed to brook no sharing.

After the second night on the way down, now out of the snow, I could no longer even carry a light pack and could barely walk. My friends said they would take the porters and all the baggage and return directly as possible to Bombay, and with a strange but total lack of hesitation I promptly turned in the other direction and managed to stumble a few miles along the pilgrim trail, when I found it, toward Gangotri. That was as far as I got on that physical journey. For the next two months I was nursed back to health in a Hindu asram on the pilgrim route, at which word arrived mysteriously from Anandamayi, who had no physical means of knowing where I was since I had told nobody about my change of plans. She merely sent word by another pilgrim that as soon as I was able to travel, I should go to her mountain asram beyond Dehra Dun and resume my "studies" (the word actually meant "duty", but that I perceived it to mean my academic duty, as, in part, it was).

Thirty years later, now an anthropologist, I undertook a round-the-world survey of tourism as a form of pilgrimage. When I reached India I was about a quarter of the way into my tour and had observed and participated in tourism in Israel, Egypt, and East Africa and observed tourists often engaged in far more than a secular quest. Remembering my various experiences of Indian pilgrimage, I now wanted to observe pilgrims and see to what extent pilgrimage as a social institution could be compared with tourism. In that frame of mind I arrived at Birla Mandir, a great, glossy, modern temple built by my old sponsor, J. K. Birla, in Delhi. The man himself was now dead, but his picture looked down on me the moment I entered the temple and sat down in the little anteroom at the entrance to take off my shoes before proceeding further. But the journey was still secular as I discussed it with a young Brahmin on the temple staff. It was still secular when he announced that he would like to come with me; I could pay his expenses, a small cost for the academic value of traveling in such company, particularly as my Hindi was still rusty, as I had only been in India less than a week and had not used the language for thirty years.

We traveled by train to Rishikesh, not far from where I was nursed through that bout of hepatitis. Since it was so late in the season and Kedarnath and Amarnath were already closed to all pilgrims by heavy snow, we made the decision that we had best take one of the last pilgrim buses that now plied the new road built to Badrinath. That trip was anything but a sacred journey for either my companion, Mohan Kumar, or me, although there were sacred moments, such as when for the first time in his young Brahmin life he felt it possible and "right" to eat not only with other castes, but with outcastes. He was a tourist all the way, at least in outward behavior, and insisted on snapshots of himself alone and with others, for which he posed in his best Western dress. But on arrival at Badrinath he, at least, had clearly arrived at a sacred place. He changed into the clothes of an orthodox pilgrim and said that he wanted to bathe in the sacred hot springs with other Brahmins; thus he politely said he did not want me with him, for the first time in a week or more of traveling together on an allegedly sacred journey. But, freshly bathed, perhaps because he was also freshly purified and strengthened in his faith, he then immediately insisted that I accompany him to worship in the sacred temple of Badri Narayan. Now the journey began to be sacred for me, though I did not share Mohan Kumar's feelings about the sanctity of the place. For one thing, the journey was now on foot, not by the assortment of buses, taxis, private cars and carts we had had to employ to negotiate the dangerously dilapidated road. In places the road had fallen completely away into the valley below so that passengers had to negotiate the rockfall on foot to where other forms of transport, stranded on the far side, could carry us to the next impasse. There is something about bare feet touching where other feet, of varying degrees of physical and spiritual cleanliness, have trod a moment before and for countless moments before, into such an ancient past.

At Badrinath I suddenly found myself once again on a sacred journey because of what I felt through my bare feet as they crossed that bridge, touched those worn stones that led up to the temple of Badri Narayan, and followed in the steps of a young Brahmin through all the slush at the temple entrance into the inner sanctum, which was at that moment being "restored," with a very secular scaffolding supporting a temporary roof. There, with my Brahmin companion, I participated in the *puja*. He seemed oblivious to the dust and rubble and noise of the workmen all around us. Before we retraced our steps toward Rishikesh, many days away, Mohan Kumar and I made another sacred journey, on our own, on foot, far down the valley floor to where, together, we could both bathe at least our feet in the icy waters of this young branch of the holy Ganga.

Without delay in Rishikesh we hired a taxi to take us as far as it could toward Jumnotri; there were no buses, and winter was fast approaching. So it was in company with a young Brahmin and a middle-aged Nepali Buddhist taxi driver that I arrived at Hanuman Chatti once again, though a physically different Hanuman Chatti from the one I had visited so long ago. It is not easy to separate one's sense of the Sacred from one's sense of the secular when visiting a place that came to mean so much so many long years ago, in days of youth and all its excitement of discovery. I enjoyed the evening's camaraderie with some of the local villagers, pleased to see us because the pilgrim season was over and both the financial gain and the entertainment value to be had from pilgrims were gone. The villagers recounted stories from the past season but were more interested in us, an unusually strange trio, they commented, while asking what had brought us together. They perceived what I had not perceived, that the Nepali taxi driver was more than that. They were not surprised, as both Mohan Kumar and I were, when he confirmed their perception that he too was making a pilgrimage to Jumnotri and was ready for the journey on foot the next day. He later told me he made that decision only when he saw a tributary to the Jumna rushing past the wooden building in which we sheltered that night. He, not Mohan Kumar, joined me there later that evening, in the moonlight, to explore the sight, sound, and smell of the water, the forest, the stones and boulders, and the leaf mold. Not a word was exchanged then, so I cannot say what he felt, but I was glad to have someone share the space and place with me, whatever he was feeling, things I had never been willing to share on that earlier trip.

On the next day, at first I laughed at myself as the other two soon caught up with me and, after a polite interval, when the going got rough, passed me and disappeared up the wooded trail. I did not laugh when I eventually had to stop, faced with yet another incredibly steep ascent that I told myself surely had not been there thirty years earlier. I tried to muster the strength to climb to the top and knew full well that would only bring me to the almost equally grueling descent to the foot of another gorge and an unknown number of further tests of endurance. At one point I lay down and recalled my first trip and decided that this time I was not going to be foolish and would simply make my way slowly back. My feet decided otherwise, it seemed, for as soon as I stood up they began to continue the ascent. Then I came to that point where I could see that cliff ledge, just as I remembered it. This time something different lay ahead for me, the certainty that Jumnotri, this time, was for me a sacred place and that all that mattered was getting there. When I rounded that most uncomfortable corner, where I had nearly fallen before, and saw the site ahead and below, it now looked rather more like a suburban dwelling with its tin-roofed tourist lodge on the stream's near side and with some European or American mountain climbers sitting there playing cards, their multicolored laundry drying on a line. My thoughts were, however, only on the sacred that I knew lay across the footbridge, where steam still rose from the hot springs. There Mohan Kumar and the taxidriver-Buddhist-pilgrim to a Hindu shrine stood, waiting for me.

There, above the temple and above the hot springs, with such an opportunity for studying both tourists and pilgrims at the same site and against all my determination to make a purely academic study of pilgrimage and its analogy with tourism, I became a pilgrim, dedicated exclusively to the quest for the Sacred. I can even point to the place the transformation began, halfway across that bridge. When I was at the mouth of a cave not many minutes later and the Nepali Buddhist rang the brass bell hanging at the entrance, I was entirely ready for the experience that followed, though none of us had any idea that Bengali Baba was in residence.

Years ago I would have dismissed him, if not as a charlatan at least as of insignificance compared with the great Hindu teachers I had met: Anandamayi, Sri Aurobindo, Ramana Maharshi. The only feeling I had, however, was the knowledge that it was right simply because it had happened. After a while, with the three of us in that small cave with Bengali Baba, there was no question about following the prescribed ritual steps that I had so ignored not only thirty years ago at this very site but only a couple of weeks ago at Badrinath. Much to my surprise, when for a fleeting moment I realized what I had done, I was stark naked, something I had never done in my life before in such assorted company, and was with my two fellow pilgrims in the stone pool filled with hot water overflowing from the hot spring above. We could barely see each other for the steam in the icy air, but we were all looking at each other, without speaking, as if to confirm that what was happening was really happening. We had bathed in a hot spring halfway along the trail, but this experience was something totally different. As if to assure us that something exceptional was indeed happening, the temple priest came out with a little bell and a censer and blessed us all, a Brahmin, a Buddhist, and a would-be agnostic academic. Our immediate reaction was far from reverent. We all laughed and set about ducking and diving in the hot water. Did the others share my relief that now there was no possible turning back? I do not know, but for me, from that moment, once again I knew that Gangotri was waiting for me, although the winter had already closed it for the season, the sacred images had been removed, and the shrines were empty. Later both my fellow-pilgrims made special mention of that moment when we were all touched by the Sacred.

This time at Jumnotri I not only ate the food but waited until it was blessed both by the priest and by Bengali Baba, who had his acolyte prepare it for us and serve it in the cave, with himself assisting. So it seemed perfectly normal when he presented me with two rare leaves he had collected from high up where vegetation is itself rare and asked me quite simply to give one to Anandamayi, as though I was returning to her, once again, in Banaras. As we made our way slowly back to Hanuman Chatti, we were together, and our conversation was exclusively about what had happened to us all up there where the icy Jumna leaps and mingles with the hot springs of Jumnotri and where strange things happen in caves and hot baths that do not seem in the least bit strange at the time and are only marvelous in retrospect. At the time they are only right, but immensely so.

We all parted company at Uttarkashi, in the main Ganges valley. The Nepali was a taxi driver again and had business to attend to. Mohan Kumar confessed that he was a city youth, and he was footsore and could go no further. Since there was no transportation to Gangotri and the shrine was closed anyway, he was more than content with what he had accomplished so early in his life and was returning to Delhi. He insisted on providing me with a Nepali porter, even though I had no more than a towel that doubled as a blanket to carry, my tourist camera, and one change of clothes.

The young porter and I traveled more or less together, one in front, then the other, as we walked and rested in our own individual time and manner. Sometimes we followed the new road that, like the road to Badrinath, had been painstakingly made but allowed to fall into disrepair, but often the foot trail was both quicker and less hazardous. We always found a small village or lone farmhouse where we were made welcome for the night and where food was gladly given and sometimes where payment was refused since I was on a sacred journey. Not once did I say that I was on such a journey, and my dress, though by now somewhat worn and dirty, was perfectly normal "casual" American wear. Nor was I once asked to discuss why I was on pilgrimage to a Hindu shrine so late in the year. It seemed that for our hosts the fact that we were making a sacred journey was both evident and sufficient in itself.

One day from Gangotri I left the porter far behind, or perhaps he too sensed what was going on and stayed far behind. When I arrived at Gangotri, two hours before sunset, I was alone in a deserted pilgrim town. I was more than content and wandered around the empty streets, visited the empty temples, and, outside the great but now empty shrine, on impulse I rang the temple bell, as should any good pilgrim. From across the river, unexpectedly, faintly, another bell answered. In this way I found lodging for the night, already getting bitter cold, and was thankfully able to abandon the corner of an open veranda into which I had bundled some old paper I had found in preparation for my stay. The bell summoned me to a small community of three Hindu monks who were proposing to spend the whole winter there and who were soon plying me with hot tea and then showed me one of the most flea-infested beds I have ever slept in, covered by a mountain of flea infested blankets. A little earlier in the season they might not have been able to spare one blanket, they said. It was only when I found myself back on the trail down to Uttarkashi in the gathering dark, lighted by the moon, that I realized my earlier fatigue had completely gone; it was nearly an hour before I found the porter slowly climbing upward, and another hour before we got back to where more hot tea and food were waiting for us.

I left before dawn, the porter following me briefly, then agreeing that it was best for me to go to Gaumukh alone. For him it was just another glacier, he said, and I would not need him. But then I had known that this journey would be made alone, the journey I had begun thirty years earlier. I remembered Anandamayi's telling me that of all the sacred places I would visit, Gaumukh would be the most sacred. Or did she really say that? Did she perhaps just speak of Gaumukh in such a way that I knew it was mine? Of course, the glacier face then was not where it was now. It did not matter, but she came to mind as I trudged out of Gangotri, beyond and above the tree line, to where the great tumble of glacial boulders begins. I quickly got lost among those towering rocks and was guided only by the sound of the river. Even that got fainter and fainter as the river got smaller and increasingly covered by ice. Then, when all sound of the river was blotted out by those massive boulders, I saw the icy top of the great glacier a bare half-mile ahead and stretching slowly up into Tibet and, had I wished, it, on to Kailasa.

The river again found me and flowed in a few places underneath a covering of ice. I followed it as best I could, though the rocks were treacherously slippery, freezing wherever touched by spray. As I rounded the last huge boulder, the face of the glacier was revealed, a massive and translucent, milky blue gateway. In the middle of its jagged face of stalactites and stalagmites was a dark gaping hole, "the mouth of the cow," and from this cavern, from the heart of that huge glacier above, poured the sacred Ganga. The stream flowed so torrentially that it was far from frozen, but the spray froze even before it fell.

Almost in the mouth itself was a small cluster of boulders in which a pole had been placed with a saffron-colored piece of cloth blowing stiffly in the icy wind. There my sacred journey would both end and begin, I knew, for there is no real end to such journeys for most of us. So, in spite of the obvious danger, from a secular viewpoint, there was no hesitation, and if my feet slipped from one rock, they slipped safely onto another until I reached the last cluster of boulders with the pole and saffron flag. There I squatted and lowered my enamel mug into the water to drink, only to find that it froze before I got it to my mouth. Moving more quickly the next time, I succeeded and so, according to the promise of the Scriptures, was assured salvation. That most assuredly was not in my mind then. It was just something that had to be done, a private goal, another step in the quest for the sacred, and a very personal experience.

A pilgrim without pretense, I was still tourist enough at such a moment, perched precariously on those ice-covered rocks, to take a photograph and, only then, with my camera still frozen to both hands, made my way back to the shore, safety, and a measure of secularity. Ahead lay a long physical journey back and months of secular research into tourism in other parts of India and on eastward. Only the outer sacred journey had ended, and with its end yet another inner pilgrimage was begun, with its own ups and downs of secularity and sanctity.

I think it is best left to the reader to decide whether or not that account of a personal experience reveals anything of wider significance for our understanding of pilgrimage as a process or if it merely tells of an experience that, because it is so intensely personal, must always remain so, perhaps of significance to other individuals, but of none for our anthropological concern with human society. I know that experience helps me in my understanding of pilgrimage both as a social process and as a social institution. I may well have omitted just that detail that might enable others to perceive the working of that essential ingredient, Spirit, the Sacred, whatever we choose to call it, as a force that is as social as it is personal. But I hope my account complements the other contributions to this volume, which show what seems to be a new sensitivity to human emotion and its power, individual as well as social.

The question was raised early on as to why pilgrimage is so prevalent in some societies and at some times in their history and so seemingly lacking in other societies and at other times. The very diversity of the topics covered, as well as the rich diversity of approaches, demonstrates the wide range of difference in the social significance of pilgrimage just as it demonstrates the difference between the various manifestations of the phenomenon in different places or in the same place at different times. These data all suggests that when considered as a process and particularly as an internal process of transformation, pilgrimage in one form or another may well be very much alive in just those societies where the outward form seems to be lacking. I have tried in the description of my own personal experience in India to demonstrate how an anthropologist's participation at the deepest possible level of personal, spiritual involvement, while not necessarily giving him any certain knowledge of the spiritual experience of others, is still likely to get him a lot closer to it than mere physical or intellectual participation. For me, at least, it broadens our understanding of the social significance of pilgrimage while, if not revealing new truths, it at least suggests new avenues to be explored.

I will end by remarking on how this volume and my own reflections on it instantly make me think anew of the one society I perhaps know and understand as well as any, including my own.

The Mbuti hunters of the tropical rain forest of eastern Zaire certainly have nothing corresponding to our understanding of pilgrimage as a formal, organized social institution. They do, however, make a very clear distinction between the Sacred and profane, and their movement in times of crisis away from the village and back into the forest, as well as their orientation of the ritual *molimo* trumpet, makes it evident that the center of the forest is the most sacred physical place of all. This fact is confirmed by a number of other observations, such as the various tabus associated with the center of the forest, notably the prohibition against hunting there. They have then, without doubt, what we might call a sacred place, and on occasion they have a conscious and organized movement toward that sacred place for the purpose of invoking spiritual aid in the resolution of crisis and conflict. The invocation may involve ritual through one or more of the musical modes among the central Mbuti or through the *molimo* festival (as well as by its specific music); but it can also be invoked, it seems, by mere proximity without ritual mediation.

These attributes are all clearly of "social" importance and something I could and should have investigated while there if such a volume as this had been available to me to stimulate my rethinking of pilgrimage as a process rather than as a social institution, to which my academic training then confined me. In my very first attempts to write about the Mbuti, their concept of the sacredness of the forest was dominant, and both many readers of *The Forest People* and I recognized the unspoken social significance of the individual act of my friend, Teleabo Kenge, when he wandered out of the camp one night into the nearby solitude of the deserted children's *bopi* (playground) and danced in such evident ecstasy. When I asked him why he was dancing alone, Kenge told me so clearly, "I am NOT dancing alone, I am dancing with the forest, dancing with the moon."

What was Kenge experiencing if not a sacred journey? His body traveled only a hundred yards or so, but it traveled away from the relative secularity (if not profanity) of the hunting camp, with all its necessarily mundane associations, to the deserted *bopi*. It so happens that this particular *bopi* was not directly between the camp and the center of the forest, but it did touch on the banks of the Lelo River, which had to be crossed to reach the center. Further, among the Mbuti the children, like elders but in some ways even more so, are considered to be closer to the spiritual source of all life than are either youths or adults; and children are charged with the vitally important duty of lighting the hunting fire, minimizing the profanity of the act of taking forest life to which all Mbuti are condemned by that primal sin, the first act of killing and eating a forest animal. Even during the daytime youths, elders, and, rarely, even adults would wander into the *bopi* for no ostensible purpose, apparently doing nothing when they got there, saying nothing. Those occasions were very different "journeys" from the ones in which they came storming into the *bopi* to reprimand the children for making too much noise, or whatever. These visits took place in any camp and any *bopi*, regardless of its orientation to the sacred physical center of the forest. Perhaps the Mbuti, too, were revitalizing their belief when they acted thus, and reifying their faith in the very existence of Spirit. Is this journeying not pilgrimage? Is a journey to a place called Lourdes or Mecca or Jerusalem or Gangotri or Bodh Gaya any more sacred than a journey to the forest, and is participation in formal divine worship any more sacred than dancing with the moon?

Even given the most materialistic interpretation of religion, we cannot deny the social and socializing force of Kenge's journey to the *bopi*, let alone the movement of whole bands of Mbuti hunters away from the periphery of the forest toward its center. How many other sacred journeys have all of us missed in our fieldwork because we were reluctant to allow ourselves the possibility that perhaps we, too, atheists or devoted believers in "another" religious system, could approach and be touched by some other Sacred or by Spirit? If we start by denying the existence of Spirit, then, indeed, there is no point in making the attempt. For some that detour is as it should be; there is plenty else to occupy any anthropologist in any field. In that case, however, I feel we should not even try to make the attempt, for it is surely a gross intellectual arrogance to suppose that we can understand a phenomenon that others say directly relates to the existence of Spirit while we openly deny it. If we do not deny it, if our approach is more that of an agnostic, then why should we not, in keeping with our participant-observer technique, take that step and open ourselves to the possibility that Spirit, as defined and recognized by others, really does exist? If we do not even make the attempt, then we are in no position to deny the existence of that Spirit and are predetermining the results of our exploration before it has begun and ordaining our own superficiality, at least in that particular branch of our study.

If our exploration of new worlds is to allow that society is more than a theoretical abstract, more than a structure, and if we are to be truly holistic and eclectic, then surely it is illogical deliberately to restrict our vision and determine in advance what we are not going to see. There is, then, no telling how accurately we do see, and there is no telling as to the magnitude of importance and social significance of what we have decided not to see. Our best of truths is likely to be but partial truth. This volume suggests to me, more than ever, that there is much room for controlled subjectivity in our field technique; there is a desperate need for it unless we are to continue to impose our own intellectual constructs on the societies we study, a complaint heard often enough from intellectuals from such societies.

For those willing to make of anthropology itself a pilgrimage, a quest for the Sacred, there is no telling where it will lead. For the true pilgrim it demands a willingness to abandon the self, both the intellectual and the religious self; it demands a total act of self-sacrifice, however momentary that may prove to be. There are pilgrims who never return from their sacred journey or who return transformed into something other than what they were. So with the anthropologist. From my own experience as an anthropologist, I can only avow that only by my working in this way can I respect and make the fullest use of the work of others, those with different goals and techniques that make up for my own deficiencies and fill in my own blind spots. Further, in terms of the personal satisfaction to which we are all entitled in our lives and in our work, no intellectual consideration has ever come near to persuading me otherwise, for if the effort has revealed anything, it is that the quest for society is one and the same thing as the quest for Self, which for some of us is also the quest for the Sacred that ultimately unites us all.

Contributors

ANNE H. BETTERIDGE received her Ph.D. in anthropology from the University of Chicago. She conducted research in Iran from 1974 to 1976 and continued residence there until early 1979. She has served as a Research Associate at the Southwest Institute for Research on Women at the University of Arizona, where she was assistant director of the faculty development project "Teaching Women's Studies from an International Perspective." She is presently Executive Director of the Middle East Studies Association of North America.

GLENN BOWMAN, a lecturer at the University of Kent at Canterbury in the interdisciplinary department of Communications and Image Studies, trained as a social anthropologist at the Institute of Social Anthropology, University of Oxford. His doctoral research on the anthropology of Jerusalem pilgrimage entailed field research in the Old City of Jerusalem between 1983 and 1985 and involved travel, with and without pilgrim groups, throughout Israel and the Occupied Territories. He has subsequently returned to the Occupied Territories a number of times to pursue research on the organization of markets, on the politics of tour guiding and of touristic development, and on the development and practice of Palestinian national-ism. He has published in *Middle East Report, New Formations,* and *Critique of Anthropology* as well as in Michael Sallnow and John Eade (eds.), *Contesting the Sacred: The Anthropology of Christian Pilgrimage* (Routledge 1991) and in David

Harrison (ed.), *International Tourism and the Less Developed Countries* (Bellhaven 1991).

ERIK COHEN is the George S. Wise Professor of Sociology and Dean, Faculty of Social Science, at the Hebrew University of Jerusalem. He has conducted studies of collective settlements and new towns in Israel, on urban life in Peru, on tourism in the Pacific and, in the last 15 years, on tourism, urban life, Christianity, and social change in Thailand. He has published about a hundred articles and edited two books. His most recent book *Thai Society in Comparative Perspective* is about to be published by White Lotus in Bangkok.

STEPHEN D. GLAZIER is Associate Professor and Chair of Sociology and Anthropology at the University of Nebraska-Kearney. He has also taught at Westmont College (Santa Barbara), Connecticut College (New London), Trinity College (Hartford), and the University of Connecticut, where he earned his Ph.D. in 1981. He is the author of four books and numerous articles dealing with religion and race relations in the Caribbean region. He has been conducting research among Trinidad's Spiritual Baptists since 1976. Glazier serves as an Associate Editor of the journal *Sociological Analysis* and is a member of the Executive Council of the Society for the Scientific Study of Religion.

ALAN MORINIS received his D.Phil. in social anthropology from Oxford University in 1980. His doctoral thesis focused on the contemporary practices and beliefs surrounding pilgrimage in the West Bengal state of India. This research was later published by Oxford University Press under the title *Pilgrimage in the Hindu Tradition*. He has published numerous articles on pilgrimage and other anthropological subjects and was instrumental in convening the seminal conference on the study of pilgrimage held at the University of Pittsburgh in 1981. In addition to editing the present volume, he has coedited *Pilgrimage in Latin America* (with N. Ross Crumrine; Greenwood 1991) and is coediting *Sacred Places, Sacred Spaces: The Geography of Pilgrimage* (with Robert Stoddard). He is currently primarily engaged in making films.

JAMES PRESTON is Professor of Anthropology and Chairman of the Religious Studies Program at the State University of New York at Oneonta. He is the author of numerous articles on various aspects of comparative religion. His publications include *Cult of the Goddess* and *Mother Worship: Theme and Variations*. He has conducted fieldwork on Hinduism in India and on Christianity among Native Americans.

JAMES B. PRUESS attended the University of Iowa and the University of Washington and received a Ph.D. in anthropology from the latter in 1974. He has taught at the University of Washington and the University of Khartoum and has conducted research in Thailand (Theravada Buddhist pilgrimage) and the Sudan (Islamic schooling). He is currently employed as a teacher and technical editor in Bangkok.

KAREN P. SINCLAIR is a Professor of Anthropology at Eastern Michigan University, Ypsilanti, Michigan. She has a Ph.D. from Brown University. She has been doing fieldwork with Maori pilgrims in New Zealand since 1972. She is currently completing a book on *Maramatanga*, which has been supported by grants from Eastern Michigan University and a Fellowship for College Teachers from the National Endowment for the Humanities. She has written several articles on this movement and on the current political situation in New Zealand. In addition to *Maramatanga*, she is interested in gender ideology, social structure, and the relationship between history and anthropology.

JOHN M. STANLEY is the Ellen Sabin Professor of Religious Studies at Lawrence University, Appleton, Wisconsin, where he has taught since 1961. Receiving his Ph.D. from Columbia University in 1966, he has conducted fieldwork research in both India and Malaysia and is the author of several articles and chapters on popular religions in western India, including "The Capitulation of Man: A Conversion Myth in the Cult of Khandoba" in Alf Hiltebeitael (ed.), *Criminal Gods and Demon Devotees* (Albany: State University of New York Press, 1989); "Gods, Ghosts and Possession" in M. Bernstsen and E. Zelliott (eds.), *The Experience of Hinduism: Essays on Religion in Maharashtra* (Albany: State University of New York Press, 1988); "*Nishkama* and *Sakama Bhakti*: Pandharpur and Jejuri" in Milton Israel and N. K. Wagle (eds.), *Religion and Society in Maharashtra*, Vol. 1 (Toronto: University of Toronto, 1987); and "Special Time, Special Power: A Study of the Fluidity of Power in a Popular Hindu Festival" (*Journal of Asian Studies*, November 1977). He is a member of Phi Beta Kappa and was the recipient of an American Institute of Indian Studies Senior Research Grant in 1975.

JAMES STEEL THAYER is an Associate Professor of Religious Studies at Oklahoma State University in Stillwater, Oklahoma. He has a B.A. (1970) and M.A. (1972) in anthropology from Indiana University and a Ph.D. in anthropology from the University of Michigan (1980). He also has a master's degree in religious studies from the Harvard Divinity School (1974). He has carried out three fieldwork projects in Africa: two in Sierra Leone (1979-1980 and 1984) and one in South Africa and the independent homeland of Transkei (1988-1989). He is the author of over a dozen articles on topics dealing with religion and culture, with particular reference to Africa.

COLIN TURNBULL studied philosophy and politics at Magdalen College, Oxford; Indian philosophy at Banaras Hindu University and Sri Anandamayi Asram, Banaras, India (1949-1951); and anthropology under Sir E. E. Evans-Pritchard at Oxford (1956-1959) and earned his D.Phil. in social anthropology from Oxford in 1964. He has taught at several universities, his most recent position being Randolph Distinguished Visiting Professor, Vassar College (1987-1988). He has done field research in Africa and Asia and is the author of numerous publications, including *The Forest People* (New York: Simon and Schuster, 1962).

PETER W. WOOD is an adjunct member of the Anthropology Department at Boston University. He received his doctoral degree in anthropology from the University of Rochester in 1986. Since 1986 he has served in various administrative positions at Boston University and is currently Assistant to the Executive Vice President.

PAUL YOUNGER was born in Pennsylvania and went to India as a student in 1958. In 1961 he married Susanna Oommen of Kerala and in 1965 finished his Ph.D. at Princeton University. He has made ten research trips to India and Sri Lanka and concentrated on the festival religion of South India and on the religious dimension of contemporary Indian politics. He has written five books and two dozen articles on the religious traditions of India. He has taught at McMaster University, Hamilton, Ontario, since 1964 and enjoys raising sheep on the family farm nearby.

References

Abu-Jaber, Kamel.
   1967. The Millet System in the Nineteenth Century Ottoman Empire. *The Muslim World*, 57:3, pp. 213-23.
Althusser, Louis.
   1971. On the Reproduction of the Conditions of Production. In *Lenin and Philosophy*. Ben Brewster (trans.). New York, pp. 123-73.
Anon.
   1950. The Vision of Necedah. *Life*, 29:9 (August 28), pp. 21-23.
Anon.
   1950. Pray and Pray Hard. *Newsweek*, 36:9 (August 28), pp. 31-32.
Anon.
   1963. Summer Guide to Shrines of Our Lady in the United States and Canada. *Our Lady's Digest*, 18, pp. 52-53.
Antoun, Richard T.
   1989. *Muslim Preacher in the Modern World*. Princeton: Princeton University Press.
Ardener, Edwin.
   1989. The Voice of Prophecy: Further Problems in the Analysis of Events. In *The Voice of Prophecy and Other Essays*. Malcolm Chapman (ed.). Oxford: Basil Blackwell, pp. 134-54.

Armanski, G.
  1978. *Die kostbarsten Tage des Jahres*. Berlin: Rotbusch.
Armstrong, Jocelyn.
  1990. Maori Christianity in the South Island. In *Christianity in the Pacific*. J.
  Barker (ed.). Lanham, Md.: University Press of America.
Atiya, Aziz S.
  1962. *Crusade, Commerce and Culture*. London: Oxford University Press.
Aziz, Barbara N.
  1982. A Pilgrimage to Amarnath: The Hindu's Search for Immortality. *Kailash:
  Journal of Himalayan Studies*, 9, pp. 2-3.
Aziz, Barbara N.
  1987. Personal Dimensions of the Sacred Journey: What Pilgrims Say. *Religious
  Studies*, 23, pp. 247-61.
Babcock, Barbara.
  1978. *The Reversible World*. Ithaca: Cornell University Press.
Balandier, Georges.
  1970. *Political Anthropology*. A. M. Sheridan (trans.). New York: Pantheon
  Books.
Basho, Matsuo.
  1966. *The Narrow Road to the Deep North and Other Travel Sketches*. Har-
  mondsworth: Penguin.
Bayly, Susan.
  1989. *Saints, Goddesses and Kings: Muslims and Christians in South Indian
  Society, 1700-1900*. Cambridge: Cambridge University Press.
Beazley, C. Raymond.
  1897. *The Dawn of Modern Geography*, Vol. 1. Edinburgh: John Murray.
Beck, Brenda E. F.
  1972. *Peasant Society in Konku: A Study of Right and Left Subcastes in South
  India*. Vancouver: University of British Columbia Press.
Beck, Brenda E. F.
  1980. The Goddess and the Demon: A Local South Indian Festival. *Pururtha*.
  Paris: Editions de l'ecole des hautes etudes en sciences sociales.
Belich, James.
  1986. *The New Zealand Wars*. Auckland: University of Auckland Press.
Berger, P. L. and Thomas Luckmann.
  1966. *The Social Construction of Reality*. Harmondsworth: Penguin.
Berliere, U.
  1890. Les pelerinages judiciaries au moyen age. *Revue Benedictine*, 7, pp. 520-26.
Bertrandon de la Brocquiere.
  1968. Travels. In *Early Travels in Palestine*. Thomas Wright (ed.). New York:
  Ktav (reprint Bohn, 1848), pp. 283-382.
Besant, Walter, and E. H. Palmer.
  1899. *Jerusalem*. London: Chatto and Windus.

Betteridge, Anne H.

1983. Muslim Women and Shrines in Shiraz. In *Mormons and Muslims*. Spencer J. Palmer (ed.). Provo, Utah: Religious Studies Center, Brigham Young University, pp. 127-38.

Bharati, Agehananda.

1963. Pilgrimage in the Indian Tradition. *History of Religions*, 31:1, pp. 135-67.

Bharati, Agehananda.

1970. Pilgrimage Sites and Indian Civilization. In *Chapters in Indian Civilization*, Vol. 1. Joseph W. Elder (ed.). Dubuque, IA: Kendall/Hunt.

Bhardwaj, Surinder.

1973. *Hindu Places of Pilgrimage*. Berkeley: University of California Press.

Bhardwaj, Surinder.

1978. Geography and Pilgrimages. Paper presented at the Tenth International Congress of Anthropological and Ethnological Sciences, New Delhi, India.

Bidyalankavara, Prince.

1954. The Buddha's Footprints. In *Selected Articles from the Siam Society Journal*, Vol. 2. Bangkok: Siam Society, pp. 37-52.

Billet, Bernard.

1973. *Le Fait Des Apparitions Non Reconnues Par L'Eglise*. Paris: P. Lethielleux.

Binney, Judith.

1986. *Nga Morehu*. Wellington: Oxford University Press.

Binney, Judith.

1987. Maori Oral Narratives, Pakeha Written Texts: Two Forms of Telling History. *New Zealand Journal of History*, 21, pp. 18-28.

Binney, Judith.

1989. The Maori and the Signing of the Treaty of Waitangi. In *Towards 1990: Seven Leading Historians Examine Significant Aspects of New Zealand History*. Auckland: Government Printer, pp. 20-31.

Binney, Judith.

1990. Amalgamation and Separation. In *The People and the Land*. Binney, Judith, Bassett and Erik Olssen (eds.). Wellington: Allen and Unwin, pp. 203-31.

Binney, Judith, Gillian Chaplin and Craig Wallace.

1979. *Mihaia*. Wellington: Oxford University Press.

Birks, J. S.

1978. *Across the Savannahs to Mecca: The Overland Pilgrimage Route from West Africa*. London: C. Hurst.

Bloch, Marc.

1962. *Feudal Society*. L. A. Manyon (trans.). London: R.K.P.

Boahen, A. Adu.

1963. Trade in the Nineteenth Century. *Journal of History*, 3:2, pp. 349-59.

Bonacich, E.

1973. A Theory of Middleman Minorities. *American Sociology Review*, 38:5, pp. 583-94.

Boorstin, D.
    1964. *The Image: A Guide to Pseudo-Events in American Society*. New York: Harper and Row.
Bordeaux Pilgrim.
    1896. *Itinerarium Burdigalense*. In *Palestine Pilgrims' Text Society Library*, Vol. 1. Aubrey Stewart (trans.). London: Palestine Pilgrims' Text Society, pp. 1-68
Bordeaux Pilgrim.
    1973. Itinerarium Burdigalense. In *Egeria's Travels*. John Wilkinson (trans.). London: S.P.C.K., pp. 153-63.
Bowman, Glenn.
    1991. The Mirror of God: The Image of the Holy Land in the Pilgrimages of the Various Christianities. In Michael Sallnow and John Eade (eds.). *Contesting the Sacred: The Anthropology of Christian Pilgrimage*. London: Routledge, pp. 98-121.
Breton, Paul Emile.
    1955. *The Big Chief of the Prairies*. Edmonton: Palm.
Brodie, F. M.
    1971. *The Devil Drives*. Harmondsworth: Penguin.
Brown, Paul
    1984. Official Ethnic Statistics in New Zealand. In *Tauiwi*. Paul Spoonley, Cluny MacPherson, David Pearson, Charles Sedgewick (eds.). Palmerston North: Dunmore Press, pp. 159-71.
Brubaker, Richard.
    1978. The Ambivalent Mistress: A Study of the South Indian Village Goddesses and Their Religious Meaning. Ph.D. diss., University of Chicago.
Burchard of Mount Sion.
    1895-1896. *Itinerary*. In *Palestine Pilgrims' Text Society Library*, Vol. 12. Aubrey Stewart (trans.). London: Palestine Pilgrims' Text Society, pp. 1-111.
Byrd, R. E.
    1935. *Discovery: The Story of the Second Byrd Antarctic Expedition*. New York: Putnam.
Campbell, Ena.
    1982. The Virgin of Guadalupe and the Female Self-Image: A Mexican Case History. In *Mother Worship: Theme and Variations*. James J. Preston (ed.). Chapel Hill: University of North Carolina Press, pp. 2-24.
Carroll, Michael P.
    1985. The Virgin Mary at La Salette and Lourdes: Whom Did the Children See? *Journal for the Scientific Study of Religion*, 24:1, pp. 56-74.
Carroll, Michael P.
    1986. *The Cult of the Virgin Mary: Psychological Origins*. Princeton: Princeton University Press.
Cauwenberghe, E. van.
    1922. Les pelerinages expiatoires et judiciaires dans le droit commun de la Belgique au moyen age. *Recueil de travaux de l'universite de Louvain*, 48.

Louvain.

Cawte, John.

1974. *Medicine Is the Law*. Honolulu: University of Hawaii Press.

Chattopadhyaya, K. C.

1937. Religious Suicide at Prayaga. *Journal of the Uttar Pradesh Historical Society*, 10, pp. 65-79.

Chittick, William C. (ed. and trans.).

1981. *A Shi'ite Anthology*. Albany: State University of New York Press.

Christaller, W.

1955. Beitrage zu einer Geographie des Fremdenverkehrs. *Erdkunde*, 9, pp. 1-19.

Christian, William.

1972. *Person and God in a Spanish Valley. Studies in Social Discontinuity*. New York: Seminar Press.

Christian, William.

1984. Religious Apparitions and The Cold War in Southern Europe. In *Religion, Power, and Protest in Local Communities: The Northern Shore of the Mediterranean*. Eric Wolf (ed.). New York: Mouton.

Clark, Paul.

1975. *HauHau: The Pai Marire Search for Maori Identity*. Auckland: Oxford University Press.

Clifford, James.

1988. *The Predicament of Culture*. Cambridge: Harvard University Press.

Clothey, Fred.

1972. Pilgrimage Centers in the Tamil Cultus of Murukan. *Journal of the American Academy of Religion*, 40, pp. 72-95.

Clothey, Fred.

1978. *The Many Faces of Murukan*. The Hague: Mouton.

Clothey, Fred.

1983. *Rhythm and Intent: Ritual Studies from South India*. Madras: Blackie and Son.

Cohen, Abner.

1968. The Politics of Mysticism in Some Local Communities in Newly Independent African States. In *Local Level Politics*. Marc Swartz (ed.). Chicago: Aldine, pp. 361-76.

Cohen, Amnon.

1984. *Jewish Life Under Islam: Jerusalem in the Sixteenth Century*. Cambridge: Harvard University Press.

Cohen, Erik.

1972. Toward a Sociology of International Tourism. *Social Research*, 39:1, pp. 164-82.

Cohen, Erik.

1973. Nomads from Affluence: Notes on the Phenomenon of Drifter Tourism. *International Journal of Comparative Sociology*, 14:1-2, pp. 89-103.

Cohen, Erik.
   1974. Who Is a Tourist? A Conceptual Clarification. *Sociology Review*, 22:4, pp.
   527-55.
Cohen, Erik.
   1979a. The Impact of Tourism on the Hill Tribes of Northern Thailand. *Internationales Asienforum*, 10:1-2, pp. 5-38.
Cohen, Erik.
   1979b. A Phenomenology of Tourist Experiences. *Sociology*, 13, pp. 179-201.
Cohen, Erik.
   1981. Comment on Nash, 1981. *Current Anthropology*, 22:5, pp. 469-70.
Cohen, Erik.
   1982a. Jungle Guides in Northern Thailand: The Dynamics of a Marginal Occupational Role. *Sociology Review*, 30:2, pp. 234-66.
Cohen, Erik.
   1982b. Marginal Paradises—Bungalow Tourism on the Islands of Southern
   Thailand. *Annals of Tourism Research*, 9:2, pp. 189-228.
Cohen, Erik.
   1982c. The Pacific Islands from Utopian Myth to Consumer Product: The Disenchantment of Paradise. *Les Cahiers du Tourisme*, Ser. B., No. 27.
Cohen, Erik.
   1983a. Hill Tribe Tourism. In *Highlanders of Thailand*. J. McKinnon and W.
   Bhruksasri (eds.). Kuala Lumpur: Oxford University Press, pp. 307-25.
Cohen, Erik.
   1983b. Insiders and Outsiders—The Dynamics of Development of Bungalow
   Tourism on the Islands of Southern Thailand. *Human Organization*, 42:2, pp.
   158-62.
Cohen, Erik.
   1984 [1986]. The Drop-Out Expatriates: A Study of Marginal Farangs in Bangkok. *Urban Anthropology*, 13:1, pp. 91-115.
Cohn, Norman.
   1970. *The Pursuit of the Millennium: Revolutionary Millenarians and Mystical
   Anarchists of the Middle Ages*. New York: Oxford University Press.
Comaroff, Jean.
   1985. *Body of Power, Spirit of Resistance*. Chicago: University of Chicago Press.
Conklin, H. C.
   1955. Hanunoo Color Categories. *Southwestern Journal of Anthropology*, 11, pp.
   339-44.
Constable, Giles.
   1976. Opposition to Pilgrimage in the Middle Ages. *Studia Gratiana*, 19:1, pp.
   123-46.
Conway, Frederick J.
   1980. Pentecostalism in Haiti: Healing and Hierarchy. In *Perspectives on Pentecostalism: Case Studies from the Caribbean and Latin America*. S. D. Glazier
   (ed.). Washington, DC: University Press of America, pp. 7-26.

Cooley, John K.
  1972. *Baal, Christ and Muhammad*. New York: Holt Rinehart Winston.
Coon, Carleton.
  1958. *Caravan: The Story of the Middle East*, revised ed. New York: Holt
    Rinehart.
Crapanzano, Vincent.
  1973. *The Hamadsha: A Study in Moroccan Ethnopsychiatry*. Berkeley: Univer-
    sity of California Press.
Cribier, F.
  1969. *La grande migration d'ete des citadins de France*. Paris: Editions de CNRS.
Crumrine, N. Ross.
  1991. Fiestas and Exchange Pilgrimages: The Yorem Pakho and Mayo Identity,
    Northwest Mexico. In *Pilgrimage in Latin America*. N. Ross Crumrine and
    Alan Morinis (eds.). Westport, CT: Greenwood, pp. 71-89.
Damrong Rajanuphap, H. H. Prince.
  1971 (originally published in 1929). *Tamnan Phra Phuttha Chedi [History of
    Buddhist Monuments]*. Bangkok: Phrae Phithaya.
Dandekar, S. V.
  1927. *Varkari Pantaca Itihasa*. n.p.
Davies, J. G.
  1988. *Pilgrimage Yesterday and Today: Why? Where? How?* London: SCM
    Press.
Davis, Wade.
  1988. *Passages of Darkness: The Ethnobiology of the Haitian Zombie*. Chapel
    Hill: University of North Carolina Press.
Delaney, John.
  1961. *A Woman Clothed With the Sun: Eight Great Appearances of Our Lady*.
    Garden City, NY: Image Books.
Deleury, G. A.
  1960. *The Cult of Vithoba*. Poona: Deccan College Press.
della Cava, Ralph.
  1970. *Miracle at Joaseiro*. New York: Columbia University Press.
Desai, A. V.
  1974. Tourism—Economic Possibilities and Politics. In *Tourism in Fiji*. Suva:
    University of the South Pacific, pp. 1-12.
Desil, Harold C.
  1967. *Une esquisse ethnosociologique de la communaute de Ville-Bonheur con-
    sideree dans ses rapports avec certains phenomenes d'order religieux*. These
    de Licence. Faculte d'Ethnologie, Universite d'Etat d'Haiti.
Desmangles, Leslie G.
  1975. *God in Haitian Vodun*. Ph.D. diss., Temple University.
Desmangles, Leslie G.
  1979. The Vodoun Way of Death: Cultural Symbiosis of Roman Catholicism and
    Vodoun in Haiti. *Journal of Religious Thought*, 36:1, pp. 5-20.

Diehl, Carl.
  1956. *Instrument and Purpose: Studies in Rites and Rituals in South India*. Lund: C.W.K. Gleerup.
Dimock, Edward C.
  1966. *The Place of the Hidden Moon*. Chicago: University of Chicago Press.
Dorsey, George A.
  1910. The Sun Dance. In *Handbook of American Indians North of Mexico*. F. W. Hodge (ed.). Bureau of American Ethnology, Bulletin 30, pp. 649-52.
Douglas, Mary.
  1973. *Natural Symbols*. London: Pelican.
Drouin, E. O.
  1973. *Lac Ste.-Anne Sakahigan*. Edmonton: Editions de l'ermitage.
Duby, Georges.
  1980. *The Three Orders: Feudal Society Imagined*. A. Goldhammer (trans.). Chicago: University of Chicago Press.
Duerr, H. P.
  1985. *Dreamtime: Concerning the Boundary Between Wilderness and Civilization*. Oxford: Blackwell.
Dumazdier, J.
  1968. Leisure. *International Encyclopaedia of the Social Sciences*, Vol. 9, pp. 248-53.
Dumont, Louis.
  1959. A Structural Definition of a Folk Deity of Tamilnad: Aiyanar the Lord, *Contributions to Indian Sociology*, 3, pp. 75-87.
Dupont, G.
  1973. Lourdes: Pilgrims or Tourists? *Manchester Guardian Weekly*. 108:23 (May 20), p. 16.
Dupront, A.
  1967. Tourisme et pelerinage: Reflexions de psychologie collective. *Communications*, 10, pp. 97-121.
Durkheim, Emile.
  1915. *The Elementary Forms of the Religious Life*. J. W. Swain (trans.). London: Allen and Unwin.
Durkheim, Emile.
  1961. *Moral Education: A Study of the Theory and Application of the Sociology of Education*. E. K. Wilson (trans.). New York: Free Press.
Dusenberry, Verne.
  1962. *The Montana Cree: A Study in Religious Persistence*. Stockholm: Almqvist and Wiksell.
Eck, Diana.
  1982. *Banaras: City of Lights*. Princeton: Princeton University Press.
Eickelman, Dale F.
  1976. *Moroccan Islam*. Austin: University of Texas Press.

Eickelman, Dale F., and James Piscatori (eds.).

1990. *Muslim Travellers: Pilgrimage, Migration and the Religious Imagination.* Berkeley: University of California Press.

Eliade, M.

1969. *Images and Symbols.* New York: Sheed and Ward.

Eliade, M.

1971. *The Myth of the Eternal Return.* Princeton: Princeton University Press.

Elmore, W. T.

1915. *Dravidian Gods in Modern Hinduism.* Lincoln: University of Nebraska.

Engblom, Philip C.

1987. Introduction. In *Palkhi, An Indian Pilgrimage.* D. B. Mokashi. Albany, NY: State University of New York Press, pp. 1-30.

Eschmann, A.

1978. Hinduization of Tribal Deities in Orissa: The Sakta and Saiva Typology. In *The Cult of Jagannath and the Regional Tradition in Orissa.* A. Eschmann, Hermann Kulke and Gaya Charan Tripathi (eds.). New Delhi: Manohar Press, pp. 79-97.

Eusebius.

1890. Life of Constantine. In *Eusebius.* Ernest Richardson (ed. and trans.). Oxford: Select Library of Nicene and Post-Nicene Fathers of the Christian Church, Vol. 1, pp. 481-559.

Eusebius.

1965. *The History of the Church.* G. A. Williamson (trans.). Harmondsworth: Penguin.

Fabri, Felix.

1893. *The Book of Wanderings of Brother Felix Fabri,* In *Palestine Pilgrims' Text Society Library,* Vol. 1. Aubrey Stewart (trans.). London: Palestine Pilgrims' Text Society.

Fairs and Festivals in Maharashtra.

1969. *Census of India 1961,* Vol. 10, part 7-B. Bombay: Maharashtra Census Office.

Falk, Nancy.

1977. To Gaze on Sacred Traces. *History of Religions,* 16:4, pp. 281-93.

Farmayan, Hafez, and Elton L. Daniel (trans. and eds.).

1990. *A Shi'ite Pilgrimage to Mecca, 1885-1886: The Safarnameh of Mirza Mohammad Hosayn Farahani.* Austin: University of Texas Press.

Fisher, Humphrey J.

1963. *Ahmadiyyah: A Study in Contemporary Islam on the West African Coast.* Oxford: Oxford University Press.

Fisher, Humphrey J.

1968. The Early Life and Pilgrimage of al-Hajj Muhammad al-Amin the Soninke (d. 1887). *Journal of African History,* 11:1, pp. 51-70.

Fitzsimons, Friar Simon.

1948. *Visit to the Holy Places of Egypt, Sinai, Palestine and Syria in 1348.* T.

Bellarinin and E. Hoade (trans.). Jerusalem: Franciscan Printing Press.

Fortes, Meyer, and E. E. Evans-Pritchard.
1940. Introduction. In *African Political Systems*. M. Fortes and E. E. Evans-Pritchard (eds.). Oxford: O.U.P., pp. 1-23.

Foy, Felician A. (ed.).
1987. *The 1988 Catholic Almanac*. Huntington, IN: Our Sunday Visitor.

Frake, Charles.
1961. The Diagnosis of Disease Among the Subanum of Mindinao. *American Anthropologist*, 63, pp. 113-32.

Frantz, Charles.
1978. Ecology and Social Organization Among Nigerian Fulbe (Fulani). In *The Nomadic Alternative*. Wolfgang Weissler (ed.). The Hague: Mouton, pp. 97-118.

Friedman, J. B.
1981. *The Monstrous Races in Medieval Art and Thought*. Cambridge: Harvard University Press.

Fuller, Christopher.
1984. *Servants of the Goddess: The Priests of a South Indian Temple*. Cambridge: Cambridge University Press.

Fussell, P.
1979. The Stationary Tourist. *Harper's Magazine*, 258: 1547, pp. 31-38.

Gauthier, Marie M.
1983. *Highways of the Faith: Relics and Reliquaries from Jerusalem to Compostella*. J. A. Underwood (trans.). Secausus: Wellfleet Press.

Geary, Patrick.
1978. *Furta Sacra: Thefts of Relics in the Central Middle Ages*. Princeton: Princeton University Press.

Geary, Patrick.
1986. Sacred Commodities: The Circulation of Medieval Relics. In *The Social Life of Things: Commodities in Cultural Perspective*. Arjun Appadurai (ed.). London: Cambridge University Press, pp. 169-91.

Geertz, Clifford.
1968. *Islam Observed: Religious Development in Morocco and Indonesia*. New Haven: Yale University Press.

Geertz, Clifford.
1972. Religion as a Cultural System. In *Reader in Comparative Religion*, 3d ed. W. A. Lessa and E. Z. Vogt (eds.). New York: Harper and Row, pp. 167-78.

Geertz, Clifford.
1983. *Local Knowledge*. New York: Basic Books.

Gell, Alfred.
1980. Gods at Play: Vertigo and Possession in Muria Religion. *Man* (n.s.), 15, pp. 219-48.

Gibb, H. A. R. and J. H. Kramers (eds.).
1953. *Shorter Encyclopaedia of Islam*. Ithaca, NY: Cornell University Press.

Gilsenan, Michael.
　1973. *Sufi and Saint in Modern Egypt*. Oxford: Clarendon Press.
Gilsenan, Michael.
　1982. *Recognizing Islam: Religion and Society in the Modern Arab World*. New York: Pantheon Books.
Glazier, Stephen D.
　1980. Commentary on Ward and Beaubrun "Trance Induction and Hallucination in Spiritual Baptist Mourning." *Journal of Psychological Anthropology*, 3:2, pp. 231-33.
Glazier, Stephen D.
　1982. African Cults and Christian Churches in Trinidad. *Journal of Religious Thought*, 39:2, pp. 17-25.
Glazier, Stephen D.
　1983. *Marchin' the Pilgrims Home: Leadership and Decision-Making in an Afro-Caribbean Faith*. Westport, CT: Greenwood.
Glazier, Stephen D.
　1985a. Mourning in the Afro-Baptist Tradition: A Comparison of Trinidad and the American South. *Southern Quarterly*, 23, pp. 141-56.
Glazier, Stephen D.
　1985b. Syncretism and Separation: Ritual Change in an Afro-Caribbean Faith. *Journal of American Folklore*, 98, pp. 49-62.
Glazier, Stephen D.
　1986. Prophecy and Ecstasy: Religion and Politics in the Caribbean. In *Prophetic Religions and Politics*. J. K. Hadden and A. D. Shupe (eds.). New York: Paragon House, pp. 430-47.
Glazier, Stephen D.
　1988. Worldwide Mission of Trinidad's Spiritual Baptists. *National Geographical Journal of India*, 34, pp. 75-78.
Goddard, Pliny Earle.
　1919. Notes on the Sun Dance of the Cree in Alberta. *Anthropological Papers of the American Museum of Natural History*, 16, pp. 295-310.
Gold, Ann Grodzins.
　1988. *Fruitful Journeys: The Ways of Rajasthani Pilgrims*. Berkeley: University of California Press.
Goodenough, Ward.
　1965. Yankee Kinship Terminology: A Problem in Componential Analysis. *American Anthropologist*, 67, part 2, pp. 259-87.
Goody, J. (ed.).
　1968. *Literacy in Traditional Societies*. Cambridge: Cambridge University Press.
Graburn, N. H. H.
　1977. Tourism: The Sacred Journey. In *Hosts and Guests*. V. L. Smith (ed.). Philadelphia: University of Pennsylvania Press, pp. 17-31.
Grady, T. J.
　1967. National Shrine of the Immaculate Conception. In *The New Catholic*

Encyclopedia, Vol. 10. New York: McGraw-Hill. pp. 238-39.

Graham, William.
1988. *Beyond the Written Word: Oral Aspects of Scripture in the History of Religion*. Cambridge: Cambridge University Press.

Gramsci, Antonio.
1971. *Selections from the Prison Notebooks*. Quintin Hoare and Geoffrey Nowell Smith (eds. and trans.). London: Lawrence and Wishart.

Greenland, Hauraki.
1984. Ethnicity as Ideology. In *Tauiwi*. Paul Spoonley, Cluny MacPherson, David Pearson, Charles Sedgewick (eds.). Palmerston North: Dunmore Press, pp. 86-102.

Gross, Daniel R.
1971. Ritual and Conformity: A Religious Pilgrimage to Northeastern Brazil. *Ethnology*, 10, pp. 129-48.

Gullick, C. J. M. R.
1981. Pilgrimage, Cults and Holy Places. *Journal of the Durham University Anthropological Society*, 6, pp. 1-13.

Habermas, J.
1979. *Communication and the Evolution of Society*. Boston: Beacon Press.

Hanson, Allan.
1989. The Making of the Maori: Culture Invention and Its Logic. *American Anthropologist*, 91, pp. 890-902.

Hanson, A., and L. Hanson.
1983. *Counterpoint in Maori Culture*. London: Routledge and Kegan Paul.

Harris, Marvin.
1968. *The Rise of Anthropological Theory*. New York: Columbia University Press.

Hart, George L. III.
1973. Women and the Sacred in Ancient Tamilnadu, *Journal of Asian Studies*, 32:2, pp. 233-50.

Hart, George L. III.
1975. *The Poems of Ancient Tamilnad: Their Milieu and Their Sanskrit Counterparts*. Berkeley: University of California Press.

Heilman, Samuel.
1984. *The Gate Behind the Wall: A Pilgrimage to Jerusalem*. New York: Penguin Books.

Henney, Jeannette H.
1974. Spirit-Possession Belief and Trance Behavior in Two Fundamentalist Groups in St. Vincent. In *Trance, Healing and Hallucination: Three Field Studies in Religious Experience*. Felicitas D. Goodman, Jeannette H. Henney, and Esther Pressel (eds.). New York: John Wiley and Sons, pp. 6-111.

Herskovits, Melville J.
1937. *Life in a Haitian Valley*. New York: Doubleday.

Herskovits, Melville J., and Frances S. Herskovits.
1947. *Trinidad Village*. New York: Alfred A. Knopf.

Hertz, Robert.

1983 [orig. 1913]. St. Besse: A Study of an Alpine Cult. In *Saints and Their Cults: Studies Religious Sociology, Folklore, and History*. Stephen Wilson (ed.). New York: Cambridge University Press, pp. 55-100.

Hickey, Joseph V., Gregory R. Staats, and Douglas B. McGaw.

1979. Factors Associated with the Mecca Pilgrimage Among the Bokkos Fulani. *Journal of Asian and African Studies*, 14, pp. 3-4.

Hiller, H. L.

1976. Escapism, Penetration, and Responses: Industrial Tourism and the Caribbean. *Caribbean Studies*, 16:2, pp. 92-116.

Hilton, Rodney (ed.).

1978. *The Transition from Feudalism to Capitalism*. London: Verso.

Hiskett, M.

1957. Material Relating to the State of Learning Among the Fulani Before Their Jihad. *Bulletin of the School of Oriental and African Studies*, 19:3, pp. 550-78.

Hiskett, M.

1977. The Nineteenth Century Jihads in West Africa. In *The Cambridge History of Africa*, Vol. 5. J. D. Fage and Roland Oliver (eds.). Cambridge: Cambridge University Press.

Hiskett, M.

1985. *The Development of Islam in West Africa*. New York: Longman.

Hohepa, P.

1978. Maori and Pakeha: The One People Myth. In *TiheMauri Ora*. M. King (ed). Wellington: Methuen, pp. 98-111.

Holloway, Julia Bolton.

1981. Semus Sumus: Joyce and Pilgrimage. *Thought*, 56:221, pp. 212-25.

Holmes, George.

1975. *Europe: Hierarchy and Revolt 1320-1450*. Hassocks: Harvester Press.

Hopkins, I. W. J.

1970. *Jerusalem: A Study in Urban Geography*. Grand Rapids: Baker House Books.

Howard, Donald R.

1980. *Writers and Pilgrims: Medieval Pilgrimage Narratives and Their Posterity*. Berkeley: University of California Press.

Howe, K. R.

1984. *Where the Waves Fall*. Honolulu: University of Hawaii Press.

Hudson, Dennis.

1978. Siva, Minaksi, Visnu—Reflections on a Popular Myth in Madurai. In *South Indian Temples*. B. Stein (ed.). New Delhi: Vikas.

Hughes, Katherine.

1911. *Father Lacombe: The Black Robe Voyageur*. Toronto: William Briggs.

Hunt, E. D.

1982. *Holy Land Pilgrimage in the Later Roman Empire A.D. 312-460*. Oxford: Clarendon Press.

Hurbon, Laennec.
   1972. *Dieu dans le Vaudou Haitien*. Paris: Payot.
Ishii, Yoneo.
   1986. *Sangha, State, and Society: Thai Buddhism in History*. Peter Hawkes (trans.). Honolulu: University of Hawaii Press.
Ismael, Tareq Y.
   1971. *The U.A.R. in Africa: Egypt's Policy Under Nasser*. Evanston, IL: North-western University Press.
Jackson, Peter.
   1989. *Buddhism, Legitimation, and Conflict: The Political Functions of Urban Thai Buddhism*. Singapore: Institute of Southeast Asian Studies.
Jameson, Frederic.
   1977. Of Islands and Trenches: Neutralization and the Production of Utopian Discourse. *Diacritics*, 7, pp. 2-22.
Jayawickrama, N. A. (ed.).
   1971. *The Chronicle of the Thupa and the Thupavamsa*. London: Pali Text Society.
Jerome.
   1893. The Letter of Paula and Eustochium to Marcella. In *Jerome*. W. H. Fremantle (trans.). Oxford: Select Library of Nicene and Post-Nicene Fathers of the Christian Church.
Jerome.
   1896. *The Pilgrimage of the Holy Paula*. Aubrey Stewart (trans.). London: Palestine Pilgrim Text Society.
Jha, Makhan.
   1971. *The Sacred Complex of Janakpur*. Allahabad: United.
Joseph, John.
   1983. *Muslim-Christian Relations and Inter-Christian Rivalries in the Middle East: The Case of the Jacobites in an Age of Transition*. Albany: State University of New York Press.
Kaba, Lansine.
   1974. *The Wahhabiyya: Islamic Reform and Politics in West Africa*. Evanston, IL: Northwestern University Press.
Kantorowicz, Ernst H.
   1957. *The King's Two Bodies: A Study in Medieval Political Theology*. Princeton: Princeton University Press.
Karve, Irawati.
   1962. On the Road: A Maharashtrian Pilgrimage. *Journal of Asian Studies*, 22, pp. 13-30.
Kavolis, V.
   1970. Post-Modern Man: Psychocultural Responses to Social Trends. *Social Problems*, 17:4, pp. 435-48.
Kee, Alistair.
   1982. *Constantine Versus Christ: The Triumph of Ideology*. London: SCM Press.

Kenny, M. G.
   1981. Mirror in the Forest: The Doboro Hunter-Gatherers as an Image of the Other. *Africa*, 51:1, pp. 477-95.
Keyes, Charles F.
   1971. Buddhism and National Integration in Thailand. *Journal of Asian Studies*, 30:3, pp. 551-68.
Kingdom of Saudi Arabia.
   1980. *Statistical Yearbook 1978*. Riyadh: Central Department of Statistics.
Konrad, Herman.
   1991. Pilgrimage as Cyclical Process: The Unending Pilgrimage of the Holy Cross of the Quintana Roo Maya. In *Pilgrimage in Latin America*. N. Ross Crumrine and Alan Morinis (eds.). Westport, CT: Greenwood, pp. 123-37.
Kosambi, D. D.
   1962. *Myth and Reality*. Bombay: Popular Prakashan.
Krey, August C.
   1921. *The First Crusade: The Accounts of Eye-Witnesses and Participants.* Princeton: Princeton University Press.
Kselman, Thomas A., and Steven Avella.
   1986. Marian Piety and the Cold War in the United States. *Catholic Historical Review*, 72:3, pp. 403-24.
Laguerre, Michel S.
   n.d. The Social Function of the Haitian Pilgrimage to the Notre-Dame-De-Saut d'Eau Shrine.
Laguerre, Michel S.
   1980. *Voodoo Heritage*. Vol. 98, Beverly Hills: Sage.
Laguerre, Michel S.
   1989. *Voodoo and Politics in Haiti*. New York: St. Martin's.
Laperriere, Guy.
   1981. Les Lieux de Pelerinages au Quebec. In *Les Pelerinages au Quebec*. Pierre Boglioni and Benoit Lacroix (eds.). Quebec: Les Presses de l'Universite de Laval.
Leff, Gordon.
   1976. *The Dissolution of the Medieval Outlook: An Essay on Intellectual and Spiritual Change in the 14th Century*. New York: New York University Press.
Levine, H. B.
   1987. The Cultural Politic of Maori Fishing: An Anthropological Perspective on the First Three Significant Waitangi Tribunal Hearings. *Journal of the Polynesian Society*, 89, pp. 421-43.
Levtzion, Nehemia.
   1979. Abd Allah b. Yasin and the Almoravids. In *Studies in West African History*, Vol. 1. J. R. Willis (ed.). London: Cass.
Levtzion, Nehemia.
   1980. *Ancient Ghana and Mali*. New York: Homes and Meier.

Leymore, V. L.
   1975. *Hidden Myth*. New York: Basic Books.
Liberty, Margot.
   1980. The Sun Dance. In *Anthropology of the Great Plains*. W. Raymond Wood
   and Margot Liberty (eds.). Lincoln: University of Nebraska Press, pp. 164-78.
Lohkande, Ajit.
   1976. *Tukaram: His Person and Religion*. Frankfurt/M: Peter Lang and Bern:
   Herbert Lang.
Long, David.
   1979. *The Hajj Today: A Survey of the Contemporary Makkah Pilgrimage*.
   Albany: State University of New York Press.
Lowenthal, D.
   1962. Tourists and Thermalists. *Geographical Review*, 52:1, pp. 124-27.
Lowenthal, Ira.
   1978. Ritual Performance and Religious Experience: A Service for the Gods in
   Southern Haiti. *Journal of Anthropological Research*, 34:3, pp. 392-414.
Lowes, John.
   1927. *The Road to Xanadu: A Study in the Ways of the Imagination*. London:
   Constable.
Lowie, R. H.
   1915. Ceremonialism in North America. In *Anthropology in North America*. F.
   Boas et. al. (eds.). New York: G. E. Stechart, pp. 229-58.
MacCannell, Dean.
   1973. Staged Authenticity: Arrangements of Social Space in Tourist Settings.
   American Journal of Sociology, 79, pp. 589-603.
MacCannell, Dean.
   1976. *The Tourist: A New Theory of the Leisure Class*. New York: Schocken
   Books.
MacCormack, Sabine.
   1972. Change and Continuity in Late Antiquity: The Ceremony of Adventus.
   Historia, 21, pp. 722-52.
McCreanor, Tim.
   1989. The Treaty of Waitangi—Responses and Responsibilities. In *Honouring the
   Treaty*. Helen Yensen, Kevin Hague and Tim McCreanor (eds.). Auckland:
   Penguin Books, pp. 34-45.
McLean, John.
   1887-1888. The Blackfoot Sun Dance. *Proceedings, Canadian Institute*, 3d series,
   6, pp. 231-37.
Mandelbaum, David G.
   1940. The Plains Cree. *Anthropological Papers of the American Museum of
   Natural History*, 37:2, pp. 154-315.
Mandeville.
   1967. *Mandeville's Travels*. M. C. Seymour (ed.). Oxford: Oxford University
   Press.

Marco Polo.
1958. *Travels*. Ronald Latham (trans.). Harmondsworth: Penguin Books.
Marglin, Frederique A.
1985. *Wives of the God King: The Rituals of the Devadasis of Puri*. Delhi: Oxford University Press.
Martin, David.
1990. *Tongues of Fire: The Explosion of Protestantism in Latin America*. Oxford: Basil Blackwell.
Martin, Richard C.
1987. Muslim Pilgrimage. In *Encyclopaedia of Religion*, Vol. 11. Mircea Eliade (ed.). New York: Macmillan.
Meintel, D. A.
1973. Strangers, Homecomers and Ordinary Men. *Anthropological Quarterly*, 46:1, pp. 47-58.
Memissi, Fatima.
1977. Women, Saints and Sanctuaries. *Signs*, 3:1, pp. 101-12.
Messerschmidt, D. A., and J. Sharma.
1981. Hindu Pilgrimage in the Nepal Himalayas. *Current Anthropology*, 22, pp. 571-72.
Metge, Joan.
1976. *The Maoris of New Zealand*. London: Routledge and Kegan Paul.
Metreaux, Alfred.
1959. *Voodoo in Haiti*. New York: Oxford University Press.
Meyerhoff, Barbara.
1974. *Peyote Hunt: The Sacred Journey of the Huichol Indians*. Ithaca: Cornell University Press.
Miskimin, Harry A.
1975. *The Economy of Early Renaissance Europe, 1300-1460*. Cambridge: Cambridge University Press.
Mokashi, D. B.
1987. *Palkhi: An Indian Pilgrimage*. Albany, New York: State University of New York Press.
Momen, Moojan.
1985. *An Introduction to Shi'i Islam: The History and Doctrines of Twelver Shi'ism*. New Haven: Yale University Press.
Moore, Alexander.
1980. Walt Disney World: Bounded Ritual Space and the Playful Pilgrimage Center. *Anthropological Quarterly*, pp. 207-18.
Morinis, Alan.
1982. Levels of Culture in Hinduism: A Case Study of Dream Incubation at a Bengali Pilgrimage Centre. *Contributions to Indian Sociology* (n.s.), 16:2, pp. 255-70.
Morinis, Alan.
1984. *Pilgrimage in the Hindu Tradition: A Case Study of West Bengal*. Delhi:

Oxford University Press.

Mulrain, George MacDonald.

    1984. *Theology and Folk Culture: The Theological Significance of Haitian Folk Religion*. New York: Peter Lang.

Murray, Gerald F.

    1980. Population Pressure, Land Tenure, and Voodoo: The Economics of Haitian Peasant Ritual. In *Beyond the Myths of Culture: Essays in Cultural Materialism*. Eric B. Ross (ed.). New York: Academic Press, pp. 295-321.

Naqar, Umar al-.

    1972. *The Pilgrimage Tradition in West Africa: An Historical Study with Special Reference to the Nineteenth Century*. Khartoum, Sudan: Khartoum University Press.

Naquin, Susan and Chun-fang Yu. (eds.).

    1992. *Pilgrims and Sacred Sites in China*. Berkeley: University of California Press.

Nash, D.

    1963. The Ethnologist as a Stranger: An Essay in the Sociology of Knowledge. *Southwestern Journal of Anthropology*, 19, pp. 149-67.

Nash, D.

    1979. Tourism in Pre-Industrial Societies. *Les Cahiers du Tourisme*. Serie C. No. 51.

Nash, D.

    1981. Tourism as an Anthropological Subject. *Current Anthropology*, 22:5, pp. 461-81.

Nasr, Seyyed Hossein.

    1966. *Ideals and Realities of Islam*. London: Allen and Unwin.

Neurgaonkar, H. B. P.

    1936. *Sadashiv: Palkhi Sohla*. Pune: Sou. Umati Sadashiv Neurgaonkar.

New Zealand Population: Change, Composition and Policy Implications.

    1986. New Zealand Planning Council Monitoring Group Report No. 4. Wellington: Government Printer.

Nibley, Hugh.

    1971. Jerusalem in Christianity. *Encyclopedia Judaica*, Vol. 9. Jerusalem: Keter, pp. 1567-75.

Niebuhr, Richard.

    1981. Address to the conference Pilgrimage: The Human Quest. Pittsburgh.

Nissan, Elizabeth.

    1988. Polity and Pilgrimage Centers in Sri Lanka. *Man* (n.s.), 23:2, pp. 253-74.

Nolan, Mary Lee, and Sidney Nolan.

    1989. *Christian Pilgrimage in Modern Western Europe. Studies in Religion*. Chapel Hill: University of North Carolina Press.

Noronha, R.

    1977. *Social and Cultural Dimensions of Tourism: A Review of the Literature in English*. Washington, DC: World Bank (Draft).

Norris, H. T. (ed.).
   1977. *The Pilgrimage of Ahmed, Son of the Little Bird of Paradise*. Warminster,
       England: Aris and Phillips.
Obeyesekere, Gananath.
   1966. The Buddhist Pantheon in Ceylon and Its Extensions. In *Anthropological
       Studies in Theravada Buddhism*. Manning Nash (ed.). New Haven: Yale
       University Southeast Asian Studies, pp. 1-26.
Oliver, Douglas.
   1989. *The Pacific Islands*. Honolulu: University of Hawaii Press.
Orange, Claudia.
   1987. *The Treaty of Waitangi*. Wellington: Allen and Unwin.
Otto, R.
   1959. *The Idea of the Holy*. Harmondsworth: Penguin.
Parry, Jonathan.
   1982. Death and Cosmogony in Kashi. In *Way of Life, King, Householder,
       Renouncer: Essays in Honour of Louis Dumont*. T. N. Madan (ed.). New Delhi:
       Vikas, pp. 337-65.
Pearson, David.
   1984. Two Paths of Colonialism. In *Tauiwi*. Paul Spoonley, Cluny MacPherson,
       David Pearson, Charles Sedgewick (eds.). Palmerston North: Dunmore Press,
       pp. 203-22.
Peper, W.
   1980. A Traveler's Lament: It's Always Too Late. *International Herald Tribune*,
       24-25:5, pp. W7-8.
Peters, F. E.
   1985. *Jerusalem: The Holy City in the Eyes of Chroniclers, Visitors, Pilgrims and
       Prophets from the Days of Abraham to the Beginnings of Modern Times*.
       Princeton: Princeton University Press.
Peters, F. E.
   1986. Jerusalem and Mecca: The Typology of the Holy City in the Near East. *New
       York University Studies in Near Eastern Civilization*, No. 11. New York: New
       York University Press.
Pfaffenberger, Bryan.
   1979. The Kataragama Pilgrimage: Hindu-Buddhist Interaction and Its Signifi-
       cance in Sri Lanka's Polyethnic Social System. *Journal of Asian Studies*, 38:2,
       pp. 253-70.
Pitt-Rivers, J.
   1964. Pilgrims and Tourists: Conflicts and Change in a Village of Southwest
       France. Presented at meeting of American Anthropological Society, Milwau-
       kee, WI, May 14-16.
Poole, Deborah A.
   1991. Rituals of Movement, Rites of Transformation: Pilgrimage and Dance in
       the Highlands of Cuzco, Peru. In *Pilgrimage in Latin America*. N. Ross
       Crumrine and Alan Morinis (eds.). Westport, CT: Greenwood, pp. 307-38.

Population of New Zealand. 1986. New Zealand Census, Vol 1.

Prahl, H. W., and A. Steinecke.

1979. *Der Millionen Urlaub.* Darmstadt: Luchterhand.

Preston, James J.

1980a. *Cult of the Goddess: Social and Religious Change in a Hindu Temple.* Prospect Heights, IL: Waveland Press.

Preston, James J.

1980b. Sacred Centers and Symbolic Networks in South Asia. *Mankind Quarterly,* 20:3-4, pp. 259-93.

Preston, James J.

1982. Conclusion: New Perspectives on Mother Worship. In *Mother Worship: Theme and Variations.* James J. Preston (ed.). Chapel Hill: University of North Carolina Press, pp. 325-43.

Preston, James J.

1983. Goddess Temples in Orissa: An Anthropological Survey. In *Religion in Modern India.* Giri Raj Gupta (ed.). *Main Currents in Indian Sociology,* Vol. 5. New Delhi: Vikas, pp. 229-47.

Preston, James J.

1984. Empiricism and the Phenomenology of Religious Experience. *Mentalities,* 2:2, pp. 10-20.

Preston, James J.

1986. Pilgrimage in America: An Address to the Catholic Shrine Directors of the United States. In *Proceedings of the First National Shrine Director's Meeting.* Washington, DC: National Conference of Catholic Bishops, pp. 1-10.

Preston, James J.

1988. The Pastoral Needs of Pilgrims in the Shrines of North America. In *Proceedings of the Second National Convention of Shrines.* Washington, DC: National Conference of Catholic Bishops, Committee on Refugees and Tourism, 19, pp. 16-27.

Preston, James J.

1990. The Rediscovery of America: Pilgrimage in the Promised Land. In Pilgrimage in the United States, *Geographia Religionum,* Vol. 5. Gisbert Rinschede and Surinder Bhardwaj (eds.). Berlin: Dietrich Reimer Verlag, pp. 15-26.

Preston, James J.

1991. The Trickster Unmasked: Anthropology and the Imagination. In *Anthropological Poetics.* Ivan Brady (ed.).Savage, MD: Rowman and Littlefield.

Price-Mars, Jean.

1928. *Ansi Parla l'Oncle.* Port-au-Prince.

Pruess, James B.

1974. Veneration and Merit-Seeking at Sacred Places: Buddhist Pilgrimage in Contemporary Thailand. Ph.D. diss., Department of Anthropology, University of Washington.

Pruess, James B.

1976a. Merit-Seeking in Public: Buddhist Pilgrimage in Northeastern Thailand.

Journal of the Siam Society, 64:1, pp. 169-206.

Pruess, James B. (ed.).

1976b. *The That Phanom Chronicle: A Shrine History and Its Interpretation.* Ithaca, NY: Cornell University Southeast Asia Program, Data Paper no. 104.

Purchas, Samuel.

1905-1907. *Hakluytus Posthumus, or Purchas, His Pilgrimes.* Glasgow: J. MacLehose.

Rahman, Fazlur.

1966. *Islam.* Chicago: University of Chicago Press.

Ramanujan, A. K.

1973. *Speaking of Shiva.* Baltimore: Penguin Books.

Rangihau, John.

1977. Being Maori. In *Te Ao Hurihuri*. M. King (ed.). New Zealand: Hicks Smith, pp. 165-75.

Rappaport, Roy A.

1973. The Sacred in Human Evolution. In *Explorations in Anthropology: Readings in Culture, Man and Nature.* Morton H. Fried (ed.).New York: Thomas Y. Crowell, pp. 23-42.

Rentz, G. S.

1969. The Wahhabis. In *Religion in the Middle East*, Vol. 2. A. J. Arberry (ed.). Cambridge: Cambridge University Press.

Rhys Davids, T. W. (trans.).

1900. *Maha-Parinibbana Suttanta.* In *Buddhist Suttas. Sacred Books of the East*, Vol. 11. Oxford: Oxford University Press

Rilke, R. M.

1972. *The Duino Elegies.* New York: Harper and Row.

Rinschede, G., and S. M. Bhardwaj (eds.).

1990. *Pilgrimage in the United States.* Berlin: Deitrich Reimer Verlag.

Robertson-Smith, W.

1889. *Lectures on the Religion of the Semites.* London: Adam and Charles Black.

Roff, W. R.

1985. Pilgrimage and the History of Religions: Theoretical Approaches to the Hajj. In *Approaches to Islam in Religious Studies.* Richard C. Martin (ed.). Tucson: University of Arizona Press.

Rohricht, Reinhold.

1890. *Bibliotheca Geographica Palestine.* Berlin.

Runciman, Steven.

1935. Charlemagne and Palestine? *English Historical Review*, 50, pp. 606-19.

Runciman, Steven.

1969a. *The Historic Role of the Christian Arabs of Palestine.* London: Longman.

Runciman, Steven.

1969b. The Pilgrimages to Palestine before 1095. In *A History of the Crusades: The First Hundred Years.* Marshall Baldwin (ed.). Madison: University of Wisconsin Press, pp. 68-79.

Runciman, Steven.
  1971. *A History of the Crusades*. 3 vols. Harmondsworth: Penguin.
Sachedina, Abdulaziz Abdulhussein.
  1981. *Islamic Messianism: The Idea of the Mahdi in Twelver Shi'ism*. Albany:
  State University of New York Press.
Sahlins, Marshall.
  1985. *Islands of History*. Chicago: University of Chicago Press.
Sallnow, Michael J.
  1981. Communitas Reconsidered: The Sociology of Andean Pilgrimage. *Man*
  (n.s.), 16, pp. 163-82.
Sallnow, Michael J.
  1987. *Pilgrims of the Andes: Regional Cults in Cusco*. Washington, DC: Smith-
  sonian Institute Press.
Sallnow, Michael J., and John Eade (eds.).
  1990. *Contesting the Sacred: The Anthropology of Christian Pilgrimage*. London:
  Routledge.
Sanguan Chotisukharat.
  1965. *Tamnan Meuang Neua [Histories of the Northern Principalities]*. Bangkok:
  Odeon.
Sargant, William.
  1974. *The Mind Possessed: A Physiology of Possession, Mysticism and Faith
  Healing*. Philadelphia: Lippincott.
Savage, Henry L.
  1977. Pilgrimages and Pilgrim Shrines in Palestine and Syria After 1095. In *A
  History of the Crusades: The Art and Architecture of the Crusader States*. Henry
  W. Hazard (ed.). Madison: University of Wisconsin Press, pp. 36-68.
Scheub, Harold.
  1975. *The Xhosa Ntsomi*. Oxford: Clarendon Press.
Schimmel, Anne-Marie.
  n.d. *Islam*. Unpublished manuscript.
Schneebaum, T.
  1969. *Keep the River on Your Right*. New York: Grove Press.
Schober, R.
  1975. Was wollen die Urlauber wirklich? In *Animation im Urlaub*. Starnberg:
  Studienkreis fur Tourismus. pp. 9-17.
Scott, D.
  1981. *Ask That Mountain*. Wellington: Heinemann.
Seymour, Michael.
  1967. Introduction. In *Mandeville's Travels*. Michael Seymour (ed.). Oxford:
  Oxford University Press.
Shore, Bradd.
  1989. Mana and Tapu. In *Developments in Polynesian Ethnology*. A. Howard and
  R. Borofsky (eds.). Honolulu: University of Hawaii Press, pp. 137-74.

Shukurzadih, Ibrahim.
    1346. *'Aqayid va rusum-e 'amih-yi mardum-i khurasan*. Intisharat-i bunyad-i farhang-i iran "23."
Shulman, David Dean.
    1979. *Tamil Temple Myths*. Princeton: Princeton University Press.
Sigaux, C.
    1966. *History of Tourism*. London: Leisure Arts.
Simmons, David.
    1976. *The Great New Zealand Myth: A Study of the Discovery and Origin Traditions of the Maori*. Wellington: Reed.
Simpson, George Eaton.
    1970. *Religious Cults of the Caribbean: Trinidad, Jamaica and Haiti*. Rio Piedras, PR: Institute of Caribbean Studies.
Sinclair, Douglas.
    1977. Land: Maori View and European Response. In *Te Ao Hurihuri*. M. King (ed.). New Zealand: Hicks Smith, pp. 107-28.
Singh, R. L., and Rana P. B. Singh (eds.).
    1987. *Trends in the Geography of Pilgrimages*. Varanasi, India: National Geographic Society of India.
Sircar, D. C.
    1973. *The Sakta Pithas*. Delhi: Motilal Banarsidass.
Siu, P. C. P.
    1952. The Sojourner. *American Journal of Sociology*, 58:1, pp. 34-44.
Skinner, Alanson.
    1914. The Sun-Dance of the Plains-Cree. *Anthropological Papers of the American Museum of Natural History*, 16:4, pp. 283-94.
Skinner, Elliott.
    1958. Christianity and Islam Among the Mossi. *American Anthropologist*, 60, pp. 1102-19.
Slater, Candace.
    1991. The Literature of Pilgrimage: Present-day Miracle Stories from Northeast Brazil. In *Pilgrimage in Latin America*. N. Ross Crumrine and Alan Morinis (eds.). Westport, CT: Greenwood, pp. 175-204.
Smith, V. L.
    1977. Introduction. In *Hosts and Guests*. V. L. Smith (ed.). Philadelphia: University of Pennsylvania Press, pp. 1-14.
Smith, Wilfred Cantwell.
    1963. *The Meaning and End of Religion*. New York: Macmillan.
Sopher, David E.
    1968. Pilgrim Circulation in Gujarat. *The Geographical Review*, 58:3, pp. 392-425.
Sorrenson, M. P. K.
    1987. Towards a Radical Reinterpretation of New Zealand History: The Role of the Waitangi Tribunal. *New Zealand Journal of History*, 21, pp. 173-88.

Southern, Sir Richard.
    1970. *Western Society and the Church in the Middle Ages*. Harmondsworth: Penguin.
Spier, Leslie.
    1921. The Sun Dance of the Plains Indians: Its Development and Diffusion. *Anthropological Papers of the American Museum of Natural History*, 16:7, pp. 451-527.
Spitzer, Leo.
    1949. The Epic Style of the Pilgrim Aetheria. *Comparative Literature*, 1:3, pp. 225-58.
Stanley, J. M.
    1977. Special Time, Special Power: The Fluidity of Power in a Popular Hindu Festival. *Journal of Asian Studies*, 37:1, pp. 27-43.
Stapleton, Ashram.
    1983. *The Birth and Growth of the Baptist Church in Trinidad and Tobago and the Caribbean*. Trinidad: Stapleton.
Statler, Oliver.
    1983. *Japanese Pilgrimage*. New York: William Morrow.
Stevens, John.
    1988. *The Marathon Monks of Hiei*. Boston: Shambhala.
Stevenson, Matilda C.
    1904. The Zuni. *Annual Report of the Bureau of American Ethnology 1901-02*. Washington, DC:
Stocking, George.
    1987. *Victorian Anthropology*. New York: Free Press.
Stoll, David.
    1990. *Is Latin America Turning Protestant?: The Politics of Evangelical Growth*. Berkeley: University of California Press.
Sumption, Jonathan.
    1975. *Pilgrimage: An Image of Medieval Religion*. London: Faber and Faber.
Tabataba'i, 'Allamah Sayyid Muhammad Husayn.
    1977. *Shi'ite Islam*. Albany: State University of New York Press.
Tambiah, S. J.
    1976. *World Conqueror and World Renouncer: A Study of Buddhism and Polity in Thailand Against a Historical Background*. Cambridge: Cambridge University Press.
Tambiah, S. J.
    1984. *The Buddhist Saints of the Forest and the Cult of Amulets: A Study in Charisma, Hagiography, Sectarianism, and Millenial Buddhism*. Cambridge: Cambridge University Press.
Tanaka, Hiroshi.
    1978. Sacredness in a Changing Buddhist Pilgrimage in Japan. Presented at the Tenth International Congress of Anthropological and Ethnological Sciences, New Delhi, India.

Tarasoff, Koozma J.

  1980. *Persistent Ceremonialism: The Plains Cree and Salteaux*. Ottawa: National Museum of Man.

Taylor, Ian.

  1986. *The Rite of Mourning in the Spiritual Baptist Faith with Emphasis on the Activity of the Spirit*. Thesis, University of the West Indies, St. Augustine, Trinidad.

Tentori, Tullio.

  1982. An Italian Religious Feast: The Fujenti Rites of the Madonna Dell' Arco, Naples. In *Mother Worship: Theme and Variations*. James J. Preston (ed.). Chapel Hill: University of North Carolina Press, pp. 95-122.

Testimonials of Pilgrims, Queen of the Holy Rosary. Mediatrix of Peace Shrine.

  1967, 1969. 2 vols. Necedah, WI: For My God and My Country.

Thomas, Rt. Rev. Eudora.

  1987. *A History of the Shouter Baptists in Trinidad and Tobago*. Ithaca, NY: Calaloux.

Tolkappiyam.

  1916. Madras: Minerva Press.

Toren, Christina.

  1988. Making the Present, Revealing the Past: The Mutability and Continuity of Tradition as Process. *Man*, n.s. 23, pp. 696-717.

Trimingham, J. Spencer.

  1962. *A History of Islam in West Africa*. Oxford: Oxford University Press.

Trimingham, J. Spencer.

  1964. *Islam in East Africa*. Oxford: Oxford University Press.

Turnbull, Colin.

  1981. A Pilgrimage to India. *Natural History*, 90:7, pp. 14-22.

Turner, Edith.

  1986. Pilgrimage: An Overview. In *Encyclopedia of Religion*, Vol. 11. Mircea Eliade (ed.). New York: Macmillan, pp. 328-30.

Turner, L., and J. Ash.

  1975. *The Golden Hordes*. London: Constable.

Turner, Victor.

  1967. "Betwixt and Between": The Liminal Period in Rites de Passage. In *Forest of Symbols*. Ithaca: Cornell University Press. pp. 93-111.

Turner, Victor.

  1969. *The Ritual Process*. Chicago: Aldine.

Turner, Victor.

  1973. The Center Out There: Pilgrim's Goal. *History of Religions*, 12:3, pp. 191-230.

Turner, Victor.

  1974a. *Dramas, Fields, and Metaphors*. Ithaca, NY: Cornell University Press.

Turner, Victor.

  1974b. From Liminal to Liminoid in Play, Flow, and Ritual: an Essay in Comparative Symbology. *Rice University Studies*, 60:3, pp. 53-92.

Turner, Victor.
1974c. Pilgrimage and Communitas. *Studia Missionalia*, 23, pp. 305-27.

Turner, Victor.
1974d. Pilgrimages as Social Processes. In *Dramas, Fields and Metaphors*. Ithaca, NY: Cornell University Press, pp. 167-230.

Turner, Victor.
1979. *Process, Performance and Pilgrimage*. Atlantic Highlands, NJ: Humanities Press.

Turner, Victor.
1982. The Post-industrial Marian Pilgrimage. In *Mother Worship: Themes and Variations*. James J. Preston (ed.). Chapel Hill, NC: University of North Carolina Press, pp. 145-73.

Turner, Victor.
1986. Social Drama in Brazilian Umbanda: The Dialectics of Meaning. In *The Anthropology of Performance*. New York: PAJ, pp. 33-71.

Turner, Victor and Edith Turner.
1978. *Image and Pilgrimage in Christian Culture: Anthropological Perspectives*. New York: Columbia University Press.

Van der Veer, P.
1984. Structure and anti-structure in Hindu Pilgrimage to Ayodhya. In *Changing South Asia: Religion and Society*. K. Ballhatchet and D. Taylor (eds.). Hong Kong: Asian Research Service for the Centre of South Asian Studies, School of Oriental and African Studies, University of London.

Van Hoof, Mary Ann.
1978. *Revelations and Messages As Given Through Mary Ann Van Hoof*. 2 vols. Necedah, WI: For My God and My Country.

Vickery, Michael.
1984. *Cambodia: 1975-1982*. Boston: South End Press.

Vidyarthi, L. P.
1961. *The Sacred Complex in Hindu Gaya*. New York: Asia.

Vidyarthi, L. P.
1979. *The Sacred Complex of Kashi*. New Delhi: Concept.

Vogel, C.
1963. Le pelerinage penitencielle. *Pellegrinaggi e culto dei santi in Europa fino alla le crociata*. Convegni del Centro di Studi sulla Spiritualita Medievale, 4. Todi.

Vogt, J. W.
1976. Wandering: Youth and Travel Behavior. *Annals of Tourism Research*, 4:1, pp. 25-41.

Voinot, L.
1948. *Les Pelerinages Judeo-Musulmans du Maroc*. Paris: Editions Larose.

Wadley, Susan (ed.).
1980. *The Powers of Tamil Women*. Syracuse: Maxwell School of Citizenship and

Public Affairs, Syracuse University.

Wagner, U.

1977. Out of Time and Place—Mass Tourism and Charter Trips. *Ethnos*, 42:1-2, pp. 38-52.

Walker, Peter.

1990. *Holy City, Holy Places: Christian Attitudes to Jerusalem and the Holy Land in the Fourth Century*. Oxford: Clarendon Press.

Walker, R.

1977. Marae: A Place to Stand. In *Te Ao Hurihuri*. M. King (ed.). New Zealand: Hicks Smith, pp. 21-30.

Walker, R.

1984. The Genesis of Maori Activism. *Journal of the Polynesian Society*, 93, pp. 267-82.

Walker, R.

1987. *Nga Tau Tohetohe*. Auckland: Penquin.

Walsh, Michael.

1967. *Knock: The Shrine of the Pilgrim People of God*. Tuam, Ireland: St. Jarlath's College.

Ward, Colleen, and Michael Beaubrun.

1979. Trance Induction and Hallucination in Spiritual Baptist Mourning. *Journal of Psychological Anthropology*, 2, pp. 479-88.

Weber, Max.

1920. *Gesammelte Aufsatze zur Religonssoziologie*, Vol. 1. Tubingen: Mohr.

Weber, Max.

1978. The Soteriology of the Underprivileged. In *Selections in Translation*. W. G. Runciman (ed.). Eric Matthews (trans.). Cambridge: Cambridge University Press, pp. 174-91.

Webster, P.

1979. *Rua and the Maori Millennium*. Wellington: Price Milburn.

Wheatley, Paul.

1967. *City as Symbol*. London: Lewis.

White, Hayden.

1978. Rhetoric and History. In *Theories of History*. Hayden White and Frank E. Manuel (eds.). Los Angeles: University of California Press, pp. 3-25.

White, Hayden.

1979. Michel Foucault. In *Structuralism and Since: Levi-Strauss to Derrida*. John Sturrock (ed.). London: Oxford University Press, pp. 81-115.

Whitehead, H.

1921. *The Village Gods of South India*. Madras: Oxford University Press.

Wilbert, Johannes.

1977. In *Navigators of the Winter Sun. The Sea in the Pre-Columbian World*. Elizabeth P. Benson (ed.). Washington, DC: Dumbarton Oaks, pp. 17-46.

Wilkinson, John.

1973. *Egeria's Travels*. London: S.P.C.K.

Wilkinson, John.
    1977. *Jerusalem Pilgrims Before the Crusades*. Warminster: Aris and Phillips.
Wilks, Ivor.
    1968. The Transmission of Islamic Learning in the Western Sudan. In *Literacy in Traditional Societies*. J. Goody (ed.). Cambridge: Cambridge University Press, pp. 161-92.
William of Tyre.
    1941. *A History of Deeds Done Beyond the Sea*. Emily Babcock and A. C. Krey (trans.). 2 vols. New York: Columbia University Press.
Willibald, Saint.
    1895. *The Hodoeporicon*. Canon Brownlow (trans.). London: Hanover Square.
Wissler, Clark.
    1914. Influence of the Horse in the Development of Plains Culture. *American Anthropologist*, 16:1, pp. 1-25.
Wissler, Clark.
    1918. The Sun Dance of the Blackfoot Indians. *Anthropological Papers of the American Museum of Natural History*, 16, pp. 223-70.
Wissler, Clark.
    1921. The Sun Dance of the Plains Indians. *Anthropological Papers of the American Museum of Natural History*, 16, pp. v-ix.
Wood, Peter W.
    1986. *Quoting Heaven: Narrative, Ritual, and Trope in an Heretical Shrine of the Virgin Mary in Rural Wisconsin*. Ph.D. Diss. Rochester, NY: University of Rochester.
Wood, Peter W.
    1988. The Practical Virgin: Time and Presence in the Apparitions of Our Lady of Necedah. Unpublished paper.
Works, J. A.
    1976. *Pilgrims in a Strange Land: Hausa Communities in Chad*. New York: Columbia University Press.
Wright, Frank Lloyd.
    1967. *The Japanese Print: An interpretation*. New York: Horizon Press.
Wright, Harrison.
    1959. *New Zealand 1769-1840: The Early Years of Western Contact*. Cambridge: Harvard University Press.
Yensen, Helen, Kevin Hague and Tim McCreanor.
    1989. Aotearoa—How Did It Become a British Colony? In *Honouring the Treaty*. Helen Yensen, Kevin Hague and Tim McCreanor.(eds.). Auckland: Penguin Books, pp. 17-26.
Younger, Paul.
    1980. A Temple Festival of Mariyamman. *Journal of the American Academy of Religion*, 48:4, pp. 495-517.
Younger, Paul.
    1982a. The Family of Siva in a South Indian Grove. *Studies in Religion*, 11:3, pp.

245-63.

Younger, Paul.

1982b. Ten Days of Wandering and Romance with Lord Rankanatan: The Pankuni Festival in Srirankam Temple, South India. *Modern South Asian Studies,* 16:2, pp. 325-58.

Younger, Paul.

1989. Hindu-Christian Worship Settings in South India: Mannarkat, Velankanni, and Pastor Sundaram's. In *Hindu-Christian Dialogue.* Harold Coward (ed.). New York: Orbis Books, pp. 191-97.

Zacher, Christian K.

1976. *Curiosity and Pilgrimage: The Literature of Discovery in 14th-Century England.* Baltimore: Johns Hopkins University Press.

Zelliot, Eleanor.

1987. A Historical Introduction to the Warkari Movement. In *Palkhi, An Indian Pilgrimage.* D. B. Mokashi. Albany, NY: State University of New York Press, pp. 31-53.

Index